Interpreting
the Gospel

Interpreting the Gospel

An Introduction to Preaching

Ronald J. Allen

Chalice Press
St. Louis, Missouri

All scripture quotations, unless otherwise indicated, are from the *New Revised Standard Version Bible,* copyright 1989, Division of Christian Education of the National Council of the Churches of Christ in the USA. Used by permission.

Cover: Michael Foley
Interior design: Elizabeth Wright
Art Direction: Michael Domínguez

This book is printed on acid-free, recycled paper.

Visit Chalice Press on the World Wide Web at
www.chalicepress.com

10 9 8 7 6 5 4 3 2   02   03

Library of Congress Cataloging-in-Publication Data

Allen, Ronald J. (Ronald James), 1949-
    Interpreting the gospel : an introduction to preaching / by Ronald J. Allen
        p.   cm.
    Includes bibliographical references.
    ISBN 0-8272-1619-X
    1. Preaching.   I. Title.
    BV4211.2.A387   1998   98-47231
    251—dc21   CIP

Printed in the United States of America

To
First Christian Church (Disciples of Christ)
Poplar Bluff, Missouri

You spoke the Word of Life to me.
You walked with me through the waters of immersion.
You led me to the Sacred Table,
And into awareness of the Living Presence of God.
I give thanks to God
For my every remembrance of you.

TABLE OF CONTENTS

PREFACE

I thank the Board of Trustees of Christian Theological Seminary for approving the research leave that expedited the writing of this book. I thank the Faculty Colloquium of the same community for a lively evening of conversation on the outline of the book. I express appreciation to the following colleagues who commented on the proposal, drafts, or partial drafts: Jon L. Berquist, John McClure, Mary Donovan Turner, Paul Scott Wilson. A group of congregational pastors in Indianapolis read most of the manuscript and spent an afternoon in conversation with me on these questions: What aspects of this book are true to your substantial experience as a pastor? What parts need to be modified to account for life in the real church? These partners in witness to the gospel include Howard E. M. Bowers, Mary Susan McDougal, Robert Riester, Linda Patrick Rosebrock, and Karen Smith. Two additional pastors read the book and discussed it with me: Mary Anne Glover and Randall Updegraff Spleth. Some of these readers have reservations about aspects of the book and made suggestions for change, that, at my peril, I have not followed. Joyce Krauser, faculty assistant at Christian Theological Seminary, provided extraordinary counsel in technical and editorial matters.

I hope that this book will join other resources in helping preachers strengthen the witness of the Christian community to the gospel. I hope that the sermon will nurture a living relationship with the living God as known through Jesus Christ. Indeed, I hope that the sermon will become encounter with God, so that the congregation feels gathered around the burning bush or standing atop the Mount of Transfiguration.

INTRODUCTION

For many students, the experience of learning to preach is a bundle of contradictions. They feel exhilaration and fear. They are excited yet are overwhelmed. They are energized to preach; however, they are almost paralyzed when they think of stepping into the pulpit the first time. They are honored to be in the company of the vital preachers whom they admire, while embarrassed that their own sermonic efforts seem feeble. They are confident that they have a word from and about God, but are aware that whatever they say about God only flickers in the awesome shadow of the Divine. They want to learn to preach, but their stomachs are in knots.

In this book, I develop a process of learning to preach that builds on a student's energy, while addressing uncertainties that haunt many beginning preachers—and that plague some of us as long as we preach. I try to help preachers discover their own voices. I encourage students to develop approaches to the preparation of the sermon that take account of their own theologies, their own contexts, their own styles of thinking, their own modes of communication. I encourage students to probe the subject of the sermon to the depth and breadth needed to preach with theological integrity and insight.

I do not offer a unique theory of preaching, nor one that contends that all sermons must be developed in a singular way. To the contrary, I build on the recognition that individuals and communities are pluralistic in the ways in which they think and feel and in the ways in which they receive and process communications. With others in the field of preaching, I contend that a pastor should conceive and develop sermons in multiple ways so that each congregant can have its best opportunity to encounter the gospel. While a minister may have preferred ways of preaching, most of us need to transcend our preferences from time to time to serve the gospel in particular settings.

In Jewish and Christian traditions, the preacher is preeminently an interpreter. The preacher helps the community interpret the significance of the gospel for the congregation, and for the larger world. When focusing upon interpretation as the organizing motif of the preacher's vocation, I follow in the trail of my learned teacher, Charles L. Rice, whose first major work is entitled *Interpretation and Imagination.*[1]

I take the gospel to be the news, revealed to the church through Jesus Christ of God's unconditional love for each and every created entity and

God's will for justice for each and every created entity.[2] The preacher helps the congregation interpret what God's unconditional love and will for justice offer each person and situation and what is required of each person and situation. The preacher leads the congregation in thinking critically about God, Christ, the Holy Spirit, the church, and the world. The preacher helps the congregation name the world from the standpoint of the gospel. The preacher hopes the sermon can become an experience of divine love and a call to justice.

I repeatedly speak of the preacher "helping" the congregation interpret the divine presence and purposes. The preacher is not the sole agent of interpretation in a local church. The congregation is a community that engages in conversation concerning how to understand and experience the gospel in order to witness within and beyond the parish. Seasoned preachers know that the best preaching often emerges from vital conversation that is taking place in the congregation. In the midst of such conversation, the community helps the preacher make sense of the divine promise and command.

I also speak repeatedly of the congregation "participating" in the preaching event. I do not mean that the congregation talks aloud during the sermon. Rather, I mean that while largely silent during the sermon, the congregation is not a collection of passive receivers, but is a community actively engaging the preacher. The community helps create the meanings of the sermon by refracting its content through their own thoughts, feelings, and behaviors.

In short, I envision the sermon as a conversation in which preacher and people search together to interpret our common life from the perspective of the gospel. I advocate preaching by mutual critical correlation—a motif explored in chapters 6–7.

I join a growing cloud of witnesses in thinking that preaching is directed less to individual Christians and more to Christian community. Of course, a sermon should both encourage and guide individuals and help form Christian community.

The book takes account of the emerging insight that every human awareness is an act of interpretation. We perceive every thought and feeling through interpretive lenses that result from the interfusion of all the elements in our worlds, e.g., gender, race, ethnicity, biological makeup, psychological structure, sociological setting, class, sexual orientation, education, political commitments, education, religion. Recent studies urge all interpreters to become critical of our interpretive frameworks. We never achieve a pristine, interpretation-free, objective awareness of ourselves or the world, but we can and should recognize many of our interpretive lenses. These lenses both hinder and help us. On the one hand, our interpretive frameworks bias how we perceive ourselves and the world. Sometimes, we need help to see and hear beyond our limited perceptions. On the other hand, we do not perceive ourselves or the world generically. Particularity is a positive point of contact. It allows us to engage and to be engaged by the particularity of others.

In this book, readers will hear echoes of the facts that I am male, middle-aged, European American, middle class, joyously married, heterosexual, a liberal democrat, father of five children ages seven to seventeen, a revisionary theologian, influenced strongly by the relational (process) movement, called to teach in a seminary, a linear thinker, and ordained in a long-established denomination—the Christian Church (Disciples of Christ). As suggested in chapter 5, I try to take critical account of these qualities in this book.

I try to engage the preaching worlds of others—especially African Americans, feminists, postliberals, evangelicals, liberation theologians, and their seemingly unending combinations. At significant points, I call attention to similarities and differences between my approaches and others. While I have clear convictions about a number of matters, I respect other viewpoints and hope to learn from them.

An introductory textbook cannot consider every aspect of sermon preparation in the depth or breadth necessary to sustain a preacher for a lifelong ministry. My modest aims are to identify a number of foundational issues, to lift up basic perspectives and resources for thinking about those issues, and to help students develop perspectives and patterns of sermon preparation and embodiment that bring the gospel to life in their communities.

The book is organized in sections. However, ideas and themes move through the book in spiral fashion. I introduce them in one section, but return to them again, and sometimes again, and again. Section 1 helps students name and deal with anxieties that beginning preachers often feel and offers a rationale for why it is important to learn to preach. Section 2 considers three contexts of preaching today: the church, the larger culture, and the life of preacher. Section 3 asks: How shall we conceive of the nature and purpose of the sermon today? What are the key elements in understanding preaching as theological interpretation? Section 4 narrows the focus. How do I decide on a direction for the sermon? Section 5 concentrates on developing the sermon itself. In order to give the congregation a good opportunity to participate in the sermon, where could it begin? How could it move? How might it end? What kinds of materials are especially helpful or frustrating to the congregation? In Sections 4 and 5, I enumerate twenty-seven steps to preparing the sermon. Section 6 deals with embodying the sermon, evaluating it through careful feedback, and miscellaneous concerns. Section 7 consists of case studies and sample sermons from four preachers: two males, two women; three are European American, one is African American. Each sermon is preceded by a description of the preacher's process of preparation, illustrating a particular approach to preaching.

A couple of persons who have read the book in manuscript form say that they find the twenty-seven steps overwhelming. I respond as follows. Pastors and students typically find that as they develop a rhythm of sermon preparation the steps go more quickly than they anticipate. Preachers often find that they have resources within their own heads and hearts to complete some steps almost as soon as they see or hear the steps. Ministers adapt the steps to their own personalities and habits of working. Different sermons call for different amounts of time and intensity on different steps. However, preaching with faithfulness and integrity calls for a preacher's best investment of time and energy. Sometimes, there are no shortcuts. Preachers need to find times of the day, places, partners, and patterns of preparation that are optimum for their own sermon preparation.

You can read this book from start to finish. That approach takes you from naming anxiety, through theological foundations, to the practical work of preparing the sermon. If you are ready today to begin preparing sermons, you can begin with section 1, then go to steps for sermon preparation in sections 4, 5, 6, and 7, concluding with theological rationale in sections 2 and 3. Or, you might begin by reading the sample sermons in section 7. You could then read earlier parts of the book to see the how this approach is exemplified in the sermons and the practical steps of sermon preparation that lead from the theology to the sermons.[3]

While I have dealt with some matters in this volume in relation to particular aspects of preaching in some of my other publications, this book is my most comprehensive approach to preaching. This book has a companion volume that illustrates in more detail the multiplicity of approaches to preaching that are taking place in our time: *Patterns for Preaching: A Sermon Sampler*, edited by Ronald J. Allen (St. Louis: Chalice Press, 1998). *Patterns for Preaching: A Sermon Sampler* contains sample sermons of many of the approaches to preaching that are discussed in *Interpreting the Gospel: An Introduction to Preaching*. References in this book help the reader coordinate the discussion in *Interpreting the Gospel* with the sermons in *Patterns for Preaching*.

SECTION ONE

Thoughts and Issues
for Beginning Preachers

I vividly remember sitting in the chancel before my first sermon. I was an undergraduate student in the College of the Bible at Phillips University. I was invited to fill the pulpit of my home church one summer Sunday while our pastor was on vacation. My heart was beating so hard I could feel it in my chest. My palms sweat. My mouth was dry. I began to shake. I wondered whether I could stand and speak. While I had experienced some nervousness in public speaking classes, this anxiety was different. Although the worshiping congregation numbered over 300, I had previously talked to larger groups. Because the church was in a small town, the people in the congregation were my everyday friends, neighbors, and relatives.

On the one hand, I knew the community supported me. I could see it in their eyes. I could feel it in their handshakes. On the other hand, speaking on behalf of God invoked a heavier sense of responsibility than giving an informative talk in speech class on repairing a flat tire on a bicycle. Although I felt a sense of call, I asked myself in dread, "What possessed me to say yes when the elders asked me preach today?"

I have since learned that many beginning preachers have similar feelings and questions. I have also learned that even the most seasoned preachers have such anxieties.

This section intends to help students name and begin to process anxieties that prevent them from giving their best attention to learning to preach. Chapter 1 is a collage of uncertainties common to beginning preachers; I offer some preliminary responses to those concerns. Chapter 2 deals with a question that is less common, but is sometimes acute: Why should I learn to preach?

CHAPTER ONE

Anxieties of Beginning Preachers

Seasoned preachers frequently tell me that the hardest sermons they have ever given were to peers and professors in preaching class. As one of my students said recently, "I am much more nervous preaching in class than when I preach in my field work site." In this chapter I list the most common anxieties in my first-year preaching classes. I also offer reports from former students and preachers to assure current students that they can successfully make their way through the briars of uncertainty to the pulpit.

Who am I to preach?

Many beginning preachers feel inadequate when they contemplate speaking in behalf of Christian tradition. Students can be perceptively aware of what they do not know about the Bible, Christian tradition, theology, and life. Students can be painfully conscious of moral shortcomings. Some students cannot name the sources of their distress, but feel it deeply. *Who am I to preach?* Seasoned preachers continue to experience such uneasiness. Yet many say the experiences of call and ordination are sufficient to move them toward the pulpit: they are claimed by a Power not their own. For some students, preaching class is a means to explore whether they are called. The Bible, church history, and conversation with contemporary ministers reveal many preachers who suffer from similar doubts. The reluctant prophet is less the exception than the rule.

I feel so vulnerable.

Many beginning preachers feel exposed — intellectually, bodily, emotionally, and spiritually. Students must preach ideas that are still tentative. The architecture of many pulpits puts the preacher's body on display. The preacher's emotions are often telegraphed through posture, tone of voice. Even when preachers do not speak directly about themselves, they reveal their spirituality through the selection of biblical texts and sermon topics, through the values that they commend, through the ways they develop sermons.

A preacher is vulnerable. The risk is great. However, preachers who identify their points of vulnerability often find taproots that are ripe for growth. For instance, when I know that I must risk a tender idea about God in a sermon, I give that idea my best thought. Often a congregation's response helps me extend that thought. Furthermore, students often find that vulnerability is a point of contact between preacher and congregation. Preachers who articulate their own questions and reservations usually find the congregation resonating with them. The congregation can grow in faith by attending to their exposed points. Of course, as noted in chapters 5 and 12, certain self-revelations are not suitable for Christian preaching.

What if I misrepresent God?

Beginning preachers are sometimes afraid that they will misrepresent God or other aspects of life. The truth, of course, is that even the best preachers occasionally misrepresent God. God, and life, are always more than we can fathom. Knowing that we can never speak fully of God, Barbara Shires Blaisdell, a pastor from California, advises preachers to speak adequately of God and life.[1] In the tension of the preaching moment, the most eloquent tongue can misspeak. I know a pastor who, in the heat of the moment, even said something that the pastor did not believe to be true.

The whole of a preacher's testimony to the gospel seldom rides on one sermon. Preachers who misinterpret God or who say something foolish can usually correct themselves in a subsequent sermon or through other avenues of congregational communication (e.g., the newsletter). When I come face to face with my own inadequate interpretations of the gospel and life, I am comforted by a statement from the book of Acts: God has never been without "witness in doing good" (Acts 14:17). When a sermon is less than it should be, God approaches the congregation through other means.

Am I too young? Am I too old?

Some younger preachers wonder whether they can say something meaningful to parishioners who are older and more experienced. Some older preachers wonder whether they can say something meaningful to younger people. My impression is that mature people in the congregation listen first for a word that is gospel-centered and life-related. Secondarily, they consider the preacher's age. Older listeners frequently want to hear from rising generations of Christians. Senior Christians sometimes interpret the presence of a youthful minister as a sign of hope. Younger people are often hungry for the wisdom of age and experience, especially when it is spoken sensitively.

To be sure, younger preachers have not lived as long as older members. However, that does not negate the importance of the younger preacher's experience. Living a long time, in itself, can add little to understanding. Learning from experience allows persons to deepen and grow. A youthful minister can frequently help older members reflect on their experience in ways that help the older group better understand the meanings of their lives. Young and old can deepen their knowledge of one another by listening to each other.

Some second-career students are anxious about the degree to which they can learn to preach. Can an old dog learn new tricks? Can a former lawyer get the difference between making a case to a jury and preaching the gospel in a congregation? Of course. The requisites are a desire to learn, the courage to risk, and the willingness to experiment. Second-career preachers draw on broad and deep life experience that is eyeball-to-eyeball with ambiguities and complexities. A grandmother said to a twenty-five-year-old preacher, "Life is just not as simple as you think." Because they tend to be secure in their own identities, older class members often accept criticism, and do not take themselves with paralyzing seriousness. I do not mean to romanticize second career students. A few are curmudgeons. Others use their age as an excuse for undisciplined work. But, at their best, they leaven the class.

Can I be myself in the pulpit?

Occasionally, students are afraid they cannot be themselves in the pulpit. They think they must imitate other preachers — often those who speak in artificial tones or manifest other unnatural mannerisms. However, listeners are most receptive when the preacher speaks and acts in the pulpit in ways that are consistent with the way the preacher talks and behaves elsewhere. When the preacher puts on a different manner of expression, listeners tend to suspect that the preacher is hiding behind the strange delivery.[2] Can we be ourselves in the pulpit? Absolutely. In fact, you should be yourself.

Preaching class aims to help students begin to discover their own voices. Many preachers take years to feel their way into a mode of preaching that is genuinely self-expressive. A student named Scott once told me, "When I began the class, I knew I had begun to develop my style; but I had no idea what a 'Scott-style' would be. Now I have some clues."

I am reluctant to criticize other preachers.

Frequently in preaching classes, students are asked to critique each other's sermons. Sermon criticism involves two dimensions: pinpointing strengths and identifying areas to be strengthened. In class, student respondents are typically generous in affirmation. Preachers need affirmation to gain confidence and to build on their strengths. However, student preachers must also claim their weaknesses in order to rectify them. A respondent hurts the preacher — and the church — by keeping silent about a concern in order to avoid causing the preacher to feel bad. A student respondent is called to help student preachers achieve full-bodied understanding of their preaching.

A student is sometimes especially hesitant to critique a preacher from a different racial, ethnic, geographical, or religious community. For instance, a European American sometimes finds it difficult to suggest changes to an African American preacher. On the one hand, cultural sensitivity is a positive sign of growing respect among different communities. On the other hand, preachers in all communities can improve. Students and teachers need to become aware of preaching expectations in the communities in the class. Class members need to hold the preacher accountable to the gospel and to highest standards in the preacher's community. For their part, preachers must not hide behind cultural difference in order to avoid facing things that they need to improve.

How can I fill twenty minutes?

On the first day of an introductory preaching course, some class members nearly always ask how they can fill twenty minutes (or whatever length is customary for the sermon). But, by the time they put together the first sermon, many of them are dismayed at the amount of material that they cannot use because they must keep their sermons within the time limits required by the class. A sermon needs to be long enough to cover the subject, but does not need to be of an artificial length. When a sermon is meaningful, a congregation is usually willing for it to be longer or shorter than usual.

Can I find something fresh to talk about every week for the next forty years?

Students can be daunted that they must come up with a fresh subject every Sunday. For a twenty-five-year-old ordinand, that could be forty years – totaling at least 2,000 sermons. However, long-term pastors report that they find a significant direction for each sermon as long as they are sensitive to the congregation and are theologically alive. Many preachers find a lectionary to point in ever new directions. The reflective pastor's problem is more likely to be narrowing on one focus from many possible foci.

Further, all sermons share a common core. The preacher seeks to examine the subject matter from the standpoint of the gospel. One of my colleagues uses the analogy of a house. People who look through different windows see the interior of the house from different points of view. Likewise, from week to week people look at the gospel and its implications from different points of view (e.g., different biblical texts, different doctrines, different practices, different situations). Preachers also have favorite themes to which they return repeatedly. Preachers need to become conscious of these themes to make sure that they have adequate theological depth to help a congregation grow in the gospel. Ministers need to be aware of these themes so as not to bore the congregation with repetition.

Every time I stand to preach, I shake like a leaf in the wind. Do I ever get over that?

With varying degrees of intensity, most pastors feel nervous before they preach, no matter how long they are in the ministry. Some shake like a leaf in the wind. Others perspire. Others get dry mouth. Some feel a knot in the pit of their stomachs. A certain amount of nervousness creates energy that the preacher can channel into positive animation. However, preachers do need to manage their physical expressions of anxiety so that those expressions do not distract the congregation from the content of the sermon. As one experienced preacher has said, "I get butterflies every time I preach, but now they fly in formation." In chapter 13 I describe some things that preachers can do to help focus their nervous energy. With experience and practice, preachers usually lose the most visible manifestations of nervousness.

Can I survive evaluation from peers and professors, especially watching the videotape?

A student classroom sermon is usually followed by an evaluation by peers and professors. Some students are more anxious about the feedback than about preaching. The evaluative remarks of students and teachers aim to help the student become the best preacher possible. Virtually all class members make their comments in ways that are collegial, warm, and caring. I have never heard a mean-spirited critique. Students and teachers seek to help students name points in their preaching that need to be improved. This part of the process can be painful. However, the hurt is similar to the pain that follows surgery. The pain is a sign of healing.

Some students claim that watching their first sermon on videotape is very hard. "I can't believe I am that person on the screen." Students usually get over the shock of seeing and hearing themselves on tape after a second or third viewing. By then, they are receptive to learning from the tape. They can identify qualities that both enhance and frustrate communication.

Will I be able to negotiate gaps between clergy and laity in the congregation?

Clergy and students are often aware of gaps between clergy and laity in the congregation, and gaps among laypeople in the community. Clergy often have different theological convictions than laity. Differences are sometimes pronounced in worldview, class, education, and many other arenas. Students are sometimes aware that these gaps can result in misunderstanding and even conflict. Through creative interaction, preachers can often find ways to bridge differences. Even when changes in perspective do not come about, clergy and laity can reach a high degree of mutual understanding and trust. Indeed, the ability to live as a community in the midst of differing perspectives, worldviews, and situations is often a powerful witness to the reign of God.

How do I deal with the fact that some people may think I do not belong in the pulpit?

The congregation sometimes contains persons who think that the pastor should not be in the pulpit. Some members resist women preachers. Congregations of one dominant racial or ethnic composition can resist the leadership of persons from other groups. For instance, European American congregations do not always welcome African American, Hispanic American, Asian

American, or Native American pastors. While some reservations derive from thoughtful theological reflection, most result from biases that the community has not critically examined.

What can preachers do to help gain acceptance? There is no simple formula that can be applied in every situation. Many ministers find that a change of climate results from developing relationships of trust with members of the congregation. In sermons, the preacher can help the church name its uneasiness and critically reflect upon it from the standpoint of the gospel. However, beginning preachers need to be forewarned that rational discussion will not always lead the congregation to a change of heart. Some resistance is nonrational and breaks apart very slowly, if at all. When some members are uneasy with the preacher because of theological conviction, the preacher can help them evaluate the adequacy of their beliefs. To be frank, everyone may not accept you. At such times you can remember, "Through ordination, the larger church has set me aside to help the community grow in the gospel. Growth is sometimes painful. I take heart in the knowledge that God is always with me."

Have I mentioned, or accurately described, your particular anxieties? If not, it might be helpful to name and characterize them. I hope that the responses to the misgivings in this chapter encourage students to face other anxieties and to take the risk of preaching. The risk is great. But helping a congregation come alive in response to the gospel is more than worth the risk.

CHAPTER TWO

Why Preaching Is Important

Many theologians begin their books or lectures with statements of why their subjects are important for the minister, the church, and even the world. Sometimes, these rationales are statements of the obvious. However, I have come to think that such thinkers have made an important discovery: Some things bear being said again and again. The subject is new to some readers. They need to hear for the first time why it is important. Others have forgotten why the subject is noteworthy. They need to be reminded. Some have a distorted view. They need to reframe their thinking. Some question the degree to which the topic is significant. They need a significant rationale for pursuing the topic.

In this chapter, I review several basic, interrelated reasons for why preaching is important. I separate them only for purposes of discussion. My short-range hope is that the importance of preaching calls beginning students to put forth their best energies in preaching class. My long-range hope is for ministers to develop a deep confidence in preaching so that year after year they will give it prime attention. Indeed, a minister can help the congregation recognize the importance of the sermon by preaching occasionally on the nature and purpose of preaching. Such sermons should help the congregation realize that they need to help the preacher have the time and resources necessary for adequate sermon preparation.

Preaching Partakes of the Nature and Purpose of the Church

The nature and purpose of the church reveals a foundational reason for learning to preach. The nature and purpose of the church extend from those of Israel. In Genesis 12:1–3, God calls Abram and Sarai so that they and their descendants will be blessed, and so that, in them, "all the families of the earth shall be blessed." A phrase in Isaiah 42:6 summarizes how the blessing is to take place. Israel is to be "a light to the nations." Israel is chosen and blessed not for its own sake, but to witness among Gentiles (the nations) to the sovereignty of God and to the ways in which God wants all people to live with one

9

another and with nature so that all will be blessed. Jesus interprets the church as an extension of this mission by saying to the disciples, "You are the light of the world" (Matthew 5:14). Luke and Paul speak for other early Christian writers in confirming that the purpose of the church is to be a channel that extends the blessing of the God of Israel into the Gentile world (e.g., Acts 3:25; Romans 14:8; Galatians 3:8; Ephesians 1:3).

In continuity with these themes, contemporary systematic theologian Clark M. Williamson offers a contemporary statement of the nature and purpose of the church.

> The church is that community of human beings called into existence by God, through the Holy Spirit, to live from and by the gospel of God, witnessing to the grace and command of the gospel of the God of Israel offered to all the world and hence to the church in Jesus Christ, and doing so both to remind itself of what it is about, and on behalf of the world, that it might one day reflect the glory of God.[1]

By nature, the church is called; the church does not constitute itself. The church is to witness to the gospel for the benefit of the world. The gospel is the news revealed to the church through Jesus Christ of God's unconditional love for each and all, and God's call for justice for each and all. The church is to model in its internal life and in its words and actions in the larger world how God makes it possible for all people to live.[2]

The nature and purpose of preaching are shaped by those of the larger church. Just as the Christian community is called, so preachers are called. Nearly every theology of the church regards preaching as central to the identity of the pastor. The title of a book by Barbara Brown Taylor, an Episcopal priest who lectures and writes widely about preaching, indicates the relationship between the preacher's being and activity: *The Preaching Life*.[3] Students learn to preach not just to perform a ministerial function, but to be fully who they are called to be.

I do not mean to leave the impression that persons ordained to the ministry of word and sacrament are the only preachers. Most churches recognize that anyone can be called to preach. Many churches make provision for laypersons to preach. Preachers occasionally are raised up outside conventional church circles. The relationship between call and ecclesiastical endorsement is complicated. For the most part, officially designated preachers faithfully represent the gospel. However, the church's sanctioned preachers can stultify the good news. At times, preachers who are not officially authorized by the church (and whom the church might even resist) appear to be called by God to regenerate the church or to voice the gospel in the larger culture. The church must sometimes wrestle painfully with the degree to which it can recognize the validity of such messages and messengers.

Preaching is a mode of witness to the gospel. The distinctive vocation of preaching is to help the congregation name and interpret the divine presence and purpose. The pastor builds up Christian communities so that they can witness with insight and power. Ministers learn to preach to help the sermon do its part within the larger aim of the church.

The whole life of the church should represent the nature and purpose of the gospel. Through its particular venue, each aspect of ministry ought to witness to God's unconditional love and call for justice: Christian education, *koinonia* events and groups, pastoral care and counseling, administrative decisions, the use of the church building, mission beyond the congregation, liturgy.

The congregation is a system of interrelated ministries and persons. In this vein, I frequently hear ministers speak broadly of one aspect of the church's life encompassing all other aspects. For instance, "Everything that we do in the church is prayer…evangelism…education…steward-ship… preaching." Such statements call attention to the systemic interrelatedness of the various elements of the church's witness. In a sense, every aspect of the congregation does the same thing. However, such thinking obscures the distinctive responsibilities of different modes of witness. In order to witness faithfully to the gospel, each element in the congregational system must manifest its particular witness to the gospel, and all elements of the congregational network must work together. It is important to learn to preach so that the sermon can make its maximum contribution to the life system of the congregation.

Preaching Is Part of Christian Practice

Preaching is a part of Christian practice. This reason has much in common with the preceding comments on the congregation as a system. However, it has distinct accents derived from a fresh notion of practice. Formerly, practice was considered "someone doing something" in order to achieve an immediate end, with little regard for traditions or communities associated with the practice.[4] An enlarged understanding of practice is emerging in the church. In this enlarged sense, practice is more than "doing something." It is a cooperative human activity with a particular history, with its own sources of knowledge. It is shaped by principles, expectations, and moral standards. A practice is "a way of life."[5] A practice is something we do that shapes who we are, how we perceive the world, and how we behave. Certain values, feelings, and behaviors are appropriate to it, while others are not. People develop a deep, existential understanding of the way of life by practice — by joining in it, by understanding the world from its point of view, by living it. Thus, Craig Dykstra, a leading interpreter of this notion of practice, concludes, "Communities do not just engage in practices; in a sense they are practices."[6]

The church is a community of the practice of Christian faith. In addition to being a practice, the Christian community includes several specific practices that mediate and embody aspects of the larger practice. "Christian practices are things Christian people do together over time in response to and in the light of God's active presence for the life of the world."[7] Dykstra identifies thirteen such practices: worship, telling the Christian story to one another, interpreting the Bible and the history of the church's experience, prayer, confession of sin to one another, tolerating and encouraging one another, carrying out acts of service and witness, suffering with and for one another, providing hospitality and care, listening attentively to one another, struggling together to become conscious of our context, criticizing and resisting the principalities and powers, working together to maintain social structures that will sustain life as God intends.[8]

Preaching is not a distinctive practice, but is a part of the practice of worship. In worship,

> we use the familiar elements of everyday life — food, water, oil, embrace, word — to proclaim and celebrate what God is doing in the world and in our lives. Worship distills the Christian meaning of the practices and holds them up for the whole community to see. We confess our failure to do them well, receive assurance of God' grace, hear stories and speak words that relate our practices to God's creative and redemptive work, and go out strengthened to live more faithfully.[9]

Preachers help the community "hear the stories and speak words that relate our practices to God's own creative and redemptive work." The work of ministers is to help the community learn Christian practice in depth and to help "make the practices happen." The sermon interprets Christian community as practice, and it interprets particular Christian practices. The preacher teaches "the inner workings and qualities of each practice" so that those "workings and qualities open up to the reality and truth on which they are founded."[10]

God Is Active in the Community through Preaching

God works in multiple modes, but the Bible and Christian tradition stress God's movement in the world through speech. The following biblical passages are representative. God creates the world by speaking (Genesis 1:3 — 2:3) and continues to work in the natural world in the same way (Psalm 147:12-20). God is with the mouths of Moses and Aaron as they confront Pharaoh (Exodus 4:10–17). God commands Israel to victory through Deborah (Judges 4:1–16). Preaching is a sign of the presence of the Spirit (Isaiah 61:1–4). God talks to and through the prophets, bringing to pass what they say (Jeremiah 7:1 — 8:3; 26:1-6). God communicates through Lady Wisdom crying in the streets to warn people against folly that leads to ruin and to show them the path to life (Proverbs 1:20–33).

These themes continue in the ministries of Jesus and the early church. Jesus' call on the lakeshore singularly transforms Peter, Andrew, James, and John from fishing into discipleship (Mark 1:16–20 and parallels). Through speech, Jesus commands nature and heals (Mark 4:35–41; 7:24–31 and parallels). Jesus promises that the gospel word that the church sows through the preaching will bear fruit (Mark 4:1–20 and parallels). Jesus catches the preacher's attention when he says, "I tell you, on the day of judgment you will have to give an account for every careless word you utter; for by your words you will be justified, and by your words you will be condemned" (Matthew 12:36-37). According to the fourth Gospel, Jesus is the word become flesh (John 1:1–18).

The first Pentecost demonstrates the potency of preaching as Peter's sermon leads 3,000 persons to repent, be baptized, and receive the Holy Spirit (Acts 2:1–42). For Paul, preaching is an act of power. "For the message about the cross is foolishness to those who are perishing, but to us who are being saved, it is the power of God" (1 Corinthians 1:18–25). Similarly, Hebrews 4:12 describes the word of God as "living and active, sharper than any two-edged sword." The apostle to the Gentiles underscores the importance of preaching when he wrote "But how are they [the Gentiles] to call on one in whom they have not believed? And how are they to believe in one of whom they have never heard? And how are they to hear without someone to proclaim him?" (Romans 10:14).

Christian tradition after the Bible repeatedly emphasizes that God can operate through preaching. John Calvin represents this confidence when he writes, God "did not entrust the ancient folk to angels but raised up teachers from the earth truly to perform the angelic office." God continues "to teach us today through human means." God was not content to give the law, "but added priests as interpreters from whose lips the people might ask its true meaning" (Malachi 2:7). In the same way today God desires us to be attentive to its reading, but also appoints instructors to help us by their efforts."[11]

Preachers continue to have the sense that God can move through preaching. African American, Hispanic, and European American pentecostal congregations testify that the Holy Spirit prompts the exuberance that often breaks forth in worship. The divine presence is usually less demonstrative in the long-established denominations, but is no less tangible. My colleague Charles Allen, a systematic theologian, says, "I've never prepared a sermon that turned out quite the way I thought it would when I began to prepare it. And I've never had a congregation respond to a sermon quite they way I expected. Lots of times, more goes on than I intend. Some of that, I'm sure, is the Spirit."

However, a preacher cannot casually claim that everything relating to a sermon is of God. Ministers sometimes speak simplistically of the sermon as "God's word." This nomenclature emphasizes that God can work through preaching. However, I have reservations about the casual use of that phrase to describe the sermon. In sermons, pastors can pawn their own idiosyncrasies and idols as God. Pastors can even use the sermon to abuse. In short, there is no guarantee that every word of every sermon is altogether God's word.

For these reasons, I think it wiser to speak of the sermon as an interpretation of the gospel. The notion of "interpretation" allows the preacher and the congregation to have a high degree of confidence that comes from critical thinking. Yet, the term interpretation invites humility on the part of the preacher. Human finitude limits a minister's capacity to perceive God's purposes and to articulate all that ought to be said about them.

The Spoken Word Can Have Power

The spoken word can have the power to create that which it speaks. This theme resonates with the preceding one and is as old as the Bible.

> For as the rain and the snow come down from heaven,
>   and do not return there until they have watered the earth,
> making it bring forth and sprout,
>   giving seed to the sower and bread to the eater,
> so shall my word be that goes out from my mouth;
>   it shall not return to me empty,
> but it shall accomplish that which I purpose,
>   and succeed in the thing for which I sent it. (Isaiah 55:10–11)

God's word has the power to affect that which it speaks.

To a degree, God's speech is a paradigm for human speech. The capacity to speak is a part of what it means to bear the image of God. The language of human beings can have power in our limited spheres in a manner similar to the power of divine speech in the cosmic sphere. Words can name, create, and destroy. Words are deeds.[12] To speak is to act. A word is an event. When one person speaks and another hears, something physical happens. According to the philosopher Alfred North Whitehead,

> in the production of sound, the lungs and throat are brought into play. Sound waves travel through space and move similarly in the eardrum in the body of the listener. The sense of the vague intimacies of organic existence is also excited.[13]

Speaking and listening stir the whole self.

Children still learn the proverb, "Sticks and stones may break my bones, but words will never hurt me." That statement simply is not true. Words can create new possibilities. Words can reshape old patterns. A young person says to another in the moonlight under the apple tree, "I love you," and the two take a step toward becoming one. Twenty-five years later, one says, "It's over," and their world is reshaped.

Preachers need to be careful not to romanticize the powerful possibilities of language. While God's speech is paradigmatic of human speech, it is potent partly because it is God's speech. All human speech in the Bible and in Christian tradition is not generative. Some human talk is informational, mundane, or trivial. Some talk works against the gospel. These negative possibilities impress the preacher with the importance of using language carefully. We want to use language in such a way that the sermon becomes a gospel event.

The Sermon Shapes Perspective

The sermon gives the preacher an opportunity afforded to very few leaders in North America: the regular opportunity to help a body of people reflect on the meaning of the whole of life from the perspective of the transcendent. This aspect of the preacher's calling coheres beautifully with the results of a study of why people come to church. They want to make sense of life from the standpoint of ultimate reality.[14] For forty-eight or more Sundays a year, a preacher has twenty minutes, or more to help people reflect on the meaning of life.

Since God is concerned about everything in the world, the preacher is called to help the congregation understand it all, too (though not usually in a single sermon). In addition to traditional religious concerns, the preacher needs to help the community ponder the implications of the gospel in personal and social relationships, in racial and ethnic matters, in political and economic affairs. Karl Barth, a prominent theologian earlier this century, coined a compelling image: the preacher broods with the Bible at one hand and the newspaper at the other.[15] Today, I suppose, we would say that the preacher broods with one eye on the Bible and other on CNN.

North America is filled with public commentators on the current scene — newspaper and magazine columnists, radio and television talk show hosts, social analysts of various kinds. However, few such commentators speak with theological insight. Personal preference is the only norm to which most popular public analysts are accountable. By contrast, the preacher is appointed, on a weekly basis, to lead other people in making sense of the world from the viewpoint of God's unconditional love and universal will for justice.

The need for thorough criticism of life is great. Many social philosophers and theologians bemoan the growing cultural and theological illiteracy of people today. These illiteracies are accompanied by a loss of critical thinking. Fewer and fewer people know how to delineate an idea or experience for analysis, identify the issues that must be investigated in order to clarify, gather data and perspectives on an issue, and come to a normative understanding. Many people derive values and make major life decisions on the basis of sound bites from talk shows, or gossip at the hair shop, or how they feel at a given moment. Weekly preaching gives the pastor opportunities to help the congregation recover the basic stories, language, practices, and norms of the Christian faith, and to develop a critical theological method for interpreting everything in life from the vision of the gospel.

Preachers in the long-established denominations sometimes lament, "There are some things I cannot talk about in the pulpit." They usually mean that some people in the congregation get upset when preachers voice their opinions on subjects such as politics, economics, or sexuality. To be sure, such situations are complex and sensitive. At the risk of alienating some readers, I must report that the difficulties are frequently as much the responsibility of the minister as of the congregation. Preachers do not always help the congregation understand that they are dealing with these areas because God is concerned. The preacher does not speak from a theological frame of reference. Consequently, the Christian preacher's message cannot always be differentiated from a political commentator on National Public Radio. Preachers seldom lead congregations through the process of reasoning that led them to their conclusion. Preachers frequently ask congregations to change their minds on important issues on the basis of nothing more than the preacher's opinion. Sermons can deal with complex issues in sound-bite fashion. Instead of dealing with such matters in depth, preachers tend to sideswipe them, perhaps with nothing more than an illustration or a passing comment. The preacher can give the congregation the impression that if they do not accept the preacher's view, they are unfaithful: "Take it or leave it. There's no room in between."

However, some preachers can talk with their congregations about almost anything. The preacher can even propose ideas that are diametrically opposed to the dominant view in the congregation, but communication continues. A study of preachers and congregations in which preachers have long histories of successfully helping congregants reflect on a wide range of issues finds that trust between preacher and people is a linchpin. Furthermore, the pastor speaks from an explicitly theological point of view. The minister helps the congregation identify a range of interpretive possibilities and the strong and weak points of all. The minister helps the congregation understand the rationale for the viewpoints the pastor is commending. Such preachers leave some elbow room for the congregation to disagree. The preacher does not demean or blast the congregation. The preacher makes it clear that pastor and people are bound together in covenant on a journey of mutually exploring what it means to be faithful to the gospel.[16] In an environment of trust, the preacher can be a provocateur — provoking the community to consider God, church, and world in fresh ways.

If the preacher is to lead the community in the holistic, theological interpretation of life, then the preacher must develop a life of study. Pastors must show that they have a current and thorough understanding of the subjects on which they are speaking. Preachers who speak without careful preparation discredit themselves and the gospel.

The Service of Worship Is the Largest Regular Gathering of the Congregation

The service of worship is the largest regular gathering of the congregation. Pastors have weekly occasion to share with the church the best of their interaction with the Bible, Christian tradition, and current life. Pastors will make fullest use of this occasion when they have a clear understanding of what can happen through the sermon and how to shape sermons to help the congregation have a good chance to interact with the gospel. Later material in this book should help students develop perspectives on these matters.

The sermon is a key to setting the tone for the Christian community. I heard someone say that congregations become like the preaching they hear. Given the fact that the congregation is a system affected by many factors, this claim is overly extravagant. However, preaching contributes to the shape of the community. For instance, a congregation nurtured on sermons portraying God as large and gracious tends to become large-minded and gracious. A congregation whose preacher depicts a God who is small, rigid, and legalistic tends to become small, rigid, and legalistic.

Despite the fact that the service of worship is the largest single congregational assembly of the week, some clergy regard preaching as an afterthought.

Sermon preparation gets lost in the flood of moment-to-moment details of ministry. Some ministers spend the whole day answering routine phone calls, talking with people who drift by the church building, picking up office supplies, and stopping by the hospital on the way home. Saturday evening comes, but they have not thought toward the sermon. Such ministers need to restructure their time management to include sermon preparation.

Furthermore, when congregations seek pastoral leadership, they nearly always place preaching at or near the top of the list of qualities that they desire in a minister. For instance, a recent seminary graduate reports that when meeting with a committee appointed by a local congregation to nominate a pastor, the chair began the interview by saying, "We want someone who can bring us a real message."

The Gospel Transforms People through Preaching

The gospel transforms people through preaching. Frederick Buechner, a minister and novelist, tells an autobiographical story, now a classic in the literature of preaching, that demonstrates the transformative possibilities in preaching. Buechner was not a practicing Christian when he visited the Madison Avenue Presbyterian Church, located at 73rd Street and Madison Avenue, in New York City.

> At twenty-seven, living alone in New York, trying with no success to start a novel and in love with a girl who was not in love with me, I went to hear a famous preacher preach one morning although I had no idea at the time that he was famous and went only on impulse — I was not a churchgoer — because his church was next door. It was around the time that Elizabeth II was crowned at Westminster Abbey, and the preacher played variations on the theme of coronation. All I remember of what he said is the very last, and that not very well, just one phrase of it, in fact, that I'm sure of. He said that Jesus Christ refused a crown when Satan offered it in the wilderness, or something like that. He said that the kingdom of Jesus was not of this world. And yet, again and again, he said, Jesus was crowned king in the hearts of those who believed in him, crowned king. I remember thinking that was a nice enough image, as images in sermons go, and I remember how the preacher looked up there in the pulpit, twitching around a good bit, it seemed to me, and plucking at the lapels of his black gown. And then he went on just a few sentences more.
>
> He said that unlike Elizabeth's coronation in the Abbey, this coronation of Jesus in the believer's heart took place among confession — and I thought, yes, yes, confession — and tears, he said — and I thought tears, yes, perfectly plausible that the coronation of Jesus in the believing heart should take place among confession and tears. And then with his head bobbing up and down so that his glasses glittered, he said in his odd, sandy voice, the voice of an old nurse, that the coronation of Jesus took place among confession and tears, and then,

as God was and is my witness, great laughter, for reasons that I have never satisfactorily understood, the great wall of China crumbled and Atlantis rose up out of the sea, and on Madison Avenue at 73rd Street, tears leapt from my eyes.[17]

As a result of a chain of events sparked by this sermon, Buechner awakened afresh to God and Christian faith. He enrolled in seminary and became a minister who is noted for his preaching. Christian themes refract through the novels that he continues to write. In short, he was converted.

To be sure, every sermon will not draw responses that are at the same level as that represented by Frederick Buechner. Some sermons do not appear to draw any response beyond the casual, "Nice sermon, Reverend." Some listeners may resist a particular sermon. A preacher, then, cannot always gauge the effect of preaching on the basis of the congregation's immediate response to a single sermon. However, the church repeatedly discovers that faithful preaching helps the gospel have room to work. Through preaching, the gospel touches individuals and communities, sometimes in singular moments, sometimes cumulatively, sometimes dramatically, sometimes almost imperceptibly.

I grew up in the Ozark Mountains in southern Missouri. When it rains, a person can seldom distinguish the individual raindrops as they descend from the sky, much less remember any of them. But the soil absorbs them. Drop by drop, they gather in pools deep in the ground. When enough water collects, it pushes its way to the surface, and a spring begins. The ground around the spring is changed. Flowers and ferns appear. Animals come to drink. The trees grow taller and faster.

Once in a while, people are touched by preaching in singular, memorable moments, as was Frederick Buechner. Nearly every Christian can vividly recall, and even reconstruct, a particular sermon or two or three. But, most of the time, the effect of preaching is more like the accumulation of raindrops in the Ozarks. One at a time, sermons filter into the congregation and gather in the depths of the heart of the community. Eventually, the character of the preaching pushes to the surface and begins to flow through the congregation. The preacher cannot force this action. But a minister can help the process by giving careful attention to the conception, preparation, and embodiment of the sermon so that as much water as possible reaches the subterranean reservoirs of the community.

My father told me about a couple in the Ozarks who lived in a house at the base of a hollow and who carried a bucket a half mile to the river for water. They worked the soil in the hollow to increase the amount of water that the soil absorbed in order to develop a spring near their cabin. At the time they died, they were still walking to the river. But years later, at the bottom of the hollow, a spring bubbled up. Preaching is often that way.

SECTION TWO

Three Contexts for Preaching Today

Preaching is never generic. It always takes place in a particular context. In fact, preaching typically takes place in multiple overlapping and interacting contexts: the preacher's personal life, the preacher's household, the local congregation, the denomination, the global Christian community, the neighborhood and city, the state and nation, the globe, and the cosmos. Contexts include elements that are physical, intellectual, emotional, and behavioral. A context is not static, but changes.

The preacher should understand the contexts of the sermon in gospel perspective. On the one hand, a minister needs to communicate in expressions that people understand. The gospel can engage a community most intensively when it comes to expression in the language of the local community. The Word becomes particular flesh. On the other hand, the gospel challenges aspects of the worldview of the context. Until the complete manifestation of the reign of God, every context can better conform to God's unconditional love and will for justice. The preacher aims to analyze the sermon's contexts so as to name the succor and requirements of the gospel with as much precision as possible.

This section discusses three contexts within which preaching takes place. I begin with the church (chapter 3) because Christian vision is the lens through which the preacher and the Christian community interpret the world. The church, of course, is not a single context but is a collage of multiple and interacting contexts. Chapter 4 deals with the larger culture as a context for preaching. I focus on implications for preaching that result from the transition from modernity to postmodernity, and on the movement of the long-established churches from the mainline of the culture to its margins. Chapter 5 explores the life of the preacher as a part of the context of preaching.

19

CHAPTER THREE

The Church as a Context for Preaching

The church is a multidimensional context for preaching. The dimensions range from ways in which the Christian community is a source of the knowledge of God, through the church's relationship with the wider society, to the fussing at the congregational meeting regarding the long distance phone bill. While congregations have many similar dynamics, each local community has qualities particular to it. These factors, and their interactions, create a charged congregational environment in which the minister rises to speak. At times, the preacher can almost feel the charge (or the apathy) in the worship space. The minister who has a broad and deep understanding of the contexts of the church can draw upon those aspects of the local situation that manifest the gospel and can challenge those that work against it.

This chapter first explores the church as the context within which preacher and congregation derive their distinctive Christian interpretations of God and the world. I then identify the characteristics of preaching that are particular to different historic Christian denominations. I turn to the relationship between the service of worship and preaching. The chapter considers an approach to discerning the ethos of a local community, and concludes by noting that multiple groups within the congregation call for multiple forms of preaching.

Preacher, People, and Christian Community

The Christian community is not only a context in which preaching is expressed. It is also a context that forms both preacher and people. As noted in chapter 2, the church is a community of practice. Christian practices are "conditions under which various kinds and forms of knowledge emerge — knowledge of God, of ourselves, and of the world; knowledge that is not only personal but also public. Christian practice forms the virtue and character and wisdom of the communities and individuals who participate in them."

21

Through "participation in practices of Christian life, the community of faith comes continually to awareness of and participation in the redemptive activity of God in the world."[1] The thirteen Christian practices (enumerated on pages 11–12) are the primary set of lenses through which the preacher and the congregation interpret the church and the world.

These practices shape the preacher and the community. The preacher develops a deep existential understanding of them by participating in them. Christian practice develops the distinctive perceptions and behaviors of the Christian community. For instance, the church learns to worship the God of Israel (in contrast to lesser gods) by engaging in Christian liturgy. Children are more likely to learn that the world is God's creation and that they are in partnership with God in its care from Bible study than from Sunday morning cartoons. The stories that Christians tell one another usually have a greater potential to develop lasting community than the stories that soap operas tell. The preacher helps the church remember Christian practice, interpret its significance, and bring it to life.

To be sure, not all these practices are unique to the church. For example, many organizations engage in service to other people. However, these practices are distinctive of Christian life and witness. Even when a church's practice is behaviorally similar to that of other organizations, Christian participation often has a distinctive character. For instance members of a service club staff a kitchen for the homeless on weekends. They do so in order to help people who are down-and-out. Christians who engage in the same activity also want to help the homeless. In addition, their service is a response to the love that they have experienced from God and a testimony to God's will for justice for all people. Ideally, Christians who serve in the soup kitchen also analyze the larger social values that lead to homelessness and take actions designed to change those values.

Within given communities, Christian practice sometimes evolves. The history of the church is, in part, a record of how the church tries to work out the implications of practice in each new situation. Christians sometimes debate how best to understand and enact Christian practice. Occasionally, the preacher must help a denomination or a congregation reinterpret Christian practice in order for the church to live up to the best insights of wider Christian practice.

Churches do not always think, feel, or behave in the best of Christian practice. Since sin is an active agent within the Christian community, the church can distort its interpretation of God, church, and world. The actions and attitudes of the church can subvert the gospel. Worship of the God of Israel can degenerate into veneration of denominational custom. Telling stories to one another can become gossip. In short, pastors cannot let themselves be mindlessly formed by all that happens in Christian community. The preacher is called to engage in critical evaluation of the ways in which Christian communities put Christian practice into practice and to call the community to reformation.

The church can learn important things from the world. Some writers in the Bible point out that knowledge of God can come through created order and through general human experience (e.g., Psalm 19:1–6; Proverbs 6:6–11; Wisdom of Solomon 13:1–9; Acts 14:8–18; 17:22–28; Romans 1:18–23; 2:12–16). The rabbis of the first centuries of the common era speak evocatively of God as the omnipresent one. The philosophical and theological traditions of natural theology hold that we can know something of God through nature, as well as through events and relationships outside of Christian community.

Since God is present at all times and in all places, a human being can come to the knowledge of God in any time and place. In the pungent phrase of Mary Catherine Hilkert (a theologian with a deep interest in preaching), a purpose of the sermon is to help the congregation "name the grace" that is present in every moment.[2] Of course, most moments in life are mixed in their interplay of grace and sin. The church sometimes has difficulty sorting out the knowledge of God that comes through experience from our own desires and fantasies. When the world sets too much of the agenda for the church, the agenda of the gospel can easily disappear.

However, the church does not have a monopoly on insight. Sources outside the Christian community can help the church interpret many situations. For instance, the church can benefit from descriptions of life found in the arts, psychology, sociology, philosophy, political analysis, economics, as well as from persons and groups who do not represent a guild but who are wise. Such sources do not imperially hand normative judgments to the church; normative conclusions result from bringing such sources into critical conversation with the gospel. However, such resources can help the church discover the dynamics of particular situations and how God's love and justice relate to those situations.

In some cases, the perspectives of the world can prompt the church to refocus, enlarge, or correct itself. For instance, for centuries, actual Christian practice in many congregations assumed women to be subordinate to men. Admittedly, some Christian thinkers and communities advocated egalitarian relationships between women and men in almost every period of history. However, the long-established denominations in North America did not widely question the subordination of women until the late 1960s when women in the world began to call for liberation. Provoked by voices outside its walls, the Christian community began to reassess its reading of the Bible, tradition, and practice in regard to the relationship of women and men. Most Christian communities in the long-established denominations conclude that the gospel itself calls for equality between the genders. At its best, Christian practice contains the seeds for its own reform.

Of course, every noise the world makes is not a call for the church to rethink its practice. But the church must remain open to the possibility that the world may call its attention to aspects of the divine will that the church overlooks or distorts. The preacher does not sit smugly in the study, looking out the window at the degraded world. The preacher looks upon the world with compassion born of God's love. The preacher listens for the word that God might be speaking amidst the many confusing and contradictory words of the world. The preacher embraces the world tenderly in the pulpit.

Historic Christian Denominations as Contexts for Preaching

Despite the strong emphasis on the importance of the formative power of Christian community in the preceding question, we cannot speak glibly of Christian practice as if it were a monolith. While Christian communities share many fundamental qualities, each community has its distinguishing marks. The practice of each historic denomination calls for preaching that is characteristic of that denomination in theological content and function (e.g., orthodoxy, Roman Catholicism, the many houses of Protestantism). In our time, the historic denominations are supplemented by contemporary theological families that cut across these historic lines. The leading contemporary families are evangelicalism, postliberalism, liberation theology, and revisionary theology. I deal now with the historic denominations and mention the contemporary families below. Chapter 6 discusses orientations to preaching in the contemporary families in more detail.

Sermons in all Christian traditions, movements, and communities should share the common focus of relating the gospel of the God of Israel to the life of the community hearing the sermon. While this requisite might seem obvious, I state it because I hear a surprising number of sermons that do not articulate an explicitly theological worldview. They offer advice for living or analysis of selected life issues, but they never help the congregation understand these matters from the perspective of the gospel. Such a sermon could as easily be a talk at a service club, a self-help seminar, or a political rally. While such talks may be helpful to listeners, they do not fulfill the calling of Christian preaching, that is, to help the congregation name and interpret the gospel of God.

At the risk of caricature, I cite leading qualities in the preaching of several Christian houses. These different approaches to preaching share the common core of seeking to help the community interpret life from the perspective of the gospel. In some cases, these different denominations use different words to talk about similar characteristics. In other cases, the denominations have genuine differences in emphasis.[3]

For the *Orthodox*, the service of worship is sacramental in its entirety. The reading of the Bible and preaching comprise the sacrament of the word. While the sermon explains aspects of the Bible and church doctrine, it is much more. A sermon functions much like an icon. An icon is a medium through which worshipers experience the truth that the icon represents. Indeed, the Orthodox sermon is not far from being an icon in flesh. A sermon renders that which it bespeaks into the present. For instance, the power of an event from the past or the future becomes actualized in the present. The Holy Spirit animates speaking and listening. The Orthodox preacher suppresses personal creativity in interpretation. The homilist seeks to be a conduit whereby the Spirit can bring the gospel of the historic church to life in the congregation.

The Second Vatican Council (1963-65) was a watershed in *Roman Catholic* understanding of preaching in the twentieth century. Prior to that council, the homily was primarily an explication of a theological doctrine. Across the year, the sermons sought to expose the congregation to the range of churchly teaching. The homily seldom related to the Bible readings or to other parts of the service. Vatican II restored four qualities to the sermon:[4] (1) The preacher is to base the sermon on sacred scripture, and is to interpret life from its standpoint, taking account of church teaching. (2) The sermon is to be liturgical in the sense of doing its part in the service and in reflecting the themes of the Christian year. The church prescribes a lectionary of Bible passages that are supposed to coordinate with seasons of the Christian year. (3) The sermon is to center in the announcement of salvation rather than in moral prescriptions. (4) The sermon is to be familiar conversation, that is, the talk of persons in their full humanity with one another, in accessible language. The homily is less a polished work of art and more a heart-to-heart moment in which the preacher shares insights from the gospel, the Bible, and Catholic teaching about concerns in the community. The preacher joins the people in common struggle with questions, doubts, fears, implications of the faith. This church does not regard preaching as a sacrament, but recognizes that word and sacrament complete one another.

An *Anglican* or an *Episcopalian* sermon is much like a Roman Catholic one. The Episcopal sermon is to be biblical, liturgical, kerygmatic, and conversational, usually in a eucharistic context. The biblical texts are assigned by a lectionary. The preacher is to relate them to the congregation in view of the major concerns of the season of the Christian year and in conjunction with Christian doctrine. However, these matters are not ends in themselves. The sermon has a sacramental quality in that through the sermon, the Holy Spirit aims to disclose the real presence of Christ in the community. The sermon is a vehicle of grace. Just as the Spirit takes the ordinary elements of bread and cup and uses them to reveal Christ, so the Spirit takes the ordinary words of the preacher for similar purpose. The preacher asks, "How do the Bible readings and the Christian year help us realize the renewing presence of Christ?" The sermon is to help the community understand the liturgy itself and especially how Christ is present through the eucharist.

Lutheran preaching, too, is biblical, indebted to a lectionary, and liturgical (though the liturgical context is infrequently eucharistic). The Lutheran sermon often takes place on the axis of law and gospel. In the Lutheran mind, the law reveals our sin and inability to save ourselves, and the good news is that God justifies us by grace. The Lutheran minister preaches nothing but Christ, i.e., the revelation that God graciously does for us what we cannot do for ourselves. The preacher frequently helps the congregation identify how to live in daily life in response to grace. Furthermore, God can speak through the sermon to seek sinners and assure them of divine acceptance. The sermon is also an instrument of conflict in which God battles the principalities and powers. One of the most pernicious enemies of God is the propensity to works righteousness. The Lutheran preacher often exposes our self-destroying efforts to save ourselves and commends God's grace.

In the *Reformed tradition*, preaching has a teaching quality. Reformed preachers who follow Calvin's example preach clearly and directly. The preacher explains how God's grace operates in the biblical passage, and how it continues to operate in the world, generating faith. Calvin's famous third use of the law has a kind of preaching corollary in that the sermon provides instruction for faithful obedience in response to grace. Reformed preachers in early generations had an affinity for *lectio continua* — preaching from continuous reading of books of the Bible. Two sermon patterns preferred by Reformed pastors have been preaching verse by verse and the Puritan plain sermon. (Both are explained in chapter 11.) The most numerous heirs of Reformed preaching are Presbyterians, the Reformed Church, segments of the United Church of Christ, as well as modified forms in the Christian Church (Disciples of Christ), the Christian Churches affiliated with the North American Christian Convention, and the Churches of Christ.

Preaching in the *Wesleyan* spirit is "plain truth for plain people."[5] Wesley turned away from the florid sermons of his day to simple preaching so that people could easily understand the gospel and feel the Spirit. Wesleyan preaching seeks to help people awaken to their need for God and to turn to Christ as the means by which God satisfies their need by showing divine love for sinners. The preacher calls the community to sanctification, i.e., to continuous growth in manifesting the fruit of justification in their personal and social worlds. The Wesleyan preacher stresses the human capacity to accept or reject the gospel. The Holy Spirit generates both inward and outward holiness, the former characterized by existential awareness of divine acceptance and the latter by works in behalf of others. These emphases can still be found in the African Methodist Episcopal Church, the African Methodist Episcopal Zion Church, the Christian Methodist Episcopal Church, the United Methodist Church, and various Wesleyan and Holiness churches.

Anabaptist liturgy is usually simple, consisting of congregational singing, extemporaneous prayers, and other acts of worship shaped by local leaders especially for the occasion, with the sermon as the focal point. In *Baptist* churches, the sermon is usually designed to lead the listeners to an awareness of God's grace made known through Jesus Christ and to a decision in response. The classic decision is to accept the grace of God. The sermon can also call for decisions in support of institutional programs, or on personal or social issues. Indeed, the service of worship is sometimes entirely planned to lead to decision. Such foci can be found in many congregations on the Baptist spectrum: American, independent, Missionary, National, Progressive, Southern, and others.

Other *churches descended from the radical reformation* approach the sermon from the ecclesiological conviction that the church is radically disjunctive from the larger world. The church is to keep itself uncorrupted from the fallen world in order to witness as purely as it can to God's grace and demand for the sake of the world. The sermon is less for evangelism than for leading the congregation in growth in discipleship. These sermons tend to stress the church as a community of mission with the Bible as the primary source for instruction. The Mennonites, for instance, follow these patterns.

Pentecostalism understands the sermon as an event led by the Holy Spirit. Occasional pentecostals make no preparation for the sermon so that their human efforts will not interfere with the message and experience that the Spirit would create in the moment of preaching. Most pentecostal preachers, however, believe that the Spirit anoints the preacher in the preparation of the sermon, as well as in the pulpit. The Spirit anoints the congregation to be receptive. While Pentecostals proclaim the grace of God through Christ as the center of Christian faith, they also stress the work of the Spirit and the importance of the congregation acting on the gifts of the Spirit. Preachers ask both how the Spirit leads them to interpret a biblical passage, and how the passage helps them interpret the presence and work of the Spirit. Such preaching is typical in the Assemblies of God, the Church of God in Christ, the United Pentecostal Church, and other pentecostal bodies.

Some meetings of the *Society of Friends* have programmed worship that includes a sermon. George Fox, founder of the Friends, preached on certain occasions. Other Friends' meetings have unprogrammed worship. Such services take place largely in the famous Quaker silence and rely upon the direct movement of the Spirit in the assembly to lead members to speak in its behalf.

In addition, we need to speak today of the *community churches* and the *Bible churches*. Congregations with these and similar names are multiplying in North America. They do not have a long history as a movement, nor are these congregations in covenant with one another, though they often cooperate on certain tasks. Like many reform movements in the past, many of these churches want to leave behind the denominational accretions that are secondary to faith and return to simplified Christianity in keeping with the spirit of the earliest churches. Since the Bible is the source of faith, doctrine, and practice, their preachers explain the Bible, often in the form of verse by verse exposition. In fifty years, historians of preaching will have a clearer idea than they do today of whether the preaching in this movement coheres sufficiently to be called a tradition.

In the contemporary world, the previous categories are being supplemented, and in some cases supplanted, by theological families that are shared by people across traditional denominational boundaries. Evangelicals, postliberals, liberation theologians, and revisionary thinkers are found in almost all of the above-mentioned groups. The *raison d'être* of the *evangelical* sermon is explaining the Bible and applying it to life. The Bible, divinely inspired, is the preeminent source of the knowledge of God. For *postliberals*, the preacher's task is to help the congregation describe the world from the standpoint of Christian tradition and language. In *liberation theology,* the sermon helps the congregation name and join God's liberating purpose.

Revisionary thinking regards the preaching task as mutual critical correlation between the Christian tradition and the contemporary setting. The preacher correlates the gospel with the contemporary world while criticizing the contemporary world from the viewpoint of the gospel and Christian tradition. The preacher also critiques Christian tradition from the perspective of fresh understanding of God's will.

Particular racial and ethnic communities adapt these traditions to their own customs and mores. For instance, an African American pastor in a Reformed congregation might preach Reformed theology from a liberation perspective in the energetic pattern of call and response found in much African American preaching.

The perspectives of a particular historic denomination or contemporary family does not always provide the depth or breadth necessary for full-bodied growth in Christian faith and witness. Preachers must sometimes go outside their denominational and theological communities for theological supplement. The gospel itself is the final norm against which to evaluate every aspect of every tradition's notion of preaching.

The Service of Worship as a Context for Preaching

The service of worship is the immediate context of preaching.[6] The primary purpose of worship is revealed in the etymologies of a Hebrew word, *shachah*, and a Greek word, *proskuneo*, both of which are often translated "to worship" but more precisely mean "to bow down" or even "to prostrate oneself." The Hebrew *kabad* and the Greek *latreuo* are also used of worship and come from roots meaning "to serve." The fundamental purpose of worship is to honor God.

The sermon is seldom directed to God. However, preaching honors God when it encourages the congregation to consider the service of worship, the Christian community, and the world in gospel perspective. On the model of some of the psalms, the preacher may speak an occasional sermon to God, especially if the community is struggling with God's intention in a particular text, doctrine, or situation. Even when a sermon is not directed to God, God is affected by the sermon because God is present in worship.

The liturgy helps form the community's vision of God, church, and world. What we say and do in the service of worship teaches ideas, feelings, and actions that are consistent with Christian vision and those that are not. These qualities are communicated through the content and tone of the hymns and the prayers, the movements and symbols, who participates in leadership (and who does not), the Bible readings, the sermon. "Worship is to daily life, a wise pastor has said, as consommé is to broth. In liturgy at its best…the meaning of all the practices appears in a form that is thick and tasty, darker and richer than what we get in most everyday situations." In a provocative image, worship is "'practicing the practices' the same way a child practices catching the ball or playing the scales."[7] When a community has worshiped well, it is better able to enflesh the gospel in its daily relationships and situations.

A generation ago, many pastors thought of the sermon as the crown jewel of the service of worship. The rest of the liturgy was a velvet backdrop. Less elegantly, some congregations spoke of the first part of the service as "preliminaries." While this thinking pertains in some quarters, many communities are changing. The Second Vatican Council sparked the liturgical renewal that is spreading through Roman Catholicism and into congregations in many protestant communions (e.g., African Methodist Episcopal Church, African Methodist Episcopal Church Zion, some Baptist bodies, Christian Church [Disciples of Christ], Christian Methodist Episcopal Church, Episcopal Church, Presbyterian Church (U.S.A.), Reformed Church in America, United Church of Christ, The United Methodist Church).

This movement rightly emphasizes that the sermon makes its best contribution to worship when it is integrated into the service. The homily is a part of the liturgy. Of course, the sermon speaks its distinctive word. The sermon is more than a component of liturgy. But it speaks in concert with the movement of worship. The sermon draws from preceding elements of the service and contributes to the flow of subsequent parts. The language of the liturgy can inform the sermon. The language of the sermon can inform the language of the liturgy. Language can help wed pulpit and table.

According to the liturgical renewal movement, Christian worship *starts* with the community coming together for worship (call to worship, opening hymn and prayer, confession of sin). The community *remembers* the gospel (Bible readings, sermon). The people *respond* to the gospel (invitation to discipleship, affirmation of faith, prayers of the people, baptism). Christ *renews* the church through the Lord's supper. The people are *sent* into the world for mission. The liturgically sensitive sermon frequently echoes thoughts and images from earlier in the service (e.g., particular sins that the congregation confesses). It helps the congregation respond in confidence with an affirmation of faith. It points to the table.

Since I am a member of the Christian Church (Disciples of Christ) — a community that partakes of the Lord's Supper every Sunday — the reader will not be surprised that I regard the weekly observance of the supper as a norm for worship. Disciples, Roman Catholics, and Episcopalians are not alone in this call. The liturgical renewal movement is moving toward consensus that the Lord's supper should be constitutive of Christian worship. The sermon helps the community make its way to the table.

These emphases are consistent with the practices of the earliest Christian communities. They are also consistent with the dominant understanding of the relationship of preaching and the sacraments in Christian history. Both word and sacrament are means of proclamation. The sermon is the gospel spoken. The sacraments are the gospel represented in loaf and cup. Both word and sacrament embody the gospel. Augustine, a leader of the church in the fourth and fifth centuries, gives the church a famous expression: "Take away the word, and what is the water except water? The word is added to the elemental substance, and it becomes a sacrament, also itself, as it were, a visible word."[8] The sermon is spoken sacrament.

In today's culture in North America, fewer and fewer people outside the church understand the Lord's supper. The service of worship should routinely contain a statement of the meaning and significance of the Lord's supper for the sake of newcomers to Christian community who have not been exposed to this aspect of Christian tradition, and to help rekindle the memories of established Christians whose understanding of the Lord's supper is not well formed. A pastor of a congregation that weekly attracts unchurched persons as visitors instituted such a statement in both printed form and as a part of the pastor's invitation to the table. The pastor reports that before such a statement became a regular part of the service, first-time and unchurched visitors would ask after the service, "What was the point of that interlude in the service at that table?" With only an introductory explanation, however, such persons feel preliminarily introduced and welcomed. When the sermon comes prior to the Supper, it can help interpret the significance of the events at the table.

Few congregations partake of the Lord's supper weekly outside of Roman Catholic, Episcopal, and restoration tradition circles. Nonetheless, Charles L. Rice, a professor who is greatly concerned about the relationship of preaching and worship, points out, "Simply by standing at the table for the prayers of the people and the Lord's Prayer, the presiding minister can gather the community in such a way as to connect the whole service" with the Lord's supper. "This will be all the more effective if the pastoral prayer — one more clericalism — gives way to bidding prayers that invite the congregation to do its liturgical work around the table, in a kind of 'dry Communion.'"9?

The liturgical renewal movement recommends the Christian year as the calendar within which worship takes place, with a lectionary as basis for preaching. The Christian year is an annual cycle of seasons that exemplify several (not all) leading motifs of Christian faith. I offer an overview and critical evaluation of the Christian year and the lectionary in chapter 9.

Worship planners prepare the liturgy for a given Sunday by drawing on key ideas and images in the season of the Christian year and the readings for the day, in conversation with what is needed in the congregation and its setting. Strictly speaking, the minister does not preach the text. The minister preaches theological themes of the season from the standpoint of the text in order to help the congregation interpret the service and its situation in view of the gospel. Worship planners and preachers ask, "How does this season, day, and text help us glorify the God of Israel and interpret the gospel for our situation?"

This approach to worship often results in services in which the liturgical materials and the sermon cohere around a single theme, e.g., repentance. The theme informs the selection of the hymns, the composition of the prayers, the content of the sermon, the art pieces in the sanctuary. Thematic worship can be theologically and aesthetically rich. However, if the theme is handled carelessly or repetitiously, the service can sink under the weight of the theme. When worship ends, the community is relieved that it is over.

Some preachers and Christian communities do not share the enthusiasm of the liturgical renewal movement for word and table as the normative form of Christian worship. These churches organize their worship according to other calendars. For instance, some congregations plan their worship according to civic holidays (e.g., Mother's Day, Memorial Day, Fourth of July, Labor Day, Thanksgiving), or in conjunction with special Sundays that are emphasized by their denomination (e.g., Rural Life Sunday, Week of Compassion). A few Christian communions minimize the importance of the sacraments. Although the Society of Friends has ritual ways of encountering the holy, Friends depart from conventional Christian sacramentalism. Nonetheless, many worship leaders in Christian communions that have a minimalist view of the sacraments develop services and sermons that work together.

The Contemporary Service as a Context for Preaching

An increasing number of congregations add contemporary services of worship as alternatives to traditional services to the weekly schedule. Some congregations worship exclusively in contemporary style. Contemporary services are usually designed in order to appeal to persons who are relatively young (Boomers, Generation 13) or who want to worship in a more current idiom than afforded by most traditional liturgies. At their most faithful, contemporary services seek to represent the theological essence of Christian worship while adapting the approach of the service to today's modes of expression. At its worst, it baptizes aspects of the culture that work against the gospel.

In content and form, contemporary worship is still evolving, even experimental. The tone of most services is relaxed. Participants and worship leaders dress casually. The worship bulletins (when used) contain a minimum of material. The service moves at the direction of the worship leaders, with input and prompting from the congregation. The service is frequently conducted in a space with flexible seating, perhaps a fellowship hall. The music has a contemporary beat. The service moves informally. Contemporary services sometimes include dance or body movement, dramatic skits performed by members of the community, and video clips from television, cinema, or other media. Sometimes people talk out loud to the worship leader or to one another. Some contemporary services are held at times other than Sunday morning (e.g., Thursday night, Saturday night, Sunday night). Some are held at 9:30 on Sunday morning with the traditional service at 11:00. Congregations with sufficient leadership can hold traditional and contemporary services concurrently, though in different parts of the building. A congregation in Indianapolis holds its contemporary service in a dinner theater. The people sit at tables (yes, drinking coffee and orange juice and eating breads and fruit) with the service led from the stage.

At their optimum, contemporary services manifest essential elements of Christian worship. They include praise, confession of sin, reading from the Bible, preaching, affirmation of faith, various forms of prayer, offering, the

Lord's supper. They can move in the classic way from starting through re-membering, response, and renewal, to sending forth. They can personify the themes of particular theological families. For instance, a contemporary ser-vice can be spoken, sung, and enacted in the Wesleyan spirit.

Contrariwise, a contemporary service can be a mish-mash of random impulses governed by nothing more than the feeling of the participants at the moment. Theologically unreflective planners can create a contemporary ser-vice that only mirrors degenerate cultural trends.

The sermon in the contemporary service has the same purpose as the sermon in the traditional service: to help the Christian community interpret its life and the life of the world from the perspective of the gospel. The essen-tial theological content of preaching at the contemporary service is no differ-ent than the content of the sermon at a traditional service. Indeed, some pastors who preach at both contemporary and traditional services on the same weekend use much the same sermon.

In keeping with the mood of the contemporary service, preachers are often more informal, less tied to notes. When the service is in a fellowship hall, a preacher may not have a pulpit, but may use a music stand. Some pastors abandon a note stand altogether. Some preachers sit. These innova-tions sometimes create an intimate and engaging atmosphere.

In some contemporary services, the congregation feels free to interject their comments and questions into the sermon. Some preachers plan for people to talk aloud during the sermon, responding to questions, speaking with one another in small groups, sharing experiences with the whole com-munity. Some pastors handle these occurrences well. Others do not. Frankly, I am seldom in a European American worship setting in a congregation in a long-established denomination when out-loud interaction enhances the ser-mon. (In African American, Hispanic, and Pentecostal services, out-loud inter-action is often the typical pattern.) Very few people can generate insightful comments on the spot. When I am involved in such settings, people seem to do little more than share their preexisting thoughts, feelings, experiences, bi-ases, even prejudices, with little theological reference or opportunity for trans-formation. Such direct interaction seems better saved for other settings in the Christian community (e.g., small group Bible study).

Some preachers make use of overhead projectors during the sermon. Projection serves the gospel purposes of some sermons, but not all. When the purpose of the sermon is to communicate information, the preacher might help the congregation remember it by projecting it. For instance, if the preacher is drawing a series of lessons from a particular doctrine, the preacher might write the lessons on an overhead screen. A pastor might project a map or a drawing of an artifact to help the congregation catch a theological point from a geographical location or object. A preacher might project some data (e.g., on street crime in the neighborhood) to help the con-gregation sense the urgency of a situation. The minister might project a slide of a painting or photograph to help the congregation visualize and feel a scene. Some preachers outline all their sermons on overhead screens. This approach serves the informational dimensions of some sermons; however, not all sermons are informational in character or are well served by outlining the message on an overhead projector. For instance, a sermon whose purpose is to evoke experience of the gospel can easily be undermined by an overhead projection. A preacher can use technology so as to depersonalize the communication that takes place in the sermon. When using such media, the preacher needs to be careful that the technology does not interfere with the gospel event.

Disciplined pastors who plan their sermons in advance can bring contemporary forms of expression into the sermon. Some ministers use video clips, slides, or moments of drama. Such materials typically introduce an issue, bring an idea to life, help the congregation experience a situation or claim, or voice points of view for the congregation to consider. These moments can work well when they serve the aim of the sermon, when they are carefully planned, and when they do not overwhelm the sermon. When poorly conceived, they distract the congregation.

We need to distinguish between seeker services and contemporary services that aim to be full-bodied Christian worship. Seeker services are an evangelistic strategy. They are designed to introduce the gospel to persons who have never made an affirmation of faith or have drifted away from the Christian faith or community. The seeker service is for people who are seeking a more meaningful life. The service uses contemporary approaches to suggest ways the gospel can satisfy that longing.

Some ministers and theologians criticize seeker services as "theology-lite." The critique is sometimes correct. However, it needs to be balanced by the awareness that the seeker service intends to be a port of entry into the gospel. It offers the gospel as a promising possibility that the seeker can explore more fully in other settings. Congregations with seeker services need to provide full-bodied worship. They also need to offer a range of learning opportunities to introduce seekers more fully into Christian faith and life.

The Congregation as Social Context

Preaching textbooks have long encouraged the preacher to be attentive to the congregation to help determine what kinds of encounters the community needs to have with the gospel and how to facilitate those encounters. In an eloquent statement, Leander Keck, a penetrating scholar of the second Testament, describes this aspect of ministry as "priestly listening." The minister listens to the Bible and the tradition "as part of his or her office. The preacher listens for a word not only as a private citizen but as a representative of the church. The preacher's listening and hearing is a priestly act." In addition, preachers listen to the congregation and to themselves. "Just as the preacher's own listening/hearing evokes questions, doubts, resistance, or hostility toward the text," and toward other aspects of the developing sermon, "so the congregation will respond in various ways." Vicarious listeners know "what these responses are likely to be when," they have "genuine solidarity with the people, on the one hand," and when they are "in sufficient touch with" their humanity "to be able to extrapolate from their own responses on the other." Keck is direct. "Extrapolating from one's own experience without having solidarity with the people leads to projecting one's own problems onto the congregation; purely vicarious listening/hearing (without involving one's self-hood) leads to manipulation."[10] The priestly listener is able to hear what a congregation consciously wants, what the congregation needs in order to mature in the gospel, and the kinds of communication the congregation is likely to receive positively or to tune out. This listener helps the congregation evaluate and reformulate its Christian understanding, life, and witness.

In the last fifteen years, the discipline of congregational studies has emerged as an important resource to help a preacher understand the local context.[11] Congregational studies seeks to help a preacher develop a "thick" description of the community, that is a description that accounts for patterns of thinking, personal and social behaviors, history, values, myths and symbols, feelings, and traditions — all of which interpenetrate in a community. Such analysis helps the preacher discover why people are the way they are. The preacher can then try to initiate a conversation with the community about the gospel in language that is indigenous to the people and that deals with local concerns in ways that will be inviting and not off-putting.

Leonora Tubbs Tisdale, professor of preaching at Princeton Theological Seminary, describes a process of "congregational exegesis" that examines symbols that reveal local congregational culture.[12] The pastor conducts an exegesis of the congregation that is similar to the exegesis of a biblical text by paying attention to the qualities listed below. This process takes time, attention, and patient listening.

Each of the sermons in chapters 16, 17, 18, and 19 is preceded by a summary of the preacher's congregational exegesis in preparation for the sermon. They illustrate analyses of four different settings: a small town congregation (chapter 16), a regional church meeting (chapter 17), a largely European American metropolitan congregation (chapter 18), a largely African American urban congregation (chapter 19).

Stories and interviews. The stories that the congregation tells about its own life reveal much about its identity. The pastor hears these stories both in the course of everyday ministry (especially pastoral calling) as well as by deliberately striving to find them. A pastor can usually identify several persons within the congregation who can tell story after story. When Tisdale was a pastor, a seventy-year-old dairy farmer named Sam accompanied her on many pastoral visits. As they drove from place to place to place and called on people, she discovered that Sam was a depository of local lore. Asking Sam a question was like pushing the play button on a talking book. The pastor needs to listen to a variety of voices in order to discover the stories that come most often to expression. The pastor also needs to pay attention to stories that appear to be significant but that are told only by one or two people. The following categories are among those that can help pastors catalogue the stories and develop a systematic picture of congregational life.

- What are the important theological ideas in the stories? Why are these ideas important? How do they impact congregational life?
- Which events seem to be turning points for the congregation? Why? How do these events affect the congregation?
- What values seem most motivating for the community?
- What behaviors are most respected or, are looked upon with suspicion?
- Who are the heroes, heroines, and villains of community life and what makes them so?
- What are the silences — the stories about which everyone knows but about which people say nothing? Why are they silent?
- Do some stories or images recur? What makes them important to retell?
- What seem to be the dreams and hopes that are common to most in the congregation?

Using such data, the pastor can plot the story of the community like the plot of a novel.

The pastor can also engage in structured interviews of individuals and groups. Many pastors conduct such interviews in small-group meetings at the beginning of their ministries. Pastors can also interview established groups (e.g., the board of directors, the choirs, support groups) and groups that are convened for particular purposes (e.g., congregation-wide small groups to review the community's mission statement). In addition to questions such as ones used to analyze congregational stories above, the following are examples of questions that can help structure interview sessions.[13]

- What is happening in the church today?
- What changes have you noticed in the congregation in the past?
- Which changes have pleased you? Which have displeased you?
- What holds this congregation together?
- What has the most potential to cause this congregation to fall apart?
- What makes your congregation different from other nearby congregations?
- What kinds of programs are empowering and frustrating in this congregation?
- What are the qualities of members that win the community's respect? What qualities embarrass the community?

The pastor listens to both the obvious and latent dimensions of meaning in the responses. An experienced pastor counsels listening especially to the stories of those who are marginalized in the congregation.

Archival materials include official church histories, minutes of official meetings, publications (e.g., yearbooks, church directories, worship bulletins, the church newsletter, materials printed for stewardship campaigns), financial records, letters, pictures, audio and videocassette recordings. Some materials will be found in official files, while others are in the hands of individual members. The pastor can interpret such materials using categories like the ones listed for *stories and interviews*. These things can feed directly into a sermon when a pastor quotes from a source or describes a frayed picture from an earlier era.

The study of a congregation's *demographic composition* tells the pastor who is present (and who is not) and ties the congregation's story into the stories of similar and dissimilar groups. With the help of survey forms distributed to the congregation, a membership directory, and in consultation with members who know about such things, the pastor can quickly determine the composition of the congregation according to age, race, ethnicity, gender, household composition, education, social class, economic situation, political philosophy, sexual orientation, roles in the larger community. This data often reveals, indirectly, concerns of the community. For instance, a congregation that is predominately composed of persons over sixty years old is likely to be interested in sermons that deal with Christian thinking on aging. A pastor can note demographics past, present, and projected to help interpret stasis and change in gospel perspective. The pastor can compare and contrast the demographics of the church with those of the area that the congregation serves and reflect on these matters from the gospel. For example, a church that is demarcated from its area by arbitrary qualities (such as race, ethnicity, or social class) may need to be encouraged to broaden its witness to God's love for all.

Architecture and the *visual arts* can tell much about a congregation. The location and condition of the church building and grounds, the design of the building, and its decor often signal much about the character of a Christian community. What understandings of Christian faith, community, and mission are represented in the architecture of the building and the art pieces in it? A church building both reflects and creates congregational ethos. The preacher needs to ask the question of the degree to which the building and its aesthetic environment coincide with congregational life. I have been in many a congregation who abandoned an old Akron-plan sanctuary, with its semicircular seating pattern that creates a strong community-feeling, for a long, narrow, cathedral-like sanctuary, only to discover that the congregation's sense of relatedness to one another is not well served by the two long sets of pews in which worshipers can only see the backs of the heads of the other worshipers.

Some of a congregation's *rituals* take place in worship, but many occur in other settings. Some rituals take place in accordance with the calendar, such as the Christian year with its movement from Advent through Christ the Cosmic Ruler. Many congregations have annual rituals that are not a part of the Christian year, e.g., the mother-daughter tea, fund-raising events, the youth group summer mission trip. The church calendar is often affected by other calendars with occasions that the church marks ritually, such as the school year, the planting and harvesting seasons, manufacturing cycles, seasons for sports. In Nebraska, for instance, football is nearly a statewide sacrament. Other rituals are episodic. They are significant but take place in response to exceptional circumstances, e.g., baptism, major life transitions (birth, marriage, divorce, death), hospitalization. The preacher can learn much about a congregation by observing what they do (and do not do) on these occasions. Nora Tubbs Tisdale, for instance, noticed that the women in her congregation always placed a potted plant on the Lord's table when a child was baptized. After the service, they transferred the plant from the pot to the church grounds. Tisdale discovered that this act telegraphed the high esteem of the congregation for children, the earth, flowers, fruits, and the continuity of the generations.

Useful indices of a community's values are often provided by the resources that a Christian community puts into its *events* and *activities*. Here are some questions by which to reflect on what a preacher can learn from this aspect of the congregational world.

- What activities are most intensively supported and most neglected?

- In which events does the congregation take the most (and have the least) pride? Are some happenings controversial? If so, what are the dynamics of the controversy?

- Do recently added activities point to future directions in which the congregation is moving? Do events that are receiving less support or are being dropped indicate changes in the community's climate?

- Can a preacher sense incongruity between what a community says is really important and the actual investment of its personnel and other resources?

The preacher must ask whether a church's life makes an adequate witness to the gospel.

People are presumed in all lines of analysis. However, Tisdale suggests that the preacher pay particular attention to people whom the congregation regards as sages and those on the margins of the community. Sages are persons to whom the congregation listens because they represent the best of the community's self-perception. Discovering why the marginalized are on the edges of the community can often help a pastor discern the social boundary lines of the community. A community's boundaries for differentiating "us" and "them" needs to be evaluated by God's love and God's will for justice.

A pastor must often be in a community for a long time before its members trust the pastor with the deepest secrets of their hearts. However, pastors who begin their ministries by paying attention to these qualities will begin immediately to get a sense of the congregation's worldview, values, and ethos. In chapters 10 and 11 we will see that such sensitivity is necessary as the preacher considers possible directions for sermons.

Multiple Communities Within the Congregation

While congregations cohere as communities around the gospel, they are diverse in many other ways. Most congregations contain several subgroups. These groups can be identified along lines such as gender, age, race, ethnicity, Sunday school class, theological viewpoint (e.g., conservative, liberal), interpretations of the Bible, social relationships, psychological makeup, personality type, place in the congregational power structure, economic status, political affiliation, shared values, patterns of processing communications. Each group has its own qualities that frequently make it more receptive to some approaches to the sermon and less receptive to others. For example, some people participate most fully in sermons that are evocative, imaginative, and associative. Other people enter most directly into sermons that are propositional, linear, and direct. A preacher can ask, "How can I shape the sermon so that its interpretation of the gospel has a good opportunity to be received by each group in the congregation?"

To take a simple example, I once heard a parishioner say, "I know nothing about sports. I do not care at all about sports. But my pastor only uses sports illustrations in the sermons. If I hear another golf story, I'll walk out."

To take a more complex example, Mary Field Belenky and a group of colleagues who researched woman's patterns of coming to knowledge find that women cannot be casually grouped in the ways in which they come to knowledge. Belenky and her colleagues identify five different patterns.[14] These patterns are significantly related to women's self-perceptions and their relationships with others. The patterns are not related to intelligence or theological viewpoint. Women of different intelligence quotients and different theological viewpoints appear in each pattern. A woman can move from one pattern to another in accordance with changing life experience and relational patterns. However, within each way of knowing, women are better able to participate in certain kinds of sermons than others.

Some women are *silent* because they are not aware that they can think and act independently. They often feel oppressed by other powers. These women need to know that God, and the preacher, understand their silence. This woman is often distrustful of speech because it has been used to keep her silent. In order to believe the gospel and to develop confidence that she is an independent agent, the silent woman needs an empathetic word in the midst of a supportive and listening community. The *receiving* woman understands knowledge as receiving from others. She does not know that she can think for herself. This woman needs to receive the gospel in a direct and certain way from the preacher. Ironically, the preacher can straightforwardly help receiving women realize that they are capable of thinking for themselves. A woman tends to move from receiving to subjective knowledge in response to a crisis of authority. The old, exterior,sources of knowledge are no longer trustworthy. The *subjective* knower is aware of her internal authority. She relies principally on intuition. This woman has a hunch that a certain behavior or way of thinking is reliable and tries it. The sermon that communicates with this woman pays attention to feeling. While the preacher wants to help the subjective knower develop as an independent agent, the preacher needs to help the subjective knower recognize the limits and dangers of perception that is based largely on intuition and feeling. *Procedural* knowledge results from recognized procedures for gathering data from a wide range of sources as the basis for decision making. They listen to interior voices and to external authorities. For some procedural knowers, knowledge comes through established patterns of processing data and recognized norms. For others, the recognized procedure is collaboration with others. *Constructed* knowledge results when women critique and transcend established systems of knowledge gathering. These women recognize the biases inherent in each method of knowing and are able to construct a sense of self and world that accounts for inherent ambiguities. The preacher who wishes to be taken seriously by the constructed knower must acknowledge the complexity of issues in the sermon.

To take another example, James Fowler — a professor who studies the ways in which people develop in faith — notices that people think about faith in six different ways.[15] These patterns are partly developmental in that they begin with childhood and continue into adulthood. However, few people pass through all six stages; most people plateau at a stage (usually stage 3 or 4). Fowler emphasizes that the stages are not a hierarchy of value; each stage is simply a different mode of mental functioning. The stages are not related to intelligence, nor are they inherently related to theological viewpoint. Although people settle at certain stages, they can often move to the next stage.

To put it crudely, we might say that each person is programmed to receive and process certain styles of communication better than others. Persons are most receptive to communications that come to them on their channels. Consequently, preachers need to be able to speak to different stages. Congregation and preacher often experience communication loss when the preacher consistently speaks at one stage (e.g., stage 5) when many in the congregation function at a different stage (e.g., stage 3).

In stage 1 (roughly ages 2–8), children are still learning how to think. The stage 2 (beginning about age 8) thinker is a rule follower. This thinker responds positively to sermons that state the rules, how to follow them, and the rewards (and punishments) that follow. The stage 3 (beginning in adolescence) person sees issues as clearly defined on the basis of family/tribal/ church authority. The sermon that appeals to this thinker defines the world into the conventional terms of acceptable and unacceptable. In stage 4 (usually beginning in late adolescence or early adulthood), people also have a clear sense of right and wrong, but think through the reasons for these categories. When hearing a sermon, they want to know the reasons for the preacher's opinion. Most adults come to rest in stages 3 or 4, and they most easily respond to sermons that are direct and propositional. Stage 5 is reached by relatively few persons and typically not until the middle or golden years. Such people think critically and live in the midst of ambiguity. They need for a sermon to offer transcendent perspective on making their way through the complexities of life. Only a handful of people reach stage 6, for example Mother Teresa, Gandhi, Martin Luther King, Jr., Abraham Heschel. The stage 6 thinker has a universal vision of the interconnectedness of all things. Persons at this stage tend to be prophets.

I do not suggest that the preacher sugarcoat the message or tell people what they want to hear by sanding off the rough edges of the gospel. I simply urge the preacher to frame sermons so that listener orientation becomes a port of entry into the sermon.

A preacher might respond to this pluralism in several ways. (1) A preacher could prepare a sermon (or a series of sermons) with particular groups in mind. For instance, a pastor might prepare a message for Boomers as the persons most in need of a certain sermon. (2) Within a single sermon, a preacher can include material that connects with several different groups. (3) Over a season of preaching, a pastor can give attention to a wide range of variables in patterns of congregational perception. Randy Updegraff Spleth, a pastor in Indiana, refers to these approaches as "layering," that is, including material in the sermon that speaks to people at different layers of life and Christian faith.

From time to time, a pastor may find it helpful to create a grid, such as Table 1, that coordinates groups in the congregation with sermons (or parts of sermons) that take account of each subcommunity's characteristics. I recommend that every four months a preacher review previous and upcoming sermons to see that sermons consider the qualities of the various groups.

A pastor that I know has turned a part of the Pastor's Report to the Ministerial Support Committee into a time of reflection on such matters. Whereas this minister formerly reported statistical information (e.g., the number of sermons preached, calls made), the pastor now tells this body the breadth of scripture texts from which the sermons grow, the direction of the sermons, the kind of conversation the preacher is trying to generate in the congregation, those in the congregation whom the preacher is particularly wishing to engage. The governing body then reflects with the pastor their perception of the theological adequacy and timeliness of the sermons, and on the degree to which the sermons embrace the whole congregation. The pastor says, "This process is, for me, a teaching and accountability tool."

The picture is even more complicated. Individuals are complex interweavings of multiple categories. For instance, an African American woman might be a Boomer, a theological conservative, an Extrovert-Sensate-Thinker-Perceiver among the Myers-Briggs personality types, a liberal democrat in the upper middle-class who is deeply invested in the congregational committee system. Furthermore, people are not trapped by their predilections. Persons can transcend their categories.

A minister can never preach a sermon that takes account of every listener's every quality. Indeed, a preacher who tries to blend every listener characteristic into every sermon will implode. The preacher probably needs to gauge which characteristics seem most important to be included at a given moment for a specific sermon. Over time, the preacher can develop sermons that include all in the congregation.

The gospel, the preacher, and the sermon can transcend listener peculiarities. Out of the many diversities in the congregation, some sermons can create a community of one heart, mind, and will. Even when that does not happen, the sermon can still bring people together in a community of conversation in which the many grow together in the gospel.

The table on pages 42–43 coordinates generational characteristics with selected other qualities present in a congregation.[16] Preachers might review their sermons over a four-month period and place a check in the boxes each time a sermon includes material for each group. A minister could set up a grid using other motifs. For purposes of illustration, I have used some categories discussed in this section of the chapter, and have added categories that are discussed in chapter 12, especially, pages 213–214. The latter are aspects of the world of the congregation, and the larger world that the preacher needs to address.

The concentration of checkmarks indicates the groups to which the preacher is consciously or unconsciously giving the most attention and the groups that are relatively neglected.

TABLE 1: Chart Coordinating the Characteristics of Community Members with the Appearance of Those Characteristics in Sermons

	Children	Youth	Generation 13 (born 1961–81)	Boomers (born 1943–60)	Silents (born 1925–42)	Builders (born 1901–24)
Male						
Female						
European American						
African American						
Hispanic American						
Asian American						
Native American						
Persons from other nations						
Silent knower						
Received knower						
Subjective knower						
Procedural knower						
Constructed knower						

	Children	Youth	Generation 13 (born 1961–81)	Boomers (born 1943–60)	Silents (born 1925–42)	Builders (born 1901–24)
Material from home life						
School						
Blue-collar workplace						
Unemployed						
White-collar workplace						
Single people						
Married people						
Partners						
States of health and disability						
Lower-class people						
Middle-class people						
Racial, ethnic, and national groups other than the predominant one in the community						

CHAPTER FOUR

The Larger World as a Context for Preaching

Factors in the world beyond the church affect the environment in which the sermon is spoken and heard. The Christian community must determine the degree to which it can affirm larger cultural forces and the degree to which it must critique them. Some qualities of the emerging world can help the church's witness, while other qualities subvert the gospel and the quality of life in the world. This chapter identifies several factors in the larger world that directly influence how the preacher and congregation understand the sermon. I overview the transition from the modern to postmodern worldviews taking place in many quarters of North America. I then consider changes that are taking place in the church's relationship to the larger social setting and their relationship to the sermon.

Preaching in the Transition from Modernity to Postmodernity

Western culture is divided into three eras: premodern, modern, and postmodern.[1] The premodern era lasted from the dawn of civilization to the Enlightenment. The modern world began with the Enlightenment and continues in many sectors of the contemporary world. Postmodernity has come to be widely recognized only in the last twenty years. The transition from modernity to postmodernity is still in process and its outcome uncertain. Many congregations contain members who are modern and others who are postmodern.

Walter Ong, who is giving his life to the study of human communication, points that communication patterns among human beings have evolved in eras that are roughly comparable in time and theme to the three major eras of Western culture.[2] Oral-aural communication is typical of premodernity. Print-based communication is associated with modernity. Multi-media communication is postmodern. However, the communication patterns are not segregated by historical period. Oral-aural and print-based communication continues into the present, although modified by multi-media phenomena.

Preaching in the Premodern World

In the premodern world, authority is lodged in the community's tradition. The tradition contains the wisdom necessary for life. Premoderns assume the authority of the Bible, the church, the preacher. For premodern people, truth is the correspondence of appearance and reality. To know is to be initiated into the community's myths and mores. Knowledge is relational: to know is to relate to self and others in ways that are consistent with community values. Identity in the premodern era is communal. To be is to be a member of a community. An individual carries community consciousness within the self. Individuals represent the community wherever they go and whatever they do. Nature is animate. To premoderns, the cosmos is a vast community in which the elements of nature and humankind are mutually responsive. Story is a common mode of communication.

Premodern culture is largely oral-aural. Communication takes place primarily through face-to-face speech. While the alphabet and writing come into being, one of their most important uses is to keep business lists. Written documents are received and processed as if they are speech. For instance, when Paul's letters are read in the ancient church, they are considered a manifestation of the presence of the apostle.

In an oral-aural setting, sound is the primary medium of communication. Spoken words have an electric quality for both speaker and hearer. As noted in connection with the world of the Bible (page 14), language in oral-aural culture is powerful. While memory is highly developed, those who preserved community memory often felt free to add interpretive remarks. Oral-aural communication is highly situational; it is charged with the sense of context in which it comes to expression. Oral-aural culture makes use of many mnemonic devices, especially repetition, formulaic speech, the use of simple sentences, narrative (especially myth) and proverbs. Both speaker and hearer have an immediate sense of affecting and being affected by each other. Oral-aural culture continues in many segments of North American society. For example, many African American communities are primarily oral-aural, as are many blue-collar European American communities.[3]

The premodern preacher helps the community learn its traditions, and interpret how the traditions help the community fit together the many pieces of life. The preacher helps people discover how to relate, as a community, with God, with other communities, and with nature. Premodern preaching shares many characteristics of oral-aural communication, including extensive use of narrative, repetition, formulae, proverbs. Oral-aural preaching has the quality of direct encounter between preacher and listener.

Preaching in the Modern World

In the modern world, tradition recedes as an authority. Some moderns debunk traditions from the premodern world as primitive, even superstitious. For moderns, truth is still the conformity of appearance and reality, but the criteria for determining such conformity are now (1) the scientific method that results in data that is empirically verified through the five senses, or (2) first principles — self-evident first truths from which all else is deduced. Beginning with the scientific method and inviolate first principles, moderns believe that they can reason their way to universal truth. Knowledge is possession of facts. Emphasis on communality gives way to individualism. Moderns view nature as a resource to be exploited for human pleasure. Progress is technological expansion.

Modernity is accompanied by the rise of print-based culture, beginning with the invention of the printing press. The printed page gradually becomes the norm for communication. The eye, with its relatively low-energy physiology, is the primary organ used to receive and process the page. Engagement with print is usually less intense than in face-to-face encounter. While the reader can be conscious of others who are in and behind the material being read, reading is typically a solitary activity. Print leads to communication that is linear and less spontaneous than in the oral-aural period. Print results in sentences that, for the sake of variety, become longer and more complex.

Modern linguists divide language into two categories: propositional language that is reliable because it communicates facts and mythic language that may be entertaining but is unreliable when its picture of the world does not accord with empirical observation or first principles. Moderns use the term "myth" to denote that which is untrue.

Modernity creates a crisis for the church. Why should modern people trust Christian tradition when this tradition originated in the primitive premodern era and is filled with stories that violate human reason? A sea opens? Resurrection from the dead? Really? How can one speak reliably about God when God's existence cannot be confirmed through empirical observation and is not a necessary first principle?

Theologians coined the term "hermeneutical gap" to refer to the differences between the premodern and modern ways of understanding. One of the modern preacher's tasks is to help the congregation reconcile Christian tradition with the modern worldview. Some moderns turned to Deism as a way out of the dilemma. According to the Deists, God is a great clock maker who wound the universe and then stepped aside. The world proceeds according to natural law without further divine interference. Other modern congregations attempt to show that Christian claims are true in modern terms. For instance, some Christians seek to prove that the events of the Bible happened as reported. While natural law governs everyday operations in the world, God intervenes in those operations through supernatural means. Other Christians demythologize the Bible. The preacher separates elements that are trustworthy from their mythological, but unnecessary, husk. For instance, a modern person may not believe that Jesus physically calmed the stormy sea of Galilee, but the story reveals that God can calm the metaphorical storms that afflict modern people. When confronted by such difficulties, other preachers collapse intellectually. They say, "God is a mystery. We cannot understand." Still other moderns give up religion.

The modern sermon is directed to the individual. The sermon is informational, propositional, and often deals with aspects of what moderns can believe. Many modern preachers conceive of the sermon as a written essay. This sermon tends to be highly rational in content, logical in structure, and analytical in method. Myth disappears from preaching (except as it is demythologized). Stories appear as illustrations of conceptual points. The goal of the sermon is to put ideas together persuasively to lead to a clear, truthful conclusion. The caricature of the sermon as three points and poem is taken from modern preaching. While some preachers consider these approaches to the sermon altogether outdated, I think they can still play a useful role in preaching, though they must now be supplemented by other ideas.

Preaching in the Postmodern Ethos

The modern synthesis is breaking apart. Few people continue to have unrestrained confidence in science. The unreflective use of science contributes to many current problems. We cannot assemble a set of first principles on which the human family agrees. Each community interprets the world through its own particular lenses. Experience is pluralistic. The contemporary world has no universal standard by which to adjudicate all questions of interpretation of God and the cosmos. In the graphic phrase of systematic theologian Edward Farley, the traditional house of authority has collapsed.[4]

One of the difficulties of discussing postmodernism is that the term means many things to many people. I find it helpful to think of postmodernity as less a tight philosophical construct and more as an ethos. Charles W. Allen, another systematic theologian (and not related to me) summarizes one leading quality. "To be postmodern is to be constantly and consistently aware of the relativity of all human thinking and acting."[5] Postmodern people are cognizant of their own particularities of context, orientation, preference, even bias. A second, related, leading quality of postmodernity is diversity. The melting pot was a popular image for modern culture: The ideal world was a melting together of different ideals, races, ethnicities, and customs in which each element lost many of its distinctive characteristics as a new, common identity came about. The salad bowl is a better image for postmodernity, suggesting both distinctiveness and relatedness: Each ingredient retains its own flavor, color, and texture, while all ingredients share a common bowl.

The postmodern world does not turn its back on modernity. "Some of the gains of modernity are irreversible."[6] For example, modernity's emphasis on logical consistency guards postmoderns against contradiction. For another, science has spawned a continuing series of breakthroughs in medical treatment that few people want to forego. At the same time, many postmodern people are recovering some premodern notions. Postmoderns value tradition and wisdom born from the experience of previous generations. Postmodernism turns away from the radical individualism of modernity and regards the self as a self-in-community. The postmodern ethos regards nature not as an inanimate resource but as a living realm with its own integrity.

Nonetheless, postmodernism is more than an amalgam of selected themes from premodern and modern worlds.

Postmodernism's sense of the relativity that permeates human perception helps the preacher and the church by encouraging us not to idolize our theological formulations. This relativity vexes the Christian community in that the church cannot assume that its interpretation of God and the world are optimum. Postmodern inclinations challenge the Christian community continually to assess its interpretations. However, while the church should respect other communities and viewpoints, postmodernity's relativity ought not lead the church to endorse all other possibilities for understanding and acting. From time to time, the church must critique and even protest other ways of thinking and behaving.

The preacher in a postmodern ethos must first help the church understand the particularities of Christian interpretation of the world. I describe five aspects of this task at the end of the next section. A caveat: Even though Christian communities have many viewpoints and customs in common, we cannot blithely speak of "the" Christian interpretation of the world. For each Christian community has its own spin on details of how best to understand God, church, and world.

Premodern preachers could simply invoke Christian tradition as basis for their construals. The modern preacher could invoke the authority of science or rational deduction. The preacher in a postmodern setting must help the congregation explore why a Christian interpretation of life is trustworthy. The preacher cannot rely on external sources of authority but must help the community develop internal reasons for having confidence in the Christian gospel. Toward this end, postmodernity offers two resources. For one, as noted previously, many postmoderns have a high respect for positive values in the past. The preacher can appeal to the fact that the Christian tradition has helped many people and communities in the past. For another, postmodern people place a high value on experience. Where moderns tended to limit experience to perception received through the five senses, many postmodern people acknowledge that experience has depth dimensions that cannot be satisfactorily described in traditional terms of sight, sound, touch, taste, and smell. As philosopher and theologian Bernard Meland says, "perceptual experience is a richer event than conception can possibly be, providing every occurrence of awareness with a 'fringe,' implying a 'more,' much of which evades conceptualization."[7] While the meaning of experience is hotly debated in contemporary theological and philosophical circles, the pastor can still cite the experience of people past and present that confirms the reliability of Christian witness. Furthermore, the gospel may enlarge and deepen the experience of persons in the postmodern ethos.

The electronic media play a significant role in shaping perception and communication in the postmodern ethos. These media recover the oral-aural reliance upon sound. Television, cinema, and even the computer add a visual dimension. The electronic media create multimedia worlds into which people enter. These experiences often use a narrative format with music, visuals, dialogue, and action to elicit specific responses.

Preaching is a multimedia event in that it involves both sound and sight. Many ministers believe that preaching should move away from modernism's concern for conceptuality and should become an experience. The sermon should be something like a television show in that it is an image or a series of interlocking images designed to touch people. Such preachers believe the media have created a culture in which people no longer perceive through rational thought, but through imagery.

On the one hand, the preacher in the postmodern setting can welcome and make use of the recent rediscovery of story and experience. Preachers can create sermons with narrative structures. Many sermons can contain experiential moments that help bring the gospel alive in hearts of the congregation. On the other hand, the preacher needs to be cautious. The sermon that communicates in the manner of the electronic media can easily fall into the same traps as the media. Neil Postman, a commentator on contemporary media, demonstrates how under the governance of the printing press discourse in America was different from what it is now. It was "generally coherent, serious, and rational." Today, "under the governance of television, [discourse] has become shriveled and absurd."[8] Listeners may subtly associate media-like sermons with such discourse. Further, media communication can be manipulative, reducing complex issues to sound-bites. It discourages critical engagement. It can encourage listener passivity. While the media-like sermon can entice people to accept its image of the world, it does not always help provide the foundations that will help the community struggle with questions about the adequacy of the image. In any event, people today have the capacity to follow rational discourse, even for long periods of time, when the communication is clear and related to life, and when the communicator is engaging.[9] Consequently, preachers who take their sermonic cues from the media need to do so cautiously and with an ever watchful eye on the degree to which a sermon might drift toward negative qualities of media-shaped communication.

Some people think that postmodernism's permeating relativity has obviated the category of truth. To be sure, a preacher can no longer imperially declare things to be true or untrue on the basis of the degree to which they conform to universally acknowledged standards. However, the preacher must commend an interpretation of the gospel that the pastor and the church can really believe. The integrity and trustworthiness of the gospel is at stake. The pastor can use an adaptation of the notion of truth as conformance of appearance and reality by speaking of ways in which the Christian message has been confirmed in the experience of the community (past and present, in this place and in other places). The gospel can reframe and enlarge the community's experience. In humility, the church can offer this testimony to others in the world. The church can dialogue with other communities, probing for the most adequate understandings of the Transcendent.

In the modern period, the preacher sought "the" correct interpretation of a biblical text, Christian doctrine, or Christian action on the basis of allegedly value-neutral, historical-critical interpretation. Postmodern preachers recognize that all interpretation is biased by interpretive lenses. We cannot achieve objective, impartial interpretation. We tend to see what our lenses predispose us to see. Preachers can, however, become cognizant and critical of our interpretive lenses. We can note points at which our lenses benefit us and points at which they contribute to marginalization and exploitation. Preachers need to keep grinding and regrinding our lenses on the wheel of the gospel.

The preacher in the postmodern ethos hopes for the congregation to come to a clear understanding of the claims of Christian community. The congregation needs clarity as to what is (and is not) acceptable in the Christian house in order to reflect critically on its own life and on its relationship to other communities and movements in the world. The preacher hopes for the community to develop the enlarged and deeply experiential sense of knowledge — the "more" described above. Experience empowers conceptuality with depth dimensions. Conceptual thinking interprets the "more."

The modern preacher regarded the congregation as a collection of individuals. The postmodern preacher envisions the congregation as community and intends the sermon to help the church form as community.

Philip Wheelwright, an influential literary theorist, uses the terms "stenic" and "tensive" to describe the two main understandings of language in the postmodern world.[10] Stenic language is propositional and informational. Its great value is precision. Furthermore, ideas can be powerful. I encounter ideas that are transformative. The community must be able to name and critically evaluate its experience in order to gauge the degree to which its experience is adequate to the gospel. Indeed, the preacher needs to help the congregation learn how to think critically from the perspective of the gospel.

Tensive language is charged with awareness of the depth dimensions of life. It creates an imaginative experience. Many postmoderns can enter a narrative world and experience it as true in that its interpretation of experience conforms to their own, even when elements of the stories are not factual according to the standards of empirical observation. For instance, whether or not a snake actually approached Adam and Eve in Eden, the story of the Fall helps us understand that the world today is not the kind of place God intends it to be (Genesis 3:1–17). We, too, hear the tempting voice of the snake.

The preacher in the postmodern world can use language in ways that are both propositional and imaginative in accordance with the purpose of a specific sermon. A particular sermon may call for the preacher to explore a doctrine with precision as to what the church can and cannot believe. Another sermon may call for the preacher to create an experience for the congregation. Most sermons contain both stenic and tensive elements.

A particular challenge for many pastors is the fact that congregations contain some persons who are modern in their outlooks, others who are postmodern, as well as many who feel the pull of changes in cultural undercurrents, but who cannot name these forces. As necessary, sermons can draw upon the multiple modes of authority, concern, and discourse that appeal to moderns and postmoderns and can critique aspects of the same when they run counter to the gospel.

Preaching as the Church Moves from the Mainline to the Margins

The United States has long had legal separation of church and state. However, through the middle of the twentieth century in Euro-America an informal but powerful alliance existed between the religious community and the prevalent culture. To be a citizen of the United States was to be Christian or Jewish and vice versa. Religious and civic communities believed that their values were supportive. The church propped up the culture by pronouncing God's blessing over it; the culture propped up the church by feeding it a constant stream of members and power. This perception is still alive among some people.

This way of thinking and acting was commonplace in popular culture. For example, the minister was often on the platform at public events, offering prayer that portrayed God's blessing of civic endeavors. The social structure of the church frequently mirrored the social structure of the community – with physicians, lawyers, business executives, and civic leaders in positions of leadership. I heard a certain congregation described as "the Board of Directors of the Country Club on its knees at prayer." The church discussed ecclesial issues in the same terms and criteria used by corporate and civil boards. Democracy in the church assumed that the vote of the people is the voice of God. Cultural holidays organized the congregation's year – e.g., President's Day, Mother's Day, Memorial Day, Fourth of July, Labor Day, Thanksgiving. Churches used the same standards to gauge their success as did other institutions: growth in membership, expansion of influence in the community, financial power. Preachers interpreted aspects of the Christian tradition so as to raise the hand of blessing on cultural proclivities. I heard a sermon that used the parable of the talents to justify capitalism. The church was high priest of the culture.

This alliance benefited the church in certain ways. Many people joined the church in response to the culture's expectation. Many towns had a mid-week "church night" when they did not schedule other events. (Some communities still have such a night.) Sunday morning was reserved for church. The church could serve as the conscience of the culture.

This alliance also created significant problems for the church's witness to the gospel. It resulted in civil religion in which the popular church was used to validate popular culture. The church understood its role as helping people make their way through the existing social order. The church seldom offered prophetic critique of the nation's life. The church was complicit in various forms of injustice – the most infamous case being the church's interpretation of the enslavement of Africans as the will of God. The middle-class, grass-roots European American church did not widely teach a sense of Christian identity as distinct from identity of nation, class, or social group. Nor did the church reflect on its own community or the larger world from the standpoint of distinctively Christian norms.

This alliance has been coming apart since the 1960s. The United States was never as homogenous as European Americans assumed in the heyday of civil religion. Pluralism in Western society in conjunction with the separation of church and state, no longer allows an informal church-synagogue-state establishment. The church is moving from the mainstream of the culture to its margins. In the mall of human loyalties, the church will increasingly live as one religious community alongside others.

Many congregations closely allied with the culture are having difficulty negotiating the transition from the mainline to the margins. Many of these congregations are declining in size and vitality. The reasons for decline are complicated, ranging from factors such as low birth rate, aging memberships, being located in declining population areas, keeping more accurate membership rolls, to lethargy in membership recruitment, unimaginative programming, and theology-lite preaching. Through empirical study of persons in and out of the church, sociologists Wade Clark Roof and William McKinney discovered that large numbers of people leave the church because the church does not offer a vision that is sufficiently compelling and distinctive for them to continue to participate.[11] They believe that they can get the same help for living from other sources (e.g., American Association of University Women, Kiwanis, *Psychology Today,* the National Association of Social Workers, the softball league, *The Mother Earth News*) as they do from the church.

Preaching contributes to this difficulty. Marsha Clark Witten, another sociologist with an interest in religion, finds that in Baptist and Presbyterian pulpits, "transcendent, majestic, awesome God of Luther and Calvin — whose image informed early Protestant visions of the relationship between human beings and the divine — has undergone a softening of demeanor throughout the American experience of Protestantism, with only minor interruptions."[12] God is now a cosmic therapist who counsels persons to cope with their individual lives. The message is little different from other psychological messages in secular culture. While Witten's conclusions are drawn from Baptist and Presbyterian pulpits, I am confident they apply to many other communions. Consequently, Clark M. Williamson, a theologian, comments, "Middle class values and mainstream culture are available outside the churches. The failure of church life to offer a vision transcending the culture undercuts any reason for participating in the church."[13]

I join a growing number of Christians in hoping that the disestablishment of the church can actually help the church revitalize its life and witness. As the Christian community is less beholden to the culture for members, status, and money, the church is more likely to feel free to name the differences between its vision of the blessed community, and the visions that prevail in the current culture. The church is less likely to assume that its life should imitate the corporate world. The church may be able to gauge its faithfulness less on statistical indicators, and more in terms of its witness to the gospel. The church may be able to move further toward letting its life demonstrate the rule of God.

Preaching can play a significant role in this revival of theological identity and mission. D. Newell Williams, Dean of Christian Theological Seminary, points out that preaching in the church today needs to help the Christian community discover the distinctive qualities of the gospel, the Christian faith, and the church.[14] Toward this end, preaching in a disestablished church calls for five particular emphases.

First, the preacher can help the church *name its changing relationship with the culture.* A fair number of people within the church, particularly lifelong members, continue to think of the church as warp and woof in the established order. Many other Christians are tempted to think that Christianity is a simple additive that makes life better (much like a mechanic adds STP to automobile oil). The Christian community needs to have a clear sense of itself as modeling alternatives to many aspects of existing community.

Second, sermons need to *help the community learn the formative language* of the Bible and Christian tradition. Biblical and theological literacy are at low levels. The preacher cannot casually refer to the story of Deborah and assume that people will fill in the details. Preachers need to help the congregation acquire basic information as well as methods of interpreting it.

Third, the preacher can help the church *articulate its distinctive vision of the world* as a community in which God promises all created entities unconditional love and calls for justice in all relationships. The contemporary world is pluralistic. In order to think and act coherently, the Christian community needs a clear grasp of a theological center that will help it mediate among the various pluralisms in which it finds itself.

Fourth, the preacher can encourage the church to *identify points of similarity and difference between its vision of the world and the culture's visions.* While I emphasize the importance of articulating differences between Christian vision and the culture, it is also important for the preacher to help the congregation name moments and movements in the larger world that are consistent with the gospel. The world outside the church is not one vast antagonism to the gospel. Because God is omnipresent, it can also manifest the divine will. The preacher needs to help the church recognize and claim such values and occasions.

Fifth, preaching in a church moving to the margins of the culture needs to *emphasize the promise that accrues from Christian faith and community* while keeping sight of the demands of the gospel. The gospel is, by nature, good news. The sermon, then, should concentrate on how the good news of the gospel can renew community. In addition, the candid fact is that most people are motivated to self-understanding, commitment, and action on the basis of promise. The church needs to name and interpret the benefits of participating in a community with counter-cultural qualities.

Preaching cannot bear sole responsibility for developing these qualities in the Christian community, but as part of the most visible event in the church, it can help keep them bubbling on the top of the church's consciousness.

CHAPTER FIVE

The Life of the Preacher as a Context for Preaching

The life of the preacher is a part of the context for preaching. The sermon is affected (whether or not the preacher is consciously aware) by the preacher's life. On the one hand, we need to be aware of our lives so that we can critically evaluate the relationship between our personal lives and our preaching. The life of the preacher can be a source not only of material for the sermon, but of the knowledge of God. On the other hand, this discussion can easily drift toward the narcissism that plagues our time. We need to be self-aware, but not self-preoccupied.

Since this chapter revolves around the nature of experience and since I take account of experience in my discussion of theological method in the next chapters, I begin with that topic. The chapter then turns to the relationship between theology and experience. The chapter explores ways in which the preacher's experience participates in sermon preparation. I conclude by urging preachers to participate in Christian practices that can help form our hearts, minds, and behaviors.

What Is Experience?

Experience is the full range of awareness of all in which we participate. It includes that which happens to us and in us. It includes all that we perceive through the five senses. It includes all that we think, feel, and intuit. It is physical, mental, and emotional. A preacher does not exist as an isolated individual, but as a self-in-community. Experience encompasses the thick web of social relationships and communities in which we live. As noted previously, experience has depths that are powerful, but that we perceive only dimly, and about which we cannot always speak precisely.[1]

All experience is interpretive. We have no pure awareness. We cannot achieve a state of value-neutral objectivity when observing ourselves. The very act of claiming to be value-neutral is itself an interpretation. As Alfred North Whitehead, a philosopher, says, "If we desire a record of uninterpreted experience, we must ask a stone to record its autobiography."[2] From the moment of birth we are in an interpreted and interpreting world. Our experience is a grid of lenses of thought, feeling, and intuition shaped by elements such as the following:

- gender
- race
- ethnicity
- family history
- physical condition
- home life
- relationships outside the home
- emotional conditions
- psychological make-up
- interests outside the church
- communities of which one is part

- religious vision
- sexual orientation
- geographical location
- social class
- economic situation
- aesthetic inclination
- influence of books, the media (e.g., movies)
- etc.

Periodically, it is helpful for ministers to reflect on how these factors (and others) predispose us to God, the Bible, Christian tradition, the church, and the world. However, we can never isolate all the parts of the self. The self is more than an accumulation of parts. It is a *gestalt*, a whole in which all parts affect one another to create a being with its own interior life and its own ways of relating to the world beyond the self.

Theorists debate the degree to which such a self may be inherent or may be the result of socialization. Whatever the case, human beings are not entrapped by experience, but have significant measures of freedom to decide which experiences will play dominant roles in the self and which will not. For example, although I am male, I choose not to conform in every respect to characteristic or stereotypical male attitudes and behavior for my culture. Nonetheless, as a male, I tend to notice qualities that benefit me as a male in biblical texts, in Christian tradition and doctrine, and in personal and social situations. Of course, we cannot choose some things. We cannot always be conscious of our experience and its effects on us. But when we are aware of things affecting us, we can choose how we respond.

Experience as a Theological Source

By definition, experience is always a medium for theological reflection. All theological conversation takes place in experience. Beyond being a medium for reflection, experience can also be a source of theological discovery. Indeed, because God is omnipresent, any moment of experience can be a source of the knowledge of God. Consequently, Mary Catherine Hilkert, a systematic theologian who reflects extensively on the relationship between experience and theology, points out that when preachers listen to human experience, "they are listening for an echo of the gospel."[3] At the same time, because sin permeates the world, experiences can turn away from the divine will. Few experiences are altogether revelatory of the divine will, or deformed by sin. Most experiences contain traces of both divine purpose and its corruption.

Hilkert also points out that while all experience occurs within frameworks of meaning that have been handed on, "New experiences may call for modification, change, or even rejection of previous horizons."[4] Consequently, we need always to reflect on our experience, to try to name as clearly as possible what happens to us and how we should value it. We may discover that parts of our pre-existing experiential grids are inadequate and need to be repaired or replaced.

A purpose of preaching is to provide language to name our experience in terms of the gospel. The preacher tries to sort out those aspects of experience that are consistent with the gospel, and even reveal it, from those portions of life that work against the gospel. In Chapter 7, I draw upon three criteria to help grind an interpretive lens that the preacher can use in doing so: (1) appropriateness to the gospel; (2) intelligibility; (3) moral plausibility. An aside: We need to be careful not to rush these moves. Time and perspective sometimes cause us to understand experiences more clearly than when we are in the midst of them.

The life of the preacher seldom unfolds as a series of discreet experiences that the preacher can evaluate theologically in the sequence — and at the time — that they occur. The life of the preacher is a collage of experiences, some of which take place serially and others simultaneously. The flow of life carries us from one experience to another. To reflect on experience, preachers need to bring it into consciousness. Occasional moments are bold and clear. They clamor for interpretation. At other times, we feel a tug that seems to suggest that we pause and consider what a particular moment may reveal to us. From time to time, we preachers need to discipline ourselves to reflect on our experiences so as to understand how they are influencing us and our preaching. At times, we quickly resolve how to understand an experience. At other times, reflection itself may yield no more than the intuition, that something is important, though we cannot now name just how.

For instance, something may happen in the life of the church that seems immediately to reveal God's unconditional love. The preacher can immediately name the experience. Or, the preacher may see a picture in a news magazine that brings a feeling of revulsion to the preacher's stomach. The feeling causes the preacher to ask whether something in the picture or the story is inconsistent with God's love for all and God's will for justice for all.

The Minister's Experience and Sermon Preparation

The preacher is not a *tabula rasa*, a blank slate, when beginning to prepare the sermon. The preacher's experience affects all that the preacher sees, hears, thinks, and feels. Of course, experience need not arbitrarily determine how a preacher approaches a biblical text, a Christian doctrine, or a personal or social situation. However, experience plays a role in predisposing the preacher toward ideas, approaches, and events that are congenial with the preacher's experience and away from those that are not. For instance, a preacher's experience may urge a preacher, week after week, to select a certain kind of biblical text.

The inevitability of experience playing a part in the environment of sermon preparation can be both a hindrance and a help. Preachers who think about their experience from the perspective of the gospel are more likely for their experience to be a help than a hindrance. Preachers who do not weigh their experience on the scales of the gospel sometimes let their experience play a role that is unsuitable to a context, to an interpretive move, or to Christian witness. For instance, as a comfortable member of the middle class, I tend to be drawn to aspects of the biblical witness and Christian convention that allow me to continue in my middle-class comfort zone. I resist aspects of the gospel that suggest that God wants more than a middle-class life for people in this world. I especially resist the Christian community's suggestion that my own life might be disturbed in order for God's will for justice for all to take effect.

To take another example, many of my students grew up in the forests of southern Indiana; hence, when they hear about a wilderness in the Bible, they imagine an area that is thickly wooded and is almost impassable because of bushes, vines, and other undergrowth. They need to learn that many wilderness lands in the world of the Bible are arid or semiarid. For still another instance, I know a preacher whose experience of disappointment and anger with the church clouded this person's sermons to the point that the gospel's possibilities for renewal were lost. In sermons, the preacher "took it out" on the congregation until a colleague helped the preacher recognize this pattern. Preachers sometimes need to transcend our experience.

Experience can also be a help, especially as a positive point of contact and as a source of stories. Preachers who are in touch with pain that they have felt are often sensitive to the pain behind, in, and caused by Bible passages, Christian tradition, and personal and social situations. A preacher who has experienced racism is likely to pick up nuances in Christian material that critique racism and offer alternatives to racism. Such a person is also likely to notice (and critique) aspects of the Bible and other material that could be used in support of racism. A preacher whose home life is difficult may be able to pick up qualities of biblical texts, Christian thinking, and life experiences that help people deal with such stress.

In connection with each sermon, a preacher might ask the following questions:

- What is my experience with the subject of the sermon — biblical text, Christian doctrine, practice, personal or social situation? What is on the surface of my consciousness? What is more hidden?

- How does my experience help me deal with this subject?

- How does my experience hinder me from encountering this text, doctrine, or situation?

Such reflection will likely turn up thoughts, feelings, and behaviors.

Although a preacher's experience generates material that could be directly useful in a sermon, a minister needs to handle such material with care. For instance, the pastor may witness reconciliation between two board members who had threatened each other with excommunication during a hot business meeting. When preparing a sermon on reconciliation, the preacher remembers the incident. It brings the major thrust of the sermon to life. In chapter 12, I note criteria by which a preacher may gauge the degree to which it is advisable to use material from personal experience in the pulpit. For now, I note that the minister cannot simply rush into the pulpit with the story of the reconciliation of the two church leaders, but can proceed only with the permission of all concerned. At times, a preacher must keep confidence, even with a story that is perfect for a sermon. At other times, a preacher cannot recount the event in a straightforward way in the pulpit, but may be able to rework the event, or allude to it, so that its experiential power is conveyed without embarrassing or calling attention to the parties involved.

A preacher also needs to be careful when telling stories from a previous pastorate. An incident from another congregation ten years ago may bring an aspect of the sermon to life. But, hearing such a story, the present congregation may wonder, "Are we going to be in the pastor's sermons ten years from now when the pastor is serving another congregation?" Such questions can distract the congregation and even erode trust in the pastor. Consequently, I recommend that, generally, a preacher not tell the congregation that a story derives from a previous pastorate. If such an experience is just right for a sermon, the preacher can tell it without tying it to a prior ministry.

In the heat of sermon preparation, some preachers have a hard time remembering particular experiences that would help the sermon. In chapter 15, I mention some practical ways that preachers can keep a record of significant experiences.

It is important to remember that the preacher's life is the preacher's life and not a series of sermon resources. We make the best "use" of our experience when we live as fully and deeply as we can. When we too quickly glom onto the preaching possibilities of a particular moment, we may violate the integrity of the moment. The event is no longer an event in its own right, but merely a sermon resource. Such a preacher is a cannibal.

A better approach is to live and to reflect on life. When I go to a movie, I do not enter the theater with the idea that the movie will furnish me with a sermon illustration. I watch the movie to help me engage life. Reflection on experience often helps me better understand myself, the congregation, the larger world, and it helps me better see, hear, and feel the divine presence.

The preacher can often directly and indirectly draw on experience in the sermon. For instance, in my sermon in chapter 16 I refer to an experience of being lost as a part of applying the story of the lost sheep to our setting (pages 266–267). While Mary Donovan Turner does not refer directly to her experience as a part of the sermon in chapter 17, her own struggles as a disciple clearly lay behind the sermon (pages 271–273). In chapter 18, René Rodgers Jensen closes her sermon with a tender but revelatory personal experience (page 285). Reginald Holmes experience as an African American urban pastor repeatedly comes to the surface in his sermon in chapter 19 (pages 288–295).

As pointed out earlier, many contemporary listeners would prefer to hear "evidential experience" in order to accept a preacher's claim.[5] An evidential experience is a report of a person — present or past — with whom listeners can identify and who has had an experience that is similar to the experience that the preacher commends. Congregations are most impressed when preachers themselves can report such experience.

A caution: Aspects of my experience help me understand the experiences of others, and relate the gospel to them. However, preachers cannot assume that all listeners share, understand, or even appreciate the preacher's experience. Nor can we assume that our experience is (or ought to be) representative or normative. Preachers need always to function as priestly listeners to the experience of others (pages 33–34). As theologian Mary Catherine Hilkert says above, the experience of others can enlarge our experience, help us reframe it, or even cause us to realize that what we have assumed to be normative is not so. Consequently, the preacher needs to listen as carefully and widely as possible to the experience of others. Such listening can take place through face-to-face conversation, books and other printed matter, the electronic media (television, movies, radio, musical recordings), the visual and kinesthetic arts.

While a person can never completely understand the experience of another, the minister's empathy and imagination can allow the preacher to penetrate the experience of others with considerable fullness. By entering imaginatively into the experience of others, the preacher's reservoir of experience is increased in breadth and depth. Likewise, by means of the imagination, the sermon can add to the experience of the community.

In a sermon entitled "The View from Mt. Nebo," Joseph Sittler (a Lutheran pastor and theologian who taught at the University of Chicago) points out that preachers must sometimes preach beyond their immediate experience.[6] Sittler compares the preacher to Moses who led the Israelites to the edge of the promised land. Moses will not enter the land. However, from

Nebo, Moses sees the land and announces its blessing to the people. Like Moses, preachers must sometimes proclaim promise and judgment, that we do not personally experience, but that are inherent in the gospel.

Experience That is Sensitive to the Divine Presence

Some elements of experience simply occur in the course of everyday living. You wake up in the morning and the sunlight is streaming on the pillow and you feel the security of the everlasting arms. You are in the hospital holding the hand of a senior member at the moment of death and you feel the transience of human life. You turn on the late news and are confronted by a moral outrage and you remember the gospel's demand for justice.

However, preachers can also cultivate aspects of experience that are particularly promising for the development of spiritual life and sermons. In particular, preachers need to cultivate the thirteen Christian practices enumerated on pages 11–12. Regularly engaging in these practices helps the minister (and other Christians) develop life experience that is infused with the gospel. The minister feeds the soul with Christian nutrients. Consequently, the minister is better able to be sensitive to traces of the gospel in everyday experience.

Worship, Bible study, meditating on the Christian tradition, confession of sin, tolerating and encouraging one another, providing (and experiencing) hospitality and care, listening attentively — these and the other practices can help ministers develop the language, concepts, modes of thinking, and behaviors that are necessary for Christian existence. They also develop the minister's interior landscape. They help shape the minister's life of feeling. They add to the dim, deep parts of the pastoral self in ways that are sometimes difficult to describe, but that help shape the pastor's receptivity toward God and the world. Christians sometimes develop intuition as to God's presence and leading.

Some preachers prefer certain practices more than others. Indeed, some preachers put the practices in a hierarchy of importance. For instance, some clergy say that prayer is most important. Preferences evolve naturally in individual clergy because of personality, theological commitment, and community orientation. While ministers can participate in some practices more than others, the wisdom of Christian tradition is that all are necessary in the Christian life. Indeed, the practices have complementary effects on one another. The practices of the interior life nourish the inner self, while the practices external to the self and community prevent the interior practices from becoming ingrown. The practices external to self and community make Christian witness in the larger world, while the interior practices remind them of their ultimate purpose and empower them.

Preachers need to find ways of engaging in the practices that are congenial to their personalities, theological orientations, and communities. For example, while the tradition calls for prayer that includes adoration, confession of sin, thanksgiving, intercession, and petition, the tradition does not prescribe a singular form of prayer. Some Christian communities find the need for prayer satisfied by contemplative prayer with its extended periods of silence. Some people keep silence for fifteen minutes a day, others for an hour a day, still others for a week, or a month, or a year. Other people respect the contemplative tradition, but find that the silence itself is distracting — no matter how long and hard they keep it. For them, the purpose of prayer is fulfilled through active engagement with God and others. Still other traditions find that the use of a prayer book provides a satisfying and revealing structure for prayer.

I pause over a matter that frequently comes up in seminary classes and in discussions among clergy colleagues. When engaging in the practices for devotional (and other formative) purposes, do I suspend what I have learned in seminary? For instance, when reading a psalm for the day, do I try to read the psalm as if I know nothing about the historical-critical and literary-critical interpretations of the psalm? Certainly not. The critical study of the Bible is intended to place one in a position to engage a Biblical text (or other Christian manifestation) as a genuine other with its own witness. I ask, How does interaction with this text help me conceive and recognize God's presence and leading in my setting today? To particularize the example further, How does a psalm of lament help me name and express the lamentation in my life and community? How does the psalm help me hear and respond to the lamentations of others? How does my reaction to the psalm help me identify God's presence and purposes in the situations that prompt lamentation?

I return briefly to an earlier theme. The practices themselves sometimes contain elements of ambiguity. For instance, contemplative persons sometimes emerge from periods of silence with clear visions of what they think God wills in particular situations. To be sure, the rarefied atmosphere of contemplation can help one become sympathetic to the deep movement of the Spirit. However, sin can warp even sublime moments of contemplation. Even the most sincere contemplative's vision can turn toward the vested interests of the contemplative rather than the gospel. The same thing, of course, is true of modes of prayer that involve direct conversation with God and others. In corporate prayer, we can chat up ourselves to God in such a way as to suggest that our desires are God's desires for us. While a prayer book can provide structure and security within which to relate to God, it can also become an insulator from God. Consequently, preachers need to test the insights that emerge from particular experiences of Christian practice against the experience and thinking of the broader Christian community.

Preaching is inevitably autobiographical. The autobiographical elements may be indirect as when they guide us in the selection of texts and subject matters. They may be overt as when we explicitly name our own experience. The preacher's responsibility is to think critically about experience so that the sermon will not become an exercise in personal preference or idiosyncrasy, but will witness to the gospel of God.

SECTION THREE

Preaching as Theological Interpretation

The church is called to witness to the gospel in all its life. The church makes a Christian witness in many ways: in worship, in Christian teaching and learning, in programs that the church sponsors, in the process and decisions of the governing body, in the uses of the building, in the relationships of members with one another and with persons outside the community, in the Christian community's association with other communities, and in the stands the congregation takes on public issues.

At the same time that the church makes the Christian witness, it must also reflect on the content of that witness to gauge the degree to which its witness measures up to the fullness of the gospel. The congregation is a community of theological interpretation. The preacher is called to help the community both make and criticize its witness. The pastor is not the only theologian in a congregation. Indeed, all Christians should be theologians. Most preachers can recall occasions when their theological perception was clarified by grandmothers, day-laborers, physicians, and neighborhood children. However, the church sets the preacher aside so that someone in the community is specifically responsible for helping the church reflect theologically on its life and witness.

Chapter 6 considers the nature and purposes of the sermon. What should happen in the process of sermon preparation, in the event of preaching, and in the afterglow of the sermon? The sermon is theological interpretation through conversation. Chapter 7 develops a theological method centered in three criteria that the preacher and community can use in theological analysis of a text, doctrine, practice, or personal or social situation. It also identifies possible hermeneutical relationships between the gospel and the community that can result from such analysis.

CHAPTER SIX

Preaching as Theological Interpretation through Conversation

Preachers need to have a clear idea of what a sermon is, what is supposed to happen in a congregation when preaching takes place, and how to evaluate the success of the event of preaching. Two experiences highlight the importance of such clarity.

For a Lenten service of worship at a seminary (not at Christian Theological Seminary), the planners replaced the Lord's table and the pulpit with a campsite: a tent, a sleeping bag, a camp stool. For the homily, the student preacher sat on the stool and read from a journal that the student had kept while camping. It described the clouds that the camper had seen in the sky during an afternoon of lying in a field. The reading did not mention God. The language was beautiful but without point.

Later, I asked the student to tell me the purpose of the homily. The camper replied, "I wanted to share my feelings with the community." Further conversation revealed that the student believed that the reading would communicate an implicit theological message. However, even after the speaker's explanation, I was puzzled as to what a description of summertime clouds in the Rocky Mountains three years ago had to do with God and with our community in February in a grimy urban setting.

Another sermon took place on the second Sunday of Advent. The text was John the Baptist's call to repentance. The preacher sketched John's setting and recalled the meaning of repentance and its importance in the Christian life. The preacher explained that repentance is not a work that we perform but a gift that God provides. The preacher outlined benefits that come about for self and community when we repent. The preacher then described several situations for which the listening community should repent and offered us the opportunity to do so. I was moved to repent.

The first case is extreme. Nonetheless, it demonstrates the confusion that can result when a preacher does not have a clear grasp of the purpose of Christian preaching. The second case illustrates that clarity can result in purposeful encounter with the gospel.

In this chapter, I develop an understanding of the sermon as theological interpretation that takes place through conversation. I mention the partners in the conversation. The chapter concludes by calling attention to turns that the preaching conversation takes in four major contemporary theological families – revisionary theology with its method of mutual critical correlation, postliberalism, liberation theology, and evangelicalism.

The chapter is based on three theological presuppositions. First, God created the world to be an Eden, a delight. However, second, as we learn from Genesis 3, sin now distorts God's purposes. The world is not fully the place God would like for it to be. Among the many manifestations of sin are self-service, idolatry, falsehood, exploitation, broken relationships, and violence. Third, God is at work to restore the world so that all creatures, natural elements, and relationships will conform to the divine purpose in every way. A common biblical expression for this renewed world is the rule (NRSV: kingdom) of God.

The church comes to know and experience redemption through the story of Israel and through Jesus Christ. The story of Israel is the paradigm of divine presence, purpose, and activity through which the church understands the story of Jesus Christ. These stories reveal the gospel of God's unconditional love for each and all and God's call for justice for each and all. Because of the creative power of language, the sermon can be an active agent in this restoration. The sermon can re-create aspects of the world.

Preaching as Theological Interpretation through Conversation

The vocation of the preacher is to help the congregation interpret the significance of the gospel for the sake of the congregation and the world. The preacher helps the Christian community interpret the divine character, the situation of the world, God's relationship to it, and how to respond in ways that are consistent with the gospel. From the perspective of the theological convictions articulated immediately above, the preacher helps the congregation name the world in three important respects. First, the preacher helps the community remember the Great Creator's purposes of love and justice for people and nature. Second, the minister helps the congregation name sin and its effects and agents. The minister encourages the congregation to recognize its own brokenness, the distance of the world from the purposes of God, its complicity in the ways of sin, and its impotence to make things right. Third, the preacher helps the community understand how the gospel offers hope for the congregation and the world. What does God's love offer each person, community, and situation? What does God's will for justice require?

In the strict sense, the minister preaches the gospel. The minister does not preach the Bible, a Christian doctrine, or practice. The Bible, affirmations of faith, Christian practices, and other voices in the Christian tradition are witnesses. They typically testify to the gospel (although, as I note in the next chapter, a few of them actually work against the gospel). The preacher uses them to help the community discover — or rediscover — aspects of Christian tradition and identity that are essential for today's community. The Bible and other elements of Christian tradition help the preacher focus the gospel for a particular aspect of the life of the contemporary church and world. However, the preacher does not simply preach a Bible text. The preacher seeks ways in which an encounter with the text can help the congregation encounter the gospel. Thus, the key question to ask of the sermon is not "Is it true to the biblical text?" but "Is the sermon true to the gospel?"

To borrow an image from Justo and Catherine Gonzalez, professors who are committed to ministerial preparation, a preacher is not a lone-ranger interpreter.[1] At its best, interpretation takes place through conversation in community. The conversation begins in sermon preparation, is manifest in preaching itself, and continues after the preacher finishes speaking. Over the past twenty-five years, systematic theologians have increasingly used the term conversation to describe the process of theological interpretation. Preachers have now begun to use it to describe the process of preparing a sermon, preaching, and its aftereffects.[2] John McClure, professor of preaching at Louisville Presbyterian Theological Seminary, in particular, has developed a process of collaborative preaching in which preacher and community meet to study the biblical text before the preacher prepares the sermon. Lucy Atkinson Rose, who taught preaching at Columbia Theological Seminary, speaks of the church as a round table that has neither head nor foot.

My approach shares much with these two pioneers. I agree with McClure that face-to-face collaboration can be useful, but I lay a little less stress on it. I agree with Rose that all partners in the conversation need to be heard. In some ways, my approach brings her work to practical expression. With a difference in nuance, however, I think (with McClure) that ordination bestows a special role on the preacher as representative of both tradition and community. The church ordains the pastor to help make sure that certain voices are represented in the conversation and to help the church think its way through the pluralism of voices to theological conclusion. In the conversation, such voices may challenge, correct, and even chastise the preacher.

Conversation is mutual exploration of ideas, feelings, and behaviors with the goal of coming to as promising an understanding as is possible at a given moment. In the church, the conversation of preaching aims for an adequate interpretation of the significance of the gospel for the life of the ecclesial community and the world. By preaching as conversation, at least in European American congregations, I think less of an actual give-and-take between the preacher and the congregation in the act of preaching and more of a feeling of mutual interaction. The sermon itself is typically monological in form. However, long ago, Reuel Howe pointed out that a sermon that is spoken by a single person can have a dialogical character when the speaker "feels responsible for and responds to the patterns of experience and understanding" of the listeners.[3] A sermon is conversational when the community recognizes itself in the sermon.[4] In two contexts, however, preaching as conversation often involves direct, spoken communication between the minister and the people. In pentecostal churches of all races and ethnicities, the congregation sometimes speaks out loud during the sermon. Some of these remarks and expressions are direct engagement with the sermon. Others are more formulaic. In most African American communities, the call and the response is mutual engagement. The people participate in the sermon by responding aloud. Many African American preachers reshape the sermon, while they are preaching in response to the congregation's participation. Whether the congregation actually speaks aloud, a sermon can have a conversational quality when the community feels engaged in the give-and-take of the development of the sermon.

Hans-Georg Gadamer, a philosopher of language, points out that "the first condition of the art of conversation is to ensure that the other person is with us."[5] Each person is a genuine other whose integrity must be respected. "A conversation is a process of two people understanding each other."[6] Conversations can involve others in the forms of texts and other phenomena. In order for the conversation to move toward its deepest possibilities, each participant must respect the otherness of all involved. This requirement means not hearing the other only from the perspective of my preunderstanding, entangled as I am in my own projections and biases. I am morally obligated to listen to, and respect, the other as other. In "true conversation" all participants open themselves to the others in interchange, consider the viewpoints, and try to understand the issue from the points of view of the others.[7]

The heart of conversation is listening and probing. As David Tracy, a widely respected theologian, says, we "learn to give in to the movement required by questions worth exploring." Indeed, "Neither my present opinions on the question nor the text's original response to the question, but the question itself, must control every conversation." A conversation "is not a confrontation. It is not a debate. It is not an exam. It is questioning itself. It is a willingness to follow the question wherever it may go. It is dialogue."[8] Consequently, conversation has

> hard rules: say only what you mean; say it as accurately as you can; listen to and respect what the other says, however different or other; be willing to correct or defend your opinions if challenged by the conversation partner; be willing to argue, if necessary, to confront if demanded, to endure necessary conflict, to change your mind if the evidence suggests it.[9]

While a conversational approach mandates that all participants listen carefully to one another, that respect does not mean that one shuts down one's critical faculties. Clark M. Williamson, a systematic theologian who has spent years reflecting on these matters, notes, "Lest one's mind become a garbage heap of accumulated meanings deposited there by one's conversation partners, one must critically integrate these meanings with the values and perspectives that one brought to the conversation. Commitment to a more supreme and embracing good facilitates this kind of integration."[10] A conversation may result with a participant concluding that another has a false self-understanding or a false understanding of the world. In the next chapter, I indicate three criteria (appropriateness to the gospel, intelligibility, moral plausibility) by which preachers can reflect critically on the contributions to a conversation.

The first goal of a conversation is to identify the community's preunderstanding of the subject so that the preunderstanding will not inappropriately prejudge the conclusion to which the conversation will come. The community lists and clarifies the various viewpoints and experiences of the subject. This aspect of the conversation may reveal points that are unsettled, points at which the community has little information or perspective, or points at which the community has little experience. Congregational exegesis described in chapter 4 (pages 33–38) can be very helpful with this task, as can pastoral listening, the human sciences, and the arts. In John McClure's collaborative preaching, the stage of "topic-setting" often brings preunderstanding to light.[11]

The next task is to identify and secure relevant material that the community needs to make sense of the subject — questions to be pursued, information, feelings, behaviors that arise in connection with the subject. The conversation partners listen to the subject, and to the various pieces of data, and to one another.

The heart of the conversation is identifying the various interpretive possibilities. The community compares and contrasts the various interpretations with one another and decides which one(s) make the most sense in the light of the gospel, and the community's experience, and understanding of the subject. Sometimes new possibilities for interpretation emerge from the conversation.

Conversations include many different forms of content, such as questions, stories, logical arguments, data from empirical research, citations from official and folk authorities, statements and descriptions of feelings, expostulations. Participants in the conversation must sometimes call one another into question. At key moments, silence is sometimes the most important contribution to a conversation.

All members of the conversation offer their interpretations. The participants seek to clarify these proposals, draw out their implications, assess them, and come to a relatively adequate conclusion.

> If one demands certainty, one is assured of failure. We can never possess absolute certainty. But we can achieve a good — that is, a relatively adequate — interpretation: relative to the power of disclosure and concealment of the text, relative to the skills and attentiveness

of the interpreter, relative to the kind of conversation possible for the interpreter in a particular culture at a particular time.[12]

The notion that the sermon is an interpretation of the gospel emerging from conversation and resulting in a relatively adequate witness may initially seem unsatisfying to some preachers. To those who are uneasy with my description of the nature and purpose of the sermon, I reply that I am only making explicit approaches to the sermon that are a part of most preaching. Even the pastor who insists that the preacher's words are, breath by breath, God's words, must acknowledge that Bible scholars, church historians, and systematic theologians disagree among themselves as to how to interpret biblical passages and Christian doctrines. Preachers interpret when they prefer the opinion of one scholar to the opinion of another. By calling attention to the interpretive and conversational dynamics that are inherent parts of preaching, I hope to make them available for critical discussion.

The simple fact is that a degree of relativity is inherent in the whole process of preaching. As I have repeatedly stressed, all perception takes place through interpretive lenses. Because human beings are finite, we cannot fathom all of God. In addition, sin distorts our capacity to perceive clearly. Revelation itself has an interpretive dimension for we receive revelation through our ingrained interpretive lenses in a sin-distorted world. Furthermore, the human family encounters preachers who profess to have messages from God and sometimes turn out to use the power emanating from such claims for ends that are self-serving and communally destructive. In an earlier publication, I carelessly wrote that the preacher seeks "full knowledge of God." Scott Black Johnston, who teaches preaching, correctly rejoins,

> We cannot...have "full knowledge" at this time. Yet, we must not despair, for preachers are called to pursue sufficient knowledge of God — knowledge that will sustain the faithful even as we await the eschaton and the full revelation of the divine.[13]

Because our lenses are tinted, smudged, and cracked, preachers need conversation with others to help us enlarge our perception. Others help us see things that we may not see in texts, in doctrines, in practices, in personal and social situations, and in our own lives. I am seldom so imperceptive as I am regarding my own imperceptions.

Most of the time, a conversation that is pursued with enough honesty, depth, imagination, and rigor will result in a clear, credible, and authoritative interpretive possibility. Some conversations seem not to come to resolution; their effect is to keep dialogue alive. Occasional conversations are so fractious and mean-spirited that they end exchange, at least temporarily. Once in a great while preacher and community must admit that the data and our reading of it are too confusing for us to reach a conclusion at the present time. We need to continue to live in ambiguity and to continue to engage with one another and the subject matter until we achieve more confidence.

A conversational approach to interpretation is not foolproof. A group of conversation partners, much like an individual, can be insensitive, imperceptive, self-serving, and idolatrous. A preacher may be subtly seduced into going along with the majority opinion in the conversational group. A community that cannot reach a consensus on an issue may too quickly use that lacuna as an excuse to hide from the issue (particularly if the matter is controversial). The preacher needs to keep alert to the possibility that a community consensus may be mistaken. The best contribution a sermon may make in a congregational conversation is to go against the community's thinking.

Leading Partners in the Preaching Conversation

Conversation can be characteristic of all phases of the sermon's life: from the moments of conceiving the message, through preparation and preaching, to the afterglow. The partners in the conversation include God, the gospel, the Bible, Christian tradition, the congregation, the wider Christian community, the world, and the preacher. The preacher seeks to listen to each of these partners as a part of interpreting every text, doctrine, Christian practice, ethical possibility, or personal or social situation.

The preaching conversation can take many forms. The preacher will sometimes engage the various members of the conversational community in a flesh-to-flesh setting. For instance, the pastor may organize a group in the congregation to help with sermon preparation or may visit authorities on the subject of the sermon. Other weeks, the minister will work alone in the study, but will still be in conversation with others through reading or through the electronic media.

God, through the Holy Spirit, is active in all phases of the life of the sermon. In my view, the Spirit does not have a script of the sermon to fax to the preacher, but is a partner with the preacher. The Spirit encourages the preacher to be sensitive to the optimum possibilities for helping the community to realize God's unconditional love and to respond to God's vision for a just world. (The theological criteria in chapter 7 can help the preacher identify the presence and leading of the Spirit in the preparation of the sermon.) To be sure, the preacher can ignore, misconstrue, or reject the prompting of the Spirit. However, if the preacher distorts or turns away from the lure of the Holy Spirit, the Spirit then works with the preacher, the sermon, and the congregation in order to make the most of the possibilities that result from the choices of the preacher and the congregation. The Holy Spirit never gives up on a preacher, a message, or a church.

In order to be an adequate partner in the community of interpretation, the preacher must have a crisp and critically considered understanding of the *gospel.* I take the gospel to be the news revealed to the church through Jesus Christ of the promise of God's unconditional love for each and all and the call of God for justice for each and all.

The gospel may be expressed in other formulations. But, whatever its precise articulation, preachers need to have a deep understanding of the origins, meanings, strengths, and weaknesses of their expressions of the gospel.

Week by week, the *Bible* is a theological conversation partner. The Bible is a library of primal witnesses to the presence and purposes of God. I call it a library because, while its many books contain perspectives in common, the different bodies of literature within the Bible have their own voices in the conversation, e.g., priestly writings, wisdom literature, apocalypticism, Pauline and post-Pauline schools, Johannine community. The preaching conversation is often enriched as the community listens to different perspectives within the Bible itself. For example, if I were dealing with 2 Peter 3, which depicts the completion of God's purposes as an apocalyptic cataclysm, I would want to explore how others in the biblical world understand the fulfillment of the divine purposes. How do the Deuteronomists, the sages, and the Johannine school view the goal of the divine will? Such comparison and contrast often help the preacher and community come to clarity as to which aspects of the Bible are most illuminating and why.

Voices from the *Christian history and tradition* extend from the world of the Bible into the present. These voices include those that the church has regarded as marginal or even heretical. Like the Bible, Christian tradition is neither a monolith nor static, but is a great cloud of witnesses who speak in multiple voices from many times and places. The tradition includes personal contributions as well as communal voices that range from councils and affirmations of faith to denominations, theological movements, and ad hoc groups. Careful attention to the tradition reveals that it is constantly in the process of critically rethinking itself. The contemporary community's conversation continues the tradition into the present.

While it may seem paralyzing to consider consulting persons and communities from across the vast range and complexity of Christian history, a preacher can usually identify key voices who speak forcefully on particular texts, doctrines, issues, or situations. These voices should include the historic denomination and the preacher's contemporary theological family (revisionary, postliberal, liberation, evangelical). A preacher can listen to voices as different as Chalcedon, Origen, the Cappadocians, Augustine, Abelard, Hildegard, Julian of Norwich, Luther, Calvin, Teresa of Avila, the Council of Trent, Henry Highland Garnett, Karl Barth, Paul Tillich, Martin Luther King, Jr., the Second Vatican Council, Gustavo Guiterriez, James Cone, Mary Daly, C. S. Song, Letty Russell, Jacquelyn Grant, perspectives from a General Synod, General Assembly, or Council of Bishops.

The *congregation* seldom speaks out loud in the sermon. However, the congregation can be a partner in sermon preparation. Chapter 4 introduces priestly listening as a means whereby the preacher can discover how the congregation relates to the subject of the sermon. Many preachers, as I note in chapter 13, involve members of the congregation in sermon feed-forward groups. Preachers who are sensitive to the congregation during the act of preaching report that some members of the congregation can shout at the preacher (in both positive and negative ways) without saying a word.

Voices from the *wider world* are also present. Past and current events, movies, media images, hopes and tensions in the community, insights from politics, sociology, psychology — each is a genuine other who may contribute insights, questions, experiences, and images to the conversation. For example, a sociologist's research on spouse abuse should not singularly dictate a sermon, but it may help the preacher realize who needs to hear the news of God's love and how God's call for justice needs to be focused.

As noted in the previous chapter, the *life of the preacher* is a part of the preaching conversation. Ministers need to be aware of how their own experiences affect their interpretation of the matters that are central to the sermon. Because we so often take ourselves for granted, it may be important for preachers to take a moment specifically to identify how their autobiographies shape their engagement with the developing sermon.

On the one hand, the conversation that results from such an interchange can be exhilarating. On the other hand, a preacher can be overwhelmed by the prospect of attending to so many voices from so many times and places. Chapters 9 and 10 offer a plan for facilitating a wide-ranging conversation in a way that is manageable.

Turns in the Preaching Conversation

In chapter 3, I note that certain emphases are characteristic in the preaching of the historic denominations, e.g., Orthodoxy, Roman Catholic, Lutheran, Episcopalian, Reformed, Wesleyan, Anabaptist, Pentecostal. The preaching conversation tends to develop in the direction of the major emphases in these families. For example, a Lutheran conversation might explore the relationship between law and gospel in a particular text or topic, while a Pentecostal conversation could seek the leading of the Spirit.

In addition, four contemporary approaches to theology cut across these traditional communities: revisionary, postliberal, liberation, and evangelical theologies. Each of these newer approaches can be found within most of the historic denominations. We should not think of these contemporary approaches as if they are mutually exclusive. Speaking of a tendency in contemporary theology to pose revisionary theology and postliberalism as polar alternatives, Walter Brueggemann, a major biblical expositor, cautions that "except for a few devotees, I imagine that no one who engages in serious practice is fully at ease with either such position, and does not in fact in any case operate with a pure method of interpretation."[14] This qualification can be extended to the relationships of all of these (and other) theological families. Nevertheless, each approach takes the preaching conversation in a different direction.

In my view, the *revisionary* theological movement with its *preaching by means of mutual critical correlation* is the most satisfactory approach because it seeks to make a witness that is recognizably Christian and that is intellectually and morally credible in the contemporary world.[15] Revisionary theologians recognize two loci of authority – Christian tradition and contemporary experience. Tradition includes the gamut of the Bible, Christian history, affirmations of faith, doctrine, and practice, as well as Christian ethical prescriptions. Revisionary thinkers acknowledge that both Christian tradition and contemporary experience are thoroughly interpretive. The term "revisionary" is key. These theologians revise their understanding of the world (and its possibilities) in light of Christian tradition, and they revise aspects of their understanding of Christian tradition in light of experience.

Revisionary theology proceeds by the method of mutual critical correlation. Following the lead of Paul Tillich (a systematic theologian steeped in philosophy), revisionary Christians seek to correlate elements of Christian tradition – e.g., claims, ethical behaviors – with elements of the contemporary situation. The correlation is mutual and critical. It is mutual because it presumes that both Christian tradition and contemporaneity can inform and critique one another. It is critical because the Christian tradition criticizes the contemporary setting, even while aspects of today's community criticize the claims, behaviors, and worldview of the tradition.

In preaching that is consistent with this theological method, the pastor generates a conversation that helps the congregation affect a mutual, critical correlation between aspects of the tradition and the situation. What are the claims of this biblical text, doctrine, practice, or prescription? What are the abiding values in it? How can these be correlated with the contemporary setting? Does this text, doctrine, or practice challenge aspects of the contemporary world? Does it ask us to enlarge or rethink our vision of what is possible? Do aspects of this text, doctrine, practice, or prescription strain intellectual, theological, or moral credibility? If so, should we think again?

An example: In Isaiah 40–55, the prophet anticipated that the return from exile would be even more glorious than the exodus from slavery in Egypt (e.g., Isaiah 43:19–20). However, when they returned to Palestine, they found much of it in ruins. Farms and cities needed rebuilding. Drought set in. Many people became dispirited. Isaiah 56–66 encourages the community to continue to trust God's promises.

In the climactic oracle of salvation, Isaiah 66:6–16, the prophet uses a series of feminine images to remind the community that God's promises to restore Zion are still good.[16] Isaiah compares Zion (the community) to a woman who gives birth in the form of a renewed nation (vv. 7–8). This birth is remarkable in that it takes place before the onset of labor pains. The curse of pain in childbearing that resulted from the transgression of Adam and Eve (Genesis 3:16) is reversed: The restored land will be a new Eden. Susan Ackerman, in *The Women's Bible Commentary*, notes that, in verse 9, "birth imagery is assimilated to the deity; so that Yahweh identifies with Zion's delivery."[17] Zion breastfeeds the community (v. 11). Jerusalem is mother for the infant community: nursing, carrying, bouncing on her knees. God says, "As a mother comforts her child, so I will comfort you" (v. 13). The community will flourish (v. 14). However, as God comforts the faithful as a mother, so God comes in a storm of judgment on the unfaithful. Isaiah uses the imagery of a storm to describe God coming "in fury." For by fire God will execute judgment, "and by [the] sword, on all flesh; and those slain by the LORD shall be many" (vv. 15–16).

Preaching in the mode of critical correlation presses us to consider ways in which the text correlates positively with our situation. We, too, can be discouraged in ways that are similar to the discouragement of the community that returned from the exile. Our lives, the church, and the world are less than we believe God wants them to be. In such situations, the text functions as a sign of hope. It wants us to believe that God is present and working in our behalf like a mother: offering new life, feeding, nurturing. The text challenges us to anticipate world regeneration. The world as we know it is not the world that God wants it to be. What can we do to join God in giving birth to the new age?

The method of mutual critical correlation also notes discrepancy between the promise of immediate, painless restoration and the situation of the community as described by writers in the time of the return from exile (e.g., Haggai, Zechariah, Obadiah, Malachi, Ezra, Nehemiah). The rebuilding was difficult in almost every way—economically, socially, and environmentally (drought). The temple languished. The community did not become a second Eden. Indeed, the history of the Jewish people, especially since the separation of Judaism and Christianity, has been difficult and even torturous. The community cannot count on God to intervene in history in singular, dramatic ways. Initially, then, the text strains the contemporary community's sense of credibility.

The conversation needs to take account of these differing themes in the text. The church does have some evidential experience that periods of renewal can replace periods of discouragement. In this regard, the text invites us to revise our attitudes of pessimism and determinism. However, few such changes are immediate or painless. In this respect, experience asks us to revise an aspect of our understanding of the text.

The revisionary conversation remembers that the most frequent designations for God in Christian tradition (Father, Lord, King) are male. The permeating presence of masculine language has the effect of authorizing male status and power. The presence of the feminine dimension of the divine in this text calls for the community to revise its use of language and its social presumptions concerning the roles of women and men.

A revisionary theologian might also note that the text concludes with the plain statement that God will slay many of God's enemies. This affirmation is contrary to the gospel's promise of unconditional love and the call for justice for all. The revisionary theologian could still help the community find a positive value in this part of the text. While God may not directly slay many by the sword, communities that yield to discouragement often collapse from within. Our actions create their own consequences.

Revisionary theology has its soft spots. Revisionary thinkers can easily become captive to the *Zeitgeist* and can so accommodate Christian witness to the contemporary setting that the distinctiveness of Christian sensibility is lost. Revisionist preachers can suggest revisions in understanding Christian tradition on the basis of nothing more than the latest pop trends in the culture. Persistent reinterpretation may leave some members of the community unsettled. "On what can we really count?" The revisionary preacher needs to be cautious not to compromise the essence of Christian faith. A thorough conversation is the best safeguard against such dangers.

The *postliberals* believe that the Christian community is to interpret its life and the world on the basis of its own stories, presuppositions, doctrines, and practices.[18]

Postliberals protest the Christian community submitting its witness to standards outside of itself. Postliberals particularly protest subjecting Christian stories and claims to modern criteria — e.g., verification through experience. Indeed, the designation "postliberal" indicates this movement's dissatisfaction with liberalism in the modern period and its reliance upon experience as a standard for truth. Postliberals presuppose that the Christian interpretation of the world, especially as articulated in the Bible, is normative for the Christian community. The church is to let the Bible and other orthodox Christian texts, especially the Chalcedonian formulation, describe the world. The church "is not to make the gospel credible to the modern world, but to make the world credible to the gospel.[19]

The community of faith is to read the Bible as it does any realistic narrative; it recognizes that some of the details in the Bible are not factually accurate but the description of life that comes to expression in the narrative is still trustworthy in that it narrates God's character and purpose. The church does not try to justify the credibility of Christian faith. Rather, the church teaches itself the language of Christian faith. This language can re-create the church's view of the world to be in harmony with that of the Bible. People who assent to the Bible's vision of the world become a community. Indeed, according to the postliberals, individualism was one of the most rancid developments in modernity. Preaching the biblical story is one means whereby community is created.

The purpose of the preaching conversation, then, is to help the pastor and the community describe the world as it is narrated by the Bible and other orthodox Christian texts, doctrines, and practices. The sermon is to help contemporary listeners understand how their stories are absorbed into the biblical story. Preaching does not so much interpret the Christian tradition as it helps the community understand how the Christian tradition interprets the life of the community.

In the case of Isaiah 66:6–16, the postliberal preacher helps the congregation understand the story of the text as our story. We do not find our stories in the biblical text; to the contrary, the preacher invites us to let the story of the passage become our story. The postliberal, like the revisionist, would notice the dominant emphasis of the text is assurance that God renews discouraged communities. While postliberals acknowledge that renewal does not always take place quickly or painlessly (like birth before labor pains) and does not always result in Edenic circumstances, they are not troubled by these discrepancies. If the postliberal preacher concludes that we belong in the story of the text as the faithful in need of encouragement, the sermon would help us recognize and embrace God's presence and work. If the postliberal conversation concludes that we belong in the world of the text as people under judgment, then the preacher would help us interpret why that is so and, perhaps, pose repentance as a way whereby to avoid judgment.

The postliberal sermon could retell of the story of the text with sufficient elaboration for us to find our places in it. Of course, as Charles Campbell, who has written most extensively about a postliberal approach to preaching, makes clear, the postliberal preacher is not limited to a narrative sermon form. The minister could preach this text in one of any number of sermon forms provided that the form makes explicit the language by which the story names our interpretation of life.[20]

The postliberals remind the church not to sell its distinctive Christian identity for a mess of *Zeitgeist* pottage. However, the postliberal approach has its soft spots. Neither the Bible nor subsequent Christian tradition is univocal. Postliberalism has difficulty dealing with the pluralism within the Christian tradition itself. For example, the wisdom tradition, apocalypticism, and Chalcedonianism are rather different worlds. The postliberal preacher has difficulty mediating among the authority of different narratives. The question of truth is even more troubling. Postliberals have few standards by which to help a congregation understand why their construal of reality is true. In the end, their reasoning is circular: You should accept the Bible's version of life because it is the version of life that is at the center of our religious community. Postliberals have difficulty in making Christian sense out of theologically or morally problematic texts.

Liberation theology assumes that God's purpose is to liberate the world from oppression.[21] In this model, oppression is a form of sin in which one person or a group of people take advantage of other persons or groups (or elements of the natural world) by keeping the latter group repressed. Oppressive forces are often systemic, that is, they are not simply the result of individual human choices but are manifest in social patterns of thought and behavior. Some oppressors are not even conscious that they oppress. Some of the most visible forms of oppression are racism, sexism, poverty, classicism, ageism, handicappism, ecological abuse. Religion can even be a form of oppression. While liberation theologians recognize that all forms of oppression are systemically linked, liberation thinkers tend to group according to particular concerns: African American liberation, womanist liberation, feminist liberation, third-world liberation (with special foci on the Caribbean, Latin America, Asia, Africa).

According to theologians in this family, God is working through historical processes to release the world from oppression, and to establish conditions for all people to have dignity, freedom, work, material resources. Liberation theologians recognize that oppressors experience oppression — often unconsciously — by their involvement in oppression. Oppressors need to be liberated from the compulsion to oppress. Most liberation theologians believe that God is working to create a new social world in which all people are together in a community of shared power and abundance.

A liberation approach to preaching seeks to help the community name oppression in particular situations. The preaching conversation in this community aims to identify the historical persons and processes through which God is working for liberation. The preacher announces liberation and draws out its implications. The sermon needs, further, to help the community respond to the divine movement of liberation. Some people need to accept the fact of liberation and to live in its joy. Others need to commit themselves to the historical struggle for liberation. Others need to renounce their oppressive ways.

In connection with Isaiah 66:6–16, liberation preachers notice that the forces of oppression continue to operate in the community after the return from exile. While the Babylonians were an external repressive force, members of the community now struggle with the internal repression of discouragement. Furthermore, poverty is repressive. The text implies that God will rebuild the social world of the community so that groups within the community will not need to establish their own superiority. Furthermore, the renewal of land and cities will create an era of material prosperity, ending the limitation of poverty. By rebuilding the community's social world and reversing the curse of Eden, God not only provides for the immediate needs of the community, but changes the structures of the community and nature from life-denial to life-support.

Like the revisionary preacher, the liberation theologian is struck by the fact that the dominant images for God in Christian history are male and have been used to suppress women. The text's presentation of God as a woman is a critique of male oppression and an assertion of the worth and social equality of women.

The text does not contain a direct call to the community to engage in liberating activity. However, the liberation conversation notices that the contrast between the faithful who receive the promise of assurance, and the unfaithful who are under threat of judgment results from active worship of the one God and lives that manifest justice. Thus, the text implicitly calls the community to action. Through what historical processes today is God acting for liberation? How can the church respond?

The great danger of a liberation approach is that, when practiced in caricature, the preacher can think in bifurcated terms of the righteous oppressed whom God loves and the evil oppressors who will be thrown down in judgment. This caricature ignores the fact that even the oppressed are mixtures of good and evil. Oppressors need to repent of their evil and to make restitution for the good of the community. But simply reversing their situation only creates a new oppressed group. Liberation theologians sometimes unwittingly contribute to the oppression of the Jewish community when they portray Pharisaism and other forms of Judaism as systemic evils from which Jesus liberates us. By concentrating upon material, social, and political aspects of liberation, these preachers sometimes overlook other aspects of the human self and spirit.

The *evangelical* theological family is diverse. Nevertheless, evangelical family members share several key perspectives.[22] Evangelicals agree that God inspired the Bible, even while having different notions of the meaning, mode, and degree of inspiration. The Bible is the preeminent source of the knowledge of God. Many evangelicals regard the Bible as a body of self-consistent revelation that is valid in every time and place. Evangelicals tend to think that the Bible and orthodox Christian tradition are in unbroken, trinitarian continuity. The Bible and the tradition are a fixed deposit of beliefs on which the community can draw. Classical evangelicals operate with a modern view of truth as the correspondence of statement and reality. The Bible is true because its propositions conform to reality. Indeed, many evangelical preachers help their communities understand why this way of thinking is important and plausible.

These believers acknowledge that the Bible must be interpreted in the sense that the community must extrapolate the meaning of the Bible. Although the Bible is divinely inspired, its human interpreters can make mistakes. Interpretive conversation in the evangelical community focuses on how to understand the Bible so as to minimize the dangers of human misinterpretation. When the community understands the Bible, the community can then apply biblical truths. Evangelical conversation helps the community listen to the Bible, and figure out how the Bible should shape the community's life.

At one time, the evangelical approach to preaching was largely propositional. Most evangelicals believed that each biblical text contained truths that could be stated propositionally. The purpose of the sermon was to identify the propositions lodged in the text and to present them to the congregation clearly and persuasively. A favorite preaching form is the verse-by-verse sermon in which the preacher states the lessons from the text as they unfold. Recently, many evangelical scholars and preachers are queuing into the wider insight that the form of a biblical text is a part of the meaning of the text. To extrapolate a proposition is to change the form, and hence, the meaning of the message. So, some evangelicals are moving away from distilling propositions from the text and are creating sermons in the shape of scripture.

Evangelicals tend to view Isaiah 66:6–16 as a report of an event that will take place. Participants in the evangelical preaching conversation ask, "When and how can we look forward to the day when Zion will be renewed in the way described by the text?" Many evangelicals realize that biblical Zion represents the community of people who acknowledge the sovereignty of God.

Consequently, these evangelicals look forward to the day when God will regenerate the communities of all who trust in God. The evangelical conversation may help the congregation articulate reasons why they can continue to hope for such a renewal, even though 2,500 years have passed since Isaiah wrote.

Evangelicals ask what they can learn from the text. The text reveals the superiority of the God of the Bible over the other deities. The story reveals the extent of God's graciousness. After all, God had brought the people home from exile, only to have them lose confidence; but that does not prevent God from willing good for them. The story shows that God wants people to have resources for abundant life and that God has the power to provide for our needs. The evangelical preacher will remind those in the community to conform to God's promise of love and God's call for justice or face the divine anger.

The strength of the evangelical approach is its thoroughgoing Christian orientation. I am also deeply impressed by the passion of many evangelical preachers and by their hard work in the biblical languages and in reference books as they make every effort to understand the text. Many evangelical sermons have a teaching quality that is much needed in today's church. My reservations about the evangelical movement are similar to those that were raised above in connection with postliberalism. Evangelicals deny the pluralism that seems evident in the Bible and in Christian tradition. Most troubling to me are difficulties with moral and intellectual credibility. Evangelicalism does not take adequate account of differences of interpretation of experience in the world of the Bible and today. Few evangelicals see a contradiction between God's fury (even for remediation) and God's love.

These communities are related much like different households in a large family. They have a common bloodline in their desire to witness to the gospel. But each has its own pattern of dinner table conversation. Preachers and communities who are clear about the character and direction of the conversations taking place around their tables are likely to create sermons that promote continuing conversation in which all the family want to be involved. When the households get together for a family reunion, conversations can be mutually enriching.

Christian Preaching Is Good News

The Greek word that we translate gospel (*euaggelion*) means "good news," and thereby reveals the character of the sermon. Christian preaching is good news from (and about) God that is intended to help the congregation and the world understand itself as beloved of God and to live so as to manifest justice in each and all relationships. Indeed, a useful question to put to the sermon at its various stages of development is, "What is the good news from God for the congregation and the world in this sermon?"

Of course, as Edmund Steimle used to say to students at Union Theological Seminary in New York City, preaching must have "guts," that is, it must look full in the face at the worst life has to offer, and it must not flinch. By emphasizing the sermon as good news, I do not mean that the preacher should downplay or bypass sin and its agents. The gospel is news precisely because the world is so permeated by sin and its destructive effects. The gospel is good news because it originates in God, whose character is unconditional love. The preacher will often need to help the congregation recognize the presence, power, and effects of sin, so that the community will understand their predicament, their complicity in sin, and the need to repent. For example, the typical European American church needs both to understand that racism deforms God's desire for human community and to confront the ways in which it is implicated in racism. Only thus, can it repent of its racist attitudes and behaviors and open itself to the healing of the racial divide that the gospel brings about.

Even though it is necessary to look bare-eyed at sin, sin is only the penultimate word that the preacher is called to speak. The ultimate word is that God's love is unconditional and God's will for justice is unremitting. The preacher needs to help the congregation understand how this news offers hope to the situation of the congregation and the world. Of course, the congregation will not long take seriously a preacher who is a Pollyanna — speaking too loosely of forgiveness, love, and new life. The preacher must speak of these things in full recognition of the complexity, ambiguity, bitterness, pain, and idolatries in the situation of the congregation. But the sermon that goes no farther than naming these qualities is not faithful to God's character and promises.

Theological Criteria and Interpretative Relationships in the Preaching Conversation

Some biblical texts, Christian doctrines, Christian practices, and personal and social situations seem so straightforward that the preacher can take them straight into the pulpit. For instance, Psalm 136 declares twenty-six times in twenty-six verses that God's steadfast love endures forever. The doctrine of justification by grace through faith can almost speak for itself. In today's lonely world of isolated individualism, a sermon about the Christian practice of mutual encouragement creates an immediate hearing.

However, some Christian materials are more opaque. God says to Moses, "I will be gracious to whom I will be gracious, and will show mercy on whom I will show mercy" (Exodus 33:19). Does this passage mean that God is arbitrarily gracious and merciful to some, but not to others?

In the Gospel of Mark, Jesus repeatedly performs mighty works and then enjoins the disciples to silence (e.g., Mark 1:43). Why?

The Apostles' Creed declares that, after his crucifixion, Jesus descended to the dead. What does that mean?

Christian practice calls for us to tolerate one another. Are there no limits to what can be tolerated in the Christian community?

The Christian witness calls for the creation of a just social world. I am convinced that affirmative action is an important step in that direction. However, some Christians who say that they seek an inclusive society, want to end affirmative action because they believe that it undercuts the purpose it is supposed to serve. Does the gospel mandate that the church support affirmative action?

Still other Christian texts and themes are morally and theologically troubling. For instance, Ananias and Sapphira do not turn all of their money over to the common treasury of the earliest Christian community, but keep some.

They lie about it. God strikes them dead (Acts 5:1–10). Dead? Because they lied? Christian attorneys are among national leaders who call for the resurgence of the death penalty in the United States. Is that viewpoint consistent with Christian notions of love and justice?

Even texts that initially sound straightforward often turn out to be more complicated when we listen to them carefully. Psalm 136 declares that God's steadfast love endures forever. However, the same psalm rejoices that God struck down the firstborn of the Egyptians, drowned Pharaoh's army in the sea, and killed several famous monarchs. These actions are strange expressions of steadfast love.

As a part of the preaching conversation, the preacher needs theological criteria by which to reflect on texts, doctrines, and situations. I pose three such criteria. The chapter then recommends listening for both the surface and deeper dimensions of texts, doctrines, and practices in order to have a full understanding of the text. I conclude by suggesting that preacher and congregation usually have one of four possible interpretive relationships with a text, a doctrine, a Christian practice, or a personal or social situation.

Three Theological Criteria for Preaching[1]

The preacher and others in the community can apply the following criteria to all aspects of the preaching conversation – the thoughts, feelings, and actions of the voices in the preparation of the sermon, the relationships of those involved in the preparation and preaching, the content and embodiment of the sermon, and the responses in the community to the sermon. These norms and this particular formulation of them are not sacrosanct. The process of thinking together about the sermon may cause the community to rethink the criteria themselves.

1. *Appropriateness to the gospel.* The church seeks to determine the degree to which every biblical text, Christian doctrine and practice, ethical action, personal and social situation, and every voice in the preaching conversation is appropriate to (or consistent with) the gospel. "Is this text, etc. appropriate to the news of God's unconditional love promised to each and all and God's call for justice for each and all as the church comes to know these realities through Jesus Christ?"

My colleague Clark M. Williamson (a systematic theologian) states the importance of this norm. "The church lives by and from the proclamation of the gospel." The only reason for preaching is to witness to the gospel. "The church claims to be proclaiming the gospel." The criterion

> asks if whether this is really so. The church can be so eager to be popular and accepted, or so zealous to be contextualized in a given culture or ethos, that it forgets that the word it is given to proclaim transcends and criticizes all cultures as it also calls for being critically contextualized in them. We are always in danger in the church of running amok with our latest cliché.[2]

The preacher will usually find that many voices in the conversation are appropriate to the gospel. They declare God's unconditional love and they seek justice. In Isaiah 49:14–18, for instance, Israel laments that God has forgotten them. Using maternal imagery, God replies, "Can a woman forget her nursing child, or show no compassion for the child of her womb? Even these may forget, yet I will not forget you. See, I have inscribed you on the palms of my hands...." The text is a remarkable assurance of unremitting love. Ephesians 1:9 is cosmic in its declaration of God's universal intention, "to gather up all things . . . in heaven and things on earth."

By casting the conversational net widely and carefully, the preacher will often discover insights that clarify materials that initially seem opaque. For instance, in its literary context, Exodus 33:19 ("I will be gracious to whom I will be gracious, and I will show mercy on whom I will show mercy") is not a statement of divine arbitrariness. To the contrary, it assures Israel that God's grace and mercy are altogether trustworthy.

However, the preacher must conclude that some witnesses (or parts thereof) are inappropriate to the gospel, for they deny that God loves all or wills justice for all. The most infamous case of inappropriateness is Psalm 137:8–9. The psalm begins with the Israelite community lamenting the destruction of Jerusalem by the Babylonians. It concludes, "O daughter Babylon, you devastator! Happy shall they be who pay you back what you have done to us! Happy shall be they who take your little ones and dash them against the rock!" This attitude is not confined to the First Testament. The Christian martyrs cry, "Sovereign Lord, holy and true, how long will it be before you judge and avenge our blood on the inhabitants of the earth?" (Revelation 6:10).

Christians sometimes interpret appropriate materials in inappropriate ways. The problem is not with the witness of the text, doctrine, or practice, but with the interpretation. Two common forms of perverting the gospel are works-righteousness and cheap grace. For instance, the doctrine of justification by grace through faith assumes that we are justified by grace. Faith is our response to the gift of grace. Some communities, however, effectively interpret faith as a work that we must perform in order to receive grace, turning the doctrine of justification by grace into a doctrine of justification by works! The doctrine of justification by grace through faith calls us to treat others as beloved by God. We cheapen grace when we accept God's love for ourselves but do not respond by loving others with the love that God shows for us. The preacher needs to help the community recover an interpretation that is appropriate to the gospel and to the intent of the doctrine itself.

In the sample sermons at the end of this book, René Rodgers Jensen finds that a popular image of God in contemporary North America is not appropriate to the gospel. By turning to scripture, tradition, and contemporary theology, she offers an image of God that is appropriate to the gospel (pages 281–285).

2. *Intelligibility.* The church must make a witness that is intelligible to Christian community in the contemporary setting. "The simplest defense of

the criterion of intelligibility is to point out that there is no alternative to it other than incoherence and meaninglessness."[3] Intelligibility has three dimensions.

(a) The message of the sermon must be *clear enough for people to understand it.* People need to be able to get the point. The preacher may need to provide basic information. For example, when Paul says that Christ was "put forward as a sacrifice of atonement by his blood" (Romans 3:25), we need to know how to understand the phrase "sacrifice of atonement by his blood." When preaching on the phrase from the Apostles' Creed that says Jesus descended to the dead, the preacher and congregation need to know how that phrase was understood in antiquity, as well as how it might be understood today.

Incidentally, given the relative biblical and theological illiteracy of many congregations today, I recommend a simple rule in both negative and positive forms. In the negative mode: do not assume that the congregation understands even basic Christian vocabulary, practice, and convictions, e.g., law, grace or faith, expiation or sanctification. In the positive form: take every opportunity to explain terms, events, and practices.

(b) The sermon must be *logically consistent* within itself, and it must be logically consistent with other things that the Christian believes, says, and does. "Preachers who do not have some systematic, coherent way" of dealing with the pluralism of the Bible and the wider Christian world can easily "proclaim messages that contradict and undercut one another. If preachers are blown this way and that by every wind of thought and feeling that comes along, indeed, by diverse texts from week to week, what will happen to their hearers?"[4] The congregation's view of the integrity and trustworthiness of God is at stake. Contradiction undercuts the congregation's trust in God.

The criterion of appropriateness to the gospel is a help in moving toward sermons that are coherent with one another. The church seeks to make a witness that is logically consistent with God's love and call for justice. The preacher can commend witnesses that are logically consistent with the gospel. When voices in the preaching conversation are inconsistent with the gospel, the preacher can help the congregation understand the discrepancy between the gospel and the witnesses, and can help the community envision what to do and say to be consistent with the gospel.

For instance, Psalm 136 declares twenty-six times in twenty-six verses that God's steadfast love endures forever. That refrain clearly means that God's steadfast love endures for Israel. The psalm calls the community to give thanks for many events in which God has shown steadfast love. These events include striking dead the firstborn of the Egyptians, drowning Pharaoh's army in the sea, killing great and famous kings and taking their land for Israel. While these divine actions liberated and protected Israel, they did not demonstrate steadfast love toward the victims. A thoughtful listener might well ask, "If God would strike dead the firstborn of the Egyptians because of their participation in oppression, what would prevent God from striking my firstborn dead because of my participation in oppression?" The text implicitly calls God's universal reliability into question.

Difference does not always imply contradiction. Take, for example, the multiple understandings of sin in the Christian tradition. For some biblical authors, sin is cultic defilement. For Paul, sin is an autonomous power. For some Christians sin is misbehavior. For Tillich, sin is alienation. These views are not all mutually exclusive, but the community needs to be clear about their differences and how they relate to one another.

This criterion applies to the life of the congregation beyond the sermon as well. The behavior of the congregation needs to be logically coherent with what is said from the pulpit. For instance, when the sermon describes the congregation as a community that practices mutual encouragement, the sermon is validated when persons actually encourage one another. The sermon is undercut when the community is not mutually encouraging.

(c) The sermon must be *believable*. We must be able to count on the sermon's claims in everyday life. It must make sense, given how we interpret the world and its operation. "It is important to observe that in being concerned with intelligibility, we are not importing into the [Christian] tradition something from outside it. A living tradition is always concerned with intelligibility, with 'making sense' of the situation and the inheritance of faith." Indeed, "that the scriptures themselves represent a process of reinterpretation through five major cultural epochs itself testifies to the fact that the biblical tradition persistently sought to 'make sense' of itself in new situations, as well as to make sense of new situations in the light of its legacy of faith." This aspect of the criterion of intelligibility "is a way of showing that the Christian faith is commendable."[5]

This subcriterion must be handled delicately. On the one hand, the preacher's claims about God's activity in the world should be believable within our interpretation of experience. When the church urges people to disclaim what they otherwise think is true or to believe what they otherwise think is untrue, Christian witness moves into the realm of the nonintelligible and nonbelievable. Preaching that which is unbelievable destroys the credibility of the Christian faith. For instance, in connection with Elijah and the widow of Zarephath (1 Kings 17:8–16), few people in North America today find that God miraculously fills our kitchen jars with meal and pantry jugs with oil. The preacher who suggests that God will do so sets up the congregation for disappointment. What will I think about God if I pray for God to fill my jar and jug, but go to the kitchen to find them empty? If the preacher claims that God can intervene in history in the way described in the text, but does not do so, another difficulty comes into view. How can God be moral if God has the capacity miraculously to feed hungry people and yet allows people on every continent to starve?

On the other hand, the claims of a doctrine or a practice may ask us to enlarge or reframe our understanding of the world and God's activity in it. The gospel sometimes asks us to recognize that our interpretation of the possibilities of experience is too limited. In the next section, I distinguish between surface elements that may be objectionable, and elements that are deeper and more abiding. Some interpreters take this approach in connection with the story of Elijah and the widow of Zarephath. At the surface level, God does not fill the jars and jugs in my kitchen. At the deeper level, the story testifies that with God in the world, situations are not closed circles. God does provide.

The application of this criterion is thus an exercise in continual contextual interpretation and reinterpretation. Communities in the West change their understandings of the world as they discover fresh data and perspectives. As noted in chapter 4, the modern interpretation of the world is flawed. Science continually revises its ways of explaining various phenomena. To cite a well-known example, Newtonian physics has given way to quantum physics. In the emerging postmodern era, the global population does not subscribe to a single, universal interpretation of the world and its operation. Whereas modern people thought they could objectively interpret the world, many citizens today think that all statements about the world are affected by a community's perceptions and contain elements of relativity. Consequently, the compatibility of Christian witness with contemporary perception of the world cannot function as an imperial criterion by which to measure the church's witness. At the same time, the church's witness needs to be credible in its own context so that people can count on it and act on it. A sermon ought to be able to confirm a claim at some level of the community's experience.

As a way of negotiating between the need for credibility in the Christian witness, and the plurality of interpretations of the world, a community can take its own interpretation of experience in the world as a starting point for evaluating the degree to which a claim is believable. The community can compare and contrast its understanding of experience with those of other communities. In the give-and-take of the conversation, the preacher and community may discover that their understanding is adequate. They can proceed with confidence. They may discover that they need to rethink some aspect of their understanding of the world. In the latter case, they need to sort out what they can commend with confidence.[6] This approach gives the church a place to stand while it thinks through other notions of the world and God's operation in it. It also leaves the church with some elbow room to refine its thinking in the light of fresh insights.

3. *Moral plausibility.* This criterion is closely related to the norm of appropriateness. The gospel contains a strong moral imperative with its promise of God's love given freely for all and its insistence on justice for each and all. The norm of moral plausibility does not introduce a new theme into the criteria but explicitly invites the participants in the conversation to consider the implications for the moral treatment of all involved in the world of the sermon. Clark M. Williamson, who has an eye for the practical outcome of theological reflection, pungently shows the usefulness of this criterion.

Frequently there is in the text itself an attitude toward, e.g., women, or Jews, or slavery which simply must be rejected by any Christian who even remotely tries to live a Christian life. After hundreds of years of experience with slavery in this country and *apartheid* in South African, after thousands of years of anti-Judaism, or pogroms and Holocaust, after millennia of the oppression of women, one must simply say "no" to all attitudes from the past that would justify and reinforce such prejudices today.[7]

While Williamson writes specifically of biblical texts, his point can be extended to Christian doctrines, writings, practices, and behaviors. More than saying no, the preacher needs to help the congregation envision how the gospel can create a world in which all persons and elements of nature experience love and justice.

In one of the sample sermons at the end of this book, Reginald Holmes notices that many people and institutions in the United States have an understanding of justice that is inadequate, and that, when combined with racism, leads to a situation of moral implausibility (pages 288–295). Pastor Holmes turns to the Bible, Christian history, and contemporary theology and ethics to point toward a community that is just for people of all races and ethnicities.

The contemporary theological families mentioned in the previous chapter (revisionary, postliberal, liberation, evangelical) lay different stresses on these criteria. Revisionary thinkers weigh all three about equally. Postliberals place less stress on intelligibility, though they, too, emphasize the importance of being able to understand Christian witness and of the various elements of Christian witness cohering logically. Liberation preachers are especially interested in moral plausibility. Evangelicals, like the revisionary theologians, place great stress on all three criteria, though their understanding of these criteria is modified to fit their theological worldview.

Surface and Depth Dimensions in Christian Witnesses

The preacher can understand the claims of most witnesses in the preaching conversation straightforwardly. When interpreted in their historical and literary contexts, their possibilities for the current community are clear. The preacher can determine their appropriateness to the gospel, intelligibility, and moral plausibility. Most of the time, preachers and their conversation partners need to draw out the positive implications of biblical texts, Christian doctrines, practices, movements, and authors. Sometimes, however, preachers need to help the community reformulate, or say no to witnesses that are inappropriate, unintelligible, or morally implausible.

In other cases, the distinction between the surface and deeper meanings of a text will help a preaching conversation find positive meaning in a voice that appears to be troubling theologically, intellectually, or morally. The surface meaning is the witness of the text in its language, imagery, culture, presuppositions, and worldview. The deeper meanings are those aspects of the text that transcend the particular cultural accoutrements of the text and whose significance abides.

This typology notices that aspects of language, imagery, cultural forms, presuppositions, and worldview differ between our setting and other settings. It also notices underlying currents of experience are often similar between our world and other worlds. Similar concerns go by different names. Conversation helps the preacher and the community perceive points of deeper contact so that the community can have a suitable relationship with witnesses from other times and places. The conversation needs to help the contemporary community learn the language by which Christian tradition names these experiences so that today's community can participate fully in the conversation.

This distinction is particularly helpful when dealing with problems of unintelligibility that result from differing slants in worldview. For instance, in Psalm 75, God says, "When the earth totters, with all its inhabitants, it is I who keep its pillars steady" (v. 3). On the surface, the psalm assumes that the earth is a flat plate held above a primeval, chaotic sea by mighty pillars. This view is not good science. However, at a deeper level, the pillars are an image of God's trustworthiness. The psalm assures those who feel their worlds collapsing that God will sustain them.

In 1 Corinthians 8, Paul deals with a conflict in the Corinthian community resulting from food that has been offered to idols. In Corinth, as elsewhere in the Mediterranean world of antiquity, many people would sacrifice a pinch of food to an idol in order to bring the idol's blessing on all who ate the food. One group in the Corinthian community said that they could eat the food that had been offered to idols because the idols have no real power. Another group in the community objected to this practice because they wanted no traffic with idolatry, perhaps believing that idols were inhabited by demons. Paul acknowledges that the first group is free to eat the food that has been offered to idols. However, he cautions them not to do so because their exercise of freedom destroys the community. Such freedom destroys those in the second group (whom Paul characterizes as those "for whom Christ died") and sins against Christ.

At the surface level, 1 Corinthians 8 seems far removed from us. I know of no Christian congregations in North America today that are disturbed by the problem of food offered to idols. However, at the deeper level, the text helps the church. The text articulates two interrelated principles: (a) all behavior of Christians should build up the community; (b) each Christian should regard others as those for whom Christ died. These principles can be conversation partners in any conflict in the church in which some insist on their "rights" at the expense of the upbuilding of the community. How can we engage in behavior that builds up the community? How can we behave in such a way as to honor the fact that Christ died for all? However, the positive, deeper dimensions of the text do not solve all hermeneutical and preaching problems. Unwillingness to violate the conscience of others in the community can be paralyzing. Do times come when the church must speak or act, even at the risk of ripping the fabric of Christian community?

The distinction between surface and deeper witnesses can be instructive in the case of texts that are theologically and morally troubling, as well. For instance, Amos indicts Israel for breach of covenant, especially for idolatry and exploiting the poor. Amos announces that God will invoke punishing judgment on the community. The nation will be invaded and captured. Many Israelites will be killed. The temple will be destroyed. The people will be exiled. The land itself will cease to be fertile. On the surface level, God is the author of these actions. The Christian tradition is clear that persons and communities need to acknowledge their sin and repent, but, the near-destruction of the community and the pain inflicted on many of its members goes against the grain of the notions that God is loving and that God wills justice. To be blunt, I do not believe that God actively inflicts such pain on persons or communities. However, on a deeper level, the text is instructive. When we violate God's prescriptions for justice, community collapses. God does not directly punish a people, but we suffer the consequences of our destructive behavior. Further, to the prophets judgment is not an end in itself. Judgment is intended to awaken the community to the need for repentance.

At the surface level, several strands in Jewish apocalypticism, 300 B.C.E. to 200 C.E., assumed that this present, sinful age of world history would end in a cosmic apocalyptic cataclysm. After the cataclysm, God would create a new world, often called the rule (NRSV: kingdom) of God. Immediately preceding the apocalyptic cataclysm, a time of massive suffering (through dislocation and violence in nature and society) would occur as the demons and powers of the old age dug in their heels to fight God's repossession of the world. Jesus' teaching in the final discourse on the Mount of Olives (Matthew 24:1–27 and parallels) assumes this plan. However, many Christians today do not think that the world is heading toward an apocalyptic cataclysm, much less one preceded by such a tribulation. At a deeper level, however, the notion of tribulation reminds the reader that many in the world resist the gospel. Unconditional love and justice in the world would dislodge some powers who profit from exploitation. Hence, they resist the church's witness to God's love and justice. The notion of the tribulation is a pastoral reminder to the church to be prepared for conflict and even suffering when the church's witness to God's love and justice calls for radical personal and social change.

The pastor and others in the preaching conversation need to be careful not to bypass critique of aspects of texts by turning too quickly to the distinction between surface and deeper dimensions. Some witnesses (or parts of witnesses) need to be publicly critiqued or they will continue to do damage. For instance, in Mark some of the Pharisees take issue with the disciples of Jesus eating grain on the Sabbath (2:23–28). Mark presents the Pharisees very negatively — as legalistic, rigid, and "images of everything bad in religion."[8] Preachers have frequently turned this depiction of the Pharisees against the church by encouraging the congregation to see how we,

Christians, are legalistic, rigid, and destructive of true religion. However, the repeated presentation of the Pharisees (and many other Jewish leaders) in this way reinforces the church's tendency to anti-Judaism. This portrayal of the Pharisees results from antagonism between the synagogue and the church in the years following the fall of Jerusalem and is intended to discredit the Pharisees. It does not accurately represent Pharisees in the first century. It is a polemical caricature. The preacher is advised to critique the presentation of Judaism in the text. Without defaming Jewish people, the sermon can help the congregation recognize (and repent of) its own legalistic, rigid, and destructive tendencies.

Interpretative Relationships with Christian Witnesses

The preaching conversation usually results in a pastor and community coming to one of four possible interpretative relationships with biblical passages, Christian doctrines, practices, authors, or movements. This relationship determines whether the preacher (1) runs with the text, doctrine, practice, or situation, with a minimum of explanation; (2) must engage in considerable exploration of surface and depth dimensions; (3) must take issue with some aspect of the witness; or (4) ignores the text. While I discuss these relationships as alternatives, in actual practice they often drift into one another.

1. *Running with the text, doctrine, practice, or situation, with a minimum of explanation.* In this case, the witness is appropriate to the gospel, intelligible, and morally plausible. The witness — whether a biblical text, doctrine, practice, author, event, movement, or situation — voices the gospel. The pastor can preach the gospel by preaching the text. The preacher nearly always needs to explain elements of the voice, e.g., theological, historical, literary, sociological, psychological. However, the possibility(ies) that the witness offers to the contemporary community is clear. The sermon needs to help the community identify these possibilities and figure out how to respond to them in ways that are consistent with the gospel.

Proverbs 8, like many passages in the wisdom literature, illustrates this possibility. The text is about how human beings know wisdom, about what wisdom offers, and how wisdom is manifest. In the passage, wisdom is personified as a woman. While wisdom is distinct from God, she represents the divine presence and purposes in the world. The text begins by describing wisdom "on the heights, beside the way, at the crossroads . . . beside the gates" (vv. 1–4). These are scenes from everyday life in antiquity. Wisdom is omnipresent. In harmony with much other wisdom literature, this passage teaches that we learn wisdom by paying attention to the creation and experience. For God has ordered the world to reveal the divine aim for life. Wisdom reveals what is right, i.e., in accord with God's designs (vv. 5–9). The poem lists several qualities of life that emanate from wisdom: living with prudence, discretion, disassociating oneself from evil, avoiding pride and arrogance and perverse speech. (vv. 12–4). Political leaders enact wisdom by governing justly (vv. 15–16). The NRSV concludes the poem by noting wisdom rewards those who follow her with "prosperity" (vv. 17–21). The term translated "prosperity" is usually rendered "righteousness" and indicates being in right relationship with God and others.

A sermon on Proverbs 8 might help the community recognize how we encounter wisdom. The preacher could identify qualities of life that emanate from wisdom and the benefits that accrue to the community from the practice of wisdom in personal and corporate affairs. The sermon itself might become an occasion in which the congregation hears wisdom speaking. The preacher would need to explain key terms and assumptions, such as wisdom, prudence, discretion, perverted speech, and righteousness. But the preacher would not need to struggle with the presiding theological vision of the text.

A sermon on the Christian practice of confessing sin to one another is another example of a phenomenon that is appropriate to the gospel, intelligible, and morally plausible. The sermon can move straightforwardly. The preacher would need to explain the Christian communities' understandings of sin and the corrosive effects of sin in personal and corporate life. The sermon should help the community understand why it is important to confess sin. The community might need to know what to expect from God and from others in the community as a result of confession. Because many churches have recently only offered opportunities for private confession of sin, the preacher probably needs to help the community recognize the importance of confessing sin to one another. Some Christians need guidance in how to confess sin, both to God and to one another.

The sample sermons by Mary Donovan Turner and Ronald J. Allen at the end of this book (pages 276–278, 262–267) illustrate this option. In each case, the message of the text is straightforward and appropriate to the gospel, intelligible, and morally plausible. The preacher's primary responsibility is to help the congregation discover points of contact between the world of the text and the world of the congregation.

2. *Arriving at a positive interpretation of the passage by moving from the surface to deeper dimensions.* This case usually results from Christian witnesses that appear on the surface to be unintelligible. Probing deeper, however, reveals that the biblical passage, doctrine, practice, writer, community or movement is intelligible. Using this approach can also help the church hear a message in some voices in the church whose surface witness seems to be inappropriate to the gospel or morally implausible. When I was a parish pastor, and preaching weekly, this interpretive relationship was most frequent. The sermon needs to help the congregation think through the interpretation and retrieval of the passage. This part of the sermon not only helps the community think about the passage, it also helps the community develop an interpretive method that it can apply to other passages.

To take an example, the world of the Gospel of Mark assumes that demons are personal beings who inhabit the universe, who represent Satan, and who operate by moving into the body of a human being (or other entity).

They take over that person. The possessed child at the foot of the mountain on which Jesus was transfigured (Mark 9:14–29) is possessed. Few people today accept this surface notion of demons. However, at a deeper level, we know people who experience "possession" by forces outside of themselves. The partners in the conversation might think of persons addicted to alcohol, drugs, and other substances. They might also think of persons who are psychologically dysfunctional and who engage in behavior that is destructive of themselves and others. Communities can be possessed. What community in its right mind would consider a group of people inferior because of skin color? The sermon must go beyond identifying ways in which we have experiences that parallel those represented in the demons. The text affirms that Jesus released the child from the power of the demons. The sermon, therefore, needs to help the congregation discover how Jesus' liberating power releases today's community from the grip of the contemporary demons.

The Nicene Affirmation of Faith says that "for us and for our salvation," Jesus "came down from heaven, was incarnate of the Holy Spirit and the Virgin Mary and became truly human." Many Christians accept at face value, the notion that Jesus was born of the Virgin Mary. Some Christians insist that such acceptance is essential for Christian identity. For other Christians, the possibility of virginal conception seems unlikely. At the surface level, they could easily dismiss that part of the Nicene formulation. However, when we consider this idea at a deeper level, we notice that the notion of virginal conception is from language in the early centuries C.E. that denotes special relationship and purpose. The early church uses this language to account for the special quality of relationship with God that it experienced through Jesus. It explains how the incarnation took place. The remarkable character of Jesus' conception assures believers that Jesus is trustworthy in representing God. At the same time, the virginal conception confirms Jesus' full humanity. Through Jesus, God is fully empathetic with the world. God is fully active as an agent for salvation within the world. In some ancient contexts, the virgin birth was a part of the church's refutation of the heresy that Jesus only appeared to be a human being. The sermon could help the Christian community by focusing on ways in which this part of the Nicene affirmation functions.

3. Taking issue with a witness. A preacher must sometimes take issue with voice (or some part of a voice) in the Christian community. To rephrase theologian Clark Williamson's stronger language from above, the church must sometimes say no to aspects of a text, doctrine, practice, or a situation. This case usually results when elements of the witness are inappropriate to the gospel, or are morally implausible.

For instance, 1 Peter 2:18–25 admonishes slaves not only to be obedient in every way to their masters, but to suffer in the example of Christ. Now, we should not read the experience of African American slaves in the southern part of the United States into the world of slavery in the first century. Slavery in the Mediterranean world was typically less harsh. Some people sold themselves into voluntary slavery because that offered them a way to pull themselves up the social and economic ladder. Nonetheless, the institution of slavery contradicts both the gospel's promise of love and its call for justice. The pastor preaches the gospel, in part, by preaching against a strand of Christian tradition.

John 9 tells the story of someone born blind. Jesus' disciples want to know if the blindness is the result of the person's own sin or the sin of the parents. Jesus replies that neither the person nor the parents sinned. This person "was born blind so that God's works might be revealed" (v. 3). God made the person blind so that, when Jesus came into the world, the works of God might be revealed. While I can understand the use of this motif as a literary device, it is unthinkable that the God of unconditional love who wishes justice for all would cause a person to be blind for most of a lifetime in order to teach a lesson. The preacher who does not challenge this text opens the door for the congregation to understand any number of tragic circumstances as the direct agency of God.

In the case studies in chapters 18 and 19, both preachers take issue with popular ideas in the church and the culture. Reginald Holmes exposes an inadequate understanding of justice held by many people. René Rodgers Jensen describes a popular image of God with which the gospel takes exception.

Many congregations are unaccustomed to hearing the preacher or other leaders of the church say that aspects of the Christian tradition are misguided. Some in the congregation will greet such a sermon with relief. As a person said to me after such a sermon, "I've always wanted to think that way, but I didn't know it was possible." However, some church members will be nervous about such a message. The sermon will usually be well served by disagreeing with a biblical text or other aspect of Christian witness in a gentle and probing way. The preacher should avoid a superior, even inflammatory, attitude. The preacher should carefully explain what is at stake and why the sermon has taken the tack that it has. Many people in the congregation are receptive to critical evaluation of elements of Christian tradition when the preacher points out that lively discussion and disagreement are part of the biblical tradition itself. For instance, the attitude that obedience brings blessing and disobedience results in curse (e.g., Deuteronomy 11:26–28; 30:15–20) is dramatically questioned by Job and Ecclesiastes. The gospel itself — with its emphasis on love — should prevent the preacher from running roughshod. To do so is to make an inappropriate witness.

4. *Ignoring a witness.* Preachers and congregations can ignore a biblical passage, a doctrine, a practice, an author, or a situation. Sometimes we benignly ignore witnesses; we don't even know about them. We ignore some voices because they seem thin and frivolous. We turn away from some materials because we are finite and cannot engage all possible conversation partners. We choose to speak about some issues but not others, based on our sense of their importance or our willingness to be vulnerable to them. Sometimes we ignore witnesses because we disagree with them. We avoid conflict

by not talking. At other times, we ignore witnesses because we know that they are hard to understand, or that they make claims over which we agonize.

Even communities who discipline their worship with the use of a lectionary find that the lectionary leads them to ignore many parts of the Bible. The lectionaries have a tendency to omit passages that, at least on the surface, are theologically or morally problematic. Here are some passages that contain difficult elements that are omitted from the Revised Common Lectionary: God tries to kill Moses (Exodus 4:21–26); Jephthah sacrifices his daughter (Judges 11:1–40); the Johannine Jesus calls some Jewish people children of the devil (John 8:39–47); Paul turns Hymenaeus and Alexander over to Satan (1 Timothy 1:18–20). Even within passages that are included in the lectionary, a single passage is often sliced and diced so as to remove difficult materials.[9]

I close with a strong appeal for the preaching conversation not to ignore Christian witnesses, particularly difficult ones. While such a witness may not articulate the gospel itself, the church's encounter with a perplexing text, doctrine, or practice may provide a powerful occasion for the church to reflect on its understanding of the gospel and on why it cannot endorse the witness of a particular text. A bothersome text may provide the preacher and the congregation with a remarkable learning moment.

SECTION FOUR

Establishing and Developing a Direction for the Sermon

In order to set the stage on which to discuss establishing and developing the direction of the sermon in sections 4 and 5, we now review a traditional way of classifying sermons. Sermon classification is not for its own sake, but because classification categories help preachers understand different starting points for preparing the sermon, different processes of preparation, and different patterns of developing the sermon. Each mode has its own strengths and weaknesses. Each serves some sermons and occasions better than others do. The preacher who has a critical grasp of such matters is in a strong position to help the preaching conversation described in the previous chapters result in a sermon that is not only appropriate to the gospel, intelligible, and morally plausible, but is also contextually specific. It can help the word become particular flesh.

Sermons are traditionally classified along two axes: content and movement. I shall say more about these categories in succeeding chapters. For now it is enough to note that sermons are typically centered either in the exposition of a biblical text or in the theological analysis of a topic. Sermons are typically organized either deductively or inductively. Using these categories, we distinguish four kinds of sermons:

- Expository-deductive sermon
- Expository-inductive sermon
- Topical-deductive sermon
- Topical-inductive sermon

These kinds of sermons and their variations are discussed in the next chapters and illustrated in section 7. All four kinds of sermons share the common purpose of helping the congregation interpret aspects of life from the

97

perspective of the gospel. However, the nuances of purpose and the patterns of preparation for each of these four kinds of sermons have distinct accents.

How does the preacher decide which kind of sermon to develop for a specific Sunday? The experienced preacher is often so aware of the Bible, doctrine, Christian practices, and the situation of the community that the preacher can imagine several different sermon possibilities. However, the preaching conversation will help the preacher recognize why some options are preferable to others at a given moment in a congregation's life. Preachers select a particular type of sermon for a particular occasion because they anticipate that the qualities of that sermon's content and movement have a good opportunity to help the congregation encounter the gospel.

In order to start the process of sermon preparation, the preacher must choose whether to begin the sermon from exegesis of a biblical text or from analysis of a topic. During the process of sermon preparation, the preacher must also choose whether to develop the sermon deductively or inductively. When the preacher has settled on a focus, the pastor develops the sermon by engaging in conversation of the type described in the previous chapter. Chapter 8 considers selecting a starting point for sermon preparation. Chapter 9 offers a process by which a preacher might develop a direction for the sermon.

If I were speaking with you in a live classroom, I would now glance out the door to see if anyone in the hallway is listening. I would speak in a hushed voice. "You know, what I have just told you is true, but it isn't the whole story." The fact is that few sermons are pure examples of a single type. The sample sermons in section 7 illustrate these four types of sermons. However, most sermons combine elements of these different qualities. For example, a sermon that is largely topical-inductive might contain exegetical content and a paragraph of deductive logic. You should not think less of yourself if you put together a sermon that intermingles categories. However, for purposes of discussion and illustration we consider these types as distinct.

CHAPTER EIGHT

Starting Points for Sermon Preparation

I overheard the following conversation one Friday in the seminary lunchroom. Pat and Chris are student pastors who preach every week in small congregations.

PAT: So, what are you preaching this Sunday?

CHRIS: Well…uh…ah…oh…hmm…

PAT: I don't know either. I'll look at the lectionary. Some of the folks want me to do a sermon on the family. I could turn some of the lectures in my psalms course into a sermon series.

CHRIS: How will you decide? I mean, this is Friday, and you've got to preach on Sunday. Maybe you have the power to stop Sunday from coming, but I don't. For me, the hardest part of preparing the sermon is deciding what to preach about.

PAT: Yeah. Sometimes I sit for hours in front of the blank computer screen, my mind as empty as the screen.

Experienced preachers typically find it easier to settle on a starting point for a sermon. However, even experienced pastors need to evaluate their options for developing a sermon for a particular Sunday so that the sermon and the occasion are mutually appropriate.

This chapter discusses the two starting points for sermon preparation: the Bible or a topic. I consider the possibilities and limitations of each approach. The chapter meditates on how the preacher decides on a beginning point for a particular Sunday.

The Importance of Preaching from the Bible

Expository preaching needs to be the backbone of regular parish preaching. Expository sermons center in the exposition of the meaning(s) of a biblical text. The pastor leads the congregation in a conversation in which the community explores the meaning(s) of a biblical passage and the implications of the congregation's encounter with the text. Chapter 16 furnishes an example of an expository deductive sermon on the parable of the lost sheep (pages 262–267). Chapter 17 provides an example of an expository-inductive sermon based on Jesus' last words to the disciples (the Great Commission) in the Gospel of Matthew (pages 276–278).

There are many entwined reasons for expository preaching. *Conversation with the Bible alerts us to the presence and purposes of God in the world.* It is not obvious that a Benevolent Other is in the universe, especially when we daily experience the stunning miracles of technology, the unending and bitter cries of human suffering, and unapologetic human pride. Even in the church we can easily forget God as we get caught up in institutional preoccupation. The Bible reminds us that the cosmos is not left to its own devices. It is permeated by a Transcendent Power not our own. The Bible helps us name God.

Each text offers an interpretation of how God is present in the world of the Bible. Exposition seeks to help the congregation recognize how the text understands God to be present and our response. Through the preaching conversation, preacher and community determine the degree to which a biblical passage is instructive for us. For instance, is our church similar to the community of Israel when Solomon was in the height of his glory and Israel was institutionally robust and culturally powerful? Are we in a situation of exile and in need of reassurance? Or, are we more like the people who returned from Babylonia to Palestine to rebuild our worlds? Or, is our situation different yet?

The Bible puts us in touch with the formative expressions and experiences of Christian faith. The *Bible* teaches us the essential language of the Christian faith. This language helps name God and form our worldview. Expository sermons help the church develop positive content and experiential association with primal Christian notions, e.g., God, Christ, the Holy Spirit, grace, sin, law, righteousness, death, heaven, hell. Particular biblical texts generate (or contribute to) many of the church's stories, ideas, and images. Exposition helps the congregation sharpen and deepen its awareness of the specific contributions and dimensions of texts (and their histories of interpretation) to the church's perception of Christian life and the world.

The Bible often helps us interpret our situation from the perspective of the gospel. We cannot always name the depth of sin, or the height of divine grace, or the breadth of God's call to us. The Bible helps us name these things in our settings. Lectionary preachers, for instance, often report that a text assigned by a lectionary helps them perceive qualities that they had not seen in themselves, in the congregation, or in the larger world.

Biblical exposition helps form the identity, life, and witness of the church. The Bible helps the Christian community respond to two of the most important questions of life. Who are we? What are we to do? We live in a world created by a gracious God. We share in responsibility for that world. We are Gentiles, who know the God of Israel through Jesus Christ. We are with Abram and

Sarai journeying to an unknown destination. We are with Jacob wrestling with God by the River Jabbok. We hear Jesus speak to us, "I tell you, do not worry about your life, what you will eat, or about your body, what you will wear." Will we carry the gospel to the Macedonias of our world? The church continues the story prompted by the Bible. The Bible helps the church keep its ongoing story continuous with the main themes of Christian faith.

The expository preacher helps the church remember that which is essential in biblical texts and themes, even while helping the congregation adapt their understanding of biblical material to new situations. James A. Sanders, a biblical scholar who gives considerable attention to preaching, points out that the Bible is both stable and adaptable in helping the church understand its identity and mission. The Bible is stable in that it preserves texts that are fundamental to the church. The Bible is adaptable in that its promises and calls can be heard afresh in each situation.[1] For instance, when the church forgets that we are loved unconditionally, the Bible encourages us. When we forget that God's love and justice are for all, the Bible challenges us to enlarge our vision.

Expository preaching can help the church reclaim biblical language that has lost some of its power. Biblical expressions are vivid and powerful in their ancient settings. However, even the most vivid language can lose its power through overuse, misuse, nonuse, or change of circumstance. For instance, the expression "bearing your cross" is commonplace in Christian speech. The expository sermon helps the congregation realize that, in its setting in the story of Jesus, this phrase refers to voluntary sacrifice that one undertakes to witness to God's rule. The preacher helps the congregation understand that involuntary suffering (e.g., as a result of illness) is not bearing one's cross. A sensitive pastor will help the community understand how God relates to each kind of suffering.

Encounters with the Bible often play a key role in the renewal of the church. When the church becomes sluggish, the church often revives under the impetus of expository preaching. Augustine, for instance, was converted by reading the book of Romans. At a time when the church was wandering in the fields of works righteousness, Luther's exegesis of the same book led him to rediscover justification by grace. Luther's expository preaching transformed parts of the church. In a time of stiff formality in the church, John Wesley felt his heart "strangely warmed" while reading the Bible (again, Romans). The small cell groups spawned by Wesley's movement centered in Bible study. The open air preaching of the Wesleyans regenerated many Christian communities. Two generations ago, Karl Barth's study of Romans initiated massive theological renewal. The centrality of preaching for Barth is revealed in the first part of his thirteen volume *Church Dogmatics* when he says that massive project is intended to serve proclamation.[2] Base Christian communities in Latin America today are empowered for liberation through searching the Bible.

Preaching from the Bible gives the congregation a point of reference for gauging the development of Christian doctrine. Doctrine is the comprehensive and coherent statement of what Christians believe about God, Christ, the Holy

Spirit, the church, the Christian life, and the world. Most doctrines are inspired by biblical themes. In formalizing doctrine, church councils, theologians, and other Christian bodies often take the Bible and elaborate it, make explicit material that the church considers implicit in the Bible. The expository sermon helps the church identify benchmarks by which to identify how doctrine amplifies, reshapes, or diminishes biblical impulses. The community can then ponder the degree to which doctrinal developments enhance or frustrate gospel witness.

Expository preaching helps the long-established churches rectify their biblical and theological illiteracy. The exposition of the text helps the congregation become familiar with the content of the text. The process of exposition models responsible approaches to the interpretation of biblical passages both exegetically and theologically.

Expository preaching reminds the preacher to make the sermon particular. Many biblical texts express a particular word to a particular community. We can reconstruct the histories of some ancient communities with a fair amount of confidence. For instance, scholars widely agree on the broad lines of the situation in Corinth. However, scholars point out that we do not have access to the histories of many ancient communities. For example, we do not really know the circumstances that prompted the book of Romans. Even when we can posit a credible historical reconstruction, the meaning(s) of the text in its ancient context may not exhaust the possibilities of meaning for today. Scholars say that a text has a "surplus of meaning," that is, a text has more realities for meaning than can be isolated in a given moment. Nonetheless, the particularity of the text reminds the preacher to be as specific in struggling to understand God's purposes in our setting as the biblical writers were in their settings. How can the preacher bring the gospel to bear on a situation today that is as specific as Paul's discussion of sexual difficulties in Corinth?

The expository sermon symbolizes the congregation's commonality with other Christians, and with Jewish and Muslim communities. Expository preaching can have an inherent ecumenical character. The Bible is one of the most important things shared by all Christians. Christians further share the First Testament as sacred scripture with Judaism and with Muslims. The expository sermon reminds the congregation of the fact that the community is conjoined with other communities in a great cloud of witnesses. In a time of increasing tribalism, genocide, and ecological crisis, this quality is potent. Of course, communities disagree on how to interpret aspects of the Bible. However, when this disagreement is marked by respect and mutuality in the search for understanding, the way in which the communities seek to resolve their differences is itself a reconciling witness.

Preaching with texts from different parts of the Bible helps the congregation deal with the diversity of the Bible. Expository preaching should help the community identify the Bible's spectrum of options for interpreting God's character and activity in the world. For example, the God of the Gospel of Mark is an apocalyptic warrior who, through Jesus Christ, invades the world to do battle with the devil in the last days before the apocalypse. The God of Proverbs is a cosmic sage who has charged the world with wisdom that we encounter through experience. These points of view are not mutually exclusive, but they are different. Which, if either, is authoritative for us? And how?

As noted repeatedly, the Bible is not the only source of our knowledge of God. The church must often supplement the witness of particular passages in the Bible with later historical and theological reflections, as well as with insight that comes from the natural world, the social sciences, the arts, and everyday human experience. But, season in and season out, the church discovers that the Bible is an indispensable partner for helping the church remember and recognize the divine presence in the world. By declaring the Bible "canon," the church says, "We cannot live without this book."

In the strict sense, the pastor does not "preach the text" in the expository sermon. The pastor preaches the gospel, using the exposition of the text as a lens through which to focus the congregation's encounter with the gospel for a particular sermon. The test of the expository sermon is not the question, "Did the pastor preach the text?" After all, as noted in the previous chapter, some texts are not altogether reliable witnesses. A better test is, "Did the pastor preach the gospel through the community's encounter with the text?"

Edmund A. Steimle was famous for saying to his students at Union Theological Seminary, New York, "The sermon that starts in the Bible and stays in the Bible is not biblical." To be biblical, in the broad sense, is to do in our time what the people of the Bible did in their times: to come to as clear an understanding as we can of the divine initiatives for the world, and to respond accordingly.

There is no single form for an expository sermon. Among the most familiar expository forms (several are discussed in chapter 11) are the Puritan Plain Style sermon and the verse-by-verse sermon.[3] A recent movement calls attention to ways in which the literary and rhetorical qualities of a biblical text can help shape the form and function of the sermon.[4] Expository sermons can take many other forms, as well.

Most expository sermons will contain exegesis of the biblical text directly in the sermon. The preacher does not try to say everything exegetically that could be said about the text; the sermon is not long enough for that. The preacher usually brings into the sermon elements of exegesis that are pertinent to the development of that particular sermon. However, some expository sermons contain a minimum of actual exegetical discussion. Through story or image, the sermon will offer an exposition of the significance of the text.

Lectionaries, Themes, or Free Selection

Most expository sermons focus on a particular biblical passage. The preacher identifies a biblical text as a starting point for sermon preparation in one of three ways: a selected lectionary, a continuous lectionary, or preacher's free choice. Each starting point has advantages and disadvantages.

Preaching from a Selected Lectionary

The name *selected lectionary* (*lectio selecta*) derives from the Latin words *lectio*, "reading," and *selecta*, "selected." The scripture readings are selected from different parts of the Bible in order to serve the larger purposes of the lectionary. Most selected lectionaries are designed to coordinate with the theological emphases of the Christian year. The Christian year is made up of seasons that dramatize several important doctrines of Christian faith. Each season has distinct theological motifs.

- *Advent* is from a Latin word that means "coming." The early Sundays of Advent help the congregation anticipate the final (eschatological) coming of God into the world to end injustice and bring salvation. Later Sundays encourage the congregation to remember God's coming in Christ. Advent helps the church prepare for God's comings.

- *Christmas* honors the incarnation and gives the preacher the opportunity to interpret the significance of Christ for the church.

- *Epiphany*, from a Greek term for "manifestation," recollects the visit of the magi to Jesus with a focus on the manifestation of God's grace to Gentiles through Christ.

- *Ordinary Time* is found in two sequences in the Christian year: in the days after Epiphany to Ash Wednesday, and after Pentecost. After Epiphany, Ordinary Time focuses on the baptism of Jesus and the manifestation of the gospel to Gentiles.

- *Lent* derives from an Anglo-Saxon term for the "lengthening" of the days as winter yields to spring. Lent begins with Ash Wednesday and is a time of preparation for Easter, often by reflecting on the community's complicity with sin, the need to repent, and the resources that God provides through Christ for a way forward. Lent climaxes with Palm Sunday, and Holy Week. Many churches have special services on Maundy Thursday to commemorate the Last Supper and on Good Friday to interpret the crucifixion. On Holy Saturday, many congregations have an Easter Vigil, tracing the broad lines of holy history from creation through the final consummation.

- *Easter* celebrates the resurrection of Jesus as prefiguration of the rule of God in its fullness, when everything in life conforms to God's purposes. For seven Sundays after Easter, the church meditates on the significance of the resurrection and the rule of God.

- *Pentecost* is not a season, but a day that honors the outpouring of the Holy Spirit on the church. The church is renewed by recalling the presence and activity of the Spirit.

- *Ordinary time* resumes after Pentecost and continues until the last Sunday of the Christian year, Christ the Cosmic Ruler. We consider the Trinity, and growth in discipleship. Eschatology is the theme of both the final Sundays of Ordinary Time and the beginning of Advent, thus linking the starting and ending points of the Christian interpretation of life and reminding us that redemption is not complete.

A congregation and preacher need not subscribe to a selected lectionary, in order to follow the Christian year. A congregation can structure its life according to the seasons of the year and follow continuous readings of the Bible or free selection of Bible passages.

Most congregations that order themselves after the Christian year also follow a *lectio selecta*. The Revised Common Lectionary (RCL) is the most widely used table of readings today.[5] The RCL assigns four Bible readings to every Sunday of the year. The biblical passages in the lectionary were chosen by an ecumenical committee. In Advent-Christmas-Epiphany and in Lent-Easter-Pentecost, the lectionary assigns one passage each from a gospel, an epistle, a psalm, and the First Testament (except on the Sundays after Easter when the First Testament is replaced by readings from Acts). During Ordinary Time, the lectionary provides two sets of readings for the psalm and First Testament; one set coordinates with the gospel lesson; the other set excerpts from key materials in the First Testament. Any text (or combination thereof) can be the basis for the sermon. The psalm is intended for liturgical use, but the minister can preach from it. The readings follow three cycles of one year each. Year A centers in Matthew, year B in Mark, year C in Luke. Readings from the fourth gospel appear sporadically each year.

In the RCL, when the reading from the First Testament (other than the psalm) coordinates with the gospel reading, the readings from the two testaments relate in one of three ways: (1) parallel situations between the situations in the two texts; (2) contrast between the situations in the two texts; (3) typology, in which the passage from the First Testament is a type of an aspect of the story of Jesus.

The preacher must decide which of these lessons will be the focus of the sermon. The pastor makes this decision on the basis of which reading(s) seems to offer the greatest possibility for helping the gospel come alive in a way that correlates with the community's deepest needs. A pastor may preach on only one reading or may bring two or more of the readings into the sermon. However, preachers normally have their hands full with the exegetical and theological details that come with interpreting one lesson in a given sermon. When the preacher tries to focus on two or three lessons, the homily often becomes complicated and hard to follow. Worse, when bringing multiple readings into a single sermon, the preacher often posits relationships among the readings that are tenuous, even forced. When the lessons relate easily to one another, the sermon can clearly draw connections among the readings. This last possibility is especially promising when the reading from the First Testament and the gospel directly relate.

When preaching from a lectionary in the Christian year, the minister does more than interpret the text. The preacher uses the text in order to help interpret the major theological emphases of the season of the year. On the second Sunday of Advent, for instance, the gospel lection is the story of John the Baptist prior to the baptism of Jesus. The preacher wants to help the congregation consider how the reading helps the congregation prepare for the coming of God.

Potential Advantages of Preaching from a Selected Lectionary

1. Lectionaries intend to represent the fullness of the gospel with its dual motifs of the promise of God's unconditional love and the call of God for justice.

2. A lectionary, in the context of the Christian year, helps the congregation systematically encounter theological themes and biblical texts that are foundational to Christian faith, especially as these themes and texts tell the story of Jesus Christ.

3. A lectionary helps the congregation remember Christian identity and vocation. We live in the midst of many calendars — the calendar year, the fiscal year, the academic year, the agricultural cycle, the civic days. The Christian year and the lectionary do not quite coordinate with these other calendars, thus reminding the congregation that the gospel is omnipresent. Yet, it does not serve other interests, but transcends them.

4. A lectionary broadens the range of theological themes and biblical passages that most pastors and congregations would consider. When freely selecting preaching foci, many pastors turn repeatedly to the same doctrines, themes, or passages. Limited patterns of selection leave the congregation theologically deprived. A lectionary helps prevent the preacher from turning too often to a limited world of sermon subjects.

5. A lectionary gives the congregation a weekly opportunity to hear a part of the First Testament. Many Christian communities are latently Marcionite. Today, however, Christians are rediscovering the importance of the First Testament. Church and synagogue are moving toward a new rapport. The regular hearing of the First Testament helps facilitate this recovery and reconciliation.

6. A lectionary often brings pastor and people eyeball to eyeball with difficult texts that they would otherwise avoid. These encounters often help the community grow in its understanding of God, the Bible, Christian belief, and practice.

7. The use of a lectionary helps form the church as a community. A lectionary helps counteract the narcissism and tribalism that permeate North American society today.

8. The use of a lectionary symbolizes the unity of the church. Many congregations use the Revised Common Lectionary. Some lectionaries are used worldwide. A lectionary helps the congregation have the sense of being a part of an international witness. Also, Christians from different congregations can talk with one another about the common passages that they encounter in their separate services.

9. A lectionary gives the preacher a place to start sermon preparation. Preachers do not have to flip and flop in search of a place to mobilize their sermonic energy.

10. Publishers generate a plethora of exegetical and theological resources to help the preacher and the community interact with the Revised Common Lectionary.

11. A lectionary facilitates planning for worship and preaching. Worship planners know the central focus of services long in advance, and, consequently, have plenty of time to develop liturgical materials. Advance knowledge of the biblical texts for Sundays also facilitates communally based conversation in sermon preparation.

12. The Revised Common Lectionary combines the approaches of *lectio selecta* (especially during Advent-Christmas-Epiphany and Lent-Easter-Pentecost) and *lectio continua* (Ordinary Time). The congregation thus has some of the advantages of both patterns.

13. The Revised Common Lectionary is designed for use in a service with the Lord's supper. The use of this lectionary thus implicitly encourages churches to recover the full pattern of weekly word and sacrament.

Potential Disadvantages of Preaching from a Selected Lectionary

1. While lectionaries stress the gospel's promise of unconditional love, they give comparatively less emphasis to texts that stress justice in community.

2. While a lectionary leads a community to many important Christian themes, it does not cover all theological motifs that are important for the Christian community. For instance, the lectionary does not give sustained attention to the created world. When ecocide is a possibility in our age, this omission is regrettable. Furthermore, lectionaries subordinate the Bible to the doctrinal emphases of the Christian year. Biblical texts seldom speak in their own voices.

3. The relationship between particular lections and particular days and seasons of the Christian year is not always clear. In Advent-Christmas-Epiphany and in Lent-Easter-Pentecost, the gospel readings jump from one book or passage to another without obvious sequence. This pattern (or lack thereof) can be confusing.

4. While the lectionary broadens the purview of many preachers, preachers can still ride their hobby horses, especially in the selection of texts. I know preachers, for instance, who always preach from the gospel. The lectionary also has a limited selection of texts. The same texts are read over and over again as the lectionary is repeated. The First Testament is four times the length of the Second Testament, yet comprises not quite half the readings in the lectionary When the psalms — which usually serve a liturgical function — are excluded, the First Testament comprises less than one third of the readings. This is problematic because the

Christian community understands the story of Jesus and the Second Testament in the background of the First Testament.

5. The First Testament is disadvantaged in most lectionaries. As noted just above, it does not appear in the lectionary in the same proportion that it is found in the Bible. Furthermore, the congregation never hears the story of the Bible in sequence from Genesis to Revelation. (This absence prompts biblical scholar James A. Sanders to suggest that churches should develop a lectionary cycle that tells the story of the Bible in sequence).[6] The congregation usually hears the First Testament in disconnected bits and pieces. Few Christians have an opportunity to develop a sense of biblical chronology. From this standpoint, lectionaries reinforce aspects of biblical illiteracy. Furthermore, the lectionary provides a Christocentric reading of the First Testament. The readings from First Testament are nearly always subordinated to those from the Second Testament during Advent-Christmas-Epiphany, Lent-Easter-Pentecost, and in the First Testament readings in Ordinary Time that coordinate with the Gospel. The congregation seldom hears the First Testament in its own right. In the major liturgical cycles, the most common means of relating the two testaments is by means of promise-fulfillment. This pattern has the effect of devaluing the First Testament itself, as well as Jewish people, practices, institutions, and sacred texts. In a powerful but unfortunate symbol, the Revised Common Lectionary, dispenses with the readings from the First Testament (except for the psalms) in the Sundays after Easter.

6. While a lectionary calls difficult texts to the attention of the congregation, many of the most challenging texts are missing.

7. The readings for a particular Sunday do not always fit the immediate context of the community's life. To be candid, from time to time, a preacher may need to depart from the lectionary to another biblical text or to a topical sermon.

8. In an irony, the use of the Christian year and lectionary can remind the church of its division. Many Christian communities do not subscribe to the Christian year or a lectionary. Some pastors and congregations object to participation (or lack thereof) in the Christian year and the lectionary is a contested point with some pastors and congregations.

9. While a lectionary gives the preacher a place to start the sermon, the beginning and ending points of some of the lessons are not always satisfactory. Eugene Lowry, a creative thinker in the field of preaching, points out that the preacher needs to be particularly wary when single texts are broken into excerpts, as when a text is given in the form of Jonah 3:1–5, 10, but verses 6–9 are missing.[7] The excluded material needs to be heard if the text is to be understood as a literary and theological unity. Jonah 3:6–9, the command of the ruler of Nineveh for the people to repent, provides essential theological perspective not only on the pericope, but on the book of Jonah as a whole. Consequently, the preacher needs

always to see that the lections begin and end at natural points, and whether they include all the material necessary to understand them. The preacher may have to add (or exclude) material at the beginning, middle, or end of a lection. If, as I recommend, the preacher deals with only one lesson from the Bible in the sermon, two or three lessons are often read but not interpreted. Interpretive silence can leave the congregation confused. They hear a reading, perhaps a difficult one, but are not given any help with how to make sense of it. Consequently, they may interpret it without reference to historical, literary, or theological context.

10. While many printed aids for lectionary preaching are substantial, the preacher is sometimes tempted to use them for quick fixes.[8] Instead of engaging the text itself, the pastor engages the predigested preaching help. The preacher needs to learn how to use these aids as conversation partners and not as conversation stoppers.

A lectionary does not automatically bless or curse preaching. The contribution of the lectionary to a congregation's life depends on how the preacher and congregation relate to it. Occasionally, I come across a pastor who suffers from lectionary idolatry. This pastor is committed to preaching the lectionary every Sunday, no matter what happens in the world. While lectionaries usually provide timely readings for helping a community interpret its situation from the perspective of the gospel, Sundays come when the lectionary frustrates such an encounter. Preachers need to remember that a lectionary is a servant of witness, and not its master. A preacher should feel the freedom to depart from the lectionary as needed.

Preaching from a Continuous Lectionary

The oldest lectionary approach in the Jewish-Christian tradition is *lectio continua*, the practice of preaching sequentially through a book of the Bible or through a part of a book. For instance, the preacher might begin with 1 Corinthians 1:1 and preach through 1 Corinthians 16:24. Or, the preacher might select a part of 1 Corinthians, such as Paul's discussion of the Holy Spirit in 1 Corinthians 12–14, for a series of sermons that move sequentially through those three chapters. One could preach from the books of a single author. or from books that cohere around a common motif (e.g., the writings attributed to Peter, the preexilic prophets). By the time of Jesus, the synagogue had a lectionary pattern of reading through the books of Moses in a three-year cycle. The Reformers, especially Luther and Calvin, preached through whole books of the Bible segment by segment. *Lectio continua* often accompanies regeneration in the church. For instance, *lectio continua* was a staple in the preaching of the Reformation. Barth's theological rediscovery took place in conjunction with preaching through Romans. Today, *lectio continua* is a part of the regeneration of many Christian communities, especially in the evangelical sector of the church. This pattern could be at home in liberation, postliberal, and revisionary communities, as well.

The congregation that adopts continuous reading need not commit itself to this pattern forever. My impression is that the attention span of congregations in the long-established denominations for such preaching is usually 6–8 weeks. Some books, e.g., Ephesians, fit beautifully into this time frame. The preacher may need to adapt longer books for semicontinuous reading — selecting key passages from books for detailed exposition, and summarizing other passages in the teaching moment that accompanies the reading of the Bible or in the sermon itself.

When preaching *lectio continua*, the preacher should divide the book into passages with natural beginning and ending points. Each sermon should treat a meaningful unit of material. Because many people are not in worship every week, each sermon needs to stand on its own. Worship planners can include a printed description of the series in the worship bulletin and church newsletter and add a brief teaching moment to the reading of the Bible that explains the series and the literary context of the passage.

Many preachers think of verse-by-verse expository preaching as the kind of sermon that is most frequently associated with *lectio continua*. However, the preacher who is working sequentially through a book of the Bible is not limited to the verse-by-verse model. Continuous reading and preaching can take any expository form.

The Revised Common Lectionary makes use of continuous reading in Ordinary Time. The gospel lections move serially through Matthew, Mark, and Luke. In the readings from the epistles and the First Testament that do not correlate with the gospel, some of the readings are semi-continuous. For instance, the congregation reads through most of the Thessalonian correspondence. Segments from the stories of the ancestral families of Genesis are heard semicontinuously in year A.

Significant benefits can accrue to the community that participates in *lectio continua*. This approach allows a sustained conversation with a particular part of the Bible. For instance, when a church is dispirited, many congregations have found that returning sequentially to Philippians is an excellent means to help the community recover its spirit. When a congregation is complicit in injustice, continuous listening and preaching from Amos is often a wake-up call. A congregation that knows little about the period of the monarchy in Israel would profit from a series on the books of Samuel and Kings. Some parts of the Bible contain material that is so foundational to Christian identity that it needs regular exposition. The themes of Romans, for example, are indispensable to Christian worldview. I am convinced that pastors and congregations should work their way through Romans at least every five years.

Through *lectio continua*, a church has a chance to get a part of the Bible integrated into our consciousness by living for a time in its historical, literary, and theological world. Continuous reading can help the community perceive the distinctive voices of the different biblical writings. In this model, the congregation hears more of the Bible in its own voice and less through the filtration of the Christian year. Sermons can model how to study a section of the

Bible, taking account of historical, literary, rhetorical, theological, and herme-neutical considerations. Continuous preaching allows worship planners and preachers to work far ahead in the selection of liturgical materials, music, and sermon foci. Continuous reading creates an easy-to-use agenda for sermon feedforward groups.

Continuous reading also has potential limitations. The preacher can eas-ily become so fascinated with exegetical details that the sermon never leaves the past or never helps the congregation get the big picture of the text. The selection of books for exposition may limit the congregation's exposure to the breadth of the Bible, especially if the preacher turns again and again to a limited corpus. Without careful planning, continuous reading can run roughshod over holy days and seasons of the Christian faith. Of course, with forethought, planners can coordinate the readings with major Christian festivals.

Preaching from a Theme from the Bible

Most expository sermons concentrate on a single passage. However, some ideas, images, concerns, and behaviors recur in multiple parts of the Bible. While not a technical term from biblical scholarship, the word "theme" refers to these similar motifs. The congregation often benefits from a consid-eration of a theme as it comes to expression in different texts and contexts. Multiple appearances may deepen the motif, look at it from different points of view, provide comparisons and contrasts.

A theme may appear in a single corpus. For instance, Luke-Acts develops the role of women in the ministry of Jesus and in early Christian literature. A theme may stretch across several books and even testaments. For example, the topic of covenant appears with differing nuances in connection with Noah, Abraham and Sarah, Sinai, David, and early Christian literature. Each of these notions highlights a different aspect of covenant. The preacher could orient the congregation to the meaning(s) of the notion of covenant in the biblical world and could concentrate on the qualities of the different covenants.

The preacher may develop a single sermon that traces a theme through the Bible and that helps the community interpret the significance of the theme for the community's present life. Or, the preacher might put together a series of sermons in which each message highlights a different text or aspect of the theme.[9] For instance, while Mary Donovan Turner began to prepare her sermon on the great commission pages (268–278) with a single text, she develops the sermon in such a way as to trace the theme of discipleship through the Gospel of Matthew.

Thematic sermons help the congregation develop an overarching picture of the biblical narrative. The congregation gets a sense of how the pieces of the Bible relate together. Sermons on themes also help the congregation hear how the distinctive voices of the Bible are in conversation with one another. For instance, the Deuteronomic theologians are convinced that obedience brings blessing, while disobedience brings curse. On the same theme, the book of Job rises up with an impassioned and painful, "No!" Preaching either motif in isolation from the other is an injustice to both the Bible and the contemporary community. Of course, the preacher must help the congregation wrestle with the question of how these approaches can or cannot help today's people consider similar issues.

Edward Farley, a noted theologian, points out that the preacher does a disservice to the congregation by preaching from bits and pieces of the Bible without bringing them into relationship with larger theological convictions.[10] Christians can accumulate a grab bag of texts, images, and ideas, but may never create a systematic Christian vision. Preaching on biblical themes can contribute to a big picture within which to understand the bits and pieces of the Bible, Christian tradition, and experience.

As with *lectio continua*, a preacher might turn to a theme because it is especially fitting for questions that are alive in a congregation. For example, in a community that is puzzling over how to interpret the death of Jesus, a preacher might profitably develop a series on different interpretations of the death of Jesus in early Christian literature.

When a preacher develops a series on a theme, the congregation's published materials and worship leaders need to alert the congregation to the progress of the series. This allows all in the sanctuary to hear the sermon both in its individuality and in its relationship to the larger progression of the series.

Free Selection of Texts

By free selection of texts, I mean that the preacher chooses from week to week the text that is the starting point for sermon preparation. This possibility is often joined to a selection process that Thomas G. Long, who speaks and writes extensively about preaching today, terms "local plan."[11] In this case, worship planners structure liturgy, biblical texts, and sermons around events that are important in the local community, e.g., Christmas, Easter, days that are important in the culture — especially the birthday of Martin Luther King, Jr., Black History Month, Mother's Day, Memorial Day, the Fourth of July, Labor Day, and Thanksgiving. These days are frequently joined by days that are significant to the church, such as Homecoming Sunday, the pastor's anniversary, the stewardship campaign, special days honoring youth, women, men, or laity.[12]

The great value of this approach is that the preacher can select a biblical text that directly helps interpret the significance of the gospel for the present situation in the congregation. The potential problems, however, are many. Preachers who rely on free selection sometimes turn repeatedly to the same biblical texts to the neglect of large parts of the canon and Christian doctrine. The theological vision of the preacher and the congregation thus, unwittingly, shrinks to the size of this functional canon within a canon. Free selection and local plan requires a preacher and a worship planning team who have a thorough grasp of the content of the Bible. Otherwise, they may detour to the same texts or spend an inordinate amount of time thumbing through the Bible to find a text. In free selection and local plan, preachers and worship leaders have a tendency to select texts that encourage the congregation to feel good and to avoid texts and themes that are ethically challenging. Consequently, free selection and local plan often have the effect of reinforcing the theological, intellectual, moral, and institutional status quo.

Topical Preaching as a Supplement to Expository Preaching

Expository sermons are the backbone of regular parish preaching. However, topical preaching can be a significant supplement to expository sermons. By topical preaching, I mean a sermon that interprets a topic from the standpoint of the gospel, but without centering in the exposition of a biblical text. A topic is a need, an issue, or a situation that is significant to the congregation and that needs to be interpreted from the perspective of the gospel, and that can be better interpreted from the standpoint of the gospel itself rather than from the exposition of a biblical passage or theme. The topical sermon may include discussion of biblical texts, but the topical sermon is not controlled by the interpretation of the text. Chapter 18 contains a topical-deductive sermon on the doctrine of God from René Rodgers Jensen. Chapter 19 furnishes an example of a topical-inductive sermon on injustice that results from racism by Reginald C. Holmes.[13]

In the early and middle years of the twentieth century, topical preaching was widespread, but came under severe criticism. Some topical preachers suffered from theological amnesia. Such preachers relied only on the social sciences as sources and norms for the sermon and neglected theology. Some preachers conceived of topical preaching as pastoral counseling on a group scale or as providing self-help for dealing with individual life issues. Some topical sermons addressed topics that are not of central concern to the community or to Christian faith. When topical preachers addressed social issues, they often did so without extensive reference to Christian criteria. Consequently, they often sounded little different from social commentators in the local newspaper. However, misuse of topical preaching does not mean that the topical approach to preaching is fundamentally flawed. When managed by a responsible theological method, the topical sermon can allow the preacher to bring the gospel to bear quickly and directly on an important need or issue.

Several occasions might call for topical preaching. The Bible is silent on many issues that face today's congregation. The preacher cannot always find a suitable analogy between the world of the Bible and the contemporary world. A topical sermon can allow the preacher to speak directly about a matter on which the Bible is silent. For instance, women in the world of the Bible did not have the array of life choices that women face today. How does the gospel help a contemporary woman decide whether to remain single, to commit her life to a relationship with another person, or to remain in a relationship when it deteriorates? How does the gospel help a woman decide whether to center her life in the home or in the workplace? How does the gospel help this woman when she realizes that finitude means that she can't have it all?

Some topics are larger than a single biblical text or theme. Biblical resources may be helpful, but need to be supplemented. A topical sermon should allow the congregation to hear the Bible's perspective(s) on the issue in the context of a larger consideration. For example, the church today struggles with how to relate to the state. The letter of 1 Peter calls the community to "accept the authority of every human institution" (2:13). The book of Revelation regards the Roman government as the great whore of Babylon. Luke-Acts takes a mediating position. None of these perspectives resolves the issue for today's church. A topical sermon would allow the preacher to consider these witnesses in the context of a conversation that seeks a more adequate understanding of that relationship.

Some preachers use a word, an idea, or an image in a biblical text as nothing more than a springboard to get to a topic. I heard a Tillichian preacher bump into the word "faith" in Hebrews 11 and zoom immediately to Tillich's creative proposal of faith as the courage to be. The sermon never paused at the text's understanding of faith as "the assurance of things hoped for, the conviction of things not seen." The preacher spoke as if Hebrews employs Tillich's definition of faith. Such sermons give the impression that they are interpreting the text when they are not.

An idea, word, image, practice, or event mentioned in the Bible can prompt the pastor to realize that a broader consideration of that motif is necessary than is afforded by a traditional expository sermon. The preacher alerts the congregation to the interpretive move, thus respecting the historical, literary, and theological integrity of the text as well as the situation of the congregation. I can imagine a situation in which reading Hebrews 11 would prompt the preacher to realize that Tillich's definition of faith is particularly compelling for a contemporary setting. The preacher could help the community get Hebrews' point and then compare and contrast it with the Tillichian model.

A topical sermon might serve a congregation well when a crisis interrupts the life of a community, and a preacher does not have time to give adequate exegetical attention to a biblical text. Suppose a tornado sweeps through town on Thursday. People want to know how God relates to natural disaster. The Bible's testimonies are multivoiced and complicated. The preacher does not have much time. A topical sermon is a direct route to the pastoral interpretation of the relationship of God and natural disaster.

On some issues, the Christian community has not come to a decisive conclusion. A topical sermon can often help the community name such issues, identify the points that are unresolved, the resources that can be used to resolve them, and assess the status of the community's perception. For instance, the United States is in the midst of an involved discussion on the character of public assistance for persons who are economically disadvantaged. Some Christians think that prolonged welfare support is an optimum means to help the poor. Others think that persons should receive assistance only for short periods of time. They can then either work or go hungry. A few people want to put responsibility for the poor in the hands of the religious community and other nongovernmental associations. A topical sermon helps the congregation realize that the United States has not reached an adequate understanding of public responsibility and economic disadvantage. A topical sermon can help the church to consider the strengths and weaknesses of the various options and perhaps to envision possibilities that transcend present visions.

For some topics, a single sermon is sufficient. For instance, I know a congregation that was perplexed by the "Toronto blessing," an experience of laughter inspired by the Holy Spirit. Some members of the congregation wondered whether all Christians should receive the blessing. One sermon was sufficient to describe the phenomenon, to relate it to other experiences of the Holy Spirit in Christian history, and to help the congregation determine that the "Toronto blessing" is not normative for all Christians.

For other topics, a preacher might need a series of sermons to cover the topic well. When a plant closes, leaving many community members out of work, the preacher probably needs to deal pastorally with the grief that accompanies the loss of jobs, income, status, and security. Beyond that, the preacher would want to help the congregation consider the larger question of the relationship between the gospel and economic systems in our world that leave people unemployed. This consideration would require a series.

The preaching conversation often leads the preacher to consider biblical viewpoints on the topic, how the church has understood the topic in tradition, how the contemporary community relates to the topic, and how the gospel leads the church to interpret the topic today. Does the gospel reinforce the church's present understanding of the topic and relationship to it? Does the gospel call for a change? A preacher may find it useful to think of topical sermons as falling into three categories: (1) Christian doctrine or practice; (2) personal needs, issues, or situations; or (3) social needs, issues, or situations.

A topical sermon that focuses on *Christian doctrine* would help the community understand what the church believes about a particular tenet of Christian faith. As noted above, René Rodgers Jensen's sermon on pages 281–285 illustrates preaching in this vein.[14] For instance, the Statement of Faith of the United Church of Canada declares that God "has come in Jesus, the Word made flesh, to reconcile and make new." A preacher in that church might help the congregation come to clarity regarding what the church means when it says that Jesus "reconciles and makes new." A preacher might develop a similar series on the marks of the church (one, holy, catholic, apostolic).

A topical sermon on a *Christian practice* might help the church interpret that practice.[15] A preacher might lead a conversation on one of the thirteen Christian practices mentioned on pages 11–12. For instance, many congregations would benefit from topical sermons on how the church can work within itself and with other communities in the world to maintain social structures that will sustain life as God intends. In such sermons, the doctrine or practice is the starting point of sermon preparation. The doctrinal statement or the Christian practice functions in the sermon much like a biblical text functions in an expository message.

Doctrines and practices often lend themselves to series of sermons. Such series allow the preacher and the congregation to review the basic content of the Christian faith, or some aspect of it, in a concise and coherent way, in just a few Sundays. In today's theologically unsophisticated church, these series can help develop the congregation recover fundamental Christian perceptions. A preacher might develop a series treating each article of the Nicene formulation on a separate Sunday. The Statement of Faith of the United Church of Christ summarizes that denomination's doctrine of the church in a series of clauses declaring that God calls Christians into the church "to accept the cost and joy of discipleship, to be your servants in the service of others, to proclaim the gospel to all the world, to resist the powers of evil, to share in Christ's baptism and eat at his table, to join him in his passion and victory." Each clause could focus a sermon.

David Buttrick wisely points out that *personal* and *social* situations cannot be sharply differentiated.[16] Individuals are inherently affected by larger social systems. Wide-ranging social forces can be affected by individuals. A sermon can often help a church by concentrating on one or the other element, while keeping the larger (or narrower) dimension in view. In wrestling with a Christian perspective on divorce, for example, a preacher could help members recognize how the gospel interprets factors that go into the personal decision on whether or not to divorce or on how to relate to divorced family members and friends. The preacher would also want to help the community critically evaluate the larger social forces that affect current attitudes toward marriage and divorce.

A topical sermon on a *personal situation* usually focuses on a matter in which individuals need to clarify aspects of their immediate worlds.[17] A personal situation is one in which the individual has a high degree of personal agency. How can I think and act so as to be consistent with the gospel? For instance, when I am in an estranged relationship, how does Christian faith help me interpret the estrangement? What does the gospel call me to do? How do Christian resources help me do what I need to do?

A topical sermon on a *social situation* focuses on a matter that is systemic in character.[18] The community needs to know how to interpret and respond to larger social forces and movements. Individuals are responsible for Christian witness in their individual actions, but the issue itself extends beyond one's personal world. In North America, racism is such an issue. This topic calls for series of sermons that would help the community define racism and understand how racism today differs from racism in the world of the Bible. It would lead the church to understand how racism is manifest historically and today. It would analyze racism from the perspective of the gospel and suggest practical steps to expose the injustice of racism and to witness for a just world.

How Does the Preacher Decide on a Starting Point?

Sermon possibilities occur to the preacher and the community in many ways. Sermons can be suggested by a lectionary reading, a situation in the community, a novel, a cinema, a painting, a piece of music, or a report from a church agency. Sermons can be prompted by devotional Bible reading, by images that appear in the news, by encounters in personal relationships, by feelings and impressions from the preacher's life, or by an evening with friends sipping cider through a straw.

Preachers who use a lectionary report that the reading of an assigned text often helps them interpret their congregation's situation from the perspective of the gospel. The text helps them identify a gospel word that the congregation needs to hear.

Some starting points claim the preacher's attention in luminous moments. The preacher is electrified by an idea, or an image, or a feeling. From the moment the preacher sits down at the desk (or wherever sermon preparation takes place), the pastor's energies are mobilized toward developing that particular sermon.

Other sermons begin in subterranean depths of self and community. The pastor becomes aware of a possibility for a sermon only gradually. I know other preachers who awaken to such an idea for a sermon and discover (to their glad surprise) that a whole sermon is almost fully developed, just below the surface of consciousness. The preacher then has to work to bring inchoate awareness into sermonic form.

The critically thinking pastor usually settles on a focus for a particular sermon (or a particular series of sermons) by considering the situation of the congregation in relationship to possibilities for developing a sermon in a given week. Acting as a priestly listener and advised by the preaching conversation, the pastor asks, "Which starting points are the most promising for helping the congregation encounter the gospel in our setting this week? Should I start with a biblical text from a lectionary? with a biblical text from outside the lectionary? with a Christian doctrine or practice? with a personal or social situation? with an insight from a novel, a TV show, the report of a public agency?"

Deciding on a beginning point is not always a matter of analysis. In order to respond to the preceding questions, the preacher takes into account what is happening in the congregation, the situation of the larger social world, the theological orientations of the historic denomination and theological family of which the congregation is a part, what is going on (or not going on) in the preacher's life, and the opportunities for communicating the gospel afforded by the different kinds of preaching. The sensitive, critically reflective preacher knows the resources of the gospel, the situation of the community, and how to bring them into conversation.

Some weeks or seasons, a preacher will have a very clear sense of what the congregation needs in order to grow in gospel. Most weeks, a preacher can imagine several different possibilities for promising sermons. When faced with multiple possibilities, the preacher selects a direction that promises to provide a rendezvous with the gospel. Once in a while a preacher is stuck sitting before an empty screen. In this last case, a recourse is to turn to a lectionary or other predetermined source of sermon starts. Once in a while, a preacher starts a sermon on little more than an intuition, a hunch, to find that the idea grows in clarity as the preacher works with it. Sometimes the starting point of a sermon appears to be sheer mystery. The possibility for the sermon — a thought, an image, an experience, a question — simply comes to the surface of consciousness at the right time. With respect to selecting a starting point for a sermon, a former colleague stated a useful theological method: Be faithful to God and open to the possibilities.

Whether the starting point is the result of analytical choice, a stunning moment of discovery, or a quiet gestation, the preacher needs to evaluate the degree to which the starting point promises a sermon that is theologically appropriate, intelligible, morally plausible, contextually specific, genuinely helpful to the congregation, and of sufficient size and importance to take up a preacher's most sustained opportunity to dialogue with the whole congregation in a given week.

The preacher may begin sermon preparation with a specific purpose in mind. The sermon may well unfold just as the minister intends. However, sermon preparation has a way of taking on a life of its own. The sermon may develop in directions that are very different from the preacher's anticipation. Most weeks, the pastor will develop the sermon as envisioned at the beginning of sermon preparation. The preacher whose starting point is a text will develop an expository sermon. The preacher who starts with a topic will develop a topical sermon. From time to time, however, the process of preparing the sermon will cause the preacher to switch from one track to another or to combine them. For instance, the preacher might realize that the sermon that started in the exposition of a biblical text will only allow a side-glance at a topic in which the congregation is in immediate pain. In order to help the congregation deal adequately with the subject, the preacher could shift gears from an expository sermon to a topical one.

CHAPTER NINE

Developing the Direction
of the Sermon

After the minister has settled on a starting point for sermon preparation, the detailed process of developing the direction of the sermon begins. This chapter identifies essential issues that the preacher needs to consider in order to develop a direction for the sermon. How does a preacher figure out what to say about a biblical text, a practice, a doctrine, or a personal or social issue? The next chapter focuses on putting together the sermon itself. Since I am a linear thinker, I envision sermon preparation as a series of twenty-seven sequential steps as outlined below. However, many students and pastors are more associative thinkers. One question or insight leads to another, often without apparent logical connection. For associative thinkers, a sequence of steps may be a straitjacket. Most preachers combine these two approaches. They appreciate a certain amount of structure, yet interrupt the sequence of steps when they become aware of a question, insight, image, or hunch that comes to them outside the linear progression of development.

Finding a Time, Place, and Pattern to Prepare the Sermon

Many preachers find that they are most able to give themselves to the process of sermon preparation if they have particular times and places at which they turn their attention to the sermon. The pastor associates the setting with creativity. Each pastor needs to find the time and setting that provides maximum freedom to take part in the conversation. Many pastors close the door to the study, Monday through Friday, at 8:00 a.m. and work without interruption until 10:00 a.m. They put their phones on voicemail. They perform particular tasks each day. Other pastors find that they work best in one extended sitting: They begin at an early hour and work until late in the evening. They reserve one whole day a week for sermon preparation. Some pastors can work in the study at the church building. Others have a space at home. I know a pastor who goes to a place away from home and church for one day each week for sermon preparation. Some pastors are most generative at times outside the 8:00 a.m. to 5:00 p.m. workday. For instance, I am at my mental peak from 5:00 a.m. to 7:00 a.m. If I haven't had a good idea by 7:00 a.m., I am unlikely to have one that day. Many of my clergy friends are most alive at night. Fred Craddock, perhaps the most well-known preacher in European America, has a rocking chair in a quiet part of the house for aspects of sermon preparation. I have a friend who works on certain preaching tasks while mowing the lawn. Preachers need to find the times and places that work best for them, for their significant others, and for the congregation.

Most preachers benefit from having the direction of the sermon in mind early in the week. Spaghetti sauce that is cooked one day often tastes better the next, after the flavors have had a chance to steep. In a similar way, sermons usually improve if they have time for the ideas and images to mulch in the heart and mind of the preacher. Time allows the mind and heart of the preacher, consciously and unconsciously, to remember things forgotten, to make connections, to let the full weight of feelings settle, to generate images. This fermentation keeps contributing to the sermon almost to the moment of embodiment.

Paul Scott Wilson, a leading writer about preaching, recommends that the minister assign specific aspects of sermon preparation to each day, with the goal of having the sermon largely in hand by Thursday or Friday.[1] For the sake of preachers who find such patterns helpful, I adapt Wilson's fine model to the sequence of steps below. Preachers, of course, need to allow for a day off, and can adjust the work pattern accordingly.

- *Monday:* establish a focus, name preassociations with the subject of the sermon, identify specific tasks, develop familiarity with key words, concepts, images (steps 1–4, begin steps 5–8).

- *Tuesday:* research the subject of the sermon from the standpoints of exegetical disciplines, social sciences, philosophy, arts, and congregation (steps 5-13).

- *Wednesday:* list interpretive options, evaluate them theologically, and establish a direction for the sermon, clarifying what you hope will happen in the sermon (steps 14–19).

- *Thursday* and *Friday:* decide how to put the sermon together, taking account of the congregational context, so as to help the community have a good opportunity to enter into the preaching conversation (steps 20–27).

- *Saturday* and *Sunday morning:* practice the sermon and adapt its contents to material that has emerged from percolation.

From sermon to sermon, the preacher may distribute tasks differently.

Steps to Developing a Direction for the Sermon

The following steps help identify essential elements in the preaching conversation. The preacher interacts with others through print, through imagination, and through encounter with other living beings. Particular preachers will adapt and supplement steps to their own patterns of sermon preparation. Pastors can work on these assignments by themselves, with feed-forward groups in the congregation (a feed-forward group is one that helps the preacher prepare the sermon), or with clergy colleague groups. I illustrate the practicality of the steps by following one biblical text — the story of Jesus healing the woman with the issue of blood in Mark 5:24b–34. I also illustrate from occasional Christian doctrines, practices, personal and social situations. While I discuss these steps separately, their tasks sometimes interrelate.

Beginning students who see twenty-seven steps are often overwhelmed by their number. However, students usually find that they go faster than expected. Experienced preachers who have worked extensively with the Bible and Christian doctrine and practice may find that they already have in hand many pieces of information that are called for below.

Each sermon in chapters 16–19 is preceded by a description of factors that the preachers took into account while preparing the sermon. These chapters also include statements of how the preachers hoped the sermons would enter into congregational conversation on matters related to the issues addressed in the sermons. Mary Donovan Turner provides an exceptionally rich and detailed narrative of how she prepared her sermon.

1. Open yourself to the divine presence through prayer.

As noted in chapter 6, the Holy Spirit is a partner in the preaching conversation. God is omnipresent in all aspects of sermon preparation, whether or not we pray. However, prayer is the intentional opening of the self to the divine presence. Prayer makes us more receptive. We do not pray to ask God to be with us, for God is already present. We pray to be open to God's presence and for God to help us move past distractions, self-absorptions, misperceptions, and idolatries toward the gospel.

I speak for a number of preachers when I confess that I must pray for God to help me minimize particular demons. One demon is the potentially destructive desire to be liked. I get a powerful sense of affirmation when people tell me that they liked the sermon. This can subtly lead me to shape the sermon so that people will say things that are preacher-affirming. In order to win affirmation, I may forego a challenging gospel word. Another demon is that I sometimes assume that ideas and images that come to me in prayer are sparked by the Spirit. They may be. But, given the permeating power of sin, they may not be. Prayer is not an excuse for bypassing critical thought. Another demon is a tendency to assume that the gospel only confirms my current life. I pray to be open to the possibility that the gospel may call for transformation in my personal life and in the church and the world. Still another demon is self-absorption with creativity in preaching. I can want to be so fresh and imaginative that sermonic cleverness becomes an end in itself. I know that I cross this boundary when a saint says, "Brother Allen, you have such a way with words." With John Wesley, I pray for God to help me speak plain truth. What are the particular concerns for which you need to pray?

Prayer can work against openness to the Spirit. The familiarity of praying can insulate us from unexpected qualities in divine leading. We may create the god to whom we pray in our own images. Prayer may leave us prepared to receive only that for which we pray. We can use prayer to bless the ideas that we already had for the sermon, without being genuinely open to the fresh stirring of the spirit. Consequently, many preachers need to pray for God to help prayer itself not become a barrier to the Spirit.

2. Before reading, or otherwise directly engaging, the biblical text, doctrine, practice, or situation, describe your preassociations, and those of the congregation.

A preacher and others in the congregation frequently have preexisting associations with a text, doctrine, practice, or situation. Preassociations can take many forms — ideas, feelings, memories, intuitions, and experiences. They lie in the mind and heart in various states — from the unreflective and playful to the solidly buttressed. The preacher cognizant of such preassociations can evaluate critically the role they play in sermon preparation.

Awareness of preassociation is especially useful if the development of the sermon causes the preacher to come to a different way of perceiving the subject of the sermon than is present in preassociations. "When I began to work on this sermon, I thought…, but now, after considering the subject more fully, I think.…"

The following questions and exercises may help participants in sermon preparation (including you) bring preassociations into consciousness.

a. Let your mind and heart associate freely with the subject of the sermon. What comes to you? Jot down your uncensored initial associations. What do these preassociations tell you about your relationship with the subject?

b. What emotions does the subject of the sermon stir? Do these predispose you toward the subject in any way?

c. What images come to the screen of your mind in connection with the sermon subject? Do these images preorient you to the focus of the sermon?

d. Can you recollect experiences, memories, awareness of what others have said about the subject?

e. Suppose a member of the congregation looks into your eyes and asks, "Pastor, what do you think about this topic right now?" What do you say? Are you willing to risk the possibility that the conversation could cause you to change?

f. As you meditate on the subject of the sermon, what questions come to you? Are you curious? unsettled? dissatisfied with a previous perspective?

g. Do you have an intuition about where this sermon might go? Eventually you need to reflect critically on such hunches, but begin by getting them on the screen.

h. Do you care about the subject of the sermon? If the conversation leads you to the point that you must risk something of yourself in the sermon, do you care enough about the subject to do so and to live with possible negative congregational reaction?

i. Which of your preassociations seem most loaded, most charged, most capable of influencing the sermon?

At this stage, you need not critically evaluate anything that comes to you. You simply accumulate material. Critical reflection comes later.

For purposes of illustration, I mention only one of my preassociations with the story of the woman with the issue of blood. I remember a picture from a Sunday school quarterly when I was a youth. The picture showed a woman fearfully reaching through a crowd to touch the bottom of Jesus' prayer shawl. That picture still stirs me: Would I have enough courage to overcome my fear and do what she did to be healed?

An experienced pastor recommends reading a biblical text with laity or discussing a topic with them and listening for how they understand it. For instance, I know a minister who regularly reads the Bible passage for an upcoming sermon with persons who are in the hospital, and in other settings, and listens for what those persons hear in the passage. The pastor says that such listening often results in significant questions for the sermon and keen insights into the text. Such listening also turns up interpretations of the text (and of God, church, and world) that need to be corrected.

Consider this example. A preacher prepares a sermon on helping upper-middle-class families consider Christian witness on sending children to public or private schools. The preacher discovers that, in addition to being concerned about education several parents are latently racist and classist. The sermon needs to take these phenomena into account.

3. As possible, read aloud the pertinent material on which the sermon draws.

When a sermon draws on a passage from the Bible, an affirmation of faith, or some other textual material, the preacher and other participants in the preaching conversation usually profit from reading the pertinent material over and over. Reading the passage helps you discern what is actually in the material. Reading helps the pastor and others perceive the otherness of the text. Reading a passage helps those in the conversation develop an intuitive familiarity with the passage and its distinctive qualities.

Occasionally, a pastor begins to prepare the message before actually reading the Bible passage or other starting point. Such pastors often interpret not the text but their idea of it. They can miss or misrepresent important elements in the text.

I strongly recommend that the pastor and others involved in the preparation of the sermon read the text aloud. The preacher who reads the material out loud several times in several different vocal inflections usually discovers that the meaning(s) of the passage shifts as the preacher reads different parts of the passage with different emphases. The interpretive possibilities for the sermon thus increase. Reading aloud causes the readers and listeners to move slowly through a passage. I know a preacher who makes a tape recording of the text and listens to it on the cassette player in the car while making pastoral calls. Oral interpretation causes those in the preaching conversation to pay attention to words, phrases, and elements of structure that the fast-moving eyes of the silent reader bypass. Since many biblical texts were originally spoken and heard, reading aloud may help the interpreting community recover primal dimensions.

Reading out loud also serves as practice for the public reading of the Bible in worship. The reading of the scripture lessons is often one of the least satisfying moments in the service of worship. Some readers make mistakes in pronunciation, phrasing, and vocal inflection. Others act as if they are bored. All persons who read the Bible aloud in worship should be trained to help them read with expressive oral interpretation. During the service of worship, the preacher should read the passages that are central to the sermon. The pastor can inflect the text so that the reading begins to orient the congregation to the direction of the sermon. The preacher can then begin to orient the congregation to the direction of the sermon through the way in which the text is read. In public worship, of course, the preacher needs to be careful not to read the text with the kinds of flourishes that call attention to the reading.

A recent movement invites Bible readers to "speak" the text.[2] The reader memorizes the passage and voices the passage with expression, sometimes coming outside the pulpit or lectern in order to add to the sense that the text is a word of address from another.

4. List as much as you can that you need to know about the biblical passage, doctrine, practice, or situation in order to understand it in a satisfactory way.

Preachers may find it useful to make a list of everything they need to know about the subject of the sermon in order to make a thorough and critical gospel witness. This enumeration pushes us systematically to name issues we need to consider and the sources we need. As a wag says, "You plan your work, so that you can work your plan."

Early in the process of sermon preparation, the preacher may need to locate specialized resources. When preaching on a part of the Bible, a doctrine, or a Christian practice, a preacher should have abundant secondary resources in their own libraries. When preaching on personal or social situations, or when drawing out the implications of texts, a preacher may need to turn to the local public library, bookstore, or the Internet.

A simple plan can help students develop a library of significant lifelong partners for preaching conversation. Early in their seminary careers, students should set up a plan to buy biblical commentaries, dictionaries of the Bible and church history and doctrine, and other pertinent theological reference books and multimedia resources (such as CD-ROM reference materials). A student who buys at least two volumes a month during seminary will accumulate a significant body of conversation partners.

By taking the time to survey the landscape of the subject of the sermon, the preacher is likely to give attention to essential questions and issues. If the preacher settles on the subject of the sermon, reads the pertinent textual material aloud, and simply grabs the first reference book on the shelf, the process of sermon preparation can easily be sidetracked by the first provocative interpretive possibility.

When considering the story of the woman with the flow of blood, a preacher would want to check out at least the following. The list will grow as the preacher works.

— What are the historical, literary, and theological purposes of the Gospel of Mark and the functions of this story within those large frameworks?

— What are the functions of the story in its immediate contexts — the series of miracle stories beginning with Mark 4:35 (the stilling of the storm) and its placement in the middle of the story of the raising of Jairus' daughter (5:21–43)?

— What are the functions of the crowd in Mark, and their role here

— Is it significant that the main character (other than Jesus) is a woman?

— What is the role of women in Mark and of the woman in this passage?

— How did Jewish people understand the sources of illness and methods of healing in antiquity? For example, who were "physicians" and what did they do? What have physicians been doing that caused this woman to spend all that she had? How do these views compare and contrast with views of illness and healing in the contemporary congregation?

— What are the possible causes of this woman's hemorrhage?

— How did the Jewish people understand blood-related diseases and the personal and social consequences of such diseases?

— What is a comprehensive picture of the personal, social, and religious situation of the woman before and after the healing? What does the healing make possible for her?

— Why does the woman approach Jesus from behind?

— What part of Jesus' "cloak" did the woman touch? Does that have significance?

— What is the role of touch as the agency of healing?

— What is Mark telling us about Jesus by emphasizing that Jesus felt power go out from him at the woman's touch?

— Why does Jesus not know that the woman touched him?

— Why does he want to know who touched him?

— What prompts the woman to admit that she is the healed one?

— What does the text mean when it says that the woman came in "fear and trembling?"

— What is the significance of Jesus' address, "Daughter"?

— What is the definition of faith in this context? What is its role in the healing?

— Is faith necessary for healing?

— What does it mean to be "made well" in the world of Mark? in our world?

— Why does Jesus tell the woman, "Go in peace"?

— Why does Jesus tell the woman at the end of the story to be healed of her disease when the narrative is already clear that she is healed?

— What are the effects of this story on the listener, ancient and contemporary?

— If Jesus had unlimited power to heal, why did he heal only a handful of the multitudinous sick and infirm in Palestine?

— Do these kinds of healings happen in our world? If they do, why are they not more common? If not, how can this story help us?

— Does this story make a witness that is appropriate to the gospel, intelligible, and morally plausible?

With such questions and issues in hand, a preacher can accumulate a list of secondary resources to consult.

Consider this example. At the time of civil elections, many Christians puzzle over how best to express their faith in the voting booth. Do they vote for Republican, Democratic, or some other option? Do they vote at all? In order to develop a topical sermon (or series of sermons) helping the congregation with this matter, a preacher would need to identify the purpose of human community and the role of government in that purpose. The conversation would need to consider models of political government (e.g., monarchy, dictatorship, democracy, various forms of socialism) and the advantages and disadvantages of each. It would examine the key issues in the relationship of church and state. Which political system(s) has the best chance of helping the human community reflect the divine purposes? What are the possible relationships between the vote of the people and the will of God? In the political arena, do people make absolute choices between Christian and non-Christian alternatives, or are electoral choices often a matter of candidates and issues being relatively more or less reflective of the gospel? Those in the conversation would need to name and theologically evaluate the key issues in the campaign. On which issues is a party relatively more or less appropriate to the gospel, intelligible, and morally plausible? Should the preacher recommend that the congregation vote for a particular candidate or for a particular issue? What is the role of Christian community when an election results in officials and policies that work against the gospel? Would a political system other than democracy give a community a better opportunity to create a just community? If so, should Christians work for that system? And how should they attempt to initiate change?

5. Clarify the meanings of key words, concepts, images, characters, and other elements central to the biblical text, Christian doctrine, practice, or situation.

Words, concepts, images, and characters are context-specific. To honor the otherness of the biblical text, doctrine, practice, or situation, the preacher should clarify the meanings of these elements in the text or topic. We cannot assume that we know how a particular word is used in a particular context. Ministers and others in conversation do not unconsciously want to read their own meanings into the central notions of the text, doctrine, practice, or situation. That would be talking to oneself, not engaging an other.

The list from step 4 is a beginning point for this task. The preacher can get immediate help from the Bible helps, as well as from dictionaries of church history, theology, and from other materials that interpret the subject of the sermon.

When using a Bible dictionary or other interpretive aid, the preacher can too easily settle for a generic definition from a Bible dictionary or other resource when the use of a term in its specific context is much more vivid. The preacher also needs to avoid assuming that a collection of word studies is the same as exegetically engaging the text, doctrine, practice, or situation. Meaning emerges through words working together.

I illustrate with some key words, characters, images, and notions from the story of the woman with the issue of blood.[3] The central character, other than Jesus, is the woman. In that period, the identity of women was tied to that of men. We expect the text to mention the male who is responsible for her. The omission of a male suggests that she operates independently. Such freedom of movement for women is associated with the reign of God. The fact that she had money to spend on medical treatments for twelve years suggests that she had been a woman of means who is now impoverished.

The physicians of the ancient world likely treated her with leeches or bloodletting that resulted in anemia. They exercised power over her. They took her money. They increased her pain. But they did not help her. Her attempts to seek help through the physicians is itself a demonstration of the brokenness of the old world.

The woman has had a hemorrhage for twelve years. The text does not indicate whether this problem is an unceasing menstrual flow or some other difficulty. A flow of blood rendered a woman unclean until the hemorrhage stopped and she performed rites of purification (e.g., Leviticus 12:1–8, 15:19–30, esp. 25–27). During the period of uncleanness, the woman is to remain relatively isolated. She cannot participate in normal social functions or in religious life. Other people become unclean when they touch her, or touch furniture or utensils that she has used. When she is on the street, she is to call out so that people can avoid her. The illness allowed her only the most essential contact with males. When she approached Jesus in silence, she risked making him unclean, as well as any people whom she touched.

To us, she has a medical problem for which a physician would prescribe vitamin K, a drug, or surgery. In the first century, the illness distorted her entire world. When she is healed, not only is her body repaired, but her world is restored. The community, too, is restored by her return to full participation.

In this story, Jesus is more than a healer. The Gospel of Mark is apocalyptic in orientation (see page 90). At the start of the story, the woman's bloody life exemplifies the brokenness of life in the old order. Jesus, however, is agent of the reign of God. This story demonstrates the presence of the rule of God for the woman. Through Jesus, Mark's listeners can encounter it, too.

Reversal is an important theme in apocalypticism. The woman — who is on the bottom of the social ladder — receives healing and becomes a model of faith. Her ordinary place in ancient society is reversed.

The NRSV says that the woman "touched [Jesus'] cloak." Most scholars think that she touched the bottom of his prayer shawl. Most Bible dictionaries give a drawing of such a garment.

Jesus does not intend to heal the woman. Indeed, Jesus is on the way to Jairus' house. Jesus would not even be aware of the presence of the woman if she did not touch him. The story thus emphasizes the woman's initiative.

When the woman comes forward after the healing, she falls down "in fear and trembling." It is not clear whether this expression refers to religious awe, or to fear *qua* fear, or to an intermingling of the two.

By addressing the woman as daughter, Jesus uses a term that was not used casually in the first century. It designates kinship. This woman is part of Jesus' family, a group that is defined not by blood-kin but by responding to the manifestation of the rule of God (Mark 3:31–35). Jesus' family is a community that anticipates the new age.

In Mark, "faith" means confidence that God is manifesting the divine rule through the ministry of Jesus. The woman demonstrates faith by opening herself to the new world as it is demonstrated through Jesus. The implicit suggestion is that readers who have similar faith will also experience the power of the new world.

When Jesus says, "Go in peace," he invokes the Hebrew notion *shalom* (well-being in community). The woman is restored to her place in community. When Jesus says that she is made well, he uses a double entendre. The Greek term translated "has made you well," can also be rendered "has saved you." The healing demonstrates the rule of God that will eventuate in the salvation of the cosmos itself.

6. Insofar as possible, identify the historical context of the biblical passage, Christian doctrine, practice, or situation, and the purposes of the text or other matter in its context.

Documents emerge in particular historical contexts. Often, a knowledge of the context helps determine the dynamics of a text, doctrine, Christian practice, or situation. For instance, the awareness that Isaiah 40 was written to people in the Babylonian exile helps explain aspects of the famous poem that begins, "In the wilderness prepare the way of the Lord, make straight in the desert a highway for our God." The prophet assures the community that God is ending the Exile. As at the exodus from Egypt, God will lead the people home through the wilderness that lies between Babylonia and Israel. In their religious life, the Babylonians built a roadway through the wilderness for a procession for their deity. The exiles are to build a similar road for God ("the way of the Lord"). But God's superiority over the Babylonian deities is revealed in that the roadway will stretch all the way from Babylon to Judah and God will free the exiles.

As noted in the previous chapter, it is not always possible to specify the historical context of a biblical text, a doctrine, or a Christian practice. The easiest way for preachers and sermon preparation groups to identify what we can and cannot know about the historical context of particular materials is to turn to the introductions to the Bible, biblical commentaries, the standard works in church history, and systematic theology. The best of these resources indicate options that are available for reconstructing the historical setting of a document. They also indicate the relativities in particular reconstructions.

What does a preacher do when confronted by scholars who offer different, even contradictory, explanations of a text or situation? When such a reconstruction is important to the sermon, the preacher must choose which (if any) of the reconstructions to follow on the basis of which scholarly claims make the most sense.

Scholars have interpretive biases. Good scholars indicate their points of view and compare and contrast them with others. Some scholars, however, present their thought as if their line is the only one, or they do not treat other viewpoints fairly. When using a scholarly source, a preacher needs to appraise the viewpoint, fairness, and comprehensiveness of the source.

In an earlier generation, scholars commonly called for preachers to determine the intention of the author when writing a biblical passage. However, while we have access to texts, we do not have access to the mind of an author. We cannot ask a writer, "What did you intend in this text?" As a result, few scholars today recommend pursuing this line of inquiry. Furthermore, knowing an author's intent may not mean that the preacher completely understands a passage and all its implications. Authors say more than they intend or even know.

Scholars pose several different historical reconstructions of the Gospel of Mark. For the sake of space, I will not review and evaluate them. They are all problematic. We cannot precisely identify the time, place, or circumstances of Mark's writing. However, we can have a general sense of Mark's interpretation of the situation of his community and the purpose of the gospel. Most scholars agree that Mark is apocalyptic in theological orientation. Communities typically turn to apocalypticism when they feel uncertain, fearful, and threatened. Mark 13 suggests that the gospel was written for such a time. The Gospel of Mark, like other apocalyptic writings, encourages its readers. The story of the woman with the issue of blood is a part of this purpose as it assures the listeners that in the midst of the current age of suffering and difficulty they can experience release and can participate in the beginning of the new world through the gospel.

To take another example, some churches observe Reformation Sunday. A preacher may help the congregation understand the importance of the Reformation by sketching the historical situation, especially the indulgence system, that prompted the Reformation. The preacher who calls this situation to mind should not leave the congregation with the impression that the Roman Catholic church today is deformed by works-righteousness. The preacher needs to bring the historical situation up-to-date by helping the congregation realize that the indulgence system did not represent the best of Roman Catholic theology in its own day. Roman Catholics today view justification by grace as the center of the church.

7. Insofar as possible, identify the literary or rhetorical form, characteristics, and function of the text, doctrine, or practice.

In the last generation, preachers have learned from literary and rhetorical scholars that form and meaning are inextricably intertwined. The way something is said is part and parcel of what is said. Form and content cannot be disjoined without loss of meaning. The preacher needs to pay attention to the literary and rhetorical features and functions of the material that is central to the sermon — biblical text, Christian doctrine, or practice.

Literary and rhetorical analysis can often help a preacher understand the nature and purpose of expressions and behavior in both personal and social situations. In the current discussion of Christian interpretations of abortion in the United States, one group has adopted the label, "right to life movement." This group opposes abortion except in cases in which the health of the mother is endangered. The phrase "right to life" performs the rhetorical function of intimating that those who do not advocate the "right to life" are exponents of death. When preaching on this subject, the preacher must decide whether the rhetoric of the "right to life" movement is appropriate to the gospel, intelligible, and morally plausible for all concerned in the world of abortion.

Four questions help the preacher identify the literary form, characteristics, and function of the text, doctrine, practice, or aspects of a situation. These questions apply both to whole books or sections of the Bible, and to individual passages. An epistle, for example, is itself a literary form with particular purposes and literary characteristics. Within an epistle, we can identify smaller components that have their own characteristics and purposes (for example, the thanksgiving paragraph). The smaller forms often perform particular functions on their own and contribute to the larger form. Commentaries and reference works will often help preachers answer these questions. However, the preacher's own sensitivity will often yield fresh insights.

(a) *What is the form of the biblical text or other material that is central to the sermon?*[4] Nearly every passage of the Bible can be identified as a particular literary or rhetorical form, e.g., parable, proverb, psalm of lament, royal psalm, oracle of salvation, oracle of judgment, apocalypse, catalogue of virtues, catalogue of vices. The story of the woman with the hemorrhage is a miracle story.

(b) *What are the characteristics and movement of this form, and how are they manifest (or adapted) in the material that is central to the sermon?* A knowledge of the components of the form and of how they are adapted to the text, helps the preacher discern the purposes of the text. Do the characteristics of the form suggest similar characteristics for the sermon?

Narrative texts involve particular configurations of setting, character, and plot. A miracle story usually contains:

    (i) a description of the setting and the condition of the person in need of healing;

   (ii) an encounter with the miracle-working power;

  (iii) the miracle;

  (iv) evidence that the miracle has taken place;

   (v) a gasp of awe from the onlookers.

The listeners experience the narrative world created by the text. When they return from the narrative world into the ordinary world of everyday life, they must discern the degree to which the narrative world influences their perception of the ordinary world.

This structure is evident in story of the woman with the issue of blood. (i) The chief character in the text, other than Jesus, is the woman. Her appearance in the story evokes the associations that are described in step 5: She is a bleeding woman, socially and religiously unclean. (ii) When she comes into the sphere of Jesus' power, however, she is cleansed and restored to community. The listener knows from previous chapters in Mark that Jesus is an agent through whom God is manifesting the divine rule in the world. (iii) The text reports, but does not detail, the miracle of healing. (iv) The story demonstrates that the woman is healed. The last line, "Daughter, your faith has made you well, etc.," confirms that she is restored to community and to standing with God. In this respect, Jesus functions in the church much like the temple functions in Judaism. Faith is the agency through which the power of the rule of God is released in the woman to work its self- and community restoration. (v) This story does not conclude with a gasp of awe. However, it leaves us with the sense that we, too, can encounter the restorative power of Jesus.

(c) *In the case of a smaller unit of material (e.g., a parable, a legal saying), does the piece perform a particular function within the larger form of which it is a part? How is the larger setting affected by the individual passage?* While a sermon typically deals with a single passage, the interpretation of the passage is often affected by its place and function in its larger setting, and the larger work is affected by the smaller piece.

As noted at step 5, the story of the woman with the issue of blood demonstrates the manifestation of the new world for the woman. At one level, we can engage the story in its own right. At another level, the story is sandwiched into the larger story of the raising of Jairus' daughter, taking place after Jairus summons Jesus to come tend to Jairus' dying daughter, but before Jesus reaches Jairus' house. As such it extends and heightens the dramatic tension between Jairus' request and Jesus arrival at Jairus' house. We want to know what happens to Jairus' daughter. The power needed for the healing of the woman foreshadows the power that is necessary to raise Jairus' daughter from the dead. The woman's faith gives the listener a portrait of the kind of faith that Jairus (and the listener) should have. However, the story of the woman is told as an interruption as Jesus is on the way to tend to Jairus' daughter. Does this placement devalue the suffering of the woman by making it a side-focus on the way to the raising of Jairus' daughter?

d. *What are the effects of this text on the listener?* The preacher can often answer this question by considering both the purpose of the form in general (e.g., miracle story) and of the text in specific (the story of the woman with the flow of blood). In antiquity, a community tells a miracle story in order to gain or confirm trust in the miracle worker and the transcendent power(s) involved in the story. The miracle story reveals possibilities for human life and for the cosmos that result from the presence of the miracle-working agency in the world. The story also validates the life, claims, and power of the miracle worker. It embodies aspects of the message in the service of which the story is told.

By entering into the narrative world of the text, the listeners experience the pain and isolation of the woman, as well as the transformation that comes about when the woman comes into the sphere of the power of Jesus. However, literary and rhetorical critics point out that a story has different effects on different listeners, depending upon the persons in the world of the story with whom the listeners identify.

Many listeners identify with the woman. For Mark, the risen Jesus still performs the kinds of ministries in the postresurrection community that Jesus performs in the story. Consequently, for Mark, the story assures persons who are similar to the woman with the issue of blood that they can encounter the power of the risen Jesus that can restore them to God, self, and community. Other listeners identify with the disciples. Throughout Mark, the disciples are confused about the character of Jesus and the rule of God. The story helps these listeners realize that the ministry of Jesus demonstrates the reign of God (Mark 1:14–15). Some listeners in the world of Mark's church are uncertain about the purpose and future of the church. The story challenges such members to remember that the church is intended to be a community that welcomes and restores hemorrhaging women and persons like them.

Consideration of the literary aspects of the text sometimes suggests possible movement for a sermon. In the narrative of the woman with the flow of blood, the movement is from brokenness to healing through the agency of

Jesus, appropriated by faith. The preacher is not ready to decide on a form for the sermon at this stage of sermon preparation, but can make a note that the movement of the text suggests a possible movement for the sermon: from community situations like the one represented by the woman, through encounter with the sphere of the power of Jesus to restore community.

8. Imagine as much as you can about the world of the text, doctrine, practice, or situation. What do you see? hear? smell? taste? touch? feel? think?

A biblical text is a world that creates a sphere of perception that involves the whole of the self. Preacher and congregation want to enter the world of the text, doctrine, or practice so they have a clear idea of how it might relate to our world. We can often get a lively picture of the world of the text by imagining what we would see, hear, smell, taste, touch, feel, and think. The preacher can present such material directly in the sermon to help the text come alive for a congregation.

When engaging in this exercise, those in the conversation should discipline themselves to imagine the world of the text in ways that are consistent with the historical and literary setting of the text. When working with the text in the story of the woman with the issue of blood, I want to envision how people dressed in Palestine in the first century. I want to feel the flow of the blood in her body. I want to smell the street odors. I want to feel the weave of the prayer shawl.

Doctrines and practices are seldom as vivid as biblical texts. But we can benefit from asking what we see, hear, touch, taste, smell, and feel when we imagine the communities that generated such materials or who receive (or practice) them. For example, many affirmations of faith begin, "I believe in God…, creator of heaven and earth." The world is the creation of a Transcendent Power not our own. How does this perception affect the way in which we see, hear, touch, taste, smell, feel, and think about the world? How do our perceptions differ from those who do not regard the world as such a creation?

Many preachers find it helpful to imagine the text, doctrine, or practice from the different vantage points of different characters in the material itself or in the larger world of the material. Different characters may see, hear, smell, taste, and touch similar things. However, the different characters in the text itself and in the larger communities that hear the text can react very differently to what they see, hear, smell, taste, and touch. For instance, the Christian practice of tolerating and encouraging one another can feel very different from the standpoint of the persons who are tolerated than from the community that tolerates. The preacher can help encourage the church to become a community of toleration by helping persons in the two groups understand how the world looks, sounds, and feels to the other. The story of the woman with the issue of blood has different nuances when one identifies with the woman, with the disciples, with the crowd, with listeners in the Markan church, with non-Christian Jewish people, with non-Christian Gentiles.

Personal and social situations also come to life when the preacher imaginatively enters them. When preaching on a social uprising, for instance, the sermon can sometimes help the congregation gain a fresh perspective by imagining the situation from the inside out. For instance, on our street, police brutality against an African American sparked a protest by fifty African Americans at a particular police station. While the demonstration was peaceful, the possibility that it might escalate to violence prompted police to close the precinct street for several days and to patrol the street with armored vehicles. Many European American residents in the neighborhood did not understand why the African Americans were upset enough to protest and were annoyed by the closed street. Some European Americans began to voice racist attitudes. One European American neighborhood preacher helped the European American congregation understand the dynamics that led to the protest by helping the congregation imagine aspects of what it is like to live as an African American in that neighborhood. The sermon relied heavily upon what people see, hear, and feel from day to day. Many in the congregation experienced imaginatively something of the racism that fueled the protest.

9. Investigate how the larger church has interpreted the text, doctrine, practice, or situation in history.

Steps 9–11 deal with the history of interpretation of the subject. Step 9 is like a large portrait with broad lines in which you review the main lines of interpretation in the larger church. Steps 10 and 11 enlarge parts of the larger portrait.

Today's preaching conversation is seldom the first time that the church considers a biblical text, doctrine, practice, or situation. Positively, the preacher is often enriched by the awareness of previous interpretations of the subject of the sermon. Negatively, an acquaintance with the prior history of interpretation may help today's preacher avoid miscues of previous interpreters. René Rodgers Jensen and Reginald Holmes illustrate the value of this step in their sermons in chapters 18 and 19 respectively. Jensen shows how an understanding of the emergence of aspects of the doctrine of God helps the preacher's analysis, and how such history can be used directly in the sermon (pages 281–285). Reginald Holmes demonstrates, similarly, how awareness of the development of the concept of racism can help the preacher understand an issue and bring such material into the pulpit (pages 288–295).

This aspect of sermon preparation may require a little more time and ingenuity in research than the previous steps. Scholars have written relatively few detailed histories of the interpretation of particular passages in the Bible. Some biblical commentaries provide a short section that summarizes the history of the research on each passage. The *Word Biblical Commentary* is often helpful in this regard.[5]

I am not able to locate a concise history of the interpretation of the healing of the hemorrhaging woman. The Bible commentaries point out that in later Christian traditions, the woman is given the name Veronica or Bernice.

Legends accumulate around these later figures. In churches that know these legends, the preacher might need to help the congregation differentiate between the woman in the text of Mark and the later stories so that the congregation will not too quickly read the legends into the woman in the text. The preacher may be able to discern a relationship between the women of the Bible and the legends, but the preacher and congregation need to hear the text in its own right.

Since the text is a miracle story, I look up the article "miracle" in several dictionaries of the Bible, church history, and theology. While these articles do not rehearse the interpretation of this story in particular, they outline the major interpretations of the miracle stories in Christian history (and beyond). I easily extrapolate from the broad strokes in the articles to the specific case of the story. Based on the articles in the dictionaries, I distinguish five patterns of interpretation of the miracle stories.

(a) A pattern that is common from the biblical period to the Enlightenment assumes that the miracles took place much as reported. Miracles were unusual manifestations of divine power in order to demonstrate the claims of Jesus and the Christian tradition, to call forth trust in God. People in this period did not distinguish between natural and supernatural realms. Ancient people conceived of the cosmos as a singular, living entity in which divine power could be manifest in extraordinary ways without violating "natural law." The story of the woman with the flow of blood is such a report.

(b) Many Enlightenment thinkers concluded that we can accept as true only that which can be verified through the senses. Based on empirical observation, such thinkers formulated universal natural laws that explained how the universe operates. Miracles violate natural law. Some Enlightenment thinkers, therefore, conclude that miracles do not happen. The story of the healing of the woman with the issue of blood never took place. Consequently, the church cannot regard this story authoritatively.

(c) Other thinkers in this period created the category of supernatural to explain that miracles occurred by God's intervention in normal historical process. They explain why belief in miracles is intelligible, even in the face of Enlightenment skepticism. When believers in these latter groups conclude that miracles took place, they interpret their significance as much like those in the previous period. A few Christians promote this story as a model of faith healing that is available today.

(d) Other Enlightenment thinkers shift from the question of whether the miracle occurred to the question of how the miracle stories *qua* stories might instruct today's church. Rudolf Bultmann, for instance, conceived of such stories as composed of two layers that are related like the husk and ear of corn. The outer layer (the husk) is the story told in the worldview of antiquity in which people believed that such events took place. The inner layer (the ear) is the lasting meaning of the story that transcends the worldview in which it is told. Contemporary people do not have to believe that the event took place to appreciate the inner meaning of the story. Bultmann, a pioneering biblical scholar in the first half of this century, influenced by a philosophical movement called existentialism, believed that the story of the woman with the issue of blood is a mythical way of saying that God always offers new possibilities.

(e) Yet another movement contends that the miracle stories should be interpreted in light of the conviction that form and content are inseparable. This approach is summarized in step 7. The story creates an experience. Preachers who follow this route must eventually, like persons in patterns (b), (c), and (d), decide whether they can say that the congregation can count on direct, personal, physical events of the kind described in the story of the woman with the issue of blood. Most interpreters in this movement do not deny that such events could take place. After all, the universe is not a static entity like a machine. The universe is a living organism, and relationships among elements in the universe might sometimes result in miracles. However, such preachers do not commend miracles as patterns in life that can be activated on demand. Most preachers in this wave (e) view the transformational possibilities in the story in psychological or social terms.

Another example: When preaching on the phrase "I believe in...the life everlasting," a preacher turns to commentaries and dictionaries of the Bible, church history, and theology to discover how life beyond death was interpreted in the worlds of the Bible, across church history, and today. The preacher travels from Sheol in the Hebrew tradition through texts in the early church that seem to presuppose the resurrection of the dead, others that commend the immortality of the soul, and still others that believe that present life can manifest eternal qualities. Some in the history of the church think that everlasting life comes only with the complete manifestation of the rule of God. Others think it occurs in "heaven," which they envision as a place. Others regard heaven not as a place but as a time. In the current period, theologians debate whether the life everlasting has a subjective dimension (i.e., whether we are conscious in the life beyond the grave).

10. Note how your denomination has interpreted the text, doctrine, practice, or situation.

In today's pluralistic ecclesiastical climate, few pastors are required to interpret texts or topics from the standpoint of their denomination. However, knowledge of the denomination's tradition may help us become conscious and critical of otherwise hidden interpretive tendencies that we have inherited from our denominations. Interpreting a text through a denominational lens can help a community recover or develop a sense of being a part of a wider tradition. At times, of course, a preacher will be called to critique and even reject denominational tendencies. Reginald Holmes draws on material generated by his denomination to help the congregation reflect on the relationship between justice and racism in his sermon on pages 288–295.

Luther's interpretation of the story of the woman with the flow of blood illustrates both positive and negative dimensions of denominational interpretation. Luther places the story on the axis of law and grace, as described on pages 25–26. The physicians are exemplars of works-righteousness. They have led the woman to believe that she can be made well through her the work of buying healing. These masters of deceit profit by taking her resources.[6] Those who try to become righteous by performing works of the law "not only do not become righteous but become twice as unrighteous; that is, as I have said, through the Law they become weaker, more beggarly, and incapable of any good work."[7] The story is a paradigm of salvation by grace through faith. Jesus is grace itself. She brings nothing to Jesus except her faith. Faith does not save her. God's grace saves her. The woman's faith is the willingness to accept God's grace as the basis for her self-understanding and healing. Faith enables her to appropriate the divine gift. This story, then, models precisely what believers need to do: confess their inability to save themselves through works, recognize God's grace present for them through Jesus, and trust in that grace through faith.

This angle of interpretation helps the preacher recognize God's gracious presence. On the other hand, the text gives no suggestion that the physicians are manifestations of works-righteousness. Luther reads this element into the text. This interpretation comes perilously close to reducing the particularity of the text to an illustration of the general theological abstractions of law and grace. This reading leaves the story at the level an individual's relationship with God and does not take into account wider possibilities.

11. Note how your particular contemporary theological family (revisionary, postliberal, liberation, evangelical) orients you to interpret the text, doctrine, practice, or situation.

As noted in chapter 5, many preachers and Christian communities perceive God, the gospel, the church, and world along the lines of one of the following contemporary theological families: revisionary, postliberal, liberation, evangelical. Each theological family yields an approach to preaching that is characteristic of that family. Although few ministers or congregations are pure exponents of any position, many pastors and people are more prone to one way of interpreting Christian faith than to others. The preacher is called to be aware of these patterns and to be critical of them.

When considering the woman with the issue of blood, revisionary theologians seek mutual critical correlation between the text and the contemporary community. Revisionary theologians note that while miraculous healings were common in the world of the Bible, they are not common now. Some people in our world dismiss the story as foreign to our experience. However, the revisionary approach leads the preacher to probe for points at which the text might correlate positively with our situation. Some people and communities today are in religious, personal, and social situations much like the woman: feeling unclean, isolated, alone, marginalized. The revisionary theologian identifies such persons and groups who become aware of the presence of the restorative power of Jesus and who are returned to themselves and to participation in community. Faith is a means through which this transformation occurs. Thus, the revised understanding of the text is confirmed in our experience. The text challenges persons who deny the possibility of such transformation to revise their understanding of divine activity in the world.

Postliberal preachers would narrate us into the story of the text. The story of the woman with the issue of blood redescribes our understanding of the world. Walter Brueggemann, a well-known biblical scholar, retells the story, elaborating and contemporizing it slightly, so that listeners recognize that the text is about them.[8] The woman represents pain who comes into contact with Jesus. Jesus wants to know who has drawn power from him. The woman admits that she touched Jesus "in fear and trembling" because she expects to be punished by a traditional figure for whom power is the exercise of brute force. However, Jesus' power is touched by the woman's pain. Jesus models a new use of power when, instead of reprimanding the woman, Jesus blesses her with new possibilities. The woman is now a part of the story of Jesus. The sermon invites us to become participants in the story of Jesus. "We are all hemorrhaging women, with life bleeding out of us.… We are all of us part of the busy disciples…. We are also the bystanding folk.…" Nonetheless, the presence of Jesus makes it possible for the preacher to say to the community the same words that Jesus spoke to the woman, "Go in peace, be healed of your disease, by your faith be whole."

A liberation approach observes that the woman is oppressed. She is a woman, sick, poor, marginalized, and powerless. Liberation exegetes identify the structures in antiquity that put her in this position. Jesus brings liberation. Jesus not only performs a miracle in her behalf but changes the structures of her life. Jesus demonstrates that a new social order (the reign of God) is manifest. The act of liberation is material: The woman's body is changed and the woman's religious and social location is changed. The liberation preacher helps the community understand where and how God's liberating activity takes place today. The congregation can resist the oppression represented by the woman's situation at the beginning of the story and can join God in the process of liberation. The liberation thinker would note, further, that the story is a warrant for oppressed persons to seek liberation. A feminist suggests that the woman "may have helped the Markan Jesus to free himself from the patriarchal assumptions and male privilege of ancient culture."[9]

Many evangelicals are heirs to the strand of Enlightenment interpretation that sought to show that it is rational to believe that miracles occurred as reported. An evangelical might take the story of the woman with the issue of blood as an occasion for apologetic: helping the congregation discern why it is important to believe that the event took place as described. Evangelicals might ask what they learn from the story that is important to their understanding of God, sickness, the human situation, Jesus, healing, and Christian community. For example, the story demonstrates that Jesus is Messiah. Occasional evangelicals use the story as a model of how persons today can be healed (physically and otherwise) through faith.

12. Identify the vested interests in the Bible passage, doctrine, practice, or situation. Could these materials be used to support the interests of some at the expense of others?

People do not develop viewpoints in an objective, value-free atmosphere. Communities develop viewpoints to support certain people, practices, places, and institutions. Such viewpoints sometimes have the effect of downplaying, distancing, and even degrading other people's practices, places, and institutions. Some Christian materials were generated for this very purpose. Some Christians use texts or topics to oppress other people. Further, as Sandra Schneiders, a biblical interpreter who gives a lot of attention to hermeneutical issues, notes, some Christian materials are not only used oppressively, they are oppressive.[10] Such observations give rise to the hermeneutic of suspicion, an interpretive attempting to expose the "vested interests" that are enshrined in Christian materials, especially when these interests particularly benefit certain people or groups.[11] For instance, the household codes of early Christian literature ("Wives, be submissive to your husbands") benefit husbands while limiting life possibilities for wives. To take another example, in his sermon in chapter 19, Reginald Holmes shows how vested interests on the part of Europeans and European Americans played a significant role in the emergence of slavery and racism (pages 288–295).[12]

While we often think of vested interests in a negative way, some vested interests are positive. For example, a congregation has a vested interest in helping the preacher have the time and resources to develop sermons that encourage the congregation to grow in faith.

The preacher who is aware of the vested interests in biblical texts or topics or in the use of these texts or topics, can help the church reflect critically on the degree to which these interests are appropriate to the gospel, intelligible, and morally plausible. However, congregations are frequently unaware of the vested interests that are present in texts, doctrines, practices, or situations. We innocently receive Christian materials and order our thoughts and behaviors around them without considering their effect on all in the community. The preacher must sometimes help the community name these interests.

In order to help determine these interests, a preacher might ask simple questions. Who profits from the viewpoints in this text or topic? Do aspects of the text, doctrine, practice, or situation support the interests of some at the expense of others?

In the case of the story of the woman with the issue of blood, males benefit from viewing blood flow as unclean. The woman's condition limits her social power and presence in the community. The woman, too, benefits. The bleeding makes her unclean, which means that men cannot exploit her sexually. The physicians profit monetarily from the woman without healing her. The Jewish religious system benefits from the woman's condition in that her illness justifies the existence of that system. Religious leaders derive their vocation and their incomes by supervising the hemorrhaging woman. Under ordinary circumstances, when the bleeding ceases that system would provide the means for certifying her cleanliness and facilitating her reintegration into society. People who are "clean" sometimes use the presence of bleeding women to reinforce their own sense of cleanliness and superiority. People in situations similar to that of the woman benefit, in that the text points them toward a source of healing. The church benefits because, like Judaism, it is the most common place that the healing possibilities of the story are revealed. When the church claims that it is the only source of healing, then its benefit takes place at the expense of other communities that can also help bleeding women.

13. How is your understanding of the biblical text, doctrine, practice, or situation enriched by the social sciences (e.g., psychology, sociology, political, and economic analysis), the physical sciences, phenomenology, philosophy, and the arts?

The social sciences (e.g., psychology, sociology, political, and economic analysis), the physical sciences, philosophy, and the arts help the preacher discern dimensions of the biblical text or topic that the community might miss. Because of the high regard for the social sciences in contemporary North America, the preacher may be tempted to let data from the social sciences uncritically inform the theological direction of the sermon. When attending to these voices in the conversation, the preacher needs to analyze them theologically by means of the criteria of appropriateness to the gospel, intelligibility, and moral plausibility (step 15).

A preacher is expected to have a comprehensive collection of resources for biblical and theological interpretation. A preacher is less likely to have a large collection of resources in the social sciences, philosophy, or the arts. Consequently, for instance, when preaching on child abuse, a preacher may have to work hard to find reliable resources in these areas.

Persons in the congregation and wider community who are knowledgeable in these arenas can help the preacher understand the subject of the sermon. For example, the school psychologist who joined the congregation six months ago would be delighted to have a conversation with the preacher about child abuse.

The preacher who draws on the *social sciences* needs to have a responsible, critical understanding of the methods and conclusions. Each social science is comprised of several schools of thought. The different schools are not always compatible in method and conclusion. The preacher needs to honor the complexity of the understandings of the subject of the sermon that are found in the discipline. Otherwise, the integrity of the sermon is in question. Furthermore, the authority of the sermon is compromised when the preacher does not deal with ambiguities, contradictions, and other difficulties in data from the social sciences. Many congregations contain listeners who are knowledgeable in these areas. When the preacher mentions only one interpretation of a debated issue in this area, some in the congregation may think either that the preacher has not researched the subject sufficiently or that the preacher is trying to hide other perspectives.

When disciplines within the social sciences offer different interpretations, the preacher must decide which one(s) makes the most sense. The preacher can share with the congregation both the conclusion and the reasons for thinking it persuasive.

For instance, the question of whether homosexuality can be an appropriate sexual orientation is a lively issue for many Christian communities today and deserves thoughtful address from the pulpit. Those who do their homework soon discover that psychologists, psychiatrists, and psychobiologists are divided on whether homosexuality is a normal or abnormal condition, on whether homosexuality is the result of socialization or genetic predisposition, on whether people who consider themselves homosexual can unlearn homosexual tendencies and become heterosexual. Which conclusions are the most persuasive? Why? In the sermon, the preacher needs to help the congregation understand the range of opinion and why some points of view are convincing and others not so.

Paul Ricoeur, a well-regarded philosopher, notes that while the association of blood and uncleanness may not seem rational to the contemporary community, it was quite deep and powerful to people in antiquity. The woman herself felt stained, defiled, as did people who came into physical contact with her. The experience of defilement is "a quasi-material something that infects as a sort of filth, that harms by invisible properties, and that nevertheless works in the manner of a force in the field of our undividedly psychic and corporeal existence."[13] Indeed, the phenomenologist Rudolf Otto says, "The unclean is loathsome, that which stirs strong feelings of...disgust." Otto continues, "We have ourselves a direct experience today in our emotional reaction to the sight of flowing blood which it would be hard to say whether the element of 'disgust' or 'horror' is the stronger."[14]

The presence of an unclean person reminds the community of the precariousness of its existence. As long as the woman is unclean, she needs to be controlled to minimize the danger to the larger community. The unclean person needs to be purified. Consequently, Bruce Malina and Richard Rohrbaugh, in their *Social-Social Commentary on the Synoptic Gospels,* note that in the ancient world, healers focused on "restoring a person to a valued state of being rather than an ability to function."[15] To be unclean is to be out of place. In this story, the healing returns the woman to her proper place in the community.[16]

The preacher can also determine how the subject of the sermon is interpreted in the *arts.* Artists are frequently sensitive to aspects of a text, doctrine, practice, or situation that bypass many of us. The arts have their best effect when we encounter them in their own media, e.g., we see a painting or hear a symphony. The preacher who seeks to determine how a work of art interprets a particular subject for the sake of informing the sermon can easily cannibalize the work and the experience of encountering it. In the rush to see what in the work of art will preach, pastors can limit and even distort what they encounter. Most of the art pieces known to European American pastors are European in background. Art from other worlds is only slowly making its way into European America.

To help the congregation experience an art, a preacher might occasionally project a slide of a painting, or show a clip of a cinema, or invite a dancer into the sermon. My colleague, Frank Burch Brown, who teaches religion and the arts, develops multimedia sermons. The sermon is a series of art pieces projected, performed, or presented in its own medium with commentary.

The preacher is sometimes disadvantaged when trying to get in touch with how a passage, doctrine, practice, or situation is interpreted in the arts because there are few resources where such material is brought together. Two resources now help with this lacuna. The United Church Press has brought together a collection of paintings, poems, and songs that correlate with selected texts in the Revised Common Lectionary: *Imagining the Word.*[17] The journal *Lectionary Homiletics* contains a section describing some expressions of art that correlate with selected lectionary texts. Also, one of the most promising and convenient points of contact with the arts is the Internet. The number of electronically available resources is rapidly expanding, especially in the visual arts and music. For instance, the National Gallery of Art offers thousands of works of art at http://www.nga.gov. Preachers should continually update their familiarity with Internet resources.

A friend who was preparing a sermon on Jesus and the disciples crossing the storm-tossed sea knew that a painting of that scene appears in the Indianapolis Museum of Art. The pastor went to the museum and sat before the painting for about an hour. In the process, this minister began to feel guilty. "I thought I should be *doing* something to prepare my sermon. Finally, it dawned on me that in the act of apprehending the painting, I was doing something." A preacher should never feel guilty for viewing a painting, or listening to music, or partaking of some other aesthetic experience in connection with the sermon.

The preacher might also visit with artists in the congregation or in the larger community about what they see or hear in the text or topic and how they might paint, dance, write, sculpt, or otherwise respond to it.

When preparing a sermon on homosexuality, the preacher can easily turn to plays, movies, and novels that depict aspects of life as it has been experienced by some homosexual persons. When preaching on homosexuality, the preacher has easy access to more materials than can be used in a single sermon. However, I can locate only a handful of artistic responses to the story of the woman with the issue of blood. In her survey of women who appear in religious art, Diane Apostolos-Cappadona, an artist and historian of the arts, finds that this text is featured only in a few early Byzantine paintings. Unfortunately, copies of these paintings are not in my seminary's library.[18] The arts commentator in a recent *Lectionary Homiletics* article on the text does not comment on art pieces on this passage. However, she does describe works that focus on the relationship between faith and touch, such as Michelangelo's painting of God reaching to the first person on the ceiling of the Sistine Chapel, as well as other examples in dance, in the play *Agnes of God*, in a painting of the raising of the daughter of Jairus, and in several movies.[19] I doubt that any of these art works will take center stage in the sermon, but I can immediately imagine how one might help the congregation feel the woman's touch.

I also find references to this text in two contemporary hymns. The first stanza of a hymn, "The Scantest Touch of Grace Can Heal," by Thomas H. Troeger and Carol Doran (one of the most notable hymn-writing teams in this century) prompts me to ask myself if I have wounds that continue to bleed.[20] The hymn pushes me to ask, "Am I willing to reach beyond my pain, or have I become so accustomed to it that I fear leaving it behind?" Brian Wren, a biblical scholar, poet, and hymn writer, devotes a stanza to this story in a hymn in which each stanza tells the story of a different woman in the Bible.[21] The stanza helps me feel the woman "creeping up behind." I am struck by the sense of possibility, freedom, and agency in the phrase "touching is allowed." The tunes of the two hymns are quite different, yet as I hum them, I realize that each has rhythm and tonal qualities that are haunting, yet hopeful. I make a note to consider using the hymns in the service of worship.

14. Drawing on the previous materials, summarize your understanding of the witness of the Bible passage, Christian doctrine, practice, or situation in its historical and/or literary context.

The preacher attempts to bring the welter of information that has emerged in the previous steps into a sensible understanding of the biblical text, doctrine, practice, personal or social situation. The preacher responds to the question, "What does the text claim to be true of God, church, world?" In step 15, the preacher evaluates this possibility theologically in preparation for identifying a hermeneutical relationship in steps 16–19.

The story of the woman with the issue of blood is a narrative world into which we enter. The story has several possible interpretations that share this common thread: The story presumes that the world is not a closed system in which our sense of self and community is inevitably determined by situations like the one represented by the woman. God helps us move from being un-clean, broken, oppressed, and isolated, to cleanliness and right standing, wholeness, freedom, and community.

The more precise function of the story depends upon the character with whom we identify. If we identify with the woman, we experience the pain of the woman and the positive transformation of her world that comes about through her encounter with Jesus. We are encouraged to have faith, i.e., to take the risk of openness to the new world that is promised to us through the figure of Jesus. If we identify with the disciples, the story invites us to admit that we are often unable (or unwilling) to perceive who Jesus is and what Jesus is doing. The story encourages us to recognize that Jesus, through his continuing resurrection presence, manifests the reign of God in actions such as the healing of the woman with the issue of blood. If we disciples have faith similar to that of the woman, Jesus can help us recognize his presence and actions that demonstrate the reign of God. The larger literary world of Mark makes it clear that disciples are to continue that work (e.g., Mark 3:13–18, 6:6b–13). If we identify with the church to which Mark wrote, the story both assures us that all who are like the bleeding woman can be cleansed and restored to community, and it challenges us to help the church become a community in which God's cleansing and restoring grace is operative. We are to become a community in which persons like the woman with the issue of blood are renewed and accepted. In so doing, we embody the reign of God.

When the preacher identifies several options for understanding the text or topic, the preacher might create a spectrum of possible understandings. The preacher can then compare and contrast them, seeking to identify the mode of interpretation that is most compelling in the light of the various historical, literary, and theological factors.

15. Evaluate your understanding of the witness of the text or topic according to the criteria of appropriateness to the gospel, intelligibility, and moral plausibility.

The preacher evaluates the witness of the subject of the sermon, as summarized in the previous step, by means of the criteria of appropriateness to the gospel, intelligibility, and moral plausibility. (These criteria are discussed more fully on pages 83–88) The evaluation of the biblical text, Christian doctrine, practice, or personal or social situation plays a key role in determining the hermeneutical relationship between the subject of the sermon and the congregation (step 18).

(a) *Is the witness appropriate to the gospel?* That is, does the witness of the Bible passage, doctrine, practice, or situation manifest the gracious promise of God's unconditional love for each and all and God's call for justice for each and all? The story of the woman with the issue of blood is consistent with the gospel. God's love is freely available to all. The story does not deny God's love to anyone. The motif of faith, in fact, suggests that restoration is available for all who are in conditions similar to that of the woman. In this story, faith is not a work that one must perform in order to win God's favor. The story embodies God's will for justice. The healing allows the woman to participate fully and freely in the community in the way that God intends.

(b) *Is the witness of the text intelligible?* This criterion is comprised of three subcriteria: clarity, logical consistency, and believability.

    (i) Is the witness of the text clear? Yes, the witness of the text is clear.

    (ii) Is the text logically consistent within itself, and is it consistent with other things that Christians say and do? The answer is yes to both parts of this subcriterion. The story is consistent with the pictures of Jesus, women, the disciples, and the church that are found in the Gospel of Mark. The promise of restoration to community is certainly consistent with the Christian vision of God's love expressed for all through community.

(iii) Is the text believable? As a revisionary thinker, I note that we do not experience miracles of the kind described in this text on an everyday basis. But, because the universe is a living organism in which all elements are related, I am quite ready to believe relationships among people and the cosmos can evolve so that such events happen. However, at the present time, I am unable to say that physical miracles of the kind described in this story take place simply because a person has faith. The distinction between surface and deeper witnesses of the text (pages 88–91) move us beyond this impasse. The surface level of the text tells the story of the healing of the woman with an issue of blood. As shown in the exegetical notes in steps 4–8, the woman's experience is cast in language, imagery, and cultural assumptions of the first century. Our culture views some of those elements quite differently. A woman who is bleeding, for instance, is not considered ritually unclean and is not isolated from community. However, the experience represented in the figure of the woman transcends those particular cultural expressions. Many people today feel unclean and isolated. Through the restoring presence of Jesus, people today can become clean and part of a community. When that happens, God's reign is manifest.

At the same time, the text asks us to revise our understanding of the world. Since the world is a living organism and since God is omnipresent, situations in which we feel imprisoned are never completely determined. Even when physical circumstances do not change, the attitude of a person or community within those circumstances can change Faith can transfer us from perceiving ourselves as unclean and alone to clean and included in community.

(c) *Is the witness of the text morally plausible?* The narrative of the woman with the flow of blood is morally plausible. It does not legitimate the mistreatment of anyone in the world of the text or beyond.

I recommend that preachers regularly press texts and topics on appropriateness, intelligibility, and moral plausibility. If we are puzzled or troubled by aspects of the text, many in the congregation are likely to be. These points are frequently excellent points of contact for the sermon. Indeed, they often make good beginnings for the message. For example, does the claim of the text seem too good to be true? What reasons do we have for accepting the witness of the Christian tradition on a topic? Is a particular assertion self-serving?

16. Describe your experience with the witness of the biblical text, doctrine, practice, or situation and that of the congregation.

In step 2, the preaching conversation identifies preassociations with the subject of the sermon. This step recommends a more systematic consideration of ways in which you and the congregation encounter the subject of the sermon. The following exercises can initiate an inventory of the congregation's experience of the topic. These reflections are more disciplined than those in step 2.

(a) Review the preassociations generated in step 2. In your rumination since that step, what has emerged that seems especially important?

(b) What are your memories and those of the congregation regarding the testimony of the text, doctrine, practice, or situation? How do these memories orient you and the community positively or negatively toward that subject?

(c) Where and how do you and the congregation come into contact with text, doctrine, practice, or situation? person to person? in groups? through the media? How do these contacts affect your perception of that witness?

(d) What are the major incidents (if any) that contribute to your perception and that of the congregation concerning the text, doctrine, practice, or situation? Have the effects of these incidents lingered in the congregation?

(e) What emotions does your understanding of the text or topic arouse in you? in the congregation? How do emotions affect your relationship with the text or topic? For instance, do they get in the way? Are they a point of positive contact?

(f) What are your convictions and those of the congregation concerning the witness of the text, doctrine, practice, or situation? Are these convictions deeply held, the result of serious thought in combination with powerful emotion? Are they less deeply held, perhaps the result of inheriting an idea without reflecting on it?

(g) What are your hopes, fears, and other responses (and those of the congregation) concerning the witness of the text or topic? How do these affect you as you find yourself in the middle of preparing a sermon on that subject? How do you think they will affect the congregation's participation in the sermon?

(h) What do you anticipate to be the future of the witness of the text or topic in the congregation? For example, do you think it will be a part of the congregation's landscape for a long time to come? Is it likely to disappear with this sermon? Is the sermon likely to spark (or fan) a brushfire?

The preacher can respond to these questions on the basis of priestly listening, talking with persons in feedforward groups, interviewing people in the congregation, reading the congregation's history, and engaging in other activities of the kind described in connection with congregational analysis on pages 33–38.[22]

When I work with the story of the woman with the issue of blood in Bible study groups in congregations or in classes at the seminary, I raise these kinds of questions. Typically, few people have specific preassociations with the text. But when I move the discussion to the phenomena of uncleanness and isolation, many associations emerge. For instance, in connection with item (e), one person recalled being in a Sunday school class when a visitor arrived in wrinkled, dirty clothing. The visitor smelled. The person who reported this incident said, "I felt soiled by the presence of that visitor. I could feel the whole class grimace." The preacher might be able to use such an experience as a way of helping the congregation understand how people in the world of the first century might have responded to the woman with the issue of blood.

17. When preaching on a biblical passage, doctrine, practice, or situation, note how the context of the Christian year and the setting within the congregation's year orients the interpretation of the material.

As noted on pages 104–105, the theological themes of the Christian year are an interpretive context. When preaching from a lectionary, the pastor explores how a particular passage helps the community understand the theological themes of the season to which the passage is assigned. When preaching on a doctrine, practice, or situation in the context of the Christian year, the sermon could explore how the topic expands the congregation's understanding of the Christian year and how the Christian year helps the congregation interpret the topic.[23]

The story of the woman with the issue of blood is in Ordinary Time in year B in the Revised Common Lectionary. The passage helps the congregation deepen its growth in discipleship (the general theme of Ordinary Time). Since the readings from the gospel are semi-continuous in Ordinary Time, the preacher can help the congregation determine how the passage contributes to its growing awareness of the Markan drama.

Congregations that do not follow the Christian year often have a local plan or some other principle by which they organize their worship. These emphases also affect the way in which the preacher and the congregation hear a biblical text, a Christian doctrine, a practice, or a situation. A Father's Day observance, for instance, might prompt a preacher and a congregation to hear a text differently than on a stewardship emphasis Sunday or on a cold, snowy January Sunday. The preacher can assist the congregation to explore ways in which the text, doctrine, or practice helps the community enlarge its understanding of the day and the way in which the day helps the community explore aspects of the text, doctrine, or practice.

18. Identify the hermeneutical relationship that will guide the sermon.

Coming to clarity as to the hermeneutical relationship between the congregation and the text or topic will help the preacher know the general direction and tasks of the sermon. These can range from building a positive bridge between the congregation and the witness articulated in the previous step to taking a stand against that witness. As described more fully on pages 91–95, that relationship can take one of four general directions.

(a) *Does the preacher run with the witness with a minimum of explanation?* The witness of the text is appropriate to the gospel, intelligible, and morally plausible. The preacher can build an immediate positive bridge between the text or topic and the congregation. The main task of the sermon is to clarify the significance of the witness and to help the congregation draw out its implications. The story of the woman with the issue of blood is appropriate, intelligible, and moral. However, because I distinguish between surface and dimension witnesses of the text to come to a full-bodied understanding of its promise, I think of it in the next category (b).

(b) *Do I arrive at a positive interpretation of the text or topic by moving from surface to deeper dimensions?* The surface witness of the text or topic raises questions as to whether it is appropriate to the gospel, intelligible, or morally plausible. The question may be about one of these qualities or all three. However, upon further examination of the deeper character of the text or topic, the uncertainty is resolved by moving from the surface witness to the deeper one. Questions about the story of the woman with the issue of blood arise at the level of intelligibility. Since we do not routinely experience miracles of the kind reported, can we accept the witness of this text? An examination of the deeper dimensions of the text reveals a resolution to that issue. Further the text challenges many of us to revise our understanding of the world and to take account of the divine activity and purposes.

(c) *Does the sermon need to take issue with the witness of the biblical text, doctrine, practice, or situation?* The minister preaches against the text (or some aspect of the text) because it is inappropriate to the gospel, unintelligible, or immoral. The story of the woman with the issue of blood does not suffer from this problem.

(d) *Do I ignore the text or topic?* As indicated previously, the preacher does not need to ignore any text or topic because of its potential problems. Even a text or situation that is inappropriate, unintelligible, or immoral can become the occasion of a positive encounter with the gospel. A preacher may conclude that the context in the congregation is not ripe for an immediate consideration of a text or topic, in which case the pastor and may seek a time when the lines of receptivity are open. Preachers sometimes simply do not notice texts or topics. A preacher would find the story of the woman with the issue of blood easy to overlook because it is sandwiched into the more dramatic narrative of the raising of Jairus' daughter. Some males bypass this text because its central character is female. Although the story is found in all three synoptic Gospels, it appears in the Revised Common Lectionary only in years A (in its Matthew form) and B. Lectionaries have a disproportionately small number of texts with women as the leading characters. By assigning the story twice in the three-year cycle, the RCL does not take maximum advantage of an opportunity to feature a text with a woman in a central role. Does the lectionary unconsciously assign women a secondary place in the community of faith?

19. Formulate a compact summary of the direction of the sermon.

I recommend that a preacher formulate a compact summary of the direction of the sermon. This statement is the contribution of the sermon to the conversation. This statement summarizes the main voice that the sermon will contribute to the conversation in the congregation about the text, doctrine, practice, or personal or social situation that is at the center of the sermon. Such a statement can help the preacher develop the sermon coherently around a unified theme and purpose. It pushes the minister to become very specific about the direction of the sermon. It can help prevent the preacher from bringing material into the sermon that is extraneous and distracting. I frequently hear a sermon containing thematic units that do not relate closely to one another; these singular sermons should be divided into three or four separate messages, each with its own force and purpose. When the sermon is incoherent, the congregation may subtly think that the preacher, the church, and God are incoherent.

Preachers are divided as to whether this summary should be a single sentence that expresses the direction of the sermon, or whether it could be a softer, more general statement, perhaps expressed in as much as a paragraph. I incline toward summarizing the witness of the sermon in a single sentence. Others refer to such a statement as a proposition, the big idea, the theme statement, the thesis statement, unifying theme, controlling idea, or focus statement.[24] Ideas, stories, information, insights, and questions that relate to the sermon-in-a-sentence can be considered for the sermon. Material that does not relate to this sentence can be put in the file for use another Sunday.

The simpler the sermon-in-a-sentence, the more likely it is to help the preacher develop a sermon whose parts all work together. A simple sentence helps the preacher attain a clear perspective on the direction of the sermon. The more complex this sentence becomes, the more complicated and possibly disjointed the sermon is likely to be.

Christian preaching is first and foremost good news about God and God's activity in the world. The sermon in a sentence should usually have God as subject, God's activity as verb, and the result of God's activity as predicate. A verb in the active voice indicates that God is active and assertive, whereas a passive verb often communicates that God is passive. When the sermon calls for a particular human response (thought, feeling, or action), that response can be in the predicate.

Subject	Verb	Predicate
God	Activity of God and our response	Result of God's Activity

Articulating the human action in the predicate reminds the minister and congregation that the response is precisely that, a response to God's gracious initiative, teaching, and call. When we make ourselves and our activity in the subject/verb/predicate of the sermon, we increase the possibility that the sermon might move toward the errors of works-righteousness or moralism.

The preacher will run into urgent occasions when the sermon needs to go directly to what the congregation needs to do. In the face of an immediate moral threat, for instance, the preacher may need to urge the congregation to behave in ways that are consistent with the gospel's call for justice. However, these occasions are few.

Given the congregational analysis developed earlier, I ask the congregation to identify with the bleeding woman. I develop the following sermon in a sentence:

> God restores us to our sense of self and our place in community when we, like the bleeding woman, come into the sphere of Jesus' healing power.

This sermon would explain the meaning of restoration of self and community. It would also need to help us discover how we come into the sphere of Jesus' healing power.

A preacher could develop other foci for the sermon. If the congregation is confused about the identity of Jesus, the pastor might ask them to identify with the disciples, and the sermon could focus on who Jesus is. If the congregation is a club for upper-middle-class executive types, the preacher might ask the congregation to recognize that the church is a community in which the hemorrhaging women of the world are to be welcomed and touched.

By emphasizing the simplicity of the sermon in the sentence, I do mean that the preacher should oversimplify the complexities of the text or topic. A sermon must face into these complications. The sermon-in-a-sentence pushes the preacher to be as clear as possible about what is most important for the sermon to say and do.

Some preachers think that sermon preparation is better served by a more general perspective on where the sermon is going than the sermon-in-a-sentence. Eugene Lowry, who has given considerable thought to the formation of the sermon, notes that theme statements are designed to provide precision of sermonic purpose. This "precision is, of course, required. The question is how to achieve it."[25] A theme statement can propositionalize the sermon to the point that the sermon becomes little more than a report on what we have found out about the theme, with little existential power. Preparing a theme statement early in the process of sermon preparation may too quickly resolve the questions and tensions that are the lifeblood of creativity. "Experienced novelists and other narrative artists are likely to note that they never quite know where the story will go — or should go — until they follow it to the end. We, too, need to maximize our capacity to keep open throughout the sermon process."[26] Lowry consequently recommends that preachers think more generally through a focus statement that summarizes the issues that are at stake in the sermon and of the aim(s) of the sermon with respect to those issues and the turns that the sermon may take.[27]

At this point, the preacher is ready to begin the preparation of the sermon proper. How can the sermon be arranged, and what can go into the sermon, to facilitate the congregation's optimum participation in the preaching conversation? The next section considers these questions.

SECTION FIVE

Putting the Sermon Together

A pastor led a trip to Quebec, where French is the most frequently spoken language, with seventeen high school students from a parish in Ohio. In Quebec, all the young people were in line at a fast-food restaurant that had only one person serving. The pastor was standing at the back of the line when a person from outside the group joined the line. In English, the pastor explained that the youth were taking a long time. After apologizing, the pastor expressed the hope that the restaurant would open another register. When the newcomer did not appear to understand, the minister (who had last spoken French in high school twenty years before) attempted to translate into French. The newcomer responded with a confused look and stepped to a line at a second cash register that was just staffed.

Later, when the group arrived at the Quebec church where they were sleeping, the pastor recounted the incident to the Canadians who hosted them. A bilingual local translated, "These seventeen are my babies. As you can see, we are very strong. We're taking over this restaurant. If you know what's good for you, you'll leave now." No wonder the newcomer at the end of line looked confused.

Sermons sometimes communicate with clarity. At other times, the sermon is similar to the pastor's broken French. Preachers have an idea of the conversation they would like to have with the congregation, but the sermon does not prompt the conversation they intend. Confused, the congregation mentally shifts to another register.

This section considers things the preacher can take into account to help the congregation have a good opportunity to participate in the sermon in a positive way. I focus on factors in the macromovement of the sermon and in its microsections.

A caveat: Even the most careful sermon preparation cannot guarantee that the congregation will participate in the sermon in the way that the minister intends. Members' situations in life often orient them to engage certain themes and images but not others. Indeed, listeners can completely reshape the content of the sermon. For instance, some in the congregation bypass messages with which they disagree. They do not hear what the preacher says. Some in the congregation are predisposed to translate everything the preacher says into confirmation of their own beliefs and practices. Even when the preacher says something that contradicts their values, they do not recognize the contradiction. They may even hear the preacher as confirming their values and actions.[1]

Preachers cannot take responsibility for all that happens in the mind and heart of the congregation. However, preachers are responsible for doing all that they can to help the community have a good opportunity to participate in the sermon. More often than not, such attention will help the congregation engage the gospel.

CHAPTER TEN

Engaging the Congregation in the Sermon

In previous chapters, we considered a process for establishing and developing a direction for the sermon. The preacher now decides how to organize the sermon so that the congregation will have a good opportunity to interact with it. The preacher takes into account the purpose of the sermon, the relationship of the direction of the sermon to the congregation, the occasion, the approaches to communication that seem to help the congregation enter the world of the sermon, the preacher's preferred style of preaching. "How can I say what I need to say to help the congregation converse with the gospel?"

Pastors often develop a preaching style with which they are comfortable. However, ministers need to transcend their styles and to be multivocal. Some styles suit some purposes better than others do. The same style, week after week, can be boring. Members of the congregation have different styles of listening.

This chapter continues the steps enumerated in the previous chapter by exploring how awareness of the congregation's relationship to the direction of the sermon can help the preacher shape the sermon so that it invites people into conversation. The chapter then examines ways in which most sermons move (deductively or inductively). The chapter closes with consideration of beginning and ending the sermon.

20. Assess the relationship of the congregation to the direction of the sermon as developed in steps 14–19.

The preacher will be helped in developing the specific direction of the sermon by considering the congregation's relationship to the direction of the sermon summarized in steps 14–19. How does the congregation think, feel, and act in regard to the witness of the text, doctrine, practice, or situation? The preacher comes to this determination on the basis of priestly listening, through conversation with members in the congregation, through paying attention to the ways in which the issue is perceived in the larger culture. The preacher can tailor the sermon to account for the congregation's predilections. When the direction of the sermon and the congregation's relationship to that witness point the same way, the preacher can build in a direct and positive way on the commonality among them. When the text, gospel, and community, and the sermon run against one another, the preacher may need to help the congregation deal with resistance.

A congregation likely relates to the witness of the text or topic in one of six ways. A congregation may have listeners in more than one of these categories. Some congregations may have members in each of the six. However, most congregations have a center of gravity, a point at which more people gather than any other point.

(a) *The congregation may be informed and enthused about the direction of the sermon.* The preacher can reinforce the congregation's interest and help the community deepen its understanding or draw out implications. For example, a congregation that is aware of the negative effects of legalized gambling may be able to move quickly from that commitment to helping the congregation consider acts of protest against such gambling.

(b) *The congregation may be favorably inclined toward the direction of the sermon, but have an inadequate understanding or experience of the direction of the sermon or may not know how to act in response.* The preacher can build on the goodwill of the congregation toward the direction of the sermon, but needs to help the congregation enlarge its understanding, experience, or behavior. This category names the relationship between congregation and text in many churches in which I have led Bible studies on the story of the woman with the issue of blood. Many people intuitively identify with the woman. They are drawn to the figure by the promise of healing, but they aren't sure quite how — or whether — such healing might take place today. The sermon can help them make sense of the story for today's community.

(c) *The congregation may have a clear understanding or experience of the direction of the sermon, but they may act out of character with it.* The preacher needs to help the congregation realize the discrepancy between its awareness and its actions. What does the congregation need to do in order for its behavior to be consistent with its beliefs and feelings? For instance, many churches are generally in favor of ministry with youth. However, as the average age of membership gets older, few members have contact with youth. Unwittingly, some congregations manifest attitudes and behaviors that alienate today's youth. When developing a sermon on youth ministry in such a setting, the preacher may need to help the congregation become acquainted with youth culture today, with ways in which the congregation's behavior works against the congregation's desire to relate positively to youth, and with approaches to youth ministry that help today's young people positively encounter the gospel.

(d) *The congregation may be apathetic about the direction of the sermon.* These people are not interested in the direction of the sermon. The preacher needs to help the congregation realize why the sermon is important. For instance, an ingrown congregation may have no interest in providing hospital-ity for one another or for those outside the community. The preacher needs to help this church recognize the importance of hospitality.

(e) *The congregation may be unfavorably inclined, even resistant, toward the direction of the sermon as a result of unconscious factors.* This congregation does not consciously choose to resist the direction of the sermon on theological or ideological grounds. They passively inherit dispositions against the direction of the sermon. Frequently, they respond positively if the preacher helps them name their resistance, its source, and its incongruity with the gospel. For ex-ample Psalm 19:7–8 celebrates *torah*, law. "The law of the LORD is perfect, reviving the soul…; the precepts of the LORD are right, rejoicing the heart." Some Christians naively view law in the First Testament as a series of legalisms that one must obey to be accepted by God. These Christians have never considered whether this view of law is accurate. They passively resist *torah* by not paying attention to it. The preacher can help the congregation overcome resistance by helping them name their reservations and discover that *torah* refers to gracious instruction to help the community embody its identity. Obedience to the commandments is not designed to win God's favor, but to express one's identity as a member of the covenant people.

(f) *The congregation may be unfavorably inclined and actively resist the di-rection of the sermon on the basis of consciously considered factors.* This congre-gation resists the direction of the sermon on the basis of deep intellectual, emotional, and moral commitment. The preacher needs to help the congrega-tion critically evaluate its point of view. For instance, the preacher who wishes to advocate universal salvation might encounter profound resistance on the basis of carefully considered biblical, historical, and theological arguments. The preacher who advocates universal salvation needs to help the commu-nity reflect on the inadequacy of its understanding. The arguments and pur-poses would be reversed in the case of the preacher who wishes to advocate limited salvation in a context in which universal salvation is the prevailing viewpoint. The roots of resistance may be so deep and nonrational that the preacher cannot penetrate it in a single sermon. The preacher may be able to engage such resistance only incrementally.

21. Describe how you hope participating in the conversation will affect the congregation in thought, feeling, and will.

The sermon is not usually the last word in a congregation's conversation. However, the sermon can make a significant contribution to the conversation if the sermon is thoughtful, resonant with the feelings of the community, and offers practical suggestions and next steps. The preacher can help maximize the potential participation of the sermon in the conversation by being clear about how the preacher hopes the sermon will enter into conversation with the congregation in thought, feeling, and action.

For purposes of discussion, I suggest that pastors clarify how they hope the congregation will think, feel, and act. Anyone who has had a basic course in psychology knows that the human being is a *gestalt*, a whole. We are not trifurcated into spheres of thought, feeling, and will. A thought can provoke passion. An action can provoke critical reflection. Cold-blooded ideas can lead to dynamic actions. These qualities can be so intertwined that it is impossible to speak about them separately.

(a) *What do I hope the congregation will think as a result of participating in the sermon?* I do not mean that the preacher should try to propagandize the congregation. Quite the contrary, the preacher is called to encourage critical reflection. Toward that end, the sermon may need to help the congregation gain essential information about the text, doctrine, Christian practice, or situation. The sermon should also help the congregation identify key issues that they need to understand in order to think carefully about the sermon. The conversation can also help the congregation think through how to understand those issues in the light of the gospel and the context of the congregation.

In a sermon on the woman with the issue of blood, the congregation needs to receive essential information about the woman and her condition, the figure of Jesus in the Gospel of Mark, the effects of the healing, the effects of the healing on the woman and the community, the role of faith. Who, in our setting, is like the woman with the issue of blood? How do such people and communities encounter the restoring power of Jesus? How can the congregation welcome such people? Can the congregation itself become an agency of restoration?

(b) *What do I hope the congregation will feel?* Feeling includes emotion as well as the larger sense of feeling, that Susanne K. Langer, a contemporary philosopher, describes:

> Human feeling is a fabric, not a vague mass. It has an intricate, dynamic pattern, possible combinations, new emergent phenomena. It is a pattern of organically interdependent and interdetermined tensions and resolutions, a pattern of almost infinitely complex activation and cadence. To it belongs the whole gamut of our sensibility — the sense of straining thought, all mental attitude and motor set. Those are the deeper reaches that underlie the surface waves of our emotion and make human life a life of feeling instead of an unconscious metabolic existence interrupted by feelings.[1]

In this context, feeling "is taken in its broadest sense, meaning, everything that can be felt, from physical sensation, pain and comfort, excitement and response, to the most complex emotions, intellectual tensions, or the steady feeling tones of a conscious human life."[2]

In the story of the woman with the issue of blood, I want the congregation to feel many of the sensory qualities that are described in step 8. I hope the community will feel the situation of the woman at the beginning of the story: unclean, impoverished, desperate, alone. I hope the congregation will feel her intermingled desperation, courage, hope, and fear as she approaches

Jesus. I hope they will feel the healing take place in her body. I hope the congregation will feel her restoration to community and the community's restoration of its own brokenness by her return. I hope the congregation will feel close kinship with Jesus in the title, "Daughter." I hope that the community will feel those points at which they feel unclean, impoverished, desperate, alone. I hope they will feel Jesus' restoring presence. I hope that the congregation can feel faith as openness to the new world embodied in Jesus. I hope they will feel that openness in themselves. I hope the congregation will feel kinship with Jesus and with one another as a community whose healing of hemorrhaging women can witness to God's will for community

(c) *How do I hope the sermon will affect the congregation's will?* Some sermons aim to affect the will by prompting the congregation to a specific behavior. For example, during the stewardship emphasis, a preacher may hope to encourage a congregation to make a pledge to the stewardship campaign. A sermon on justice may call the congregation to march against the death penalty. Other sermons aim to affect the will by prompting the congregation to make a conscious decision about matters of the mind or heart. For example, in many churches, the sermon is followed by a hymn of invitation to Christian discipleship. In that context, the preacher might urge nonChristians to decide to make a confession of faith and to be baptized. The preacher might encourage other believers to reaffirm their faith during the singing of the hymn. For still other sermons, it is enough to prompt the congregation to decide to continue thinking about the subject of the sermon.

One pastor has a very useful exercise that helps with this process. This minister sits in the sanctuary and imagines how the sermon would be received by persons who customarily sit in those seats. How might they be affected in thought, mind, will? This preacher gives special attention to how the sermon might be received by persons who are in tension with the preacher over matters such as theology, visions for the church, personality.

Most individual sermons affect the will modestly. A single sermon usually has an incremental effect in changes of behavior. Over time, the effects of several sermons and considerations of the issue in other contexts in the congregation can help the congregation move toward change. Preachers will save themselves from the constant enervation of thinking that congregations do not respond to their sermons by scaling the pastor's hopes for specific sermons to what they can realistically expect to happen as a result of a single sermon or series. For instance, a preacher can seldom expect an individual sermon to prompt a congregation to repent of sexism and become an inclusive community. A single sermon might help the congregation discover a link between patterns of speech (e.g., referring to God exclusively as "Father") and aspects of sexism.

When preaching on the story of the woman with the issue of blood, I hope that members of the community who are bleeding will decide to acknowledge their brokenness. I hope they will explore ways in which to open themselves to restoration. I hope that other members of the community will resolve to seek and to welcome persons who are like the woman with the flow of blood. I hope that the sermon will provide both groups with practical steps they can take to seek healing and to welcome those in search of healing.

22. Take a time-out to list the questions, issues, perspectives, data, stories, experiences, and other materials that need to be in the sermon for the sermon to serve its purpose.[3]

Once they have decided on a general movement for the sermon (deductive or inductive), many preachers find it helpful to identify the main questions, issues, data, experiences, stories, and perspectives that need to appear in the sermon for the sermon to have an opportunity to fulfill its purpose. These things often develop into blocks of material — a paragraph here, two or three paragraphs there. The preacher can then decide the sequence in which to bring these materials into the sermon (steps 23–26). To use an athletic image, this step is a time-out before running the next play, so that the preacher can be sure all the players are on the field and know what they are to do.

Given the direction of the sermon on the woman with the flow of blood, a preacher would need material in the sermon to help the congregation to:

- grasp differences in perception of miracle in the first century and today

- understand and feel the woman and the effects of the unceasing hemorrhage — personal, social, religious

- recognize Jesus as demonstrating the rule of God in the world of the text and as a continuing presence in our world

- realize the woman's risk and courage in seeking Jesus

- discover the role of faith — the woman's and ours

- name ways in which people in our setting are in situations analogous to that of the woman

- explore ways in which we encounter the cleansing presence of Jesus

- identify risks that people today sometimes take to encounter that presence

- help people to want to experience healing and to take risks necessary for it

- perceive how experience of the presence of Jesus restores people to community, and how community is restored by their return.

In connection with several of these items, I list stories, images, quotations, and thoughts.

To continue the athletic image, the play (sermon) may not develop as planned. The preacher may need to account for changes in the evolution of the sermon.

23. Decide whether the sermon will largely move deductively or inductively.

Sermons typically move in one of two ways: deductively or inductively. In philosophy and logic, these terms are reserved for tightly defined forms of reasoning. In preaching, they refer to patterns of movement. Based on the purposes of the sermon and the congregation's relationship to the direction of the sermon, the preacher decides whether an inductive or deductive approach (or a combination of the two) will have a better chance of helping the sermon generate a conversation in which the people will participate. Chapters 16 and 18 furnish samples of sermons that move deductively. Chapters 17 and 19 contain sermons that model inductive movement.

Deductive movement is from a general premise to application of the premise in specific situations. The preacher reveals the direction of the sermon very early. In the rest of the sermon, the preacher makes deductions. The preacher makes the big point at the beginning of the sermon and then reasons from the big point. The sermon moves from the general truth or claim to particular applications and outcomes. The preacher hangs a banner at the beginning of the sermon announcing what the people will find in that sermon. Then, as if on a street, preacher and congregation walk down the street, looking at the shops along the way. You tell them what you're going to tell them.

The very first part of the sermon usually focuses the congregation's attention on the subject of the sermon. The preacher then states the direction of the sermon (from step 19 in the previous chapter). Beginning a sermon on the story of the woman with the issue of blood, the preacher might focus the congregation's attention on social and religious significance of the transformation of the woman from the beginning of the sermon to the end. The deductive preacher might say, "In one way or another, many of us feel like that woman — unclean, alone, out of relationship. But according to that story, Jesus makes us clean, and restores us for relationships and community. I want to explore how we, too, can encounter Jesus' regenerating power."

After the opening summary, the deductive sermon can go in many directions. The preacher could offer *reasons* for why the big point is true. The preacher might *apply* the big point to different spheres of life: individual, congregation, city, and world. The minister could *apply* the general claim of the sermon to different kinds of individuals, households, or communities. The body of the sermon might draw out *implications* of the big idea. The pastor can *enumerate lessons* that the congregation can learn. The preacher could *illustrate* the big point as it applies to the listeners. For instance, in a sermon on the story of the woman with the hemorrhage, the preacher might help the congregation discover different ways in which members of the church encounter Jesus' transforming power.

Clarity is a strength of deductive preaching. People have an optimum opportunity to get the point. The deductive sermon tends to be systematic, thus helping both the preacher and the congregation to organize and process material straightforwardly. Deductive preaching communicates security to the community since, from the start, the community knows where the sermon is headed. When listeners determine that the sermon is important to them, they immediately commit themselves to following the sermon.

The deductive pattern is particularly useful when the congregation has a friendly predisposition toward the direction of the sermon. The sermon can join the positive feeling of the congregation and help the congregation deepen or extend it. Deductive preaching can also serve occasions when an issue is burning in the congregation's heart, and the community is ready for direct talk about the issue in the sermon. Deductive approaches can be helpful when the community needs to know specifically what it can believe or do. Deductive preaching particularly suits linear thinkers.

The deductive sermon can have disadvantages. The deductive structure can be distant from life experience. It can artificially impose order and logic upon situations that are complex and ambiguous and that cannot be neatly resolved by simple deduction. Some critics of deductive preaching notice that deduction is only secondarily the means by which we learn. When our seven-year old-daughter arrives at a playground, she tries all the equipment and then decides which piece she likes best. The preacher makes the primary discovery and hands it over to the congregation, thus depriving people of coming to insight on their own. Many years ago, I heard deductive preaching described as predigested protein. The sermon is nutritious, but the congregation is deprived of the tastes, textures, and joys of eating the meal. Why do we need to think? The preacher does it for us.

Deductive movement may not serve the preaching event when the sermon needs to move against the grain of the congregation's thinking, feeling, or action. If the preacher challenges the congregation in the first moments of the sermon, many community members may become so alienated that they stop listening. Deductive preaching can be rigid and hierarchical. By giving the impression that the premise of the sermon is the last word on a text or topic, the sermon can work against real conversation. Indeed, deductive messages can frustrate the mood of egalitarianism and the search for authority emerging from community conversation that is characteristic of our time.

The deductive sermon can be boring. The congregation knows where the sermon is going in the first three minutes. Why, then, continue to listen?

None of these disadvantages inhere in all deductive preaching. A deductive preacher who is enthusiastic about the subject of the sermon and dialogical in spirit can infuse a deductive pattern with energy. A strong deductive sermon can be a conversation-opener in the community.

Inductive movement begins with particulars of life experience, biblical texts, doctrines, practices, or situations, and moves to a general reflection or statement. The preacher begins with issues and questions that are raised but unresolved. The preacher works through those issues and questions with the help of biblical exegesis, historical and theological analysis, data from the social sciences, artistic insight, reflection upon life experience. Toward the end of the sermon, the preacher reaches a conclusion. No banner hangs over the beginning of the message, announcing what people will find. Instead, preacher and community walk together, as if down a street — identifying issues, stopping at shops, talking with people in a restaurant, pausing in the bookstore to thumb through some magazines that explain the history and features of the street. By the end of the walk, the community has a sense of life on that street. Because they have experienced that street, they can decide whether they want to visit it again or even move into it.

In a sermon on the story of the woman with the issue of blood, the preacher might begin by helping the community recall situations in which contemporary people feel unclean. Along the way, the preacher needs to help us encounter the renewing power of Jesus and experience the transition from uncleanness to cleanness.

Inductive preaching can be used in connection with almost any occasion, text, doctrine, practice, or situation. Inductive sermons are helpful when the subject of a sermon is sensitive, complicated, or ambiguous. This approach allows the preacher to describe the complications and ambiguities in their fullness and to honor their integrity before reaching a conclusion about them. The inductive sermon can help the listeners deepen their experience of a text, doctrine, or practice. When a congregation is apathetic toward the direction of a sermon, an inductive approach can often help focus attention and raise interest. The preacher does not hand the congregation a glass of predigested protein for supper. Instead, the community gathers in the kitchen, makes the salad, peels the onions, cooks the potatoes, bakes the cake, sets the table, lights the candles, and eats together.

Inductive movement is useful when the preacher must challenge a congregation's thinking, emotions, or behavior. Rather than beginning by calling the congregation into question, the sermon helps the congregation discover thoughts and experiences that test the adequacy of the congregation's perception. Instead of being instantaneously inflamed, they have an opportunity to grow into awareness of the need for change.

Inductive movement is participatory by nature. In the expressive phrase of Fred Craddock (who helped the pulpit rediscover inductive movement), the congregation takes the journey of discovery with the preacher.[4] Because the journey is their journey, the congregation is thus likely to own the conclusions of the sermon. Inductive sermons, with their emphasis on communality in preaching are likely to be egalitarian. An inductive sermon can incorporate multiple voices into a congregation's conversation about a text, doctrine, practice, or situation. When necessary, the inductive sermon can be as systematic as the deductive sermon. Because it withholds the conclusion until the end of the sermon, inductive preaching is prone to build suspense and, hence, to hold the attention of the congregation. When caught in an unresolved tension, human beings have a propensity to want to experience resolution of the tension.

Inductive preaching requires great discipline on the part of the preacher to keep the sermon focused and moving in a single direction. I have heard some inductive sermons whose movement is stream of consciousness. In the end, I could not identify the subject of the sermon much less its witness. Furthermore, a congregation may not need to take a journey into a particular text, doctrine, practice, or topic. A congregation may need for the subject of a particular sermon to, explained as directly as possible.

Many sermons *combine both inductive and deductive* patterns. A sermon might begin inductively. In the first half of the sermon, the preacher moves to a conclusion. In the second half of the sermon the preacher makes deductions from that conclusion. Or, within a deductive sermon, a preacher might employ inductive movement in order to develop a sub-point. Preachers can combine these approaches by announcing at the beginning what the sermon is about, but withholding the conclusion until the end. For instance, in a sermon about the story of the woman with the issue of blood, the preacher might tell the congregation at the beginning that the narrative is about being unclean and clean, but reveal later how the story helps us move from feeling unclean to feeling clean.

24. Arrange the main questions, issues, resources, explanations, and data in a sequence that serves the purposes of the sermon and the relationship of the congregation to the direction of the sermon.

Many preachers find it helpful to have a sense of how to relate the various blocks of material in the sermon to one another so as to help the sermon accomplish its purpose in the congregational conversation. The pastor who makes such an arrangement has a prefiguration of where the preparation is going to be open road and where the preacher is likely to encounter construction delays. It helps the preacher gauge how much time is likely to be needed in different parts of the sermon. It helps the preacher get a sense of the intellectual and emotional rhythm of the sermon — where to tell a story, where to add a little humor, when a pause might be needed.

Most preachers create a fresh pattern of movement for each sermon. However, preachers sometimes get help by considering stock patterns of arrangement that have worked well for other preachers. Chapter 11 provides examples of standard arrangements.

In an earlier generation, preaching textbooks exhorted students to outline the sermon using the formal characteristics of outlining:

I. Major division

   A. Major subdivision

      1. Minor subdivision

      2. Minor subdivision

   B. Major subdivision

      1. Minor subdivision

      2. Minor subdivision

II. Major division

This pattern works for some preachers and some sermons, but not for all. Some preachers do not think in such categories. Many subjects do not fall into a neat, linear structure.

Another approach is prompted by a floral analogy: A preacher is much like the gardener who cuts an armload of daisies, roses, lilacs, and zinnias. The preacher spreads them on a table and tries them in different combinations to see which combination creates the best arrangement for the place where they will be displayed. I sometimes put a word or phrase describing each subsection of material going into the sermon on a notecard. I then move the cards around to get a sense of how the sermon moves, feels, and thinks when the blocks of material are arranged in different sequences. This process nearly always causes fresh material (especially stories) to come to mind.

A similar analogy is provoked from the world of painting. A preacher is like an artist who tries different colors in different relationships with one another on a canvas. Which configurations bring the eyes to see what the artist hopes the viewer will see?

I know a preacher who actually draws a map of where the sermon starts, goes, and ends. The map indicates the major roadways, towns, landmarks, and turns, but does not detail every hill, curve, run-down barn, or surprising vista.

David Buttrick, a major thinker about preaching, writes of the sermon having a plot.[5] Like a story, a sermon begins, travels from one episode to another, and ends. The preacher decides where to begin, which episodes to tell, and how to end. The pastor selects a point of view from which the congregation will hear the sermon. The preacher may draw on stock repertoires, but they are always shaped according to what the sermon is intended to do.

In *Writing on Both Sides of the Brain*, Henriette Anne Klauser (who studies human creativity) notes that many people do not think in linear flow but in terms of a trunk and branches. We think of a trunk — a central theme, idea, image, or feeling — and of how other material branches into and out of this central notion.[6] The result is a physical image that has an organic character, rather like a tree. For example, in preparation for a sermon on the doctrine of stewardship, a preacher might put together something like the following:

When such an exercise is completed, the preacher puts the various parts of the organic image into an oral sequence so that the sermon manifests the organic quality of the image.

A minister who is not a linear thinker told me about a child bringing home a "mind map" from school that helped the minister with this phase of sermon development. The preacher begins by putting the subject in a bubble in the middle of a piece of paper then puts subdivisions of the subject, questions, issues, resources in other bubbles connected to the main bubble and to one another. In a sermon on violence in the schools, the bubbles might appear as follows:

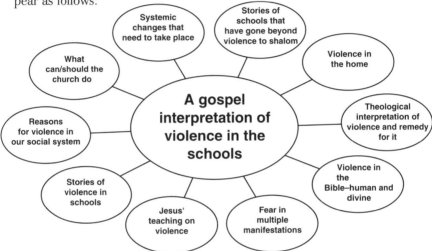

The preacher must then translate this atom-like diagram into a pattern of movement for the sermon.

A preacher might sketch line drawings of different parts of the sermon and set the drawings in different relationship with one another. The sermon is a gallery of pictures which preacher and congregation see together.

A musician might imagine the sermon as a series of musical themes and phrases. Different kinds of music create very different effects. Is a particular sermon a symphony? If so, the pieces relate to one another like the parts of a symphony. Is it a folksong? a rap? a piece of music from another culture?

As a jogger, I sometimes imagine the sermon as a jog that the preacher and congregation take together. "Now, what happens if we start one direction…these people are on the sidewalks…these yards and stores and school and playground…. What happens if we take another route that has a different character?"

25. Decide how to begin the sermon.

When the preacher steps into the pulpit to begin the sermon you can often feel the congregation's anticipation. You can see people shifting their attention. They put their hymnals away. They move in the pews to get a clear line of sight. They relax. They pass gum to the children. A hush settles over the sanctuary. No matter how many times they have been disappointed by sermons, they approach each new sermon hoping that it will help them interpret the world in a meaningful way.

A good beginning can help the congregation enter into the conversation in a way that facilitates the congregation's participation. A poor beginning can create a mood in the congregation of indifference, disappointment, or anger. The preacher has a few minutes at the beginning of the sermon to help the listeners want to join the conversation. However, we should not place too much stress on the importance of the beginning. Listeners sometimes check in and out of sermons.

At one time, preaching textbooks referred to the beginning of the sermon as the Introduction. The Introduction was a formal part of the sermon whose purpose was to arrest the attention of the congregation and introduce the subject matter of the sermon. Deductive preachers often used the Introduction to preview the sermon.

In more recent years, we have come to think of the first part of the sermon as less a formal Introduction, and more as a beginning. Since the congregation is almost innately attentive at the beginning of the sermon, the preacher does not need to arrest attention so much as to help the community focus attention to the subject of the sermon. The purpose of the beginning is to help the congregation join the conversation of the sermon.

The beginning of each sermon is particular to each sermon and is suggested by the character and purpose of that sermon. A few sermons will be well served by an opening section that previews the unfolding of the sermon, step by step. Most sermons will be served by beginnings that are less predictive and more suggestive. Some sermons call for beginnings that bring cheerleaders into the chancel as the body of the sermon comes onto the floor. Other sermons begin more quietly. Some sermons need to begin by evoking feeling, while others begin with a more detached consideration of issues.

What are some ways to begin? Common starting points include:

- telling a story from the life of the preacher or from the life of the congregation
- referring to an aspect of the Christian year
- referring to something that has happened earlier in the service
- retelling a scene from a novel, a movie, a play, or a television program
- telling a story that the preacher (or others in the community) has created
- offering an imaginative elaboration of the biblical text
- quickly summarizing the biblical text and raising a question about it, or pointing out incongruities within it, or posing an issue that it raises for us
- reading out loud a report from a newspaper, magazine, or electronic media
- describing a painting, dance, sculpture, or other art work
- recalling a situation that introduces the concern of the sermon

- creating images that lead the congregation toward the focus of the sermon
- recounting an incident in which a Christian practice takes place
- bringing forward a congregational memory or hope
- reconstructing the historical setting of a book of the Bible
- summarizing data that raise the issue with which the sermon is concerned
- providing a provocative quote from a classical or contemporary theologian or other source

As I have said in connection with several other aspects of sermon preparation, there are as many ways of beginning a sermon as there are sermons.

Most sermons begin with one of two foci. The preacher might begin by talking about contemporary experience, then moving to the text, doctrine, or practice that is at the center of the sermon. For example, in a sermon entitled "Praying through Clenched Teeth," Fred Craddock, who preaches widely in congregations, denominational meetings, and seminaries, begins a sermon with a series of contemporary images.

> I am going to say a word, and the moment I say the word, I want you to see a face, to recall a face, and a name, someone who comes to your mind when I say the word. Are you ready? The word is "bitter." Bitter. Do you see a face? I see a face. I see the face of a farmer in western Oklahoma, riding a mortgaged tractor, burning gasoline purchased on credit, moving across rented land, rearranging the dust. Bitter.

> Do you see a face? I see the face of a woman forty-seven years old. She sits out on a hillside, drawn and confused under a green canopy furnished by the mortuary. She is banked on all sides by flowers sprinkled with cards: "You have our condolences." Bitter.[7]

Craddock evokes several more images: a small-town grocer whose store is closed by the coming of a large chain supermarket, a young couple being separated by military service, a young minister who has been gratuitously given a used television set by a member in the congregation when the member purchased a new set. Craddock then connects these images with the biblical text, Paul's theologizing about his call in Galatians 1:11–24.

> Will you look at one other face? His name is Saul, Saul of Tarsus. We call him Paul. He was young and intelligent, committed to the traditions…strong and zealous for his nation.[8]

Paul is bitter about the coming of the Gentiles to the God of Israel without first becoming Jewish. The sermon explores this bitterness, and its transformation by Paul's call as apostle to the gentiles. The preacher explores how God's grace can touch our bitterness. For other examples of beginning with contemporary experiences, see the beginning of René Rodgers Jensen's sermon on page 281, in which she opens the sermon by describing a television program that she has seen. Reginald Holmes commences his sermon by referring to experiences that were common in the childhood years of many in the congregation (page 288).

Another focus for beginning is to talk immediately about the biblical text, doctrine, or practice that is at the heart of the sermon. Barbara Brown Taylor, an Episcopal priest known for her preaching, begins a sermon in this fashion on the story of the person who came to Jesus with the question, "Good Teacher, what must I do to inherit eternal life?" (Mark 10:17–27).

> Most of us know this story as the story of the rich young ruler, although Mark is the only one who suggests he is rich, Matthew is the only one who says he is young, and Luke is the only one who calls him a ruler. The fact that he shows up in all three of these gospels is a pretty good indication that the story is true, although most of us wish that he had never shown up at all. Because of him, we have one of the hardest sayings in the whole Bible, one that strikes fear in the hearts of would-be Christians everywhere: "Go, sell what you own, and give the money to the poor, and you will have treasure in heaven; then come, follow me."[9]

This beginning helps the congregation focus on the particularity of Mark's version of the story. It names uneasiness with this story and suggests the importance of the sermon to the congregation. The sermon wrestles with the relationship of money and discipleship. Of course, this beginning presumes a congregation that is acquainted with the Bible.

Mary Donovan Turner also begins her sermon in chapter 17 by referring directly to the biblical setting (page 276). By making use of a video motif in connection with the Bible, she helps us begin immediately to weave the biblical and contemporary worlds.

In a sermon on Ruth and on Jesus' admonition to "give . . . to the emperor the things that are the emperor's, and to God the things that are God's" (Matthew 22:15–22), Rita Nakashima Brock, a leading theologian, encourages the congregation to challenge principalities and powers. The sermon begins by inviting the congregation into a familiar and secure world, then asking the congregation to view that world from a different point of view.

> There was once an ordinary woman who lived in a small town near Modesto, California. She was not famous, powerful, or influential. I do not recall her name. I was told this true story about her. She was the kind of person we'd call a good neighbor. She was friendly, liked by her neighbors, and was good to her family. When the United States entered the Second World War, she supported our government — until California Supreme Court Justice Earl Warren signed an order requiring all U.S. citizens of Japanese ancestry to be interned in relocation camps.[10]

As the sermon develops, we learn that this woman challenged the government's internment of Japanese Americans. She is kin to Ruth in that, like the biblical character, she is an ordinary woman who went against the grain of convention to protest injustice and to witness to justice. The sermon helps us envision how we can do the same.

I. Carter Heyward, who is a pioneer in feminist theology, begins a sermon on the doctrine of God in a direct way:

> We are told that upon completion of "The Hallelujah Chorus," Handel fell to his knees, beside himself, overwhelmed because he had seen God — and the *beauty*, the *power*, the *majesty* of God were extraordinary.
>
> Elie Wiesel, incarcerated in a concentration camp during World War II, tells of having watched a young boy his age (about ten) being hanged by the Nazi solders As the boy writhed in agony, refusing to give in to the rope, one of the witnesses asked one another, "Where is God?" The response was silence. The boy continued to struggle, and the [person] asked again, "Where is God?" Still silence. Finally, as the boy succumbed, the [person] asked again, "Where is God?" And [a] fellow prisoner replied, "God is there. Hanging on the gallows." Wiesel speaks of the *utterly helpless* God.
>
> What of this God, this terrible good, this holy terror, this Father, Son, and Holy Spirit Trinity? This Mother Goddess giving us birth and taking us back again into her womb the earth? This God of many faces, to whom have been ascribed many name? *Who is our God?*[11]

The sermon explores the main lines of a doctrine of God that takes into account both the awesomeness and the apparent helplessness of God.

When a pastor is preaching a series of sermons, the beginning of the sermon sometimes needs only to help the community place this particular sermon in the series, as Gardner Taylor, one of the most well known and respected preachers in North America, does in a sermon preached as a part of a series that traces Jesus' last days.

> Some of you have traveled during these Sundays of Lent the whole journey on the Road to Calvary. We witnessed the nighttime betrayal in Gethsemane: the place of angels' ministry and [human] betrayal. We watched Him refusing to answer the shallow and degraded King, Herod, during His trial and we heard His gentle rebuke to some women whose sorrow was not deep enough as He trudged toward death. We came at last to Calvary, the great divide of God's amazing grace, and there under the darkening sky and above the trembling earth our hearts melted as the dying Savior and the dying thief found each other and the poor thief began the long procession of those redeemed by Calvary's death.

Now on Palm Sunday, we see Him, our Lord, at Calvary. We seek to know something of the meaning of the two final words He spoke as He came to the end of His days in the flesh.[12]

In the first paragraph, the preacher narrates us into the previous contexts. "*We* witnessed the nighttime betrayal.... *We* watched Him refusing to answer.... *We* came at last." In the second paragraph, the preacher suggests how this sermon will fit in the series.

I notice several ways that beginnings sometimes falter. For one, some beginnings are so emotionally gripping that they overpower the rest of the sermon. For instance, a student began a sermon with the poignant story of the death of a young relative. The preacher then began to talk about the biblical text. However, the story was so anguishing that the class was unable to leave the story and to engage the text. If such a story serves the purpose of the sermon, it should come later, perhaps even toward the end. The body of the sermon would provide an interpretive framework within which to hear the story.

Some sermons start too abruptly. Many preachers like to begin with a sentence that plops us into the middle of a scene. "She looked tired that day." I do not know the woman. I do not know where she is located or why she is tired. I waste energy and attention on those questions rather than entering into the world of the sermon proper. It would help me for the preacher to say, "I once talked with a teacher on the playground at the end of an August day when the temperature reached 102 degrees. She looked tired."

For another difficulty, some preachers, in the hope of winning the congregation's attention, use their most interesting material at the beginning. A preacher might tell a good story. However, the rest of the sermon is abstract and dull. The beginning suggests that the sermon will be more promising than it is. When this pattern recurs weekly, the congregation's level of engagement takes a downturn when the preacher finishes the beginning of the sermon. The preacher can presume the congregation's attentiveness at the start. The preacher can save the story to help bring alive later parts of the sermon.

For still another problem, some beginnings are dull. The preacher provides information about the biblical text, doctrine, practice, or situation in a boring way and without suggesting its importance. The sermon begins like a disembodied history lesson or social science report. As Harry Emerson Fosdick (a well-known preacher in the first half of the twentieth century) put it, "No one comes to church because they are interested in the Jebusites."[13] However, information about the Jebusites can be a positive beginning to a sermon when it is presented in an interesting way, with energy, and with an eye toward how it can help the congregation participate in the conversation.

26. If possible, decide how to end the sermon.

Preaching textbooks once described the end of the sermon as a Conclusion. However, this designation does not fit. The term Conclusion suggests that the work of the sermon is finished. Of course, the preacher must stop talking. However, the preacher hopes that the conversation will continue in the hearts, minds, and behaviors of the congregation. The end of the sermon is not as much a conclusion as it is a transition in the mode of the conversation from the preacher speaking as representative of the community to the members of the community conversing within themselves and with one another.

Endings that accomplish this purpose are usually open-ended. They leave the congregation with things to process — thoughts, feelings, possibilities for behavior.

The best endings usually have an underlying character of good news. The gospel is gospel precisely because it offers the dual promises of God's unconditional love and of God's unremitting will for justice. Regardless of the difficulty of issues faced in the sermon, the preacher is normally called, by the end of the message, to help the congregation envision the degree of promise that the gospel offers the community.

Some preachers reply that a sermon is not required to leave the community with a sense of good news, since other parts of the service bring the gospel to expression. I understand this point of view, but I urge caution. Other parts of the service have their own functions (e.g., leading the community to affirm its faith, talk with God, receive signs of assurance of God's love). The sermon is specifically designed to help the congregation reflect on its subject matter from the perspective of the gospel. Other parts of the service cannot always help the community with this task. Of course, some sermons can end in such a way that an affirmation of faith, or a time of prayer, or the Lord's supper allows the gospel to come to expression in a way that satisfies the need of the sermon.

The means of ending are much the same, though different in focus, as the ways of beginning (see pages 164–169). A preacher could spin a vision of a how a situation can be different as people respond to the gospel. A poem could end the sermon. As long as the preacher is lively, the sermon could end with a summary of the main points and an indication of where they might lead. A sermon might leave a congregation with a question to consider. If so, the question needs to be a real issue with which the congregation needs to wrestle and not a rhetorical question to which the congregation already has the answer. The former encourages interaction with the sermon; the latter closes the window to such interaction because the community can quickly answer the question.

Many preachers find it helpful to have a clear view of the end of the sermon when they are beginning the detailed work of putting the pieces of the sermon together. A clear sense of ending helps them know how to arrange the rest of the sermon so as to get to the desired stopping point. Similar to having a map on a trip, if you can see your destination and your present location, you can plot a route.

However, such forethought is not always possible. The preparation of the sermon may lead the preacher in another direction. The ending may distract the preacher from being open to other possibilities for the sermon and its ending. I know a preacher who had a story that the preacher wanted to tell, and so, in order to tell the story, created a sermon that didn't quite fit the congregation, the biblical text, or the story itself.

As noted in chapter 3, the sermon does not stand alone, but is woven into the liturgy. The ending of the sermon can often help the sermon do its part in the service by helping the congregation move toward the next things that happen in the service, e.g., a hymn, an affirmation of faith, the prayers of the community, the offering, the Lord's supper. These parts of the service can often take part in the conversation of which the sermon is a part by helping the community affirm what they believe in song or in a statement of faith, talk with God in prayer about matters raised in the sermon, sit in silence to reflect on issues raised in the sermon, receive the assurance of God's presence.

Charles R. Blaisdell, a minister in northern California, begins a sermon on the vision of the cosmic Christ in Revelation 1:12–18 by describing the breathtaking view of Manhattan from an airplane on a crisp Thanksgiving Day. On the ground, the breathtaking vista gives way to the low-level reality of "burned-out tenements, and graffiti-covered commuter trains, and the junkyards of abandoned cars, and the winos huddling over steam grates." The preacher uses this contrast to help us enter the contrast in the book of Revelation between the breathtaking world of the cosmic Christ and the everyday world of suffering. With poignancy, Blaisdell names the difficulties of living on street level and sensitively helps us see how the God of the breathtaking airborne vision moves at street level. The sermon ends concretely.

> And so I got off that plane at La Guardia Airport, and I took a cab to my friends' house where seven of us, old friends from high school and college, celebrated Thanksgiving. At the meal we asked my friend Bob to say grace. Now I must warn you that Bob's prayers can be rather, shall we say, eccentric, and yet always to the point. And this prayer was no exception, for Bob bowed his head and offered the following by way of saying grace: "I look around this table," Bob said, "and I think of similar gatherings in the past, and what has happened to each of us over the years. I see separations, divorce, new jobs, bitter leave-takings, a marriage ended by death, lives turned upside down. And yet," he continued, "my prayer is this: I raise my glass to toast us and to toast God — for like the country ham that we have tried to overcook today, and yet which has surprised us with its resilience and with its ability to taste good no matter what we have inflicted on it, we too, with God's help, have not only endured but we have prevailed. We have been brought back together in hope and in power and in new life by the one whose power shall never fail us."
>
> And Bob said, "Amen," and I said, "Amen," and we all said, "Amen." For Bob was right on that Thanksgiving Day — for each of us *had* seen, just as John had seen, just as each of you has seen, God standing there in the middle of our lives, standing there among *our* lampstands, keeping those lamps from burning out — and kindling

them, in fact, to burn even more brightly in the rich air of new beginnings, fueled with the vision that life can be lived beautifully. And not just from the aerial view, but even from the street level.[14]

The community experiences God's provision by participating in the story. The ending implicitly encourages participants to name ways in which God is provident.

I take a similar approach to my sermon in Chapter 16, devoting the last 15 percent of the sermon to a story and ending with a brief remark (pages 266–267). René Rodgers Jensen ends her message (page 285) with a moving personal story.

In a Mother's Day sermon, William Watley, pastor of St. James A.M.E. Church in Newark, New Jersey, recognizes the importance of the holiday in the culture while using it to help the congregation reflect on their discipleship. The members of the congregation can honor their mothers by living so as to show the effects of the mothers' "labor, love, prayer, teaching, and sacrifices."

> Whether honoring a mother living or dead, we can give a gift that counts. We can give the gift of a life that counts: a life that has been set free by Jesus and surrendered to his will; a life that has found its way back to the church where it was nurtured; a life that's determined not to let Satan and sin be in control; a life that says, "If the Lord wants somebody, here am I, send me. I'll go!" We can give a life that says to living mothers, "Hold your head up. Everything's going to be all right." We can give a life that says to mothers who have gone home to glory, "Sleep on and take your rest, for your living has not been in vain."[15]

The preacher casts traditional Mother's Day activities in a gospel perspective.

> Give a gift that counts. Give fruits of repentance. Give flowers of a life that is abloom with God's grace, Jesus' love, and the Holy Spirit's comfort. Send a greeting that says your name has been recorded in the Lamb's book of life. Give a gift that counts. Come back home, not only to a mother's embrace, but to God's mercy, Jesus' salvation, and the Holy Spirit's anointing.[16]

Once in a while, a preacher can introduce a theme or an image early in the sermon, and return to it at the end. When such connection is artfully done, the ending of the sermon can evoke powerful themes from earlier in the message. In a sermon on Romans 9:1–5, Fred Craddock finds that some of Paul's contemporaries accused him of becoming so caught up in the Gentile mission that he failed to care for his own Jewish people. Craddock recounts a conversation with a woman, a longtime member of the congregation, taking off her choir robe, who says, "I think I'll just hang it up and quit....I sat in the choir loft this morning, and I just looked around at the minister, and the ushers, and the elders and deacons, and all the people sitting out there. I finally said to myself what I've been thinking for years." Craddock asks, "What's that?" She replies, "Who cares?" If what she said is true, the congregation is not a church. "Caring for people is not just feeling bad about the human condition." Caring is making "a difference in somebody's life. It can be a call, a card, a visit....On that count, Paul cared."

> Centuries ago, when I was in college in General Psychology class...the textbook described an experiment. It sounds cruel to me now. In the experiment, there was a long box, a cage, in which a rat was put. In the center of the cage was an electric grill. On the other end of the cage were the young of the mother rat....The experimenter gradually increased the voltage in the grill between the mother and her young. The mother rat went to her young. She was put back. The voltage was increased. She went to her young. The voltage was increased....They watched her burn herself to death to get to her young. And the conclusion: the maternal instinct in the rat is painfully self-sacrificing.

> Paul said, "Put me here [Craddock pauses, taps the pulpit]...put the Jewish people there [tapping]...and put hell in between [tapping]." [Craddock pauses again, with the implication that Paul, like the mother rat, would cross hell for his people]. And somebody said, "He doesn't care." Like that woman at our church, "*Who cares*? Nobody cares if I'm up there in choir loft or not. Nobody ever pays any attention to me." I said to her, "You're wrong." I knew she was wrong.

> I was not surprised by her question. I've heard that comment ever since I was a youngster. My father used to say that. When the pastor would come from my mother's church to call on him, my father would say, "You don't care about me. I know how churches are. You want another name, another pledge. Isn't that the whole point of church?"...I guess I heard it a thousand times.

> One time my father didn't say it. He was in the Veteran's Hospital. He was down to 74 pounds. They had taken out his throat, put down a metal tube...cancer. I went to see him. In every window — potted plants and flowers. In every place you could sit them — potted plants and flowers. There was, by his bed, a stack of cards 10 inches deep. I read the cards, and I want to tell you that every card, every blossom, every potted plant came from Sunday school classes, women's groups, the youth group, Men's Bible Class...of my mother's church.

> My father saw me reading them. He could not speak, but he took a Kleenex box and wrote something on the side from Shakespeare's 'Hamlet:' "In this harsh world, draw your breath in pain to tell my story." I said, "What is your story, Daddy." And he wrote, "I was wrong."

That's what I said to that lady. I said, "You're wrong. I have a chance to visit churches all over the country. I know churches have their problems. There are some people who don't care, and who keep their distance, and don't give. But everywhere I go, there are people who care." She says, "I don't believe it." I said, "There really are." She said, "Really?" And I said, "Really." She said, "Name some."

She wants names. May I give her yours? May I use your name?[17]

This ending encourages the congregation to want to express care that makes a difference in the lives of people. Every time I hear this sermon on audiotape, I am moved to ask, "How can I express care for the persons in my world, and beyond?"

When the sermon is followed by the Lord's supper, the preacher can often make reference to the sacred meal in the latter stages of the sermon to help the sermon takes its part in the liturgy and to help deepen the congregation's participation in the Supper. Barbara Brown Taylor ends a sermon on "Surviving Eden" in this way. The sermon retells Genesis 3 as the story of sin that results in a world that is no longer a paradise but is "full of chips and dents and scars." In the midst of the broken world, according to legend, God taught Adam and Eve how to sew so that they could cover their nakedness. After making clothes, they built an altar, and began to use the pieces of their "broken past" in order to make "a future for themselves and their descendents."

That is our story, a story with everything human in it — promise, failure, blame, guilt, forgiveness, healing, hope — a story about us and a story about our God, who did not create us just once but goes on creating us forever, putting our pieces back together so that we are never ruined, never entirely, and never for good.

Whenever the people of God gather around an altar to be fed, they do roughly the same thing. First they hear the biblical story — their story — and then they pray, and then someone holds up the bread — the round, whole, perfect symbol of God's presence among us. Then, at the very crescendo of the service, the person holding the bread breaks it into pieces, reminding us that our wholeness does not lie behind us but ahead of us, in the company of the Lord who made us, who feeds us and clothes us, and who dwells among us this side of Eden until he can bring us home.[18]

The ending ties the experience of the world as a broken Eden to the eschatological experience of the Lord's supper. The supper then becomes a source of power for the community not only to survive Eden but to witness to the transformation of the world.

The preacher faces a special situation in congregations in which the sermon is followed by an invitation to make a confession of faith and to be baptized. The invitation is usually accompanied by the singing of an invitational hymn during which respondents make their way to the front of the sanctuary. Some churches also invite persons to come forward for recommit-ment of faith, for prayers, for healing, and for the receipt of the Holy Spirit. Many churches invite persons to transfer the record of their congregational membership to the community. If the invitation comes as a natural outgrowth of the sermon, the preacher can end the sermon with the invitation. Other sermons call for a decision on the part of Christians who are established members of the community. On such Sundays, the preacher could invite the congregation to reflect on the decisions that it needs to make during the singing of the hymn. However, not all sermons lead in a natural way to invita-tions to discipleship. Consequently, the preacher might end the sermon, pause, and then offer the invitation. This latter pattern is often facilitated if the preacher ends the sermon in the pulpit and then moves to the chancel steps to offer the invitation.

I notice difficulties that are common to the endings of many sermons. One of the most frequent is a boring ending. The preacher simply rehashes the main themes of the sermon. A preacher who ends the sermon with a summary needs to make it lively.

Another problem is a preacher's tendency to talk too long. Some preach-ers, evidently thinking that the congregation has not gotten the message, re-peat the main themes of the sermon again and again. Many in the congregation become weary and long for the sermon to end. Some are in-sulted. "Doesn't the preacher think we have any intelligence?" Endings are usually best when they are lean.

Preachers sometimes end the sermon with a prayer. A prayer can be quite a satisfactory ending when the prayer is a real prayer in which the preacher represents the congregation before God. Pastors abuse this practice and distort the purposes of Christian prayer when they use the prayer to restate the ideas that they want the congregation to get from the sermon or harangue the congregation to take a specific course of action. Indeed, a pastor can manipulate the congregation by invoking divine approval on the sermon, closing conversation. It betrays a mistrust of the conversation that takes place in the sermon.

Some sermons end on an altogether negative note. The sermon may describe a problem, but not suggest an adequate response. The sermon may leave people under judgment, even condemned. Students who take the latter tack often justify their approach on the basis that the biblical text — usually an oracle of judgment — does not contain hope. While a promissory word may not be in the passage, most oracles of judgment presume that repentance can lead to renewal. The oracle of salvation typically supersedes the oracle of judgment. However, as I noted above, the preacher may come upon a text or occasion that calls for such a sermon, with the word of renewal coming to expression in the affirmation of faith, the common prayers, or in the breaking of the bread.

Some sermons end abstractly. The preacher does not help the congrega-tion relate the sermon to the situation. As I write, I have come from a Martin Luther King, Jr. Day service. Standing on the gospel's call to justice, the preacher exhorted us to end insidious forms of racism that have taken root since Dr. King's assassination. But the sermon did not help us envision practical steps we can take to witness against racism. I am left with a responsibility, but I am frustrated by not knowing how to fulfill it.

Some preachers end their sermons by pronouncing the word "Amen." I discourage this practice. This practice often works against one of the main purposes of the ending of the sermon. That purpose is to help the congregation make a transition from engaging immediately with the preacher to reflecting on the sermon in the next phases of the service and into wider arenas of life. The word amen, when spoken as the last word in a sermon, tends to signal the community that the sermon is over. I experience it as a conversation stopper. Most of the time, the preacher is advised to conclude the sermon with a paragraph, sentence, or expression that encourages the conversation to continue.

27. Develop the whole sermon.

With the major pieces of the sermon in mind, the preacher now generates the sermon itself. This phase of preparation sometimes proceeds very smoothly. Sometimes it goes forward in fits and starts. Sometimes you sit before a blank screen or in a silent room for long periods of time when nothing seems to come. Over time, most preachers discover that this phase of sermon preparation usually follows patterns. For instance, I usually make several false beginnings and feel as though, despite everything I have done so far, I really don't have a sermon. But as I stay immersed in the process, a sermon gradually begins to emerge. Eventually my fingers on the keyboard cannot keep pace with the flow of material. Preachers who have such patterns need to learn how to work with them.

Of course, as I have repeatedly emphasized, the process of sermon preparation is organic. While developing the sermon, new material and new ways of arranging it will come to mind. When I have a sermon developing in my mind and heart, I encounter everywhere things that feed into it — comments in conversations, a scene from the novel that I am reading at bedtime, articles in magazines, lines from television programs, a sight on an evening walk, a thought in a theology tome that I am reading for a purpose unrelated to the preparation of the sermon, memories of experience. While developing the sermon itself, some of the material identified in the previous steps will recede in importance. Other material will increase in importance. Fresh perspectives will emerge.

When the process of sermon preparation takes on a life of its own, the sermon may develop in ways that I did not intend or foresee. The sermon may abandon my plan altogether. Such evolution is quite normal. However, when it occurs, the preacher does need to reflect critically on the degree to which the new developments serve the gospel in the context of the congregation.

CHAPTER 11

A Smorgasbord of Patterns of Movement for the Sermon

The preacher needs to arrange the main questions, issues, resources, explanations, and data in a sequence that serves the purposes of the sermon and the relationship of the congregation to the direction of the sermon. Once in a while, an arrangement comes to the preacher in full bloom. Most of the time, the preacher tries several arrangements before settling on one. The movement of the sermon evolves as the preacher works on the sermon. Sometimes you get stuck. You have a clear direction for the sermon, interesting exegetical material, perceptive theological insight, lively connections to the human situation, and full-bodied stories and images. However, you can't figure out how the pieces fit together.

This chapter spreads a smorgasbord of patterns for arranging sermons. In connection with each approach, I summarize its movement, indicate strengths and weaknesses, and suggest occasions when it might be useful. This catalogue is representative, not exhaustive. When a preacher is stuck, one of these patterns of movement might provide a structure. I present some of the more traditional patterns first and then some of the more innovative patterns. Because of the close relationship between form and content, these patterns are not simply interchangeable. A change in form is a change in content. A preacher seeks a pattern of movement that works with the direction of the sermon, the social context, and the person of the preacher.

When a sermon form is comprised of several parts, I indicate the approximate percentage of the sermon that is usually taken by that part. For instance, a Beginning usually takes up about 5–10 percent of the sermon. These percentages are somewhat arbitrary.

Puritan Plain Style
The Puritan Plain Style is named because it is a plain form of preaching preferred by many Puritans.[1] The Puritans developed the plain style to contrast with the ornate preaching of some of their contemporaries. This style

was adopted by many preachers in many different Christian communities in North America. I adapt the Plain Style slightly so that it can also embrace preaching on Christian doctrines and practices and to bring theological analysis more clearly to the surface of the sermon. Some sermons in this style call for explicit theological and hermeneutical analysis (as described below) when the interpretive issues are complex. However, when the theological and hermeneutical interpretation is straightforward, a preacher may be able to move directly from exposition of the text to application. Chapter 16 contains a sermon in this style.[2]

Beginning (5–10 percent). The beginning of the sermon functions as described on pages 164–170. When developing a sermon on the woman with the flow of blood, the preacher might summarize the text, or begin with a story of someone who feels unclean.

Statement of the Direction of the Sermon (less than 5 percent). The preacher directly states the subject of the sermon. Most of the time, the preacher reveals the direction of the sermon. If the beginning focuses on the biblical text, the preacher might say, "Many of us feel like that woman – unclean, alone, out of relationship. But according to that story, Jesus makes us clean, and restores us for relationships and community. I want to explore with you how we can encounter Jesus' transforming, regenerating power."

Exposition of the Biblical Text, Doctrine, or Practice (20–30 percent if the sermon needs an explicit theological and hermeneutical analysis; 30–40 percent if such a component is not required). The preacher develops an exposition of the text, doctrine, or practice that directly informs this sermon. The preacher cannot offer a comprehensive exegesis. When discussing the story of the woman with the flow of blood, the preacher would interpret the woman, the blood, the resultant isolation, her encounter with Jesus, and its transforming result.

Theological and Hermeneutical Analysis (20–30 percent if required).The preacher engages in a theological analysis that helps the congregation determine an optimum hermeneutical relationship with the text, doctrine or practice. The preacher articulates clearly and winsomely the positive witness of the sermon. What can the congregation believe about the text? When focusing on the narrative of the woman with the hemorrhage, the preacher would help the congregation note ways in which the world of the text differs from our world. We, too, encounter Jesus' regenerative presence.

Application (20–30 percent or 30–40 percent). The preacher helps the congregation apply the claims of the sermon to its life. The preacher is concrete. This part of the sermon usually includes at least one story that embodies the direction of the sermon positively. How do we encounter Jesus' cleansing presence and how such encounters affect us individually and as community.

Ending (5–10 percent). The ending of the sermon functions as described on pages 170–176. The ending of a sermon on the woman with the flow of blood might encourage us to reenter community, empowered to witness to God's restoring presence and activity.

From the standpoint of the congregation, clarity and simplicity are two virtues of the Puritan plain sermon.

These qualities of clarity and simplicity translate into ease of sermon preparation. When the preacher is working on a specific part of the sermon, the preacher's task is clearly defined. The Puritan plain sermon inevitably leads the congregation to reflect on how the gospel intersects with our world. This approach is sometimes criticized as unimaginative, dull, and predictable. It can reduce narrative and poetic texts to propositional meanings. It forces all texts, doctrines, and practices into the same sermonic form, doing violence to the way in which we encounter some texts. Our perception of a poem, for instance, does not always conform to the linear flow of this model.

This arrangement will not suit all sermons. However, in my view, all preachers need to be able to use it. It has a track record of several centuries in helping congregations encounter the gospel. It can also be an emergency vehicle, as one of my former students reports. "On Friday night, I had a lot of good ideas for the sermon, but I couldn't get them to fit together. Then, I turned to the Puritan Plain Style, and it gave a way to organize my thoughts and stories."

The Quadrilateral as Sermon Structure

The Christian community knows the so-called Wesleyan Quadrilateral as a theological method that draws on scripture, tradition, experience, and reason as sources of the knowledge of God.[3] Scripture is the preeminent source, functioning through interaction with the other three. The quadrilateral can also be a structure for sermons in which each source is a separate section of the sermon.[4]

Beginning (5–10 percent). The beginning of the sermon functions much as described on pages 164–170. In a sermon on predestination, the preacher would help the congregation focus on that doctrine, perhaps through telling a story that raises the question of whether events in this world and beyond appear to be predestined. The beginning could help the congregation define predestination with care.

Statement of the Direction of the Sermon. This statement summarizes the direction of the sermon.

Scripture (20–25 percent). The preacher discusses biblical perspectives on the subject of the sermon by pointing to key texts, themes, and images. The preacher needs to honor the pluralism of the Bible. In a sermon on predestination, the preacher would point to representative biblical passages that appear to explain this doctrine. Because pastor and people do not want to impose their understanding of predestination on the Bible, it is important to ask, "What do these passages teach about predestination?" What purposes does that notion serve in these texts? For the sake of integrity, the preacher needs also to bring forward and interpret texts that appear to presume a nonpredestinarian point of view. What do these latter passages, themes, and images presume? Is a discussion taking place within the world of the Bible on these matters? If so, where shall the contemporary community take its place in the discussion, and why?

Tradition (20–25 percent). The preaching conversation asks how the subject of the sermon has been understood in the history of the church. The community seeks to know how major voices, especially its own denomination, have understood the subject of the sermon. Because the tradition is vast, the preacher must often turn to representative voices. Integrity calls for the preacher to acknowledge pluralism. In addition to bringing formal theological views off the shelf, the preacher will frequently want to discuss popular, folk interpretations of the subject of the sermon. For folk interpretations can be quite powerful, even when at odds with the church's formal teaching. On predestination, the preacher would help the community understand how major theologians and movements in the church have understood this doctrine. In a congregation in the Reformed tradition, for instance, the preacher would want to devote considerable time to helping the congregation get a clear bead on Calvin's teaching. The sermon needs to characterize how people popularly understand predestination since such notions are often deep in the community's heart but sometimes differ from the church's teaching. The preacher needs to help the community recognize differences within the Christian community regarding how to understand predestination itself and differences between predestinarians and nonpredestinarians. The congregation will be helped by knowing the questions and issues for which predestination was a response.

Experience (20–25 percent). The preacher helps the congregation name ways in which it experiences the subject of the sermon.[5] Does experience confirm, deepen, or reframe the direction of the sermon? Does experience challenge the direction of the sermon? The preacher may also explore ways in which the doctrine needs to shape the congregation's experience. Does experience include a transrational, intuitive, component? The preacher might probe the degree to which experience seems to confirm or deny predestination. Furthermore, I once heard someone say that doctrine is experience in propositional form. The notion of predestination, for instance, gives a rationale for the experience of providence, even in circumstances in which one does not expect to experience divine care. Can the preacher who advocates predestination help the congregation recognize experiences that the doctrine of predestination helps interpret?

Reason (20–25 percent). Like the criterion of intelligibility (pages 84–87, reason as source for the knowledge of God functions on multiple levels. The community seeks to know how the Bible, tradition, and experience cohere with one another, and with other things that Christians believe and do. How does predestination square with the community's wider understanding of God's modes of activity in the world and the behavior of humankind and nature? The community seeks consistency. The community also seeks to determine how the direction of the sermon relates to its worldview. Is predestination reasonable, given the ways in which we understand the world? Or does predestination ask us to change our ways of thinking about the world in order to take account of this doctrine?

Ending (5–10 percent). The ending functions much as described on pages 170–176. If the sermon has traveled across several continents and millennia in its journey from the Bible through tradition and into the lands of reason and experience, the preacher may want to summarize what the congregation can take with them into their next phase of reflection.

As presented above, the quadrilateral is deductive. By excising the Statement of the Direction of the Sermon, the sermon can be inductive.

The quadrilateral offers a precise and comprehensive way to identify the sources of the knowledge of God. It encourages the community to come to a conclusion only after systematically engaging a spectrum of perspectives. The thoroughness of the quadrilateral can also turn into a weakness when the four sources overwhelm the community with perspectives. The preacher must draw on sources selectively and carefully. The categories (scripture, tradition, experience, reason) are sometimes artificial.

As illustrated by the doctrine of predestination above, the quadrilateral is especially useful when preaching on a Christian doctrine or practice. We can also use it to come to a Christian understanding of a situation. The preacher searches for how the Bible, tradition, experience, and reason inform our understanding of the situation. We can use it to help a congregation understand how the church interprets a biblical passage or theme. The sermon first offers an exegesis of the passage or theme, then reports on how that text or theme has been interpreted in Christian tradition. The preacher notes the intersection of the passage or theme with experience, and how we can reasonably make sense of the text or theme today.

Verse by Verse Preaching

The term "verse by verse" is a misnomer, but I use it because that phrase is popular parlance for preaching through a text segment by segment. The preacher makes a running commentary on a text. Verses are sometimes meaningful units for interpretation, but at other times, the text divides along sentences that cross verse divisions. Occasionally, a passage requires interpretation clause-by-clause, or even word-by-word.[6] While we usually think of verse by verse preaching in connection with biblical passages, this approach can be applied to any text, e.g., an affirmation of faith.[7]

The typical verse by verse sermon has a beginning, the exposition of the text in meaningful units combined with theological and hermeneutical interpretation, and an ending. The beginning provides a context for the running commentary, perhaps by recounting the historical, literary, or theological setting of the text. The beginning might include an aspect of our experience that frames the exposition. The preacher might articulate a contemporary question to which the interpretation of the text provides a response. If the sermon is part of a series of sermons in *lectio continua,* the beginning might summarize the story or themes that precede the text for the day.

In exposition, many preachers alternate between exegesis of segments of the text and drawing out the contemporary implications. The preacher offers exegesis of verse 14, then helps the congregation identify contemporary significance. The preacher then offers exegesis of verse 15, and helps the congregation identify the contemporary significance.

Like the endings discussed on pages 170–176, the ending helps the congregation continue reflecting on intersections between the world of the text and the world of the congregation.

During preparation, many preachers find it helpful to create a two-column table that charts the flow of the sermon. I illustrate with reference to a possible sermon on 2 Samuel 20:14–22, the wise woman who saves the city of Abel of Beth-Maacah.

Beginning	
Exegesis of v. 14	
	Theological and hermeneutical implications of v. 14
Exegesis of v. 15	
	Theological and hermeneutical implications of v. 15
Exegesis of vv. 16–17	
	Theological and hermeneutical implications of vv. 16–17
Exegesis of vv. 18–21	
	Theological and hermeneutical implications of vv. 18–21

Exegesis of v. 22	
	Theological and hermeneutical implications of v. 22
Ending	

The beginning of the sermon could locate the text in the narrative of 2 Samuel. The preacher might need to help the contemporary community consider why we are interested in this obscure story from such a different time and place.

In the exegesis of verse 14, the preacher could help the community identify Sheba (heir of Bichri) and the Bichrites, and the conflict between Sheba and Joab. The sermon could help the community locate Abel of Beth-Maacah, and name what is at stake in the confrontation. In the theological and hermeneutical reflection, the preacher could help the community identify persons and forces in our setting that are similar to Sheba and Bichrites. How does Sheba occupy our cities today?

The exegesis of verse 15 could help the community imagine the siege mentioned in the text. In order to eliminate the threat posed by Sheba, Joab is about to destroy the city of Abel. When drawing out theological and hermeneutical implications, the preacher might note ways in which God's witnesses today (analogues of Joab) confront Sheba. How do such confrontations threaten the communities in which they take place?

The exegesis of verses 16–17 explore the "wise woman." Few women were regarded as sages in antiquity. Hence, the source of wisdom is unexpected. In theological and hermeneutical meditation, the preacher might help the community name unexpected sources of wisdom in our culture. Are women still unexpected sources of wisdom?

The exegesis of verses 18–21 points out that the wise woman initiates a conversation with Joab to discover an alternative to the destruction of Abel while eliminating the threat posed by Sheba. The preacher might explore ways in which creative conversations initiated by unlikely sources can often help today's community redirect energy from a path toward community disruption to peaceful, community-building alternatives.

The exegesis of verse 22 would reveal that the wise woman's plan worked. In theological and hermeneutical evaluation, the preacher could point to similar instances in our culture. However, the preacher would also need to critique the beheading of Sheba from the standpoint of the gospel's promise of unconditional love for each and all.

The ending of the sermon might prompt the church to consider ways in which its community can listen to the wise women of the world and act as a wise woman.

Preaching verse by verse provides the preacher with a starting point and an easy-to-use arrangement for the sermon. It helps the community become biblically and theologically literate. The community is immersed in the world of a text. This mode especially helps the preacher and community unpack dense textual material. It models how to study a biblical passage. The congregation experiences the text in congruity with the movement of the text itself. When the minister must preach against a text, this approach helps the community understand the text, and its problems, from the inside out. Verse-by-verse preaching has a distinct danger. It can be boring, especially if the sermon gets lost in the details of the text.

Simple Inductive Movement

Some inductive forms of preaching can be outlined easily, e.g., the process of sermon preparation forming the movement of the sermon, the movement of the text shaping the movement of the sermon, the sermon as taking a trip. The simple inductive sermon is a little harder to describe because it does immediately call to mind a visual or auditory image, such as "taking a trip." However, as noted in the previous chapter, inductive preaching is characterized by the movement from particulars to a generalizing conclusion.[8] This movement may be described in the following block form.[9]

> *Beginning* (10–20 percent). The sermon might begin with particular questions, images, and issues raised by a text or topic. When preaching on the story of the hemorrhaging woman, a preacher might puzzle over the text. What kind of illness did she have? Why could it not be healed? Why did she need to touch Jesus? What is the role of faith? the significance of the healing? What does such a story have to do with us?

> *Dialogue with resources for understanding* (60–70 percent). The preacher then brings those particulars into dialogue with resources that can help the congregation gain a sense of perspective on the particulars themselves and on the larger issues to which the particulars point. What do preacher and congregation learn when turning to biblical exegesis? the way in which this story has been interpreted in the history of the church? historical and contemporary theological reflection? the social sciences? the arts? The preacher brings these resources into dialogue with the questions of the congregation. This part of the sermon is exploratory. When dealing with the woman with the issue of blood, the preacher and the community might explore the woman and the phenomenon of uncleanness. Are we similar to her? The community might imaginatively experience uncleanness. The community could approach Jesus and feel his restorative presence.

> *Ending* (10–20 percent). The preacher and the congregation summarize what they can take with them. How does the gospel, as refracted through the sermon, touch them? Where might the sermon lead them? What does it mean for a congregation of bleeding women to be healed?

By definition, of course, each inductive sermon moves in its own particular way.

This approach has several notable strengths. It is modeled in the everyday ways in which we live, talk, learn, and explore new situations. It has a built-in sense of anticipation: We do not know the outcome until the end. Congregation and preacher have the sense of wrestling together with the subject of the sermon and the resources needed to come to resolution. This quality sustains listener participation. It accounts for questions, complexities, and ambiguities. On the other hand, inductive movement must be carefully managed, or it can drift into disconnected vignettes, pieces of data, and insights. Indeed, inductive preaching can be every bit as logical as deductive preaching, though the movement of the logic is more subtle.

Simple inductive preaching can help the preacher speak with the congregation about almost any biblical text, doctrine, practice, or situation. It is especially useful when the sermon challenges the congregation's predisposition. Instead of immediately and directly telling the members of the congregation that they are wrong and need to change, the community is invited to consider particular aspects of a text, doctrine, practice, or experience that raise questions that the congregation needs to consider. Simple inductive movement can also serve occasions when the community is apathetic or bored by a matter which they need to consider. The preacher can lead the community in a process of discovering the importance of the text or topic.

The Form of the Text Shapes the Form of the Sermon

One of the most widespread movements in preaching in the last fifteen years is to let the form and movement of the text shape the form and movement of the sermon.[10] Form and content are conjoined. The experience of hearing a biblical text is a part of the meaning of the text. Loss occurs when the preacher abstracts a proposition from a text.

In order to preach in this fashion, the preacher must identify the form (or genre) of the text, the literary and rhetorical characteristics of that form, the function of that form, and, consequently, how the form, characteristics, and function might suggest a form, characteristics, and function for the sermon.[11]

This approach is simplest in the case of a long text in a clearly defined genre and function. The preacher can frequently use such a text as the pattern of arrangement for the sermon. The preacher divides the text and the sermon into the blocks of material that appear in the text. In the case of a narrative, for instance, the preacher divides the sermon into scenes; the sermon begins with a discussion of the setting, the text, and how we relate to that setting. The sermon then discusses the first scene and our place in it; the second scene, and our place in it, etc. The sermon weaves back and forth between the worlds of the text and the congregation. The text and the sermon, reach the climax simultaneously. Using the categories of the miracle story on page 131, the preacher could develop such a sermon on the story of the woman with the issue of blood.

This pattern also helps with nonnarrative passages. I illustrate with Psalm 13, an individual lament. The purpose of this lament is to express the psalmists' feelings of anguish in the midst of difficulty and to place those feelings in a larger theological frame of reference that will bolster confidence in God during a time of anguish.

> *Address to God* (Psalm 13:1a). The psalmist feels abandoned by God and voices this lament directly to God. The psalmist trusts God with the pain and honesty that follow. The preacher might voice similar feelings from the congregation. The preacher could talk with the congregation about the lament, or the preacher could make the sermon itself into a lament.

> *Complaint* (13:1b–2). With poignant honesty, the writer pours out feelings of abandonment, pain, sorrow. The preacher might help the congregation call to mind moments when they feel similarly. If the sermon is preached during a crisis, the sermon might correlate the situation with that of the psalm. Some people may need to realize that God can receive the most unvarnished and bitter sentiments. We learn from the lament that we do not need to polish or subdue our feelings when we speak them to God.

> *Request for Help* (13:3–4). The psalmist directly seeks for God to intervene. However, in my view, God is, by definition, present and helping in the midst of every circumstance. We do not need to request help from God; we need to become more cognizant of the help that God is providing.

> *Affirmation of Trust* (13:5). The psalmist expresses confidence in God. This statement is from experience: In previous difficulties, God has proven faithful. The preacher might help the congregation recall past instances of divine faithfulness. How do these memories help the congregation be confident of God?

> *Vow to Praise God* (13:6). The laments conclude with a vow to praise God when the difficulty ends. The preacher might help the congregation consider ways in which they can similarly respond to God.

Difficult situations do not always end happily. For example, people who are sick do not always get well. In such cases, the preacher may need to help the congregation understand why they can praise God, even when circumstances come to a painful conclusion.

Letting the form of the text shape the form of the sermon is more challenging with shorter texts. In these cases, the preacher might develop a sermon that honors the function of the text and incorporates literary features of the text, without corresponding to the structure of the text in a one-to-one fashion. For instance, when preaching on a proverb whose purpose is to shock the listener into an aspect of awareness of the divine presence, the preacher might develop a sermon with shock-qualities. A parable might inspire the preacher to develop the sermon parabolically.

The congregation has a holistic encounter with the text through this approach. This pattern is easy for the preacher when the text has an easily identified genre, characteristics, and structure. Since the sermon attempts to recreate the experience of the text in the contemporary community, this approach works most easily with biblical passages that are appropriate to the gospel, intelligible, and morally plausible.

The Four Pages of the Sermon

Paul Scott Wilson, a leading teacher of preaching, combines theological rigor with disciplined imagination in proposing a four-page approach to the sermon.[12] Wilson rightly notices that much contemporary preaching advocates works-righteousness in both personal and social spheres. We need to stress God's gracious activity in the world. God's grace forms the framework for understanding sin and brokenness. The awareness of the divine presence enables us to respond faithfully to God's goodness.[13]

To achieve these ends, Wilson speaks of the sermon having four pages. Each page has a distinct theological task. Wilson assigns the preacher's work on each page to a specific day of the week. Monday is Getting Started Day — selecting the focus, accumulating resources, outlining the process of preparation. Page One (Tuesday) focuses on the biblical text in its own time and literary formulation. The preacher brings out the trouble (sin or brokenness) in the world that gave rise to this text. Page Two (Wednesday) examines similar trouble in our setting. Page Three (Thursday) returns to the biblical text, but now identifying what God is doing in or behind the biblical passage to act for the good of the world. Page Three correlates God's grace with the sin and brokenness of Page One. Page Four (Friday) returns to our world. In addition to these four pages, the sermon has a beginning and an ending. The preacher can rearrange the order of the pages.

Wilson uses the term "page" figuratively. However, the preacher who works with a manuscript might prepare approximately one page of material on each task, though, for particular sermons, the tasks may not break into equal parts. With a beginning and ending of a half-page each, a preacher would have a five-page manuscript — about the length most preachers need for a twenty-minute sermon.

Wilson combines the figure of preparing a series of pages with that of the sermon as filmmaking. On each page, the preacher should show a film clip that pictures the task of that page. During preaching, the congregation sees a movie or a series of clips. On each page, the preacher creates a world that speaks to the senses as well as to the mind and heart. Page One films trouble in the Bible. Page Two films trouble in our world. Page Three films grace in the Bible. Page Four films grace in our world.

A sermon in four pages on Jeremiah 31:15–22 could unfold as follows.

Beginning (10 percent). The preacher might help the community realize that this text is a word of hope for a community that is discouraged. The image of Rachel weeping in Ramah is poignant. She is a mother of Israel, a symbol for the community, weeping. How do we, also, weep?

Page One (20 percent). This page helps the community discover the background of this passage as the collapse of the nation and the exile of Israel's leaders to Babylonia. The nation collapses because the community practices idolatry and injustice. The exile is God's discipline. For filming, a pastor might picture persons in Ramah, a site from which the exiles were deported to Babylonia (Jeremiah 40:1). The preacher might picture idolatry and injustice in Jeremiah's day. The sermon could help the congregation visualize the collapse of Judah and hear and feel Rachel weeping.

Page Two (20 percent). This page helps the congregation recognize how our world participates in idolatry and injustice. The pastor might film ways in which our communities deteriorate because of idolatry and injustice.

Page Three (20 percent). In the text, God promises restoration. Repentance is the path that Ephraim takes in order to participate in the restoration that God is bringing about. Previously, Ephraim had been like an untrained calf, but now he repents. God acts and speaks as a mother toward Judah. In maternal language deep with feeling and attachment, God speaks of the divine love for the community: "I am deeply moved," "I will have mercy on him." God "has created a new thing on the earth: a woman encompasses a man." God effects that which appears impossible: The woman, (who appears to be weak, and a victim) becomes a source of strength and protection. The circumstances that appear to be community in collapse can become the circumstances for community renewal. The preacher might film God's motherly relationship with Ephraim.

Page Four (20 percent). On this page, the preacher shows how God's mother-love restores communities that are collapsing. The preacher helps the congregation see how repentance can facilitate participation in renewal. The preacher needs to provide scenes of regeneration that are as emotionally powerful as the scenes of trouble on Page Two. For instance, to pick up imagery from the text itself, the renewal of the role of women in the church in our time demonstrates God's re-creative power. Women are unexpected agents of renewal. Who are other unanticipated agents of community restoration the preacher might film?

Ending (10 percent). The preacher wants the community to leave the sermon with a vivid sense of God's presence and promise. We need to feel God's power encompassing us as a woman encompasses a man.

While Wilson envisions this arrangement serving expository sermons, it can be adjusted for sermons on doctrines, Christian practices, and situations.

This arrangement is quite attractive. It serves multiple kinds of sermons and occasions. The pages move straightforwardly from a problem to God's gracious resolution. Congregations can easily follow this pattern. It helps the preacher connect the theological direction of the sermon to today's community. The preacher's efficiency in sermon preparation is maximized by dividing the task of sermon preparation into discrete units. When the good news is placed at the end of the sermon, the congregation leaves the sermon hopeful and empowered. This approach creates an excellent point of entry (Pages One and Two) when the preacher must help the congregation consider theological problems with texts, doctrines, practices, or its own beliefs or behaviors. On the other hand, a text or topic may not be predicated upon bad news. When filming, a preacher needs to be cautious not to create a clip that calls attention to its own artistry.

The Sermon as Plot and Moves

David Buttrick, a pioneer in contemporary preaching, contends that the sermon is to form communal consciousness. The sermon is not directed to a collection of individuals but to the church as community. Buttrick thinks that the consciousness of a group functions according to distinct patterns that the preacher must take into account in order for the sermon to form in community consciousness.[14] Toward this end, Buttrick proposes that the sermon should have a plot that is filled out by four to six carefully constructed moves.[15]

Plot is derived from literary and rhetorical criticism. The plot is the selection and ordering of material in the sermon to achieve a particular intention in the consciousness of the congregation.[16] A sermon begins. It goes from one episode to another. It ends. The preacher decides where to begin, which episodes to tell, and how to end the sermon. The pastor selects a point of view from which the congregation will hear the sermon. The preacher may draw on stock repertoires (e.g., tragedy, comedy, farce) for the logic of the sermon, or the preacher may create a plot.

A sermon should have a brief beginning that focuses the congregation toward the field of meaning in which the sermon moves. It should also have a brief ending that establishes a reflective consciousness.

A preacher who decides that the time is ripe to help the congregation reflect on national health care might design the plot of a sermon as follows:

Beginning. The beginning focuses the congregation's attention on health care as a national issue.

Move 1. Look at our situation. Vast numbers of people have no access to health care because they cannot afford it.

Move 2. Many people today see nothing wrong with this situation.

Move 3. But, let us hear what the gospel has to say about health care. The gospel promises unconditional love for each and all; the gospel calls for justice for each and all. Health care is an expression of love and justice.

Move 4. Now, we see the situation differently. The Christian community is called to work for universal health care in this country.

Move 5. So, here are some ways in which we can witness to God's will for health care for all.

Ending. The ending helps the congregation continue to reflect on the importance of acting in behalf of health care for all.

This sermon moves from a conventional understanding of health care, through Christian contention with that understanding and a reframing of it, to practical steps that Christians can take to witness to the gospel's desire for health care for all.

The plot is made up of a series of episodes (called *moves*) that build one upon another.[17] Communal consciousness functions more slowly than individual awareness. It takes three to four minutes for a single idea to form in congregational consciousness. Each move communicates an idea, e.g., "We are all sinners." A move can last three to four minutes. The plot of a twenty-minute sermon can contain only five to six moves.

Furthermore, Buttrick contends that ideas form in consciousness according to predictable patterns. Each move must be constructed in a certain way. The move begins with the statement itself. The preacher must make the statement in three to four short, direct sentences. The statement lasts about thirty seconds to a minute. In different words, each sentence says the same thing.

The central part of the move is the development. The preacher may expand on the statement. The preacher may give evidence to support the statement. The preacher may deal with difficulties. Because of television, contemporary consciousness is oriented toward visual imagery. Consequently, the development of the move should contain a visual image, a picture of the statement. Communal consciousness can handle only one image per move. Never tell two stories back-to-back.

The move ends with *closure*. The preacher returns to the theme statement in three or four brief, direct sentences. The preacher may use the same words of the statement or may restate the idea of the statement in other words. Closure is crucial. Without closure, the congregation may not be able to follow the preacher to the next move.

In a sermon on the near-sacrifice of Isaac, Buttrick develops the first move:

(Statement) At the outset, notice: Isaac is much more than an only child. *Isaac is hope*, hope wrapped up in human flesh. All the promises of God were riding on Isaac. *(Development)* Remember the story? Remember how God dropped in to tell Sarah and Abraham that

their offspring would be as many as the sands of the sea, that they would give birth to nations. Well, the old folks giggled, for, according to reliable medical advice, it's mighty tough to conceive when you're pushing ninety! Then, suddenly Isaac was born, a miracle child: God did provide! Through Isaac, there *would* be many descendents, a multitude of nations. *(Image)* An American playwright tells of how his Jewish parents scrimped and saved to give him everything. They bought him new clothes three times a year, bundled him off to private schools, paid for his college education. "Everything we've got's wrapped up in you, boy!" his mother used to say. "Everything we've got's wrapped up in you." How easy it is to focus our hopes. God gives us a land to live in and, before you know it, we're chanting, "Everything we've got is wrapped up in you, America! Or a church to belong to: Everything we've got is wrapped up in you, Presbyterian Church!" *(Closure)* Listen, Isaac was more than an only child. Isaac embodied the promises of God. "Everything we've got's wrapped up in you, boy." Isaac was hope, all the hope in the world.[18]

In subsequent moves, Buttrick leads the congregation to interpret the story as God setting Abraham — and us — free for faith.

Buttrick's system can be adapted to expository, doctrinal, and topical sermons. The preacher can create a fresh plot to serve the needs of each occasion. The plot provides a clear structure for both preacher and people. My restiveness with Buttrick's work is his insistence that all sermons must conform to his system or fail to communicate. Faith development theory (as summarized on pages 39–40) suggests that individuals know and communicate in multiple patterns.

Plot and Moves That Climax in Celebration

Henry Mitchell, a leading authority in contemporary preaching, says that Buttrick's understanding of the sermon as a series of distinct subsections developed together into a plot provides a conceptual framework to describe the movement of much traditional African American preaching. African American preaching is not derived from Buttrick's proposal. To the contrary, African American preaching in this vein predates Buttrick's publication by 350 years, but Buttrick provides a helpful way of talking about the relationship of the parts to the whole in much African American preaching. According to Mitchell, many African American sermons move from one distinct block of material to another. The movements are connected much like scenes in a plot.

In most African American preaching, the final move is celebration. The preacher celebrates God's presence and activity in the world. The last move, consequently, is not exhortatory or moralistic. It does not center on what the congregation is to do. It lifts up what God has done, is doing, and will continue to do.

Mitchell distinguishes three main types of preaching in the African American community: the "textual sermon," that is a sermon on a very short passage in which the message is structured according to the divisions of the text; an "expositional sermon," that is, a sermon on a longer text in which the message follows the larger units of material in the text; a "narrative sermon" in which, from beginning to end, the sermon is a narrative.[19] However, Mitchell notices that many African American sermons end with a *celebration* of God's presence and activity in the world. The last move (usually 25 percent of the sermon) celebrates what God is doing for the congregation.[20] A textual sermon on Hebrews 12:1−2 might unfold as follows: (a) We are surrounded by a cloud of witnesses. (b) Let us lay aside every weight and sin. (c) Let us run the race with perseverance. (d) Celebration. We can lay aside the weight and run the race because Jesus, our pioneer and perfector, sits at the right hand of God.[21]

In addition, Mitchell sees character study and group study as organizing motifs for sermons.[22] In a character study, the preacher traces the history and development of a biblical character. This sermon is similar to a sermon on a biblical theme (pages 111−112) in that the sermon focuses not on a singular biblical text, but traces a character across a body of scripture.[23] In a group study, the preacher follows a particular group across a book (or other pertinent portion) of the Bible.[24] Some sermons are organized around metaphors, similes, or analogies. Mitchell also regards the sermon as a single narrative as a part of traditional and contemporary African American preaching.

While Mitchell notes that the preceding approaches to preaching are characteristically African American, they can be used by preachers in any community.

From "Oops" to "Yeah"

Eugene Lowry, another pioneer in the narrative approach to preaching, points out that the sermon is an event. Events unfold sequentially. Individual moments follow moments, creating a plot. The sermon, then, is a plot in which a series of five moments fold into one another: Oops, Ugh, Aha, Whee, and Yeah.[25] According to Lowery, the sermon must begin with an element of ambiguity in order to generate and sustain the congregation's interest. The sermon helps the congregation name a tension, then leads the community through a series of moments toward resolution of the tension, and beyond.[26]

> *Oops: upsetting the equilibrium* (20 percent). The preacher begins by describing the problem, ambiguity, or tension that arises in connection with a Bible passage, doctrine, practice, situation, or occasion. This phase helps the congregation feel the imbalance so they will want the tension resolved. When developing a sermon for Thanksgiving Day, a preacher might wonder why we should give thanks in the face of the manifold forms of difficulty and suffering in the world.
>
> *Ugh: the plot thickens* (20 percent). The preacher analyzes the problem that upsets the equilibrium. We go "Ugh." In a sermon for Thanks-

giving, the preacher could contrast affirmations of God's goodness and providence with those aspects of experience that seem to contradict such sweeping affirmations.

Aha: disclosing the clue to resolution (20 percent). The preacher discloses perspectives that indicate how the tension can be resolved. "Aha! We see a way forward." Clues for resolution should incorporate the gospel. When preaching on Thanksgiving, the preacher might help the congregation recognize that in the Bible and Christian tradition, the community gives thanks because God proves trustworthy within difficult events.

Whee: experiencing the gospel (20 percent). The preacher enlarges upon the clue to resolution. The preacher may create a moment in which the congregation can experience the resolution. For the Thanksgiving sermon, the preacher might develop an image in which the community experiences reasons for giving thanks to God in the midst of hard circumstances.

Yeah: anticipating the future (20 percent). What difference does the resolution of the tension make for the future? Yeah, what next? How do we think, feel, or act? On Thanksgiving, the preacher might help the congregation identify ways to give thanks in all circumstances.

Each sermon is an event that develops through time.

Lowry's approach is amenable to occasions when something has happened to upset the equilibrium of the world or the congregation. This pattern allows the community to name and explore the disequilibrium from the perspective of the gospel. The approach is also especially helpful when the congregation needs to reexamine some aspect of its thought, feeling, or behavior that it had thought settled. The sermon decenters the congregation and encourages them to be open to new possibilities. This arrangement can help the congregation move from surface levels of faith and doctrine to deeper ones by pushing the community to acknowledge tensions in its faith and doctrine. On the other side of the coin, this pattern can become predictable if it is the preacher's weekly Sunday voice. Some texts, doctrines, practices, situations, occasions, and congregations do not call for an "Aha!" Once in a while a sermon needs to restate what we already know.

The Sermon as Movement of Images

One of many provocative suggestions from Thomas H. Troeger (who generates many fresh approaches to preaching) is to think of the sermon as a movement of images.[27] Troeger recognizes that ideas and propositions can have an important place in preaching. Nonetheless, he says people today are trained by the electronic media to perceive in imagery. The sermon itself could be a series of word-pictures in which the images communicate the meaning of the message. The sermon also could be a single, extended image (on the order of the single narrative discussed below). The preacher does not explain the images. The congregation enters into sights, sounds, touches, smells, tastes, and feelings of the image world. An image touches the congregation simultaneously at the levels of mind, heart, and will. When the community leaves the world of the image, they can perceive their everyday world from the perspective of the image world.

For a wedding, Troeger takes this approach when developing a sermon on the meaning of the marriage covenant. Troeger does not prosaically explain the marriage covenant in traditional sermonic prose. Instead, Troeger structures the sermon as a series of snapshots taken across the life of a marriage. Each snapshot pictures an aspect of the marriage covenant: what it means to be faithful to one's promise in situations that are better and worse, richer and poorer, in sickness and in health. The images move from the beginning of marriage, through midlife, to the golden years. The wedding vow is a refrain.

> In an *early* picture, the couple struggles economically. We see the stuffing coming out of the sofa because they cannot repair it. Refrain.

> A *few years later*, the financial situation is better (the children have ten-speed bikes), but we feel tension between the spouses. Refrain.

> *Midlife*. Frazzled and roadworn, we see them wearily sucking in their tummies as they try to squeeze into their clothes. Refrain.

> On their *forty-seventh wedding anniversary*, they don't know whether they will make fifty years together. We see him depleted from two heart attacks, and we see her joints swollen with arthritis. Troeger emphasizes the words, "in sickness . . . until death." Refrain.

Although Troeger never offers a conventional definition of covenant, by the end of the sermon the congregation experiences what it means to be a faithful and loving spouse.

A congregation may benefit from this pattern when it needs to experience an aspect of the gospel. Preaching in images has a contemporary feel. The preacher who creates an image of a biblical text, doctrine, or practice avoids reducing the fullness of that material to an anemic proposition. The congregation can "try on" what it would be like to live in the world of the image. This mode of preaching is especially appealing to congregations made up of a large percentage of persons with an aesthetic orientation or who think in patterns associated with James Fowler's Stages 4, 5, and 6 (pages 39–40).

However, some people, whose thinking patterns are described by Fowler's Stages 2 and 3, think propositionally. They want to "get the point" of the image. If they cannot extrapolate a point in propositional terms, they may be frustrated. I have heard some sermons in this mode whose lovely sensory descriptions seemed to be for their own sakes. When thinking toward the sermon as a movement of images, preachers need to be clear about what they hope the congregation will think, feel, and do in regard to the gospel.

When used by itself, this mode of preaching can short-circuit critical thought. Sometimes, a congregation needs not to enter into the world of a text or topic, but to transcend the Bible passage, doctrine, practice, or situation for the purpose of clarifying what the community can and should believe, feel, or do.

From time to time, however, a preacher may be able to combine the best of the sermon as image with the sermon as critical thought by developing an image and then reflecting upon the image in the same way that a movie critic tells the plot of a movie and then helps readers reflect critically upon it.

The Process of Sermon Preparation Can Form the Movement of the Sermon

Fred Craddock posits the process by which the preacher prepares the sermon as a movement for the sermon itself. "Why not on Sunday morning retrace the inductive trip" that the preacher takes in the study to see if the "hearers come to that same conclusion."[28]

At its simplest, the arrangement of the sermon would approximately follow the progression of the steps articulated in chapters 9 and 10. Of course, the preacher would not reproduce each step in each sermon. Such a sermon would sink beneath the weight of detail. But the preacher can help the congregation experience the discovery of the most important pieces of data and insight. The sermon might begin by identifying the subject of the sermon and identifying preassociations and questions raised by the biblical text, doctrine, practice, or situation. The preacher can help the congregation discover relevant exegetical observations, as well as pertinent themes from the history of Christian interpretation, and from the social sciences, philosophy, the arts. The community can reflect on options for understanding the text or topic in view of the gospel. The preacher can help the congregation imagine implications.

For instance, in a sermon on Christian understandings of divorce, a preacher might begin by recalling situations of divorce. What are thoughts, feelings, and behaviors that result from those situations on the part of the divorced persons, others in their families, in their circles of friends and associates? How does the community respond to divorce? The congregation could join the preacher on a journey through perspectives on divorce in the Bible, church history, and theology. What do the social sciences tell us about the frequency of and reasons for divorce today? This journey reveals multiple points of view. The preacher and congregation struggle toward a view that is appropriate to the gospel, intelligible, and moral. The sermon can help the community think about how to become a vehicle of love and justice for all in the situation.

Craddock states a particular benefit of the process of preparation suggesting the movement of the sermon. "If *they* have made the trip, then it is *their* conclusion, and the implication for their own situations is not only clear but personally inescapable. Christian responsibilities are not therefore predicated upon the exhortations of a particular minister (who can be replaced!) but upon the intrinsic force of the hearer's own reflection."[29] While this approach can be used in connection with almost any text or topic, it is especially helpful when the community must deal with a sensitive or controversial matter. At the very beginning it helps the congregation name its thoughts and feelings on the subject of the message and then brings those reactions into wider conversation. This approach might also serve sermons on texts, doctrines, practices or situations in which the congregation has little initial interest. That very preassociation could be a point of departure. "When I began to prepare this sermon, I was taking coffee intravenously to keep awake." A congregation may not need to follow a process of discovery every Sunday.

First Naiveté, Critical Reflection, Second Naiveté

Paul Ricoeur, one of the leading hermeneutical theorists of our time, posits a three-fold movement by which we can critically engage texts.[30] This movement can structure a sermon on a biblical passage, doctrine, practice, or situation. The interpreter begins with first naiveté, moves into a second phase — critical reflection, then concludes in a second naiveté.[31]

First naiveté. The preacher and the congregation first enter the world of the text, doctrine, practice, or topic precritically. The community seeks to become familiar with the text or topic on its own terms. What does the text or topic claim is true about God? the world? us? Pastor and people do not question the adequacy of the text or topic. In the sermon, the preacher might simply describe a biblical story, or what the church has believed in regard to a doctrine, or how the church engages in a particular practice, or the circumstances in a personal or social situation. In the case of the narrative of the tower of Babel, the sermon might begin by retelling the story, speaking as if the event took place on the plain in Shinar, depicting the process of building a ziggurat with mud bricks, the languages, and drawing the word-play between Babel and the Hebrew *balal*, "confused."

Critical reflection. The preacher and community now take a step back from the text and consider the distance between the text and our world. Interpreters probe the degree to which a text or topic is appropriate to the gospel, intelligible, and morally plausible. Interpreters seek to unmask the possible ways that the witness of the text or topic serves vested interests (as described on pages 138–140). The preacher looks the hardest questions directly in the eye. What can we really believe from this Bible passage, doctrine, practice, or situation? The preacher seeks to clarify the hermeneutical relationship between the congregation and the text or topic. Although Genesis 11:1–9 is told as a straightforward story, minister and congregation are not able to ascertain evidence that the event occurred as described. At a factual level, then, the story is hardly intelligible. People who think they can really build a tower to heaven? Only in a setting in which people believe in a three-story universe. However, people in antiquity told such stories in order to explain why things are the way they are. The story explains (in part) why the human race is divided into different groups. It also illustrates the consequences when human beings claim prerogatives that belong to God.

Second naiveté. Pastor and people now return to the language, symbolism, and world of the text, doctrine, practice, or situation as informed by critical reflection. We no longer confuse "fact" with symbolism. The sermon helps the congregation name its world from the perspective of the language, imagery, and symbolism of the text. The community focusing on the incident at Babel might discover ways in which the story at Babel is our story, too. How do we try to build a tower with its top in the heavens? How do such attempts disrupt our personal and communal lives?

In the unending cycles of interpretation, one generation's second naiveté may become the equivalent of a first naiveté for a subsequent generation.

This pattern of preaching replicates the contours of experience and discovery. We encounter a phenomenon and are fascinated by it. We reflect on it. This three-fold encounter is especially useful when the preacher wants to help the congregation challenge its understanding of a part of the Bible or a doctrine, practice, or situation. In first naiveté, the preacher sets out how the congregation thinks or acts. In critical reflection, the sermon critiques the congregation's thinking or behavior. In third naiveté, the preacher helps he community discern a revalued understanding or behavior. This approach can also serve occasions when the community needs to deepen though not altogether replace a perception.

The Sermon as Putting Together a Jigsaw Puzzle

Most of the other patterns in this chapter are based on models that are linear or narrative. The sermon as a jigsaw puzzle, however, is associative.[32] This sermon is made of up distinct pieces — from the Bible, Christian tradition, theology, other sources of insight, data from the media and contemporary existence. While we know that the pieces ought to relate to one another, we do not know how until we begin to fit them together.[33]

For instance, Proverbs 31:10−31 portrays a woman of worth (sometimes called a capable wife) through a collage of traits. The sermon could treat the trait as puzzle pieces. Because the text is long, the preacher might group the traits according to common themes.

Beginning (5−10 percent). The comparison of the woman with rare jewels in 31:10 echoes a similar comparison between jewels and wisdom (3:15; 8:11). Hence, the woman of worth embodies the qualities of women's wisdom in this book. The passage uses a creative, strong woman to exemplify the qualities of the wise person.

Piece One (10 percent). The responsibilities of the woman are similar to those of the ruler of Israel (Proverbs 23:23–27; 9:1–9). If the text was written after the collapse of the monarchy, the woman's work in the home seems to replace the security formerly provided by the monarchy.

Piece Two (20 percent) (vs. 11–12, 21, 23, 26, 28). She is sensitive to relationships and trustworthy in them. She seeks the good of all in the household and in the wider community. She relates to other people on the basis of the wisdom principles articulated elsewhere in Proverbs.

Piece Three (25 percent) (vss. 13-16, 18–19, 24). She is an excellent and just manager of the household, and of the family businesses. She engages in traditional women's work (e.g., spinning, weaving) as well as in roles that are sometimes assumed by men (e.g., purchasing land). According to Proverbs, such industry is one of the ways that providential care is mediated to the family, the servants, and (through sharing) with the wider community.

Piece Four (20 percent) (vs. 15, 17–19, 27). She works hard in behalf of activities that encourage community. Such hard work generates energy.

Piece Five (20 percent) (vs. 20). She is a committed member of the covenant who provides for the poor from the resources of her home. This action demonstrates her grasp of the interrelatedness of all in the community.

Piece Six (20 percent) (vs. 25–26). She is a woman of wisdom, clothed in strength and dignity, because she knows God's steadfast love. Like wisdom, the presence of this woman is a teaching witness in the community.

Ending (10 percent). The preacher might help the congregation reflect on ways in which we can manifest similar qualities of wisdom in our community.

The pieces of the sermon come together to form a collage of the wise person in community.

A variation on this approach might be to structure the sermon using the pieces of a mind-map or the pattern of writing on the right side of the brain, as discussed on pages 163–164. Each paragraph in the sermon would correspond to a bubble in the mind-map or an extension in the organic image.

This approach works well with biblical passages, doctrines, practices, and situations containing multiple images or ideas. A major danger of jigsaw puzzle preaching is that an undisciplined preacher may never bring the pieces together.

A Sermon Prepared on the Model of an Author Writing a Novel

The novelist begins with the rudiments of setting, plot, character, and atmosphere. The novelist has an idea of the storyline, along with an array of ideas, scenes, turns of plot, character development. But the writer does not know how the story will turn out until the story itself is finished. An author gives identity to the characters in a novel.[34]

> Even in the case of fictitious characters, however, the creatures are not mere puppets; their identity is a field of specific if vaguely known potentials interacting with the potentiality of their broader environment. *What is written takes on a life of its own,* so that the characters begin to author themselves, and, as every writer knows, to some extent the author. The author, giving life, bestows freedom; the creatures, given life, become creators. The creativity of the characters, however, continues in interdependence with — often in struggle with — the creativity of the author.[35]

The story, given the opportunity, will write itself.

The preacher, like the novelist, begins with the rudiments of the sermon, e.g., questions, biblical interpretation, episodes from church history, theological themes, points of contact between the direction of the sermon and the contemporary community. The preacher has an idea of where the sermon is headed and may have in mind some points to make, some images to use, and a general sense of the sermon's movement. But, as the preacher works, the sermon begins to take shape. Sometimes, the sermon develops as the preacher anticipates. Sometimes the sermon takes a very different direction.

Few sermons generated in this fashion necessarily will be actual narratives (though see below, The Sermon as a Single Narrative). More likely such a sermon will be a composite of genres: exegesis, theological analysis, social commentary, application. But the process of development will emerge in a way similar to the writing of a novel.

Eugene Lowry cautions against interjecting a "theme statement" for the sermon too early into the process of developing the message. Such a statement can be a roadblock to creativity. "In contrast, experienced novelists and other narrative artists are likely to note that they never quite know where the story will go — or should go — until they follow it to the end." Lowry urges, "We, too, need to maximize our capacity to keep open throughout the preparation process."[36] Nonetheless, toward the end of the process of writing the sermon as a novel, the preacher needs to pause to make sure that the sermon will have a good opportunity to provide a worthwhile conversation with the congregation and the gospel. The preacher needs to make sure that the sermon works as a unity.

For instance, a preacher might want to encourage the congregation to engage in resistance against the principalities and powers. The preacher does not know how the sermon will develop. The preacher ruminates on the fact that, in the biblical period, the principalities and powers are suprapersonal beings who siphon the glory that belongs to God and, in the process, to enslave humankind and nature. But then, quite unexpectedly, the preacher begins an imaginary face-off with the principalities and powers. The preacher personifies the principalities and powers, and speaks to them. "Racism, I know who you are…you are one of the principalities." The preacher is talking with the congregation as if the congregation is a third party in the face-off with the principalities. "Did you see that? Did you see how this principality caused that African American to be treated?" The preacher talks with Jesus, who liberates people from the principalities. Jesus invites the community to witness to a world in which the principalities and powers are subjugated to God. The preacher concludes by speaking to the principalities and powers and warning them to beware of actions against racism that the congregation is planning.

This pattern is especially useful when the preacher has a hunch, intuition, or feeling about a text or topic, but does not know where that hunch is leading. This mode offers the preacher a way to find out where the feeling might go. However, preachers can become so clever that their cleverness calls attention to itself and works against helping the congregation focus on the gospel.

All preachers should try this approach once in a while to shake loose our creativity. When I tried it for the first time, I suddenly found myself writing the sermon in free verse — something I had never done before, and had not planned. That pattern does not suit all my preaching, but sometimes, it is just right. Others may have similar experiences.

The Sermon as a Single Narrative

The sermon can be a single story. Some narrative sermons of this type are elaborations of a biblical narrative. Other preachers tell a narrative from a novel, a short story, or the media. Still other preachers create stories that they tell as a whole sermon. The story itself is the message. The preacher offers few interpretive remarks. The congregation derives the message of the story by entering into its narrative world and experiencing life from its standpoint. Later, they might engage in critical reflection.[37]

To prepare such a sermon, a preacher needs to create or locate a setting with which the congregation can identify. The story needs to have an engaging plot that the community can follow. The characters in the story need to be developed with the depth and complexity of real life. The resolution of the tensions in the plot need to be believable.

I once heard such a sermon on John 6, "I am the bread of life."[38] The preacher began by describing a hot afternoon. The preacher was at home, in a house that was not air-conditioned. The children were sweltering. The preacher's spouse noticed that they were out of bread. The preacher went to a store for bread. The preacher described the heat: stepping into the sun, the car that had been closed up, the hot steering wheel.

Inside the store, we feel the air conditioning with the preacher. As the preacher walks through the cool aisles, we pick up the fixings for homemade ice cream. We buy a large bag of ice, a case of soda pop, and an electric fan. The preacher drives home in the heat. We feel the blistering temperature, but we anticipate the soda pop, the breeze stirred by the fan, ice cream. The preacher enters the house and puts the purchases on the table.

After a moment of silence, the spouse asks, "But . . . where's the bread?"

The preacher looks the congregation in the eye during a long pause, and then continues, "Jesus says, 'I am the bread of life.' How can we forget the bread?" After another pause, the preacher sits down.

When well done, this type of preaching can create a narrative world in which the congregation encounters the gospel. It can help congregations experience biblical texts, doctrines, practices, and situations. The congregation can also sympathetically realize challenges to their faith, feelings and behavior by sympathetically identifying with the setting, plot, and characters of the story. However, the story must resonate with the depth and complexities of real life. It cannot be caricature, flat, or oversimplified. This approach is probably not suitable for every Sunday. The preacher must tell the story-sermon in a compelling way. The congregation soon checks out of a story-sermon when the preacher is standing in the pulpit, semireading from a manuscript in a droning voice. The preacher who would attempt a sermon as a single story may need to secure coaching from a local speech teacher or storyteller.

My impression is that this kind of preaching works best when the time for the sermon is short. For instance, at the Christmas Eve service a pastor sometimes preaches only 6–10 minutes. A single narrative has a good chance to carry the gospel freight in such a circumstance, as long as the story is well developed and well told.

Furthermore, when the preacher elaborates a story from the Bible, the preacher needs to be careful to enlarge the story only on the basis of material that is actually found in the text or is justified by our knowledge of the world of the Bible. The preacher needs to avoid unjustified psychologizing or fanciful description of setting or events.

Brief Descriptions of Other Lively Arrangements

The previous arrangements for sermons are only one table in the preaching smorgasbord. I now very briefly describe some further possibilities. Based on the previous discussions, a student can easily expand these brief remarks into fuller pictures.

Through much of the twentieth century, sermons were organized so as to *make a series of related points.* A point is typically a proposition that the preacher hopes to get across to the congregation. The point-making sermon is typically organized in one of two ways. In one model, a preacher discusses a biblical text, a topic, a practice, or situation and then draws out the points to be made about it or the lessons to be learned from it. In the other model, the sermon is a series of points from beginning to end. The preacher announces the biblical text, doctrine, practice, or situation and then, immediately, says something like, "The first thing I want to say about this text is...." Within each point, the preacher might provide reasoning to support the point, fill out its implications, and illustrate it.[39] Some contemporary preachers disparage sermons that make points. However, Paul Scott Wilson points out, "The problem with points is not points. The problem with points arises when the listeners, in hearing the points, become bored and ask, What is the point?"[40] When clear, critical thinking is needed in the church, sermons that make points can serve the purpose.

Preachers have long favored developing sermons in the pattern of *thesis-antithesis-synthesis.* The preacher begins by stating a thesis — a particular way of understanding a text, a doctrine, a practice, or a situation (or some aspect thereof). The preacher then undercuts understanding (antithesis). The sermon concludes with synthesis, that is, with the preacher helping the congregation combine elements of the thesis and antithesis with other elements into a fresh synthesis that overcomes the dichotomy between thesis and antithesis.[41] For instance,

> In the neighborhood in which our church is located, youth are in difficulty. The church is to witness to God's love and justice for youth. As a church, we need to provide Sunday school and a youth group, open a recreational center, serve as tutors, counselors, and legal advocates, challenge the city government to take a lead in urban renewal to upgrade the quality of life in our neighborhood.

Another much-used pattern is problem-solution. The preacher describes a problem then shows how the gospel offers a solution to the problem. Frank Thomas, a pastor in Illinois, nuances and expands this model. After describing a problem, the preacher assures the congregation of God's redeeming presence and activity. The last part of the sermon celebrates what God is doing and its effects in the human and cosmic worlds.[42]

Don S. Browning, who teaches ethics at the University of Chicago, has developed a pattern of *practical moral reasoning* that can become the pattern for a sermon that helps congregations wrestle with personal and social situations.[43] It can also help interpret biblical passages, doctrines, and practices. (1) The sermon briefly describes how the subject of the sermon comes to the congregation's attention, e.g., assisted suicide. (2) The preacher helps the congregation listen to the experience of the subject of the sermon. What feelings, values, actions are at work? What do they reveal? What factors prompt assisted suicide? The social sciences are often of great help in this phase of the sermon. (3) The sermon makes a critical, theological analysis of the subject of the sermon. How shall we understand assisted suicide and the factors that prompt it from the perspectives of appropriateness to the gospel, intelligibility, and moral plausibility? (4) The preacher helps the community come to a decision and formulate a strategy to act on that decision. How should the Christian community regard assisted suicide? How should the community witness to its conclusion?

An historic approach regards the sermon as *speaking to the mind, heart, and will.*[44] Step 21 (pages 155–158) becomes an arrangement for a sermon. After a beginning, the sermon is divided into three parts. The first part focuses on what the congregation can think and believe about the direction of the sermon. In a sermon on the doctrine of the communion of saints, the preacher might explain the origins of that idea in the Bible and its functions in both the history of the church and today. The second part of the sermon focuses on the heart. The preacher helps the congregation feel the subject of the sermon. In a message on the communion of saints, the preacher might help the congregation experience the continuing presence of the saints. The third part of the sermon focuses on the will. The congregation decides to act on the subject of the sermon. For instance, what can we do in our congregation to help it become more of a community within itself and with the saints? How can we express continuity with the witnesses of the saints?

H. Grady Davis, a leading Lutheran preacher in the mid-twentieth century, advocates a *"question propounded."*[45] I refer to this approach as a Socratic model because of Socrates' fame for asking questions.[46] The sermon is arranged to follow the movement of questions in pursuing the interpretation of a biblical text, doctrine, practice, or situation. The questions must be ones that the congregation needs to ask in order to come to a full-bodied interpretation of the subject of the sermon. Some such questions may be informational, while others penetrate beneath the skin to issues of feeling, value, and behavior. For example, a preacher might ask the following in a sermon that focuses on the ministry of reconciliation in 2 Corinthians 5:16–21. What does reconciliation mean? Who is reconciled to whom, and by what means? What is the church's ministry of reconciliation? How do we carry it out? What are its effects? Are we ready to live with the effects of the personal and social effects of reconciliation in the Christian community? How can the church witness to reconciliation in the larger world?

Fred Craddock compares a sermon to *taking a trip.*[47] At the beginning of the sermon, the preacher and the community start a journey together. Along the way, moments in the sermon reflect moments on a trip, e.g., smooth driving, a rest stop, a long hill that strains the engine, a detour for road construction, beautiful vistas that are not on the map, an emergency roadside stop for upchucking, arrival at the destination. The preacher could think of taking a trip with the Joseph cycle in Genesis 37–50. Each incident in Joseph's life is a different moment in the trip. This approach can help the preacher trace a theme across the Bible or the history of the church. Again, each author who contributes to the theme contributes a different quality to the travel.

A British preacher in an earlier generation, W. E. Sangster, borrowed the term *faceting* from the jewelry industry.[48] A jeweler takes a rough stone and cuts faces into it. The preacher and congregation, similarly, look at a text or topic from different faces. For instance a sermon on pacifism as a Christian ethical possibility might consider pacifism from the standpoints of (a) the pacifist, (b) violent communities on whom the pacifist does not inflict violence, (c) the community of which the pacifist is a part, (d) when pacifism seems to give monstrous evil powers the freedom to exert themselves, (e) the costs of pacifism to the pacifist, (f) the rewards of pacifism to the pacifist. A twist is for preacher and congregation to look at the subject of the sermon from *different points of view*. When preaching on the visit of the magi to the infant Jesus in Matthew 2:1–12, the preacher might consider the visit from the points of view of the astrologers, Mary and Joseph, Herod, the synagogue, Gentiles, Matthew's Christian Jewish listeners, today's church.

Charles Rice notices that *a story and a biblical text can sometimes mutually interpret one another with a minimum of commentary*.[49] The story can come from a novel, a short story, a play, a movie, a news source, a television program, the experience of the congregation or preacher. A preacher might tell a contemporary story, and follow it by speaking the biblical text. The preacher leaves the congregation to make connections between the contemporary story and the passage from the Bible. Similarly, the preacher might follow the pattern of story-text-story. The sermon tells part of a story, then speaks the text, then returns to tell the rest of the story. A preacher might tell one story, speak the text, then tell another story. This approach could be modified to bring a story and a doctrine or practice into an interpretive relationship.

Eugene L. Lowry develops four related approaches. In *running the story*, the sermon follows the flow of a biblical passage.[50] In *delaying the story*, the sermon begins with experience and delays bringing the biblical story into the sermon until the sermon needs the biblical news. In *suspending the story*, the sermon begins with the biblical passage, but then encounters theological or moral difficulty in the text. The sermon suspends the telling of the biblical story per se until the difficulty is resolved. Then, the sermon returns to the Bible. In *alternating the story* the sermon moves back and forth between the world of the text and the contemporary world.

Chiasm is a frequently employed literary and rhetorical device in the Bible that can suggest a possibility for a sermon. A chiastic passage is divided into parallel members (labelled a, b, c, a', b', c', etc.). Each rmember relates to the member with its corresponding letter: a relates to a', b to b', c to c'. The members interpret one another in one of three basic ways. In a synonymous parallelism, the members say the same thing but in different words. In synthetic parallelism, one member adds to another. In antithetical parallelism, the members oppose one another. In a sermon, the members would consist roughly of paragraphs. They might be portrayed, visually, as follows:

A
  B
    C
  B'
A'

The sermon would begin with A, go to B, C, then to B', and A'. This pattern gives the sermon a lovely symmetry.

Thomas G. Long, one of the most influential figures in contemporary preaching, brings still more patterns for the sermon "out of the stockroom."[51] A sermon can proceed *if this...then this...then this.* If God is love...then God loves all...then God loves our enemies. *This is the promise of the gospel...here is how we may live out that promise.* Paul affirms that already, in Christ, "there is no longer Jew or Greek...slave or free...male and female" (Galatians 3:28). Here is how we live out this affirmation in our homes, in our church, in the larger community. *Not this...or this...or this...but this.* Here is Job's situation. The first friend does not interpret his situation correctly, nor the second, nor the third, nor Elihu. But God interprets Job's situation aright. *Here is a prevailing view...but here is the claim of the gospel.* A prevailing view is that the purpose of evangelism is membership recruitment for the church...but the claim of the gospel is that the purpose of evangelism is to introduce persons who do not know God to the divine love, promises, and call. *This...well, what about this...then this...yes, but what about this?* The Song of Songs celebrates sexual relationships between women and men as a divine gift...yes, but problems related to sexual relationships are some of the most agonizing problems in the contemporary era (e.g., discrimination, harassment, abuse, infidelity)...well, many people in the contemporary world have only a self-serving and physical understanding of sex...yes, but the church's attitudes toward sexuality are Victorian and contribute to problems with sex today...of course, but that is a misunderstanding of the best of the Bible and Christian teaching on sexuality. *Here is a letter.* Like Paul writing to the Thessalonians, the preacher speaks a letter to the congregation, "Dear Friends in Christ..." *This...or that...both this and that.* "Disciples are wise as serpents; disciples are innocent as doves; disciples are both wise as serpents and innocent as doves."[52]

Possibilities for sermon arrangement are nearly endless. The most important consideration is for the preacher to arrange the movement of the sermon to serve the gospel in the context of the community and occasion when the sermon comes to life.

CHAPTER TWELVE

Stories, Images, and Experience in Preaching

Since Bible times, preachers have recognized remarkable power in stories. For instance, the Deuteronomic Moses preaching to the community "beyond the Jordan — in the wilderness, on the plain opposite Suph," prepares the community to enter the promised land by retelling the story of Israel, with commentary (Deuteronomy 1:1). Scholars of the First Testament point out that Torah is not first a set of commandments, but a story that bespeaks identity, within which commandments guide the community in living out its identity. Jesus' best known utterances are the parables. The four Gospels present the meaning and message of Jesus in narrative. You encounter a parishioner in a mall who repeats a story that you told in a sermon six months ago.

In the last generation, story has become one of the most widespread items in discussion about preaching. Preachers are rediscovering the importance of storytelling. Some preachers think of the sermon itself as having the character of a story. Toward the latter end, a major work is entitled *Preaching the Story.*[1]

This chapter explores stories, images, and experiences in preaching. The chapter focuses on the nature of story, image, and experience. I ponder the qualities of good stories and how they can witness to the gospel. The chapter passes along some tips from gifted storytellers. I conclude with the use of experience in the sermon.

What is a Story? An Image?

A *story* is usually made up of a setting, characters, a plot, and atmosphere (feeling-tone). The elements of the story may be real or created. A story narrates a sequence of words, actions, events, and experiences. Usually, the plot contains complications, tensions, or surprises that sustain our interest. In the case of a good story, we "understand the successive actions and thoughts and feelings of certain described characters with a peculiar directness." As we listen to the story, we are "pulled forward by this development almost against our will; we commonly appreciate, without needing to articulate to ourselves, many of the reasons and motives and interests upon which the story's development up towards its climax depends."[2] The best storytellers do not intrude upon our hearing of the story with explanatory comments, except as we need background information to understand the story.

Stephen Crites, an influential literary critic, points out that experience has narrative quality. Our everyday world is comprised of setting and characters. Our moments fold into one another like events in a story. Because experience has this narrative quality, stories have a potent capacity to shape the ways we perceive. Stories "give qualitative substance to the form of experience because it [experience] is itself an incipient story."[3] A story becomes a lens through which we interpret the world.

> The stories people hear and tell, the dramas they see performed, not to speak of the sacred stories that are absorbed without being directly heard or seen, shape in the most profound way the inner story of experience. We imbibe a sense of meaning of our own baffling dramas from these stories, and this sense of its meaning in turn affects the form of our experience and the ways in which we act.[4]

Stories offer a framework of meaning within which to understand persons, relationships, events, actions. Of course, experience is much more than narrative. But primal stories help us locate how the various pieces of life relate to one another. They help us know from whence we have come; they help us understand the present; they envision where we are headed. Stories help create our senses of self, others, community, world. They tell us who we are and point us to what we are to do. Stories form communities. Consequently, "a conversion or a social revolution that actually transforms consciousness" requires a dramatic change in the stories by which the community lives.[5]

An *image* is a word-picture. When it is spoken, it evokes or creates a scene in the mind, heart, and will of the listeners. For instance, the expression "God is a rock" is an image. It causes the listeners to transfer many associations with rocks to their thoughts and feelings about God. An image can be very short, or it can be developed in several sentences, even paragraphs. Like a narrative, an image evokes or creates a world into which listeners enter. A story can function as an image.

Thomas G. Long, a leader in thinking about the relationship between literary criticism and preaching, identifies three main types of images in sermons: simile, metaphor, and synecdoche.[6] A *simile* is an explicit comparison between two things. "God is like a woman who cares deeply enough about her friend to confront her friend with a needed change of behavior." A simile is typically a nonsurprising comparison intended to help the listener grasp and experience the first term (God) by means of the second (like a mother).

Metaphor is a word used very loosely in preaching circles to refer to almost any figure of speech. Technically, it denotes calling the familiar by the unfamiliar to provoke the listener to perceive the familiar in a fresh way. For instance, calling God a rock is a metaphor. Structurally, a metaphor is often similar to a simile, whereas a simile is a simple comparison, a metaphor often has a more surprising, even shocking quality. The feeling of surprise is a part of the experience of a metaphor. The comparison in some of the parables of Jesus is so forceful that literary critics regard them as metaphors. "The reign of heaven is like treasure hidden in a field, which someone found and hid; then, in joy that person goes and sells everything, and buys that field" [7] (Matthew 13:44). Everything? That's a shocking idea. Metaphors can be as short as a phrase or as long as a novel.

Synecdoche (pronounced soon-**eck**-doe-key) uses a part to stand for the whole or the whole to bespeak the part. Whereas simile and metaphor make comparison, synecdoche does not. Lucy Atkinson Rose taught preaching until she died of cancer at age fifty. Her journal from her last year is published as *Songs in the Night.*[8] The phrase "songs in the night" stands for all of Lucy's life in her last days.

In *personification* the preacher speaks of a nonhuman entity as if it is human. For instance, in a story of someone suffering a prolonged death from cancer, Fred Craddock personifies death as a caller with a pale, yellow face. In the early phases of the illness, death looks through the window with its pale, yellow face. As the illness proceeds, death knocks on the door. The patient's health caregivers and friends push against the door and keep death out. But eventually, death enters the room and takes away the breath of the patient.[9]

The preacher creates a world by telling a story or creating an image or using an experience. These language worlds have the power to reshape our perception and behavior in the everyday world. Fred Craddock once heard someone say that telling stories would "change the world about like breaking up concrete by throwing lightbulbs against it." But, then, Craddock testifies "I've been present when someone threw lightbulbs against concrete walls, and the walls cracked and fell...with just a word."[10]

How Can Stories, Images, and Experiences Function in Sermons?

In an earlier generation, preachers spoke of stories, images, and experiences as illustrations. The story made the point clear and vivid. For instance, in order to illustrate the notion that God blesses the single life, the preacher might tell the story of a single person whose life is blessed. Illustrations vivify the sermon. They help the congregation envision how the sermon concretely relates to them. They demonstrate the truth of the preacher's claim. They put flesh on an abstract theological assertion. Listeners move from the story the preacher tells to their own stories.

Stories, images, and experiences can still function as illustrations in sermons. In fact, most sermons would benefit from an increase of such material. However, many writers in the field of preaching point out that even when stories, images, and experiences are intended to serve as illustrations, they do much more. They create a world. The congregation that participates in a story, image, or experience imaginatively comes to understand the world through that lens. Stories, images, and experiences touch the self and community at the level of thought, feeling, and behavior. Because of this potency, Fred Craddock says that stories or anecdotes often

> *are* the point. In other words, a story may carry in its bosom the whole message rather than the illumination of a message which had already been related in another but less clear way. Removing the story is not just cutting the pictures from a history book, leaving only the text; it is removing the entire page. The story is the picture which is the text.[11]

The preacher, then, needs to be clear about the purpose of a particular story, image, or experience. Does the world created in the story or figure of speech serve the purpose of the sermon and its place in the sermon?

Stories, images, and experiences can function in sermons in several ways.[12] These materials can *establish* a world. The world created in the story assures the congregation that its everyday world is trustworthy. Either anticipating or during the exile, with the community's life threatened, the Priestly community gave form to the epic poem of creation that begins the Bible (Genesis 1:1 – 2:3). This poem, with its constant refrain, "and God saw that it was good," assures the community that the world is trustworthy. To take a contemporary example, in a sermon on the church as a community of support, a story of a person who overcomes adversity with the help of the church establishes the congregation's trust in the church as a body of support.

Stories, images, and experiences can *defend* the world. The story, image, or experience explains why the congregation's everyday world is trustworthy or why certain teachings or practices of the community are reliable, and offers an "evidential experience" (page 59), that is, an instance of the claim of the sermon. As one of its many purposes, the interaction between Peter and Cornelius (Acts 10:1–33) is part of the rationale for the Gentile mission in the book of Acts. Through Peter's dream, God initiates this mission. God then confirms the mission by filling Gentiles with the Holy Spirit (Acts 10:34–48). In a sermon on the Christian practice of interpreting the Bible and Christian tradition in a present-day church, the preacher might recount an incident from a Bible study group in which the hassle of getting to a Bible study was justified by the group's discoveries.

Story, image, and experience can prompt the congregation to want to *investigate* the everyday world. A story may raise a question about the world. It can pose an interesting possibility that the congregation may want to pursue. The prologue to the book of Job, in which Job loses animals, property, and family, places Job in precisely this situation (Job 1:1 – 2:12). Job's plight prompts the friends and God to investigate the possible meanings of Job's decimation. In a sermon seeking to help today's community interpret disaster from a Christian perspective, a preacher might recount the experience of a community through a natural disaster to raise questions for reflection.

A story may *critique a community and call for a repair* of an aspect of the everyday world. This function takes the motif of investigation a step further by pointing out that aspects of the everyday world are in disrepair. They need to be fixed. Joel uses the image of a swarm of locusts moving through Israel and devouring everything in their path (Joel 1:2–13) because Israel has turned away from the practice of true worship and justice. However, the plague is designed to motivate the community to repent so that they can be restored (Joel 2:12–27). To take a contemporary example, a congregation intends to be faithful, but uses its kitchen only for itself. In response, the preacher might develop an image of a congregation whose kitchen feeds hungry people.

A story, image, or experience may *subvert the world.* The language world urges the congregation to see that its everyday world is untrustworthy. Beyond repair, the everyday perception of the world should be replaced by a new way of perceiving the world. The goal of subversion is to help the community become open to a more adequate vision of the world. Matthew's parable of the ten bridesmaids presumes a community in which many Christians have developed the easy confidence that by recognizing Jesus as an agent of God's renewal of the world, they are relieved of moral obligation (Matthew 25:1–13). The parable subverts their easy confidence. They are waiting for the bridegroom, but they do not have enough oil (several of the ancient rabbis described deeds of love and mercy as oil). They do not let their lights shine (Matthew 5:14). They cry, "Lord, Lord," but do not live in ways that are consistent with the manifestation of God's reign (Matthew 7:21–24). Consequently, they are denied immediate access to the fullness of God's reign. The story is intended to shock such people into witness.

The same story, image, or experience may function in different ways because it interacts differently with different listeners. For instance, to those who experience the church as supportive community, the story of a person who overcomes adversity with the help of the congregation establishes world. The same story prompts investigation on the part of those who think that the church is largely an individualistic Sunday-morning affair. The story subverts those who dismiss the church as a cold institution whose interest in people is only what they contribute to the church's institutional self-survival. The preacher needs to be aware and critical of these different possibilities so that the preacher can use the story, image, or experience in the sermon to maximize the possibility that the material will contribute to the conversation in the way that the preacher hopes.

The Worlds Created, Evoked, and Authorized by Stories, Images, and Experiences

John S. McClure, a leading interpreter of contemporary preaching, sagely notices that the stories and images that we use in sermons are not casual matters. The composite of characters, issues, and activities that appear (and do not appear) in our stories and images reveal those to whom we pay attention, and those that we ignore.[13] Implicitly, the sermon signals the congregation as to whom and what the preacher believes to be more important and less important. For instance, the preacher who develops stories, images, and experiences from the lives of people of different races and classes helps the congregation realize God's love for all. A preacher who tells no stories about interpersonal relationships implicitly suggests that God is not concerned about such matters. The congregation may infer that the preacher is impersonal. The absence of personal material may create the impression that the preacher is not being authentic with the congregation.

Furthermore, preachers frequently evoke the power of cultural assumptions that lie behind the characters, activities, and issues represented in stories, images, and experiences. Preachers implicitly (and often unintentionally) authorize particular worlds (cultures) and subworlds (subcultures) by referring to them in stories and figurative language. For instance, sports stories often legitimate competition. An image from the world of capitalism indirectly places the divine imprimatur on that economic system. An experience from the military endorses conflict as a part of our common life. A single story can evoke multiple worlds. In addition to validating competition, a golf story likely legitimates the upper-middle-class lifestyle and the old boys' network that operates on the golf course.

Of course, preachers can critique the world that is evoked in the story, image, or experience. For instance, in the process of using an image from the world of sports, the preacher might criticize the competitive spirit. However, the preacher needs to be careful in these matters. I once heard a sermon entitled, "Establishing a Beachhead for Peace" in which the preacher urged the congregation to be peacemakers. However, the dominant word-picture of the sermon, "establishing a beachhead," is drawn from the sphere of war. Its use in the sermon suggests that it is legitimate for Christians to use warlike tactics, even in the service of peace.

McClure is direct. "Over time, what people hear through sermon illustrations is a culture being generated, validated, legitimized, and made into a norm."[14] This phenomenon is particularly true in long pastorates. Because the gospel is the promise of divine love for all and the call of justice for all, preachers need to plan, over a season of preaching to see that the worlds created by their stories, images, and experiences reflect the breadth of the gospel's concern for all.

On the one hand, the congregation needs to find itself in the worlds of the sermon's stories, images, and experiences so that the congregation can identify with the worlds created in preaching. On the other hand, most congregations need to enlarge their understanding of God's love and will for justice. The figurative language of the sermon can help the congregation enlarge its vision by inviting the community to experience new worlds through participation in the story.

To help the world created by the stories, images, and experiences of the sermon reflect the worlds of the congregation and the gospel, the preacher might make a chart similar to Table 1 at the end of chapter 3 (pages 42–43. Such a table would help a preacher keep a record of the worlds reflected in the preacher's stories, images, and experiences and to identify worlds that need to be included. To help the congregation hear its own life in the sermon, the preacher might list the worlds of the congregation (the early items on the table). To help the congregation enlarge its sense of world, the preacher should also list other worlds to help the community sense God's love and will for justice for all (the later items on the table).

Telling Stories and Creating Images

What are practical things to do while telling stories and creating images? In the ensuing discussion, I refer to a story told by Fred Craddock. Craddock develops this narrative as a part of a sermon on the parable of the parent and the two children (Luke 15:11–32). In the first part of the sermon, Craddock tells the story of the younger child — claiming the inheritance, squandering it the far country, returning home to the fatted calf. In the latter part, the preacher asks the congregation to identify with the older child who stayed at home tending the field and who resented the return of the prodigal.

> There were some young women in a family up the street, beautiful young people. One of them, about fourteen, matured very early and was into all kinds of difficulties. The parents were divorced, and they didn't have much home life. She was truant at school. She was just everywhere. She was hanging on the tail end of every motorcycle that roared through town. Always in trouble. Finally, she was up before the juvenile judge, charged with traffic in marijuana and other drugs. The judge sent her to a juvenile facility for young women in the southern part of the state.
>
> She was pregnant when she went. At the age of fifteen, she gave birth to the baby in the correctional facility. We heard about it back on the street. We also heard that she was coming home.
>
> The afternoon that she was to come home, all of us in the neighborhood had to mow our yards. I was mowing my yard, watching their house. I was interested in whether or not she would really come home. Would she have that baby? I was mowing the yard and she didn't come. And I was down to cutting about one blade at a time.
>
> Finally, a car pulled in, and she got out, and she had that baby — born in prison, out of wedlock. And some folks in that house came out and grabbed her and kissed her, and they grabbed that baby. They took turns holding the baby. A car pulled in, and another car, and another. They were all grabbing her and holding the baby. People

were parking in the street — so many that you couldn't get a Christian car down that street.

Well, finally, I got a little self-conscious and went in the house because it suddenly struck me: suppose someone in that family sees me down here and says, "Say, Fred, she's home. We'd like for you and Nettie [Craddock's spouse] to come. We're giving a party for her and the baby."

Would I go?[15]

Craddock returns to the text by speaking some of the key images, "And they killed the calf, and hired the musicians, and there was music and dancing, and a party.…"

Susanne K. Langer, philosopher of art, explains how stories and images work. That which makes them "quite different from any actual segment of life, is that the events in it are *simplified*, and at the same time *much more fully perceived* and evaluated than the jumble of happenings in any person's actual history."[16] The storyteller filters out distracting details and focuses the listeners only on that which is essential to entering the world of the story. Langer concludes, "The 'livingness' of a story is really much surer, and often greater than that of actual experience."[17] Craddock tells us only what we need to know about life on the block, the young woman, the party. Craddock trims away all material that is extraneous to the development of the setting, characters, and plot. Toward these ends, Charles L. Rice, a sensitive storytelling preacher, formulates a rubric, "Simply tell the story. Tell the story simply."[18]

Craddock calls attention to several qualities of good stories and images.[19] The setting and characters have a *lifelike quality*, that is, they honor the depth and complexity of life. They are not caricature. We know people like the young woman above. Many of us feel the complicated fascination-fear with which Craddock describes himself. We hear the story from a specific *point of view*. The story is told so that the listeners can *identify* with someone or something in the story itself or in its larger world. Kenneth Burke, an influential literary and rhetorical theorist, points out that identification is one of the most important means by which listeners or readers enter a story.[20] Identification takes place as we recognize something in the setting or characters with which we identify. In Craddock's story, most people in the congregation identify sympathetically with the preacher, who is identifying with the older child in the parable. From that point of view, the story pushes us to examine the degree to which we traditionally religious persons welcome prodigals.

The plot is *clear*. Even when the plot is interrupted by unexpected developments, we can follow it. The storyteller uses *sensory language* from the realms of sight, hearing, taste, touch, smell. At the same time, the story is *economical in its use of adjectives and adverbs*. Too much detail can obscure the forward movement of the story. The preacher wants to leave "something for the listener to contribute" to the story. The storyteller uses *images* that create a picture in people's minds, e.g., "She was hanging on the tail end of every motorcycle that roared through town." A narrative uses *direct address*. The storyteller creates conversation among characters. "Say Fred, she's home. We'd like for you and Nettie to come up." Direct conversation creates immediacy. It brings the community more into the world of the story than indirect address or a simple report of what was said.

The teller often needs time to create an emotional ethos. A little wait from the start of the story until its finish often heightens suspense and draws the community more deeply into the story. Note how Craddock begins with simple details (a beautiful young woman) and adds them in order of emotional complication (truant...motorcycle riding...drugs...jail...pregnant in jail). The full complexity cannot arrive too soon or it will be lost. Some preachers and some stories can develop such a sense in a sentence or two.

While I discuss timing in embodiment in the next chapter, I call attention to the fact that the preacher's timing is important in *telling* the story. Few stories and images should be rushed. For most narratives and word-pictures, the preacher needs patience in the telling. In the actual preaching of this sermon, Craddock uses great vocal variety: poignant, sorrowful, envious factual, indignant, and at the end — pensive.

The location of the story in the sermon is also important. A story at the beginning of the sermon creates an emotional and intellectual setting within which to hear the rest of the sermon. When the story is delayed, the first part of a sermon creates a setting for a story that comes later. The preacher must decide when to tell the story or develop the image so that it will have its best opportunity to engage the congregation. Generally, an emotionally powerful story makes its best contribution to the conversation in the later stages of the sermon. When such a story is used too early in the sermon, the congregation may not be ready for it.

The preacher should minimize efforts to summarize "the point" of a story or to otherwise interject explanatory comments into the story. Such comments may be necessary when a story is from another time or place or contains details that the congregation will not understand unless they are explained. However, a good story typically creates its own meaning. A preacher's commentary may actually drain the story of its power. Some people will find such comments distracting, even demeaning. "The preacher doesn't think we're smart enough to understand the story."

David Buttrick, who write extensively about story and image in preaching, recommends using stories in the sermon that are consistent with the imagery within the biblical text.[21] Thus, if the text contains agricultural imagery, the text and sermon can hold together as an image-unit by making use of agricultural imagery. The parable of the soils, for instance, suggests imagery of seeds, plants, and soils.

Buttrick points out that stories and images work best in sermons when the tone of the story matches the tone of part of the sermon in which it is used.[22] In a part of a sermon invoking divine judgment, the preacher would tell a story or develop an image that is sober. In a segment of a sermon that celebrates the peace that passes understanding, the preacher would draw on peaceful material.

Furthermore, Buttrick insists that the preacher make a positive interpretive comment on a positive story and a negative interpretive comment on negative story.[23] A preacher ought not tell a negative story and then draw a positive comment from it. The force of both the story and the interpretive remark are lost. Preachers sometimes tell a story with a negative cast and then use "reverse English" to draw a contrast to make a positive point. In a sermon on the practice of forgiveness, the following movement is confusing. "A father abused a young daughter — beat her, bruised her, drew blood, broke an arm. He stubbed out his cigarettes on her body. Every time she sees him, her stomach tightens in fear. But, God says we are to forgive." In addition to being problematic because the image of abuse is stronger than the call to forgive the image suggests, "This woman has reason to keep her distance from the man." The image does not provide a sense of theological empowerment to forgive and oversimplifies the dynamics required in achieving real forgiveness in the situation. Following the principle of keeping strength with strength, the preacher might take a tack like this. "We can forgive because God makes it possible. I even know of a case in which a young woman was abused…Through patient and sometimes painful therapy, she was able to forgive the person who abused her."

Buttrick also points out that the strength and vividness of a story or image should match the strength and importance of the material with which it is associated in the sermon.[24] If the preacher tells a story to bring alive a major point, then the preacher can pull out all the stops. If a pastor is developing an image in support of a minor part of the sermon, then the image needs to play a relatively minor role in the emotional fabric of the sermon. The preacher would not want to develop an image that captures the congregation's attention and does not allow them to join the rest of the sermon.

Many authors in the field of preaching caution against letting a story or image swallow the rest of the sermon. Unfortunately, I cannot cite a formula that will indicate when a story or image threatens to overpower the sermon. Length alone is not the issue. Indeed, a preacher may develop a whole sermon as a single narrative or as a movement of images. The problem arises when the story causes the congregation to lose sight of the connection between the story and the rest of the sermon. Distracting stories usually manifest some of the following qualities. They lack the depth of life. They are tedious. The narrative is so emotionally loaded that it overpowers the rest of the sermon. The story is cluttered with detail. The story does not fit the community in which it is told or its place in the sermon. The preacher does not know how to tell a story.

One of the best ways for preachers to improve their storytelling is to listen to good storytellers and to read good stories. For instance, Craddock is the quintessential storytelling preacher. Many of the stories of Barbara Brown Taylor have a magical quality. Garrison Keillor, radio host of "Prairie Home

Companion," is a splendid storyteller. Another way to improve one's storytelling is to join a storytelling group. Most metropolitan areas now contain groups who work together in storytelling. The Network of Biblical Storytellers, for instance, is collegial and has chapters in most large cities.[25]

The Preacher's Own Experience in the Pulpit

The question of whether preachers can refer directly to their own experience in the sermon has been a minor firestorm for the last twenty years. In chapter 5, I fanned my ember in this discussion by suggesting that because experience can be a source of the knowledge of God, preachers can speak directly about their own experience. They can use their own lives as windows on the gospel. Members of the congregation often identify with the pastor. When the preacher needs to help the community reflect on a challenging or sensitive issue, the pastor can sometimes approach the issue through the pastor's own experience. The preacher's story reflects the stories of many in the community. By so doing, the community may be able to name and sort through its own struggles. The use of the minister's experience can also help deepen the relationship between pastor and people, as pastor and people realize the depth of the humanity that they share.

However, this possibility comes with some parameters.[26] As a general rule, the pastor does not want to be the heroine or hero in the sermon. "Look at me, the model Christian!" This manner of speaking increases the distance between the preacher and the congregation. Instead, the pastor identifies with the congregation as sinner in need of grace, as broken in need of healing, as practicing injustice in need of repentance. The preacher can testify to grace, healing, and repentance flowing through the pastor's life. But the focus should be on God making these things possible. Preachers would use such experiences in the sermon only if their use would have a good chance of becoming a vehicle through which grace, healing, and repentance become available in the church.

The sermons in chapters 16–17 make use of the preacher's experience. I end my sermon with an extended story (pages 266–267). René Rodgers Jensen ends her sermon with a poignant and deeply moving narrative from her own life. Reginald Holmes draws directly on his life and work as an inner-city preacher. While Mary Donovan Turner does not overtly refer to her own life in her sermon, the sermon is very close to experiential.

David Buttrick (who thinks that preachers should never refer to their own experience in the pulpit) cautions that the use of the preacher's personal story can split the congregation's consciousness, that is, cause the congregation to focus on two things at the same time.[27] Preachers want the community to focus on the point being communicated. However, when preachers talk about themselves, the congregation's awareness sometimes splits between focusing on the point and on the person of the preacher. This split is particularly distracting when the preacher tells a story that causes the congregation to be concerned about the preacher's well-being.

To counteract split consciousness, a preacher can do several things. If the experience raises questions about the preacher's health or safety, the preacher can assure the congregation that the situation is under control. Fred Craddock recommends that when using personal material, the preacher hold the camera not on oneself, but use one's own life as a camera to film someone else.[28] Craddock tells the story of the prodigal young woman as something that he experienced. But he focuses the camera on the young woman. We identify with Craddock's view of the story. When he tells how the incident affects him, his question becomes our question: "Would I go?"

The preacher should not expose material that is too intimate. How does the preacher identify such material? Unfortunately, we have no formula. Paul Scott Wilson, who thinks responsibly about the ethics of preaching, proposes this criterion: You would not say in the pulpit something that you would otherwise say only to a counselor or in private to a family member or friend.[29] These matters include dimensions of personal relationship, private aspects of sexuality, personal finance, moral behavior, bodily functions.

When drawing on personal life, the preacher needs to be careful not to contribute to the voyeurism that is prominent in our time. Many people want to peek behind the curtains of the private lives of public figures. Personal material in the sermon should clearly serve the gospel.

Pastors cannot refer, in detail, to their own experience very frequently. Personal experience can be very powerful when it is used selectively and for well-chosen occasions. But, ministers who, week after week, tell stories from their own kitchens, workshops, bathrooms, lawns, canoe trips, and basements soon leave the congregation bored. Some in the community may think the pastor is acting out certain psychological needs. Others will think the pastor is lazy. "Our preacher never thinks or reads, just tells personal stories." A general principle that I have found helpful is to tell a detailed story from my own life no more than once a month. Of course, preachers can refer quickly to their own questions, struggles, and insights on a weekly basis.

The preacher cannot speak in the pulpit about things that have been shared only in confidence. To do so both violates ministerial ethics and undermines the relationship of trust between the congregation and the pastor that is essential for ministry.

Preachers are divided on the advisability of speaking about the experiences of their families and significant others in the pulpit. Certainly, the preacher should never talk about the members of the family or the significant other without permission. The preacher should not tell embarrassing things. The preacher should not depict household members in caricature (either positively or negatively).

A preacher can often make use of personal experience by recasting in the third person or by telling a story about "a person." The feelings, occurrences, questions, and observations of the experience are all present in the sermon, but the congregation does not identify them directly with the experience of the preacher.

Sources of Stories, Images, and Experiences

Stories, images, and experiences often occur to the preacher in the course of sermon preparation. Preachers who search for a story, image, or experience to work into the sermon often manipulate and misuse the material that they find. A pastor who is desperate for a narrative will sometimes bend almost any story to fit the sermon. Consequently, a prime way to develop a repertoire of good stories, images, and experiences is to live as fully as possible so that one's life and memory is stocked with ripe material. A key, as Fred Craddock stresses, is for the preacher to pay attention to life, not for the purpose of gathering stories for the sermon, but for the purpose of breathing deeply and enlarging one's "sympathies of spirit."[30]

Many stories and images originate in our own experiences. Laura Loving, a pastor in Wisconsin, was preparing a sermon for Mother's Day when her eye fell upon a mother spider tending her young on a web glistening with rain. That experience became the organizing image for the sermon. We can find stories, images, and experiences by paying attention to the news media, movies, novels, short stories, television programs, and stageplays.

In addition, a preacher can create a story or image. We can make it up in the same way that a fiction writer authors a short story, novel, or play. Some preachers think, "But I am not creative enough to write my own story." However, Professor Craddock recommends an exercise that is helpful both for those who have difficulty getting started and those who need to focus in a particular way.[31] Take a sheet of paper and write at the top, "What is it like to be…?" What is it like to be the woman who for eighteen years "was bent over and was quite unable to stand up straight"? (Luke 13:10–17), or a person who is homeless and who pitches a bed under the overpass on the freeway every night, or a young person who is in the confusion of puberty? Soon, the page is filling with word-pictures, ideas, questions, and memories. Similarly, one might simply start a story and keep writing or talking until it begins to take shape. This exercise works especially well in a feedforward group. The preacher or someone in the group starts a story about the text or topic, and people in the groups add to it. Typically a story creates itself on the spot. Such exercises, of course, take time.

The preacher who uses a created story needs to let the congregation know that the story is created. The preacher does not want to leave the impression that the story took place as reported. Honesty requires as much. The preacher could signal the congregation at the beginning of the story with lines such as, "Once upon a time," or "I can imagine a situation in which," or "Can you picture a soccer player?" The preacher might also alert the congregation to the fact that the story is created by the presence of details that are obviously imaginary. For example, I might describe a conversation with a 250 pound canary. Even when they are not factually accurate, created materials can be true-to-life in the sense that they resonate with the depth and complexity of life.

Books and other sources of canned sermon illustrations seldom provide the preacher with useful stories or images. Such material does not often throb with the depth and beat of real life. It is often simplistic and generic. Stories from such sources typically sound stale. They seldom fit the sermon or purpose to which they are put.

A preacher needs to save a good story for the right occasion. Preachers sometimes tell a story they have just found, and then, a few weeks later, wish that they could use it in a context that suits it better.[32] In chapter 16, I suggest ways of saving such materials.

Every sermon should have at least one story that embodies the major claim of the sermon. The rule of thumb: A preacher is ready to make a point when the preacher can tell a story that brings that point into life. If you cannot tell a story about a subject, you are not ready to preach about it. Such a story shows that the preacher has a clear view of a concrete point of contact between the sermon and the community. The congregation, then, is in a position to participate fully in the preaching conversation.

SECTION SIX

From the Study to the Pulpit and Back

Most preachers continue to think about the content of the sermon until they stand in the midst of the congregation to speak it. Many preachers toss in bed on Saturday night as they turn over the sermon in their minds. Some preachers make changes in their manuscripts, notes, or mental files while they are meeting with other worship leaders for prayer immediately prior to entering the worship space. A few pastors even touch up the sermon as they preach. The preparation of the sermon is not finished until the pastor steps out of the pulpit. Even then, the sermon continues as the congregation reflects and acts upon it.

The preacher wants the conversation that takes place in the pulpit to be consonant in tone and appearance with the content and tone of the manuscript, notes, or mental file. Few preachers are prepared to step into the pulpit just because they have written the last word on their manuscripts or notes or have made their last mental note. We need to prepare to bring the sermon alive during worship. We need to get the sermon from the page or from the mind into the heart and body so that we can voice it with clarity, energy, and passion. We need to evaluate our preaching so as to build on our strengths and compensate for our weaknesses — in both content and embodiment.

Chapter 13 focuses on embodiment. How do we express the sermon through body and voice? Chapter 14 suggests that preachers include evaluation of the sermon as a regular part of the process of preaching. What are some practical sources of feedback that can help us? Chapter 15 discusses a number of additional subjects that do not fit elsewhere in the book.

CHAPTER THIRTEEN

Embodying the Sermon

Only a generation ago, this chapter of a textbook on preaching would have been entitled "Delivery." In that pattern of thinking, the content and delivery of the sermon had the same relationship as a package and a letter carrier. The preacher delivered the content by making use of techniques for pronunciation, voice projection, and gestures. Now, however, we think of this aspect of preaching as *embodiment*. Of course, preachers must pay attention to the technical aspects of voice and body. The congregation needs to be able to hear and see. But these qualities serve bringing the sermon to life.

This chapter first explores the meaning of embodiment. It then highlights qualities of presence, voice, speaking, and moving in the pulpit that can help the sermon engage the congregation. The chapter concludes with some practical preparations for Sunday morning ranging from practicing the sermon to diet and exercise.

Embodiment

The word "embody" means "to give a body to." The sermon is not just a package that the preacher leaves in the mailbox of the congregation. The sermon grows from the preacher's mind, heart, and soul. As a person, I do not have a body. I *am* a body. Similarly, the sermon becomes a sermon only when it comes to life through the self of the preacher in living conversation with the congregation. The meaning and speaking of the sermon are integrated in the same way that the form and content in a biblical text are conjoined (pages 130–133). The preacher who embodies the sermon should show "a high degree of coherence between what the preacher says, and how he or she says it."[1] The preaching is consonant with the person of the preacher. In a sense, the sermon is incarnate through the preacher and the congregation.

Along the same lines, a group of preachers, influenced by recent developments in speech communication, speak of the preacher performing the sermon. In popular speech, the term perform often means "to put on a show" (with a slightly negative meaning). For instance, a teacher hears a young person's excuse for not completing an assignment, rolls the eyes, and says, "What a performance." However, studies in human communication use the notion of performance in the sense of its etymology (from old French): *par + fournir*, meaning, "to carry through to completion." In the act of preaching, the pastor performs the sermon by bringing it to completion. "Preaching is a performance of the sermon, that is, a vocal and physical action through which the form of the sermon becomes sound and image."[2]

Illustrating the relationship between a sermon and its embodiment or performance, a group of teachers of preaching contrast Sally's first experiences in preaching with her senior sermon. In her initial sermon, she struggled to breathe. She "clung to her manuscript, eyes and hands glued to her paper, her voice as thin as a reed." But through patient work, her senior sermon was quite different. "Her voice was so much more grounded than before." Her vocal tones rose and fell in accordance with what she was saying. She "stood tall, at home in her body, breathing deeply and effortlessly." As she sat down, the class applauded.

> The students in that senior seminar who applauded Sally were acknowledging that she seemed of one fabric with what she was saying. The line of distinction between her person and the words on her note card seemed barely discernible. Even though Sally lost her place once, flubbed a couple of lines, and looked a little distracted at first, her sermon came more from inside her than outside her, more from the depths of her soul than from the surface of her mind. The class sat up and listened because it realized that Sally was doing something far more profound than "getting a sermon said." She had the sermon beneath her skin and was operating from her own power and passion. In Sally, the sermon happened before the class's eyes. Because something clicked within her at the sermonic moment, something also clicked between herself and the rest of the class. "The word became flesh and dwelt among us."[3]

Such preaching happens when the sermon is part of the preacher's self and when the preacher allows the self to express the sermon.

Correlating the Tone of the Embodiment with the Tone of the Content

The preacher seeks for the embodiment of the sermon to create the same sense as the content of the message while being consistent with the personhood of the preacher. The integrity of the sermon is reinforced when the themes of the sermon and the tone of the embodiment work together. The integrity of the sermon is called into question when the content of the sermon says one thing but the embodiment says another. For instance, when the message is joyful, the preacher wants to be joyful. The congregation responds to the joy in the preacher, and the community becomes joyful. When the preacher talks about joy, but is dreary, the embodiment undercuts the message. The congregation may think, "If the preacher is not joyful, why should we believe that joy is possible?" Similarly, if the message is sober, then embodiment of the sermon should have a sober character. If the sermon is painful, then the preacher should speak with sensitivity and in pain shared with the community.

Sermons sometimes have one mood from start to finish. A sermon on sorrow, for instance, may have a sorrowful tone from beginning to end. Many sermons, however, change character from one part to another. For instance, a sermon begins in a mood of questioning. The mood then becomes exploratory as the preacher probes different resources for understanding the questions that were articulated at the beginning of the sermon. Along the way the preacher is disappointed as some leads come to dead ends, but sparks as other leads result in discovery. By the end of the sermon, confidence and hope pervade the sermon. In such a message, the preacher needs to embody each part of the sermon in a tone that correlates with the purpose and mood of the part.

Much African American preaching follows a distinctive pattern of embodiment. Many African American sermons begin with the preacher speaking slowly and deliberately. As the sermon progresses, the intensity builds. According to the content of each section of the sermon, the preacher may speak matter-of-factly, weep, shout, whisper, fume, and rejoice. Since the end of the sermon is typically a celebration, the preacher often exults in the goodness and power of God. The final section of the sermon often overflows with energy. Many African American preachers whoop at the end of message. Whooping goes by various names, such as tuning, intoning, or getting happy. Each preacher's whoop is different because it is shaped by that personality. Whooping combines chant, song, rhythm, stylized speech, shouting, and dance-like movement. The whooping of the preacher begets a similar response in the congregation. When whooping, preacher and the congregation become joy itself.

This principle — that the embodiment of the sermon should create the same sense as the content of the message — is qualified by the phrase, "while being consistent with the personhood of the preacher." A cardinal rule of embodiment is that ministers should be themselves in the pulpit. Ministers need to bring the sermon to life in ways that are consistent with who they are. Some clergy are naturally exuberant and forceful. Other clergy are quiet and introspective. Most clergy fall between these poles. The congregation expects that qualities native to the preacher will be manifest in the pulpit. In a sermon on Christian joy, for instance, the exuberant person may palpably light up the sanctuary. A restrained person communicates joy more quietly, but with equal depth and intensity.

Preachers who put on a persona other than their normal one while preaching cause the congregation to question the integrity of the messenger and the message. "Who is my pastor? The quiet person I meet by the water fountain or the one with the cheesy smile in the pulpit? What am I to believe from this person?"

The anxiety of preaching causes many pastors to be less than we can be when we step in the pulpit. We lose a measure of confidence and sense of control. We become self-conscious and fearful. We are afraid of embarrassing ourselves, the congregation, even God. Some of us shake like leaves in a gale. We retreat into ourselves. As I noted in chapter 1, some of these reactions subside with experience in preaching. However, even many experienced preachers are less than they can be. Consequently, many of us need to be pushed (by preaching class, by peers, and by feedback groups) to become more expressive.

Furthermore, as I point out in the next section, aspects of preaching sometimes call us to step beyond our immediate comfort zones of expression and movement. We are never asked to be other than we are. But we are sometimes called to express ourselves in ways that are initially unfamiliar and perhaps even uncomfortable.

Many preachers need to realize, as well, that our personhoods have more dimensions than we typically express. A talkative extrovert often has dimensions that are quiet and reflective, and that can serve the gospel witness when they come to expression in the pulpit. An introvert often has demonstrative qualities that are consistent with the individual's personality, and that can bring energy to a sermon.

Developing an Image of Yourself in the Act of Preaching

Having an image of oneself as a preacher is important. An image is a picture – or better, a video clip – in the mind and heart of the person you would like to be when preaching. An image gives you a pattern, a sense, of who you are, and how you can speak and move in the pulpit. Both consciously and unconsciously, your body inclines toward becoming that image while you are preaching. Toward the end of becoming a lively, engaging presence in the pulpit, you might list the qualities that you would like to embody while preaching. You can then integrate them into your embodiment.

The preacher seeks an image that is a genuine expression of that individual's personhood. In the pulpit, you want to be who you are. However, a preacher seldom generates an image out of thin air. We are influenced by other preachers (particularly those who have had a significant influence on us) and by communicators outside the church. Ministers can incorporate aspects of the pulpit styles of other preachers and speakers – as long as the incorporation is filtered through one's own personhood. In embodiment, as in other aspects of preaching, the pastor who simply imitates another preacher often comes across as a counterfeit.

Toward the end of establishing a preaching presence that is authentic to oneself, a pastor might inventory preachers and others who affect the preacher's self-perception. Such an enumeration might include beloved pastors of one's childhood or youth, famous preachers whom one admires,

teachers who were outstanding lecturers, actresses and actors, stand-up co-
medians from late-night television. While most of these figures are positive
role models, some may be negative. Particular mannerisms or styles may
prompt you to think, "I don't want to be like that!" The preacher can ask, "Am
I drawing my image of myself from these persons? If so, am I doing it in such
a way that I honor both their individuality and my own integrity? What can I
learn from them? What do I need to leave behind? What do I need to nurture
in my own self-image?"

Other people — in preaching class, in colleague groups, in the congregation — can often help in this process. They can point out connections that you
may not make between your image of yourself and its sources. They can raise
questions that may not occur to you. They can help you reflect critically on
the adequacy and authenticity of your self-perception.

The Body in Embodiment

Because of the anxieties that accompany preaching, embodiment seldom
happens in an optimum way on its own. Most preachers need consciously to
develop or deepen traits that are consistent with one's image of oneself as a
preacher and that help engage the congregation in communication.[4] When
embodying a sermon, a preacher often finds it helpful, especially at the beginning of one's preaching career, to divide the embodiment into tasks related to
different aspects of embodiment and to work on one task at a time. A
preacher must sometimes pass through a period of being self-conscious about
these matters, such as saying to one's self, "I must think to make eye contact
at this juncture of the sermon." Gradually these qualities become an intuitive
part of the preaching self.

The most important dimension of embodiment is the preacher's sense of
presence. This quality is hard to define. It is a function of the preacher's *gestalt.*
It cannot be isolated in the same way that we can catalogue eye contact, the
voice, or gestures, but it can permeate and empower them all. Presence is the
sense that the preacher is aware of the immediacy of the living God. The
preacher is fully present with the congregation. Presence is a sense of
centeredness within oneself and of bond with the community. It is called forth
by the awareness of God with us, by the community, and by the occasion.

Presence is communicated in the preacher's posture, tone of voice, and
movement. It bodies forth in the way in which the preacher stands in the
pulpit and in a sense of centeredness that emanates from the preacher. Presence shows in the way a preacher enters the worship space, handles a candidate for baptism, leads the prayer of confession, reads from sacred scripture,
presides at the breaking of bread, and pronounces the benediction. When it is
there, the congregation can feel it more than they can describe it clinically.
Without it, a preacher can bring forth a theologically and technically perfect
sermon, but with something missing. One preacher, who is senior minister on
a large staff and who does most of the preaching, always makes announcements prior to the service to help the congregation develop a sense of relationship with that person that will carry into the sermon.

The preacher cannot put on presence, like an alb or a Geneva gown. It grows from prayer and other Christian practices, from the deep knowledge of call, and from being in relationship with God and with the community. Preachers need to manifest presence in ways that are consistent with their personalities. An exuberant person will usually manifest an exuberance. A quiet person will be quiet. Your way of being in the pulpit should be an authentic expression of who you are in the service of mediating the knowledge of the presence of God.

Along these lines, I recently had a telling conversation with my colleague, Clark M. Williamson, who teaches systematic theology at Christian Theological Seminary. He asked, "Other than lack of theological clarity, do you know what I miss most in the preaching that I hear?" "No. What do you miss?" He replied, "Passion. The sense that what the preacher is saying really matters to the preacher and ought to matter to me." I tested his observation with other colleagues and with laypeople in congregations where I was teaching and preaching. Many agree. They add that they do not just mean shouting and thumping the pulpit. They think of passion as strength of conviction, an inner intensity that spills into the sermon. They feel it in the embodiment of the sermon.

The *voice* is important. People must be able to hear easily. If they have to strain to make out the preacher's words, they weary. Speech teachers use the term "projection" for speaking loudly enough so that all can hear. Many worship spaces have sophisticated electronic amplification equipment to help the preacher project. However, most sound systems work best when the preacher projects. The amplification system is a help in projection, not a replacement.

In order to project, the preacher *breathes and speaks from the diaphragm*, and not from the chest or the throat. I find it helpful to think of my voice as similar to a baseball that I throw from my diaphragm to the farthest pew or chair. Many preachers need more coaching in diaphragmatic breathing than they get from an introductory preaching textbook. However, here are basic points of reference to test whether you are breathing and speaking from the diaphragm or from the chest and throat. You can tell you are breathing from the diaphragm if you put your hand immediately underneath your sternum and feel your diaphragm move downward and if your chest and shoulders do not move upward and outward. If your chest and shoulders move upward or outward as you breathe, you are projecting with your throat. Preachers who speak from the diaphragm can preach all day at top volume. Preachers who speak from the throat last about half of a regular sermon before they begin to feel winded and their throats begin to get sore.

The preacher needs to find *a rate of speaking* that helps the congregation stay in the world of the sermon. A minister's speed of speech in the pulpit should typically be a little slower than conversation in the office, given the fact that worship spaces are large and they often echo. The preacher does not want to speak so quickly that words are hard to distinguish from one another (a particular problem in worship spaces that echo). At the same time, the preacher does not want to speak so slowly that the community naps between words.

The preacher must also *pronounce* words clearly so that people know what the preacher is saying. As indicated in the previous section, preachers want to *inflect* the sermon in tones that are consistent with the content of the message. Inflection calls for vocal variety and expression. Most preachers would benefit from working with an audio tape recorder prior to the sermon. The preacher can practice speaking the sermon in speeds, moods, and inflections that will encourage the sermon to express what the preacher wants it to express. The pastor preaches the sermon into the tape then listens for whether the sermon has the necessary inflection to communicate its meaning. Where can the preacher liven up the speaking? What needs to be toned down? Is the sermon phrased and emphasized so as to bring out the meaning? Are there places to speak more quickly, more loudly, with more pathos, more slowly, more softly, with less emphasis?

Eye contact helps the congregation feel that the preacher is speaking with them and not at them. By eye contact, I mean looking into the eyes of the members of the community. Most of the time a preacher should establish eye contact with one person and speak to that person for a few seconds before moving to another. When the preacher is looking into the eyes of a specific person, the rest of the congregation also feels a sense of personal connection with the preacher. The preacher who only reads the manuscript or notes and never looks up gives the impression of being afraid of the congregation, or unprepared, or both. The pastor should avoid looking up from the pulpit but looking over the heads of the congregation (perhaps eyeballing the wall just above their heads). That, too, can be interpreted as the preacher's fear of looking the congregation in the eye. The preacher whose eyes are constantly sweeping around the congregation and never making sustained contact with anyone communicates instability and unsettledness.

Eye contact is particularly important at the beginning of the sermon as it helps invite the congregation into the world of the sermon. It is important at the end of the sermon, as it helps the congregation move into reflective consciousness by feeling that they have been a part of a living conversation. It is important at key moments in the sermon. For example, if the sermon centers around a significant question, the preacher would want to establish eye contact when asking that question so that the congregation would feel addressed by it.

Some preachers are reluctant to make eye contact because they are afraid of losing specific wordings on which they have labored. My spouse has convinced me that, most of the time, immediacy of contact is more important than using a particular word or phrase.

Preachers who use a manuscript or notes and who speak from behind a pulpit or note stand can often enhance the congregation's sense of contact by standing 2 to 3 feet in back of the pulpit. They do not have to tilt their heads very far down toward the pulpit to see their notes. Consequently, the congregation sees more of their faces and less of the tops of their heads. Preachers who hang over the pulpit must turn their heads almost 90 degrees in order to read their notes. The congregation loses facial contact and instead sees the tops of their heads.

A preacher needs to be sensitive to the relationship between eye contact and the preaching space. A congregation where a friend pastors recently built a new sanctuary with a portable pulpit. When the pulpit is located in such a way as to be "high and lifted up," the preacher noticed that people in the front pews shied away from direct eye contact. Through conversation, he discovered that they felt intimidated when the preacher looked down at them from such a great height.

As important as eye contact is, some sermons have moments when the preacher wants to avoid it. In conversation around the kitchen table, there are times when the character of what is being said is such that speakers look at the floor, or out the window, or at the hands, or even up at the ceiling. Such moments come in preaching, too — when communication might even be interrupted by the self-consciousness of eye-to-eye contact.

Facial expressions that are lively can also help embody the message. The congregation can see as well as hear when the preacher asks a question, and looks puzzled, or speaks of happiness and looks happy. A stone face, or a face whose expression contradicts what the voice is saying, intimates that the gospel is stony or inconsistent.

Good *posture* can help the sermon. The preacher should stand upright, naturally, comfortably, and straight, but not rigidly. Pastors who stand on both feet and keep the weight distributed equally feel like they are on solid ground. They also communicate a sense of solidarity to the congregation. Preachers should avoid slouching, leaning on one foot, or standing rigidly. Some people who see a preacher who is rigid or who slouches will subtly think of God as rigid or a slouch. The preacher who habitually leans on only one foot feels unstable and communicates instability to the community.

As far as *body movement* (other than gestures) is concerned, the preacher should generally stand behind the pulpit. When the preacher moves the whole body within the space of the pulpit, the movement should correlate with a natural transition or emphasis in the content of the message. The movement visually reinforces the transition from one part of the sermon to another.

Some pastors like to preach away from the pulpit for all or part of the sermon — perhaps standing alongside the Lord's table, or in the center of the chancel, or even in a main aisle. Many preachers in contemporary services avoid pulpit-like furniture altogether. Many pastors who leave the pulpit preach all or part of the sermon without notes. Others have notes or manuscript clipped into a Bible that they hold in their hands. Pastors who preach without pulpit or note stand say that they feel less hidden, less encumbered, more free, and most of all, more immediately involved with the community. Many people in the congregation apparently share these positive responses.

Standing away from the pulpit can enhance the conversation between pastor and people. However, in many communities the pulpit is not just a piece of furniture, but is a vital theological symbol that the people associate with being addressed by the gospel. Furthermore, not all sermons call for freedom and immediacy. Some sermons call for a certain reserve and distance. Freestanding preaching ought not become an unthinking pattern any more than the unthinking use of a pulpit.

A fair number of preachers who leave the pulpit (and some who stay behind it) roam. They talk all the while — sometimes bent over slightly, with hunched shoulders, as if trying to appear to be profound — but their movements are aimless. They unintentionally suggest that the church and God are aimless. All major physical movement needs to coordinate with the movement of the sermon.

Gestures — actions of the hands and other body parts — can enliven the sermon. Like voice, face, and movement, gestures are not for their own sakes, but are for punctuating the message of the sermon. The preacher whose gestures are disconnected from the message can leave the impression that God is similarly disconnected. Preachers seek gestures that are consistent with their personalities. However, teachers of public speech formulate a principle that pushes many beginning preachers: In order to appear as big as life, a speaker's gestures must be bigger than life. Because the preacher is quite a distance from the congregation, the congregation cannot see small movements of the hand, arm, and head. To be seen, gestures must be exaggerated. Many students initially feel awkward making gestures that are larger than those they make in ordinary conversation. Some students feel so awkward and self-conscious about gesturing that they simply do not move at all. They look like talking fence posts. Preachers must often force themselves to gesture. Gradually, if you do so, I can almost guarantee that you will reach the point at which gestures in preaching, even large-size, will feel comfortable.

Pastors seek variety in gestures. With forethought and imagination, a preacher can create gestures that visually represent what the preacher is saying. Words can suggest gestures. For instance, when speaking of going up or down, the preacher can motion the arm and hand up or down. When referring to a circular argument, a pastor could make a circle. When saying, "On the one hand…on the other hand," the preacher might raise the right hand and then raise the left hand. The preacher who makes the same gestures over and over becomes boring. Some preachers make nervous gestures that do not relate to the message. The congregation may think God is repetitious, nervous, and dull.

For the sake of variety some gestures can be inside the body frame and some outside. The body frame is an imaginary door frame whose sides rise up the sides of the body. The top runs across the top of the head. If all gestures are inside the body frame, many will be lost because they are too small.

Generally, the preacher wants to make gestures that are open — that keep the arms and the torso open to the congregation. The preacher wants to keep the hands open, with the palms exposed, so the congregation can see them. Such openness implies that the preacher is forthright and vulnerable. The congregation can interpret closed arms and hands as revealing a preacher who is closed, self-protective, or authoritarian. The same danger follows the preacher who habitually makes a fist or who shapes a hand like a handgun (in the way that children form their hands like guns) and repeatedly points the index finger at the congregation. Once in a while, a preacher can make these latter gestures to emphasize a particular point, but only once in a while.

The *pause* is one of the preacher's best friends. A well-placed pause helps the congregation reflect on what has just been said. It can allow the congregation to process feelings that the sermon stirs. A pause can be oral-aural underlining that calls attention to a part of the message. Few preachers use enough pauses. The speech never breaks. The congregation never has an opportunity to take a break, reflect, gather its breath, or let a deep feeling penetrate to the bone. A person from the world of music says, "The rests are where the true art resides."[5]

Few preachers pause long enough. Many preachers feel out of control when they stop talking. In the tension of the preaching moment, a tenth of a second of silence can sound like three years to the preacher. The preacher is tempted to pause just long enough to take a breath. A congregation needs to have time to feel a pause. In order to discipline themselves into silence, many beginning preachers find it helpful to count, "one thousand, two thousand, three thousand," while pausing. The other side of the coin is that I have heard a few pauses that lasted so long that the community became restive. No single length fits all pauses. Pauses can be of different lengths in order to help the congregation in different ways. A pause needs to be long enough to help the congregation, but not so long that people become restless. Most preachers can develop a feel for how long to pause.

Before entering the worship space, the preachers may want to leave behind things with which they might play while they are preaching. For instance, a woman might finger a brooch. A man rattles keys in trouser pockets. Leave such things in the study.

Gestures can get out of hand. A preacher can become so busy that the actions are distracting. When gestures call attention to themselves, they work against the sermon.

A pastor in Indianapolis stresses that it is important for you to know your proclivities in respect to embodiment, so that you can work with your strengths and compensate for your weaknesses. For instance, this pastor says, "If I have keys in my pocket, I rattle them. I have a note on my office door reminding me to take my keys out of my pocket on the way to the pulpit."

Writing for the Ear

Preachers who prepare their sermons in their minds tend to prepare to speak in language patterns that are customary in speech. Preachers who prepare manuscripts or even notes sometimes write in a style that is more at home in written communication than in speech. Indeed, I have heard some sermons that sounded very much like an essay that the preacher had written for a composition class. The preacher's goal in this respect is for the sermon to be a genuine oral-aural event. The sermon needs to sound like spoken language.

In oral-aural communication, *sentences tend to be short and direct.* Writing teachers often urge students, for the sake of variety, to create sentences that can be quite complicated. In speech, however, we tend to avoid compound and complex sentences. Many oral sentences, in fact, consist of a subject, a verb, and a predicate. Speech tends to be direct, with relatively few adjectives. For effective use of this pattern in speech, note the excerpt from David Buttrick's sermon on page 192. I do not mean to articulate an inviolate rule such as, "No more compound or complex sentences." An articulate preacher can certainly use some such expressions. But the sermon that is made up of long and complicated sentence after long and complicated sentence can easily leave the listeners lost a mire of complexity.

Oral speech makes use of *active verbs and expressions and generally avoids passive verbs and expressions.* Verbs and expressions in the active voice are usually easy to follow, and they communicate a sense of energy and directness. When used of God, active verbs suggest that God is active and engaging. Passive expressions are often more difficult for the congregation to follow. The listeners must sometimes figure out who is doing what with whom. By the time they figure out those activities and relationships, the preacher is on another page. Furthermore, passive expressions sometimes suggest, indirectly, that God is passive. For instance, compare these two expressions. "God loves you." "You are loved by God." At times, of course, a preacher needs to use a passive in order to communicate a certain idea or feeling. However, most sentences are better served by the active voice.

In oral-aural communication, *paragraphs tend to be relatively brief.* Of course, listeners do not "see" paragraphs. However, the preacher's vocalization often follows paragraph-like units of material. When these are long, the congregation sometimes finds them tedious and hard to follow. Most oral paragraphs are four to six sentences. Again, this suggestion is not an absolute rule. Some preachers, some subjects, and some circumstances call for longer expressive bundles.

Oral-aural communication typically uses a *relatively small number of adjectives.* Of course, a preacher can use a good adjective, adverb, or a descriptive clause to help open up a part of the sermon. However, too many adjectives, adverbs, and descriptive clauses can call attention to themselves and even sound flowery. As noted in the next paragraph, good preachers are often descriptive, but they describe less by piling on adjectives and more by creative, simple expressions.

For instance, note the simplicity of language and the spare number of modifying expressions in this beginning of a sermon cited on page 166, from Fred Craddock:

I am going to say a word, and the moment I say the word, I want you to see a face, to recall a face, and a name, someone who comes to your mind when I say the word. Are you ready? The word is "bitter." Bitter. Do you see a face? I see a face. I see the face of a farmer in western Oklahoma, riding a mortgaged tractor, burning gasoline purchased on credit, moving across rented land, rearranging the dust. Bitter.

This paragraph is evocative, but it contains the smallest handful of adjectives and adverbs.

Lively speakers often make use of *figures of speech and colorful turns of phrase.* John McClure illustrates the difference in engaging quality that a preacher can make by shaping an expression to be more interactive. For example, the sentence, "Compassion attracts those who are in need" is clear. It is a simple construction of subject, verb, and predicate. But it is not as lively as "Compassion attracts company."[6] After the sermon manuscript or notes are in a fairly developed form, you might go through the manuscript and mark expressions that could be made more engaging. Of course, you need to be careful not to drift into language that is sensational or that otherwise distracts the congregation.

In speech, we often use *sentence fragments, expostulations, dangling prepositions and participles, and similar forms of expression* that are not suitable for most written expression. The speaker usually seeks language that follows conventional patterns in grammar. For instance, the subject and verb need to agree in number. The preacher needs to use proper cases. Without violating such conventions, speech is sometimes less polished and even fragmentary.

In spoken language, we also often connect sentence after sentence after sentence with the word "and." While the repeated use of "and" becomes monotonous in written material, it is often quite helpful to the speaker.

Talk often contains *repetition.* A preacher may use a theme line, or a turn of phrase, or an image several times in the sermon. Such repetition can help the community remember the sermon. Repetition can tie various pieces of the sermon together. It can bring the feelings and associations developed in one part of the sermon to another place in the sermon. On the negative side, it can also be overdone to the point of boredom.

Getting the Sermon from the Paper (or Mind) to the Heart and Body

In order to be ready to preach, the pastor needs to get the sermon from the paper (or mind) into the heart and body. Some ministers find it helpful to make notes on embodiment that they write in the margins of their manuscripts or notes. I have known one preacher who makes an "embodiment chart" for the sermon. This pastor charts possibilities for the voice, for gestures, for pauses.

One of the best ways for the preacher to become one with the sermon is to practice in the worship space. As one of my mentors said, "On Friday afternoon, I preach to the empty pews." In the process, the preacher becomes accustomed to the pulpit, note stand, or speaking space. The act of speaking the sermon out loud brings the whole body into the act of preparation. Speaking the sermon out loud helps the preacher "hear" the language and the degree to which it is oral-aural. The preacher can try different inflections, gestures, and pauses, to see which seem most natural and communicative. The minister can get a feel for pauses in that worship space. Preachers can practice to establish eye contact with persons in all parts of the sanctuary (including the choir) at various times in the sermon. In short, the preacher develops an image of how the sermon might come to life so as to engage the community in conversation.

Through practice, the body feels the sermon. The preacher practices a progression of bodily feelings through the sermon. During the preaching, these feelings unfold and often prompt the preacher to remember both the content of the message and how the preacher wants to body forth the sermon. If the preacher only stays in the office and reads over the manuscript or notes, or goes over the sermon mentally, then only the eyes and the mind are involved. Even if the preacher stands up and speaks quietly (so as not to disturb other people in the office or at home), the effect is only partially that of speaking in full voice in the space where the preaching conversation will take place.

To magnify the value of such practice, the preacher can work with an audio recorder or video recorder in the worship space. The preacher can then get an idea of sounds and movements that enhance various parts of the sermon. If presermon videotaping is not possible, the preacher can preach to a mirror.

Such practice sometimes prompts the preacher to further discoveries that affect the content of the sermon. The speaking and moving prompt the preacher to further insight. Recognizing this value, I know one preacher who speaks aloud and gestures throughout the preparation of the sermon. From the very beginning, the sermon is coming through the fullness of that pastor's body.[7]

Some preachers memorize the sermon. This pattern seems to work well for preachers who can memorize quickly and who can embody memorized material in fresh and compelling ways. The memorizing preacher needs to be one who does not frequently go blank in the pulpit and who does not speak memorized text stiffly.

Many clergy who preach without notes can simply organize the whole sermon in their minds. Others make use of various techniques to remember pieces of the sermon. Some preachers, borrowing a pattern from the old Dale Carnegie speech schools, construct a memorable, perhaps even ludicrous, visual image in their minds and associate various parts of the sermon with the elements of the image. A few preachers make use of various parts of the worship space to prompt them to remember and connect various parts of the sermon. The preacher sees the pulpit and thinks, "Beginning." The preacher sees the Lord's table and is reminded of the biblical text and its interpretation. The preacher sees the angel in the window in the balcony and remembers theological analysis.

The preacher can practice in such a way that the sermon becomes artificial or stale. We need to find ways to practice that encourage freshness and immediacy.

Other Practical Preparations Prior to Preaching

Many preachers benefit from a routine prior to preaching. They rise at a certain time, arrive at the church building at a certain time, perform certain tasks. Routine allows the preacher to anticipate a definite time to go over the sermon one last time. The preacher has a sense of security and direction. Energy is not drawn off in unexpected or unproductive anxiety. Routine provides a framework within which to handle the inevitable crisis.

However, some preachers are anesthetized by routine. They thrive in unpredictability. Chaos energizes them. Preachers need to find the ways that best help them be present to the congregation as they get from home through the office and hallways and into the worship.

Whether the preacher is driven by routine or chaos, the preacher needs to check the pulpit, note stand, or other preaching space prior to the beginning of the service to make sure that the space is prepared for preaching. Is the desktop clear and ready to receive sermon notes? Are the wires from the sound system out of the way? Does the pulpit light shine? Is the amplification system working? Is the microphone adjusted for your height? Do you know how to turn the microphone on and off? If you like to have a glass of water nearby, is it filled and fresh? If you need a throat lozenge prior to the sermon, is it on your pulpit or in your pocket? If you need a platform on which to stand to give you some additional elevation, is it in place? Is the area around the pulpit clear of flowers, flags, and other paraphernalia that might interfere with your gestures? A bathroom stop on the way to the worship space usually prevents bladder distraction during the service.

As a part of their general spirituality, clergy need to *eat well* and to *exercise*. These behaviors are especially important before preaching. For about twelve hours prior to the sermon, the preacher needs to eat foods that help your body prepare to preach. Pastors vary greatly on what they can ingest. Many ministers cannot eat heavily. If they do, they feel as though they have a wheelbarrow of wet cement in their stomachs. As their blood diverts toward digestion, they become lethargic. They need to eat sparingly. Other preachers are the opposite. Without a massive breakfast, they hunger. They may be weak or even cranky. Preachers need to find eating patterns that help them.

The embodiment of the sermon often benefits from exercise prior to preaching. Exercise increases the heart rate, blood flow, and energy level. It helps take some of the edge off of the preacher's anxiety. It loosens the throat, clears the lungs, and gets the metabolism working at a high rate of efficiency. Preachers who exercise at high intensity and who do so regularly need to complete (or reduce) their workouts so that they have plenty of time to recover before the service. Other preachers walk from home to the church building, speed walk around the building after they have arrived, or do calisthenics.

Preachers differ in how to spend *the night before preaching*. In order to have enough rest to have optimum energy for Sunday, some preachers need to have a slow evening with an early bedtime. However, I know a pastor, a young adult, who served a congregation in which the young adult group regularly got together on Saturday nights for events that lasted quite late. This pastor found that, even with a short night's sleep, the energy from this gathering carried into the pulpit on Sunday morning. As in so many other matters, pastors need to find their own way.

The preacher who is prepared to preach is usually prepared for another dimension of preaching that is risky, but sometimes well advised. During the course of the prepared sermon, the preacher sometimes receives signals from the congregation that they are not participating in the conversation. In the act of preaching, a prepared pastor can sometimes adjust the sermon to help give the community a better opportunity to join the conversation.

A wise friend in the ministry also suggests finding ways to *wind down from preaching* and to process the act of preaching. "What does one do with the feelings that a sermon generates?" this person asks. "Sometimes I am so full of joy I can hardly stand it, but don't know what to do with it. And sometimes I am so dismayed by the way the sermon went or the way the congregation reacted, I am equally at a loss." Most of the time, the preacher's response will be more moderate. At such times, some preachers need to be by themselves. Others need to find ways of talking through their response to the sermon with spouse, partner, or friends. I know a minister who repreaches the sermon in the way that it was intended or in a way that this preacher thinks would have made it a better sermon. Some ministers can store their reactions to the sermon until the sermon feedback group meets, but many cannot. Whatever one's preferred approach, it is important to name and process your response to the act of preaching your own sermon so that you can come to a healthy closure, and so that your response will not inordinately prejudge the way in which you begin the next sermon.

It can take a long time — as much as several years — for preachers to find ways of embodying the sermon that are communicative and with which they feel at home. Learning to embody the sermon, like other parts of preaching, involves experimenting with different approaches. Preachers who push themselves beyond their comfort zones frequently discover levels of expressiveness that help the whole community participate more fully in the sermon. Such gains are more than worth the anxieties and risks that are a part of this dimension of preaching.

CHAPTER FOURTEEN

Learning from the Congregation, Colleagues, and Continuing Education

This chapter is prompted by two related developments in ministry and theological education in the last fifteen years. The first is the notion that ministers are reflective practitioners.[1] A reflective practitioner engages in constant reflection on one's practice of ministry from the perspective of theological norms in order to ascertain what one does well (and why), and what one might do better (and how). A reflective practitioner regards a task in ministry (e.g., a sermon, a class, an event) as complete only when the minister, committee, or congregation reflect upon the task, note what they learned from it, and envision how they might go about a similar task in the future. Preachers, consequently, need periodically to reflect on our preaching.

Also, completing the M.Div., D.Min., or Ph.D. is only the beginning of ministerial preparation. In today's world, a theological degree cannot provide ministers with everything they need to know for service that will last twenty, thirty, or forty years. Regular participation in continuing education needs to be a part of the ministerial lifestyle. This chapter highlights ways whereby the preacher can engage in reflective practice and continuing education through the congregation, colleague groups, and formal continuing education.

Learning About One's Preaching through the Congregation

Congregations typically give two kinds of feedback on a pastor's preaching. First, many worshipers talk with the pastor about the content of the sermon. They want to continue the conversation of the sermon. They seek clarification or further information. They raise questions. They test their own perspectives. They may correct the pastor's logic, theology, or interpretation. Many pastors regularly offer a formal sermon feedback session after the service of worship in which members of the congregation can speak directly with the pastor and one another. Virtually all pastors receive informal responses to the content of the sermon from individuals or groups through the week.

The other kind of feedback is designed to help the minister identify aspects of preaching that facilitate communication and aspects that could be improved. In this mode, the pastor sets up formal mechanisms through which members of the congregation can help the pastor reflect on the preaching. The minister sets in motion a conversation about the conversations that take place through preaching.

Many ministers seek this form of feedback by organizing small groups that meet for a specific period of time (e.g., 3–6 weeks) whose purpose is to reflect on the preacher's patterns of communication.[2] The group convenes immediately after the service, or on Sunday evening, or later in the week. These groups can face obstacles. Some people are initially reluctant to say anything negative about the pastor's preaching, even when such feedback would be helpful. They may need to be initiated into the nonthreatening nature of open critical discussion. They may need to see that, by speaking candidly they strengthen the gospel witness of the sermon and the congregation. Others hesitate to talk about the pastor's preaching in the presence of the pastor. Bill Humphreys, a minister in Wisconsin, finds that members of his congregation are more relaxed in giving negative feedback if he models both giving and receiving it. Some ministers find that they should not meet with the group. Another person chairs the discussion and later talks with the pastor.

The conversation often proceeds most easily when it has a structure that helps the group focus. A structure discourages rambling, disconnected comments. Pastors who have particular questions about their preaching can work them into the conversation. The following questions represent some that a pastor might develop.

- What was the message of the sermon? (The responses to this question help the pastor ascertain whether the sermon communicated clearly.)

- What aspects of the sermon were interesting (involving, illuminating, important, helpful) to you? What helped you participate in the sermon? How did these aspects help you? (For instance, are you engaged by the stories, by the comments on the Bible, when the preacher attempts to relate the Bible to life?)

- What aspects of the sermon were not so interesting (noninvolving, dull, off-putting, unimportant, or not helpful)? What discouraged you from participating in the sermon? How did these aspects discourage you from participating in the sermon? (For instance, are the comments on the Bible dull? Does the preacher fail to relate the Bible to life? Does the preacher ruin a good story?)

- How do you respond to the preacher's embodiment of the message — the use of the voice, gestures, and pauses? Can you see the pastor easily during the sermon? Can you hear clearly? Is the minister's presence in the pulpit engaging? not engaging enough?

- What would you recommend that the pastor continue doing, or develop further, to build on strengths in the pastor's communication? What can the pastor do to make the preaching even stronger than it is now?

- What else would you like for the pastor to know about your reactions to this particular sermon or to the pastor's more general approach to preaching?

Directed conversation helps probe certain areas, but may prevent the group from bringing forward valuable perspectives that fall outside the main themes.

Many congregations contain individuals who can reflect knowledgeably on a pastor's preaching. For instance, a speech teacher who is a member of a congregation near us meets regularly to coach the pastors of that congregation. Ministers can also locate persons in the wider community with whom they can work reflectively.

A pastor might develop a written survey instrument that can be completed by members of the community. However, surveys of this kind are problematic. Researchers in the social sciences stress that the way in which the information is solicited can have profound effects on the results. The wording of questions can orient the survey group to respond to the questions in a certain way. Consequently, a survey instrument should be used only when it is prepared in consultation with persons trained in critically evaluated methods of congregational research. The preacher who uses a written survey approach should include interviews with members of the congregation to gain a more nuanced view of the data that comes in through the instrument. The preacher should also talk through the results with a small group in the church to determine whether that group thinks that the survey data fairly reflects a crosssection of the congregation's response to the pastor's preaching. Researchers who are schooled in the use of such mechanisms conclude that the preacher should give minimal weight to the responses that are the highest and the lowest. A few people say positive things, no matter what. A few people use the written survey to vent frustrations with the congregation or the minister that are unrelated to pastor's preaching.

Learning through Clergy Colleague Groups

By "colleague group" or "peer group," I mean a small community of clergy who meet regularly. Most of the colleague groups with which I am familiar are feedforward groups for sermon preparation. They meet quarterly, monthly, biweekly, or weekly to explore preaching possibilities in upcoming lectionary readings or other biblical texts.

Colleague groups can contribute to a preacher's continuing education in preaching by reading and discussing a book about preaching. For instance, a peer group might read and discuss this book. In one group, everyone read a book that advocates a particular approach to preaching. Then, each member of the group preached some sermons using that approach. Together, they processed their reactions to that approach, and how they perceived the reactions of their congregations.

A colleague group might invite someone known for strong preaching — e.g., a pastor, or a denominational official — to meet with them. A group might watch a videotape (or listen to an audiotape) of a preacher who is acclaimed as exemplary for the purpose of thinking critically about what "works" and "doesn't work." The group could also read sermons of thoughtful preachers. With careful planning, the colleague group might visit a service of worship led by a model preacher and follow that with an appointment to talk with the preacher.

Colleague groups can also be valuable sources of feedback. Preachers who prepare a manuscript or notes could make copies of a sermon available, so that the group could help the preacher evaluate. Better yet, the group can listen to an audiotape of a sermon. Still better, the group can process a videotape

Like response groups in the congregation discussed above, peer groups often find it helpful to structure their conversation. A colleague group might use questions similar to the ones listed in connection with feedback in the congregation (above). Here are sample questions that relate more directly to the content and purpose of the sermon:

- What is the good news in this sermon? Can the group state the gospel content of the sermon in a short, indicative statement?

- Does the preacher responsibly interpret the biblical text, or the doctrine, practice, or situation? Does the preacher represent fairly the viewpoints of others, especially those with whom the preacher disagrees?

- What is the purpose of the sermon? How does it affect the mind? the heart? the will?

- Is the sermon consistent with the nature and aim of preaching in the historic denomination of which the preacher is a part?

- Is the sermon consistent with the nature and aim of preaching in the contemporary theological family to which the preacher is related (e.g., revisionary theology, postliberalism, liberation theology, evangelicalism)?

- Is the witness of the sermon (a) appropriate to the gospel of God's unconditional love for each and all and God's will for justice for each and all? (b) intelligible? (c) morally plausible?

- Does the sermon continue or initiate a conversation that is significant to the community? Does participating in this sermon make a difference to the community? If so, how? If not, why not?

- Does the movement of the sermon facilitate the participation of the community in the world of the sermon? If not, what are the troublesome points, and what might the preacher do about them?

- Do the stories, images, and experiences in the sermon function as intended? Are they vivid? believable? inclusive? Do their contents correlate with their purposes? Are they well placed, and well told?
- Does the sermon begin so as to invite people into its world?
- Does the sermon establish a reflective consciousness at the end?
- Does the embodiment of the sermon cohere with its content?
- Does the preacher have a positive sense of presence? Is the voice easy to understand? inflected with the moods of the sermon? Is eye contact established at key moments? Are gestures natural, and do they enhance what the preacher says? Does the preacher pause to good effect?
- Accounting for the fact that the sermon is not designed for the colleague group, how does participating in this sermon affect the members of the group? Does it do what the preacher hopes?

As group members trust one another more and more, the level of conversation can become quite deep and significant. These questions could also be adapted for use in congregational feedback groups.

Learning through Continuing Education

Continuing education takes place in many forms ranging from books, through colleague groups, to events that are sponsored by theological seminaries, church judicatories, and independent agencies. Some denominations require clergy to participate in a specified number of hours of continuing education each year.

Some continuing education events in preaching consist of listening to another minister talk about preaching. Being a part of such an event can renew one's enthusiasm for preaching, germinate some ideas for sermons, and introduce the preacher to emerging perspectives in the field of preaching. This approach does not make great demands on the minister and is minimally threatening.

Most theological seminaries, divinity schools, and some judicatories offer continuing education events in preaching that last several days. Pastors explore contemporary theories of preaching and preach. Often these events utilize videotaping equipment that is not available in local congregations. A small group at a continuing education event often develops an excellent camaraderie and trust.

In addition to continuing education that relates directly to preaching, ministers can be helped by events that introduce them to fresh developments in biblical interpretation, church history, theology, and the implications of the social sciences and the arts. While these continuing education events may not immediately generate homilies, they help fill the wells from which preachers draw.

A pastor needs to receive such continuing education with an open and discerning spirit. At one end of the spectrum, preachers who receive unending praise need to receive it with humility. They need to avoid letting unbroken encouragement go to their heads. At the other end of the spectrum, preachers who receive strong recommendations for change need not allow their senses of self-worth to plummet. Suggestions for improvement do not discount one's self-worth or to ministry. They are just that: suggestions for improvement.

Furthermore, when preaching prior to receiving feedback, preachers need to be careful not to play to the crowd. The preacher is not called to win a favorable rating from a feedback group, but to preach the gospel. While response mechanisms are designed to help strengthen the witness of the gospel through preaching, a pastor (or a congregation) can turn them into instruments of self-promotion or to win the approval of other people. The pastor and congregation who are alert to this possibility can minimize it.

Preachers can be frightened by the prospect of learning from the congregation, colleagues, and continuing education, especially when the preachers are called upon to expose their own preaching to the evaluation of others. As I note early in this book, preaching is an extension of the self that is more intense and personal than most other aspects of theological education or ministry. Preachers can feel discomfort when congregants and colleagues suggest possible changes to improve. However, most such experiences are positive. The long-term benefits of strengthening one's gospel witness through preaching are worth the feelings of vulnerability and risk that accompany opening conversations about one's preaching.

Pastors should incorporate sabbatical leaves into the regular rhythm of ministerial life. A sabbatical can have several purposes, e.g., personal renewal, retooling in ministerial skills, exploration of an arena of ministry, and sermon planning. Many congregations provide for a three-month sabbatical leave after three years of service. Leaves are excellent occasions for expanding one's preaching world.

CHAPTER FIFTEEN

Miscellania

Many ministers assign each drawer in their desks to a different task. The wide drawer in the middle holds stationary and pens. The double-depth drawer on the right is for manila filing folders. The middle drawer on the left is for the phone book, computer manuals, and church directory. The top drawer on the right is for materials for sermons in preparation. The drawer on the bottom left, however, is for odds and ends. This chapter is an odds-and-ends drawer. The topics here do not need their own chapters. I discuss the appearance of the manuscripts and notes, handling the manuscript or notes while preaching, the length of the sermon, dress for worship, filing systems, planning ahead, titles, preaching on special occasions, and problem areas in preaching.

The Appearance of the Manuscript or Notes

Preachers who use a manuscript or notes need to have typed or handwritten material in the pulpit that helps their eyes quickly identify each part of the sermon. I want simply to glance at my notes and know where the sermon is going. Some preachers, particularly with visual problems, take advantage of the multiple sizes of fonts and letters available through the computer in order to print manuscripts with extra-large letters. For instance, I have a friend who prints sermons in 14 point type. Different kinds of marks often help the preacher's eyes follow the content down the page. Many ministers mark their manuscripts or notes extensively with regular pencils, colored pencils, pens, and highlighters. They underline with single, double, and triple lines. They circle, make boxes, draw stars, and insert exclamation points. In the margins, they write key words or make prompts for embodiment, e.g, "Leave pulpit/move to middle of chancel." I know a couple of pastors who color coordinate their manuscript markings with aspects of embodiment: blue means to speak matter-of-factly, yellow means softer, red indicates an increase in energy. Some preachers leave large white spaces in their manuscripts when they want to indicate a pause.

Most pastors find that they can most easily use a manuscript or a set of notes with which they have worked extensively prior to stepping up to preach. The preacher who prints a fresh, clean copy of the manuscript or notes on the way to the pulpit often finds that the material is strange to the eyes. The preacher loses eye contact and confidence while hunting for the place on the page.

The material should always be double-spaced. Single spacing so jams the letters, words, and sentences together that it is hard to distinguish them. The eye looks down and sees a blob of indiscriminate print.

Charles Rice, who has worked with preaching students for thirty years, recommends that preachers write manuscripts or notes on the order of free-verse in poetry. The preacher starts a sentence on the left margin then indents subsequent parts of the sentence. The indentations follow sense units. Here is a sample from one of his sermons on the second coming of Jesus (Revelation 1:7–11; 21:1–6). Rice remembers being a student at Union Theological Seminary (New York). His room overlooked the Riverside Church, on which is a statue of the angel Gabriel, face lifted to the sky, trumpet poised. The church is on the Hudson River.[1]

> For eight months I saw Gabriel every morning and night.
> I went to work and play and worship,
>   and he stood there all the while, his trumpet ready.
> The foundations of the church on which he perches
>   grab the bedrock of Manhattan
>   as if intending to stand there by the Hudson forever.
> And all the while Gabriel has his head in the clouds.
> The stained glass around his feet points to the past
>   to faraway places and antique times.
> Every Sunday Gabriel hears the same old story,
>   old to people in well-worn pews,
>   who expect to go to work on Monday
>   and come back next Sunday.
> They would be surprised to hear Gabriel toot his horn.
> The days come and go,
>   and Gabriel looks up into the sun,
>   and wind and sleet and snow.
> He sees out of the corner of his eye
>   that [people] still go down to the sea in ships,
>   that the traffic becomes a little more hectic
>   every Friday afternoon,
>   and that the park turns russet autumn after autumn.
> Summer and winter, seedtime and harvest, day and night,
>   vary no more than the traffic lights.
> But Gabriel keeps his horn ready.
> And so it must be,
>   that in the midst of our city,
>   we look for a city.[2]

This manuscript creates a visual picture of how the sermon might sound. SOME PREACHERS PRINT MANUSCRIPTS WITH ALL THE LETTERS CAPITALIZED. THEY THINK THAT THE LARGER LETTERS ARE EASIER TO SEE. HOWEVER, I FIND THAT CAPITALIZING THE WHOLE MANUSCRIPT CAUSES THE MATERIAL TO RUN TOGETHER. I FIND IT HARD TO FIND MY PLACE WHEN I AM PREACHING BECAUSE THE WORDS AND SENTENCES LOOK SO MUCH ALIKE. AS A DEMONSTRATION, STAND UP, LEAVE THE BOOK ON THE DESK AND TRY TO DELIVER THIS PARAGRAPH THAT IS PRINTED IN ALL CAPS.

Preachers can adjust the size of their pages to the size of the desktop on the pulpit or note stand and to the sizes that work best with their own eyes. Some pulpits are large enough for $8^1/_2$ x 11 inch paper. I know a preacher who prints sermons sideways and in two columns on $8^1/_2$ x 11 inch paper. Folded, these notes can fit into a Bible or can rest on a small pulpit. Others can accept only half-sheets. Note cards fit easily on most pulpits and note stands.

Several preachers whom I know print their sermons for persons who are visually impaired (in large type), or for distribution after the sermon. Many congregations make audio or videotapes of the service for distribution to shut-ins and others unable to attend.

Handling the Manuscript or Notes While Preaching

The preacher who uses a manuscript or notes needs to be able to do so without calling attention to the paper or cards. The congregation is distracted when the preacher's manuscript bobs up and down or when the preacher spends a lot of time straightening the pages into a neat stack. Most preachers find that they can most easily keep the manuscript or notes concealed by having the material in two stacks and sliding the pages from one stack to the next. The desktops of some pulpits or note stands are so small that they will not hold two stacks of manuscript pages or notes side by side. In such cases, the preacher might quietly slip the used pages into the shelf below the desktop or discreetly slide the used top page onto the bottom of the pile. The preacher who turns the pages over almost always calls attention to the manuscript.

When the desktop is large enough, a pastor may be able to spread manuscript or notes out. The preacher is not required to turn any pages.

Some preachers are taking laptop computers into the pulpit with them. They set the pagination so that by touching a single key, the computer screen projects the part of the sermon that they are preaching. Such preachers need to position to computer so that it does not distract the congregation and so that the preacher can easily see the screen.

An occasional church building is equipped with teleprompters. A teleprompter, of course, requires considerable practice for effective use.

A minister who leaves the pulpit area for preaching might clip notes in a Bible and hold the Bible in one hand. The pages of the manuscript or notes should be trimmed to fit within the Bible so that the material does not flop around. Some clergy who preach outside the pulpit hold three-by-five-inch note cards discreetly, or keep them in a pocket for security. Others have places where they leave notes, e.g., on the Lord's table, on a communion rail, or on a pew. I have heard of a free-standing preacher who makes an outline of the sermon in large letters on a piece of poster board that sits in the front pew.

The Length of the Sermon

The length of the sermon varies according to the custom of the congregation, the purpose of a sermon and the communicative ability of the preacher. Most congregations have an informal agreement as to how long the service, and the sermon, should normally last. People are socialized to expect the sermon to be a given length.

In Roman Catholic and Episcopal congregations, the sermon is often 10–15 minutes in length. While this length of time may seem perilously short to outsiders, a well-prepared priest making the most of every minute can lead the congregation to the heart of the gospel's interpretation of a significant issue with clarity and power. European American congregations in the long-established denominations think of the sermon as roughly 18–22 minutes. This length of time is sufficient to explore many texts and topics in depth and with some nuance. Preaching in African American Christian communities, in many Hispanic and Asian bodies, and in some European American Evangelical and Pentecostal groups can last 30-45 minutes, even an hour.

I sometimes read and hear preachers say that the electronic media have reduced the attention span of the contemporary congregation. Today's people, they say, cannot stay with a preacher who talks too long. I differ. People are quite willing to participate for long periods of time when the sermon makes an important connection between the gospel and their worlds, especially when the preacher is lively. Fred Craddock, for instance, seldom preaches for less than thirty minutes. Afterward, congregations marvel that so much time passed. Lyle Schaller, who studies congregations in great detail, finds that in a significant segment of congregations that are growing in faith and numbers, sermons are in the 30–40 minute range.[3]

I do not argue for longer sermons. I simply point out that the length of the sermon cannot be determined by formula. A preacher in a congregation that is socialized toward twenty minute sermons can help resocialize that community toward longer sermons if the longer messages help the community make significant connections between the gospel and life and if the preacher is lively. An insignificant, dull sermon is too long, no matter how short it is. A long sermon can be long because the preacher is undisciplined.

Dress for Preaching

What should the pastor wear while leading worship and preaching? Each style of liturgical dress has its own theological symbolism. The preacher seeks garb that is consistent with the church's ecclesiology and with the purposes of the ministry and the sermon. In some churches, the preacher's vestments are largely prescribed.

In churches oriented toward prayer-book worship, clergy often wear a cassock and surplice. A cassock is a close-fitting garment from shoulder to ankle that is open at the bottom rather like a dress. A surplice is usually white and is commodious, even billowing, as it extends from neck to slightly below the waist. When presiding at the Lord's table, the minister often wears a chasuble — a large, oval-shaped garment with a hole for the head in the center. The chasuble usually extends to the knees and is often decorated symbolically. These vestments evoke priestly aspects of ministry.

In the world of the Bible and in most other periods, the priest's vocation includes teaching and preaching (e.g., Deuteronomy 31:9–13; 33:10; 2 Chronicles 17:7–9, 30:22; 35:3; Nehemiah 8:1–8). When Israel was without a teaching priest, Israel was without *torah* (2 Chronicles 15:3). Such clergy often wear a stole — symbolic of the yoke of ministry. The stole is often the color of the liturgical season in which it is worn (purple in Advent, white in Christmas, green in Ordinary Time, purple in Lent, white in Easter, red on Pentecost).

The alb (usually white or earth-tone) is similar to the cassock. It fits fairly closely from shoulder to ankle. While it is historically typical of Roman Catholic, Anglican, Episcopal, and Lutheran ministers, some clergy in other long-established denominations now wear it. The alb evokes priestly ministry and is sometimes overlaid by a stole.

Reformed clergy often wear a Geneva gown. The name and style derives from Reformation period Geneva. The Geneva gown is a loose-fitting robe, somewhat reminiscent of an overcoat. Until the last twenty years, Geneva gowns were nearly always black. Now, however, they come in many colors. Because John Calvin conceived of the primary work of the sermon as teaching, the Geneva gown symbolizes the teaching office. The preacher often wears a stole with the Geneva gown. In the twentieth century, the Geneva gown was adopted by many of the same clergy across the spectrum of the long-established denominations.

Many ministers do not wear robes or other liturgical garments for leading worship. These clergy are often found in Assemblies of God, Baptist churches, Bible churches, Christian churches and Churches of Christ, community churches, Pentecostal churches. This pattern of dress is also followed by some ministers in denominations mentioned in previous paragraphs. At one time in these churches, male clergy routinely wore business suits, and women ministers wore dresses. But, in recent years, preaching attire has become more diverse with women in blouses and skirts and men in sports jackets. Occasionally men wear open-collar shirts and women wear pantssuits, especially in contemporary services. This pattern of clothing reminds both the minister and the congregation of their commonality. When the pastor rises from the people to speak, the pastor's dress symbolizes that all in the community are interpreters with the pastor set aside to lead the interpretation.

Regardless of dress for Sunday morning, clergy need to be careful not to wear clothes or accoutrements that call attention to themselves or otherwise distract the congregation. For instance, a preacher may like a particular piece of jewelry, but if it causes a blinding flash under the pulpit light, a preacher should not wear it when preaching. A congregation that is rubbing its eyes has difficulty concentrating on the sermon.

Filing Systems

In every preaching class, I am asked, "What filing system should I use to keep sermon ideas, insights into biblical texts, stories, memories, experiences?" A pastor finds a good thought, question, image, or story and would like to save it for future reference. However, a single approach cannot serve all preachers.

A minister whose congregation is located just a few blocks from the seminary where I serve uses a loose-leaf notebook to keep items that might be useful. This preacher has a hole punch in the study so that an article or a photocopy of a page from a book can easily be inserted into the notebook. The materials are not sorted by category. When asked, "How do you find things?" this pastor replies, "Well, I just get to know where they are."

Some pastors find it useful to keep a daily journal of experiences, readings, images, and other things that might contribute to a sermon. Other preachers keep a small notepad or a stack of three-by-five inch cards in pocket, purse, and on the bedstand. As soon as something comes to mind that might contribute to a sermon, they jot it down, even in the middle of the night. Charles Rice suggests that preachers keep a notebook in which they record the storyline and impressions of plays, movies, novels.[4] I know a pastor who keeps a tape recorder in the car to preserve ruminations that occur while driving.

When considering the use of a journal, pastors may find it helpful to distinguish between journals that they keep as a part of sermon preparation and journals that are daily journals in which they record their reactions to life. The latter may sometimes furnish material for the sermon, but its primary purpose is to give the preacher an opportunity for self-expression and to keep a record of the tides of one's life.

Some preachers develop elaborate filing systems and keep them fresh. They identify categories that are clear, e.g., key theological words (faith, grace, love, salvation), biblical texts, seasons, and Sundays of the church year. They design information-saving systems that are easy to use. Computer users can purchase ready-made programs for this purpose or design their own. The preacher enters data through the keyboard. Some preachers still use filing cabinets designed for note cards with topics arranged in alphabetical order. The preacher makes a record on a card and files it. Some preachers make the same record on multiple cards and file them in multiple categories. Some preachers use a regular filing cabinet with manila folders. Pastors who can manage these systems marvel that other preachers live without them.

Many pastors find such elaborate mechanisms difficult to organize, maintain, and use. Can one neatly distinguish between grace, love, and salvation as categories? It takes a lot of time to enter data through the keyboard onto a card or into a file. It can take a long time to retrieve material. A preacher can sometimes vaguely remember an insight or a story, but cannot recollect where it is filed. Ideas and images can grow stale in a file.

Some pastors who plan their sermons in advance coordinate their filing systems with their upcoming sermons. For each sermon, a preacher sets aside a computer file, or a manila folder, or a notebook. The preacher files ideas, experiences, exegetical leads, scenes from the news or novels in folders for specific sermons.

I have never found a filing system that is altogether satisfactory. The energy expended in keeping the system going seems greater than the benefits. But I have developed a pattern of preserving and sorting material that works. I have a long-range anticipation of my preaching opportunities. These sermons are in the back of my mind as I am reading theology, watching the news, going to the movies, teaching. I have a drawer in which I store materials. If I sense a possible connection between an article in a periodical and an upcoming sermon, I rip the article out of the journal, make a marginal note to help me remember the sermon or theme. I stuff it in the drawer. If I see a movie that is suggestive, I make a few notes, or I tear a review out of the paper. If I find a pertinent passage in a book, I plunk the book into the drawer. If the book will not fit in the drawer, I photocopy the passage. Periodically, I go through the drawer and see if its contents still seem to promise help with sermons. Frequently, I find that after pieces have stayed in the drawer awhile, my sense of the sermon has changed, or the material itself loses some of its attractiveness. At that point, I dispose of it. This procedure is sloppy, but it keeps my preaching file fresh.

The pastor who does not have some means of preserving good quality material lives week by week, from hand to mouth. Such a preacher often grabs a thought from a commentary, a story and a quote from a preaching help, a joke from a service club luncheon on Thursday and ties them together into a sermon. In the process, the sermon may not reach optimum depth. Some material may get jammed into a purpose which it does not serve.

One of my colleagues has a photographic memory and can describe where on the specific page (top, middle, bottom) an author discusses a topic. We who are not so blessed need to experiment until we find storage systems that work for us.

Filing systems of the kind I have described presume a lone pastor in a private study. Increasingly, pastors seek and share information and stories through the Internet and other communication systems. Many ministers circulate stories by e-mail. Someone will send forth a request, such as, "Does anyone in this group know a story on…?" Online data bases are now emerging as a source for sermon material.

Planning Ahead

Many preachers find it helpful to determine texts, topics, and themes a few weeks (or more) ahead. An advance look gives the subject time to mulch in the mind and heart. The preacher can research aspects of the sermon that need patient consideration. The preacher can order materials through interlibrary loan or similar source. A lot of life passes under the preacher's bridge between the time the preacher chooses the subject and the time of preaching, thus giving the preacher many opportunities to make connections between the sermon and the everyday world. The preacher and worship planners can select hymns and other worship materials without the pressure of an immediate deadline.

Preachers vary as to how far in advance they work. Some preachers plan a year in advance, others a quarter, others a month. When thinking ahead, the preacher seldom plans the whole sermon, but makes basic decisions, e.g., the choice of biblical text, doctrine, practice, or personal or social situations. Sermon series require advance planning. Preachers who use the Revised Common Lectionary can select which text(s) will inform the sermon. When working in the mode *lectio continua* a preacher can divide the book into meaningful units. Pastors who utilize free selection of text and topic can make their selections. Preachers can record initial thoughts and can note the season of Christian year and other calendars within which the sermon takes place — church, school, calendar, fiscal. Preachers can soon coordinate with worship planners (especially musicians) so that the service and the sermon can work together.

This approach comes with two caveats. For one, the preacher's initial thoughts about the sermon may change radically as the preacher delves into the world of the biblical text, doctrine, practice, or situation. The preacher needs to be open to fresh insights as the sermon develops. For the other, the preacher can deviate from the long-range plan when circumstances call for immediate interpretation in the light of the gospel.

Several pastors I know take 1–2 day retreats to sketch future sermons. Others plan in their offices. Some preachers work singly, others in small groups.

Advance Notice for the Sermon, and Titles

A congregation often benefits from advance notice about the subject of the sermon. People can anticipate the conversation with the preacher. They may begin to talk among one another. They may invite persons from outside the church for whom they know the direction of the sermon is important. The newsletter, web site, and bulletin board on the church lawn, as well as the congregation's presence in the electronic media and local newspapers, can contain a few sentences noting the subject of the sermon and its significance to the community. An increasing number of congregations shape their presence in the public media, including their announcements about the sermon, to appeal to persons who do not understand themselves and the world from the perspective of God's love for all and God's will for justice.

Public notice might name issues central to the sermon and pose questions for readers and listeners to ponder. The minister can regularly publish biblical text(s) and other materials related to the sermon so that the congregation can prepare. The preacher wants such material to raise the interest of readers and listeners and to orient them to the sermon but not to reveal the whole conclusion of the sermon.

A sermon does not need a title. A worship bulletin can simply say, "Sermon...Pastor." Some preachers, thinking that the term "sermon" is outdated or tainted, turn to other ways of speaking that they hope communicate more of the purpose of the pastor's conversation with the congregation, e.g., "The Good News," "The Word of Life."

However, a title can serve positive functions. It can orient readers and listeners to the subject of the sermon, and it can stimulate them to begin thinking toward the sermon. It can give the preacher a line of sight on the direction of the sermon. A provocative title can stir the imagination of the preacher and the community.

A good title is typically short — no more than a dozen or so words. It clues the readers or hearers to the subject of the sermon. It provokes thought. It contains an element of promise, as if to say, "This sermon can help this community."

When the title will be seen mainly by persons who are already in the Christian community, the preacher can often make use of familiar Christian language. For example: "The Prodigal Father" (a title from Barbara Brown Taylor), "When Faith Bogs Down" (Sandy F. Ray), "You Are Not My God, Jehovah" (Peggy Ann Way), "Praying Through Clenched Teeth" (Fred B. Craddock), "An Easter Faith in a Good Friday World" (William D. Watley), "Disturbed by Joy" (Edmund A. Steimle), "Up Against the Powers That Be" (David G. Buttrick), "Let Pharoah Go" (Nancy Hastings Sehested).

Titles that communicate with persons outside the Christian community avoid insider language while intimating that the sermon can be of help. For example, "Overhearing Love's Music in a Brutal World" (Thomas H. Troeger), "Owning Your Own Shadow" (Barbara Brown Taylor), "Things Are Not Always What They Seem" (Herbert O. Edwards, Jr.), "Finding Our Margin of Freedom" (Samuel D. Proctor), "Praying with Your Eyes Open" (Patrick Willson). Still a classic is "The Importance of Doubting our Doubts" (Harry Emerson Fosdick).

A poor title can dampen listener interest. A dull title can suggest that the sermon is dull or insignificant. It can be so diffuse as to suggest that the preacher's vision of the sermon is unclear. It may be so cute as to be frivolous. The title "Love" is too large and unfocused. It sounds as though the preacher has not settled on which aspects of that vast subject will be the focus for the week's conversation. It is better to not have a title than to use one that discourages the community.

A preacher who uses a title in the newsletter, web sites, or other media must report the title well in advance of the completion of the sermon. As noted several times previously, when sermon preparation takes on a life of its own, the sermon can develop differently from the preacher's expectation. On such occasions a preacher can simply note in the worship bulletin or in the service that such a change has taken place.

Preaching at Funerals, Weddings, and Other Occasions Outside the Regular Service of Worship

Preaching at the funeral, the wedding, and other occasions outside the regular service of worship has the same purpose as all preaching: to interpret the occasion from the perspective of the gospel. The preacher takes into account the specific dynamics, questions, and issues that are a part of each distinct occasion.[5]

A *funeral* is a service of worship whose purpose is to honor God. Consequently, a funeral should focused on the gospel with its promise and claim, not on the decedent.[6] A funeral is also a personal occasion. The decedent, relatives, friends, and community are particular people. The funeral should not be generic. The service and the sermon should help the congregation deal with the particularity of death.

The minister helps the congregation interpret the life of the deceased from the perspective of the gospel. A preacher might select a biblical passage, a doctrine, or a Christian practice that serves as a lens through which to consider how the gospel makes sense of the person's life. How did the minister and the congregation see the gospel materialize in the life of the one now passed away? How does the gospel's promise of unconditional love and its call for justice help the minister and the community make sense of that person's thoughts, feelings, actions? The preacher can use material from the life of the decedent — stories, images, experiences, traits, ideas, mannerisms.

To represent the life of a person accurately the preacher needs to visit pastorally with the family, talking with them about the decedent. The pastor can ask the family and friends for certain things they would like for the pastor to mention (or not to mention) during the sermon. Despite the personal character of the funeral homily, the preacher needs to remember that the aim of speaking about the person who died is to help the congregation perceive the gospel on this occasion.

From the perspective of the gospel, the minister also helps the congregation name and frame its feelings and thoughts at the time of death and in its immediate and long-range futures. The preacher often performs a significant ministry by leading the community to name their feelings, e.g., grief, loss, abandonment, shock, questions. The immediate occasion of death is not the time for complicated theological analysis.

The dominant tone of the funeral homily is assurance. The pastor can assure the community of God's presence and love. The pastor can help the community remember how the life of the deceased mediated that love and can point the congregation to signs that God's love continues. The preacher can help the congregation acknowledge the depth of its sorrow and also suggest that, as time passes, they will be able to continue to live with meaning and purpose. God is still with them and doing all that God can do to help them create a future that is different from one they had previously envisioned, but is still a future in which they can know God's love and justice. The preacher may need to help the community recognize that the time of adjustment may be long and difficult. The funeral is a prime occasion to state forthrightly the church's ultimate hope.

When the death is accompanied by enervating questions, the preacher can help the community acknowledge the importance of the questions, the difficulty of thinking clearly about them now, and promise more detailed discussion after the waves of feeling subside. Such questions are often raised by suicide, by deaths that take place in shocking ways, by death that is long and painful, by premature death (especially of the unborn, children, and youth), by death that could have been avoided. In order to keep faith with the pledge to take up these questions at a later time, a preacher could make a note on the church calendar to return to them in preaching, teaching, and pastoral calling.

In most European American Christian communities, a funeral meditation is brief −6–10 minutes. In many African American communities, and in some Hispanic and Asian churches, a funeral sermon is the length of the usual Sunday morning message.

A local pastor who is known and trusted in the wider community is frequently called for funerals of persons who are not members of the congregation, some of whom are altogether unknown to the pastor. In such cases, the preacher needs to make a special effort to visit the family well in advance of the service in order to be able to speak personally about the decedent. While preachers must handle such cases from the standpoints of their own theologies, the preacher is never called to pass ultimate judgment on a dead person. That prerogative belongs to God. The preacher's task is to find out as much as possible about the deceased and to help the family and friends recognize God's faithfulness in that life, as well as God's promises to the survivors.

The *wedding* is a service of worship. The primary function of a wedding homily is to help the community interpret marriage from the standpoint of the gospel.[7] What is a marriage relationship? How does God's promise of God's love to each and all and the call of God for justice to each and all affect the ways in which the couple should relate to one another? to their families and friends? to the wider world? A preacher can often interpret the significance of marriage by viewing it through the lens of a particular biblical text, a doctrine, a practice, or some aspect of the couple's relationship or hopes.

The homily is not a private message to the happy couple. (The pastor can deliver such wisdom in premarital counseling.) The homily is for the benefit of the community. However, because a wedding involves two specific people, the pastor should refer to them. The preacher can draw on their histories, qualities, wider familial and social worlds, and hopes. The marriage may have circumstances that call for particular interpretation, e.g., factors created by vocation, physical health, or the blending of two (or more) previous families, or other factors. The preacher should discuss these themes with the couple prior to the wedding service so that the bride and the groom are not surprised, embarrassed, or angry when such matters come to expression in the wedding meditation.

The preacher can bring a touch of realism to the occasion by speaking honestly of the difficulties faced by the institution of marriage in our time and of the difficulties that couples face when living with one another day after day, month after month, year after year. The preacher can help the couple and the community develop a vision of God's continuing presence through the full spectrum of marriage, including its difficulties. Not only is such straightforward talk pastorally helpful, it lends credibility to the sermon for divorced persons who are present. They, especially, know that marriage can be difficult. When the preacher pretends otherwise, the sermon loses believability. A wedding homily is normally brief — perhaps 5–7 minutes.

Pastors are invited to preach at assemblies or conventions of middle and upper level judicatories, at the community Thanksgiving service, community Lenten Services, the community Good Friday Service. As a part of a pulpit exchange, a pastor may preach at a regular service of worship in another congregation. Some congregations invite a guest pastor to preach at special services held for a weekend or for several evenings during the week. These services are usually either for the renewal of the congregation or for evangelism. They go by various names. e.g., Week of Renewal, Week of Preaching, Revival. Ministers are sometimes invited to preach at services for Baccalaureate, Memorial Day, or celebration of national independence. I refer to these opportunities as "one-shot preaching assignments" because the minister has only one chance to embody the gospel in the community that gathers for worship.[8]

In each case, the preacher tries to carry out a congregational analysis similar to the one described on pages 33–38. The preacher identifies the purpose of the service, the persons present, their concerns and worldviews. The preacher may need to seek information from pastors, other persons, newspapers, and histories from the locale where the sermon will body forth. The preacher locates a biblical passage, a doctrine, a Christian practice, or a theological theme to help the community correlate the gospel with the purposes and character of the occasion.

A preacher has an unusual opportunity during the one-shot preaching assignment. People sometimes pay more attention to a fresh face than to the familiar pastor. Consequently, a guest preacher can sometimes help a congregation think afresh about some aspect of relationship of the gospel to its situation. At an Independence Day sermon, for instance, a one-shot preacher might be able to help a community reevaluate its understanding of the purpose and configuration of national, local, and state government given God's call for justice for each and all. Is our governmental structure just? Does our government mediate justice for all?

Giving Credit When Using Material from Others

As a matter of integrity, a preacher is obliged to acknowledge material from another source. For example, a preacher needs to indicate a quotation from a poem or a passage from a volume of systematic theology. A preacher does not need to give credit when drawing on a theme that is found in several sources and therefore appears to be commonly accepted. For example, a preacher who makes use of an idea that is found in several Bible dictionaries does not need to indicate outside authorship.

When the name of the source will be recognized by the congregation, the preacher might give the name directly. "John Wesley, the founder of our movement, has the insight.…" When the name of the source is unfamiliar and may cause the congregation to be distracted, the minister may simply say, "As someone says…" or "As a respected scholar of the Bible has found.…"

Pastors sometimes add to the authority of data or perspectives in the sermon by identifying the credential of the source. When doing so, the identification should be brief and to the point. For example, "A study of this problem by the respected researchers at the Center For Disease Control in Atlanta finds that.…"

Occasionally a pastor wants to preach a whole sermon from another pastor. Once in a great while, this practice is acceptable if the sermon fits the context and if the preacher acknowledges the source of the sermon.

Who Are the Great Preachers Today?

Professors of preaching are often asked, "Who are the great preachers today?" Without pausing to think, I can rattle off a list of well-known preachers today whose sermons pastors can profitably study. For example: Joanna Adams, Charles G. Adams, L. Susan Bond, Jana Childers, Fred Craddock, James A. Forbes, H. Beecher Hicks, Jr., Joseph R. Jeter, Jr., Leontyne Kelley, Thomas G. Long, Henry H. Mitchell, Ella Pearson Mitchell, Charles L. Rice, Barbara Brown Taylor, Gardner Taylor, Thomas H. Troeger, Mary Donovan Turner, William Watley, William Willimon, Patrick Willson, Paul Scott Wilson. By listening to the sermons of these preachers, one may get a spark for a sermon, or an insight into how the preacher handles a text, or a perspective on how a sermon moves, or how to shape a story. But these preachers would be the first to encourage local preachers to find their own voices.

However, my impression is that the really great preaching today is being done by pastors who will never be well-known outside the congregations and cities they serve. After all, great preaching is preaching that helps a community interpret its specific situation from the standpoint of the promise of God's love for each and all and God's call for justice for each and all. This preaching is born from a deep and clear understanding of the gospel, faithful pastoral work, carried out day-by-day, sensitivity to the people, disciplined preparation, imagination, and prayer.

SECTION SEVEN

Case Studies of Sample Sermons

This section provides four case studies of the development of sample sermons from four preachers. Each preacher describes the setting for which the sermon was prepared and reviews the processes of interpretation that led to the sermon — from the selection of the subject, and the investigation of the subject, through the theological interpretation, and formulation of the direction, to the creation of the sermon itself. In addition, I annotate each sermon to reflect on how the sermon and its various parts helps the congregation interact with it. What does the preacher do and why to facilitate the congregation's participation in the preaching conversation?

The four sermons illustrate the four general classifications of sermons (pages 97–98). I prepared chapter 16, an expository-deductive sermon from the parable of the lost sheep in the Gospel of Matthew. Mary Donovan Turner develops an expository inductive sermon in chapter 17 on the Great Commission. René Rodgers Jensen contributes a topical-deductive sermon on the doctrine of God in chapter 18. Reginald Holmes prepares a topical-inductive sermon on in chapter 19.

CHAPTER SIXTEEN

An Expository-Deductive Sermon
Ronald J. Allen

This chapter offers an expository-deductive sermon (see pages 99–113, 159–160). The text is Matthew 18:10–14, the parable of the lost sheep. Jesus says,

> (10) Take care that you do not despise one of these little ones; for, I tell you, in heaven their angels continually see the face of my father in heaven. (12) What do you think? If a shepherd has a hundred sheep, and one of them has gone astray, does he not leave the ninety-nine on the mountains and go in search of the one that went astray? (13) And if he finds it, truly I tell you, he rejoices over it more than over the ninety-nine that never went astray. (14) So it is not the will of your Father in heaven that one of these little ones should be lost.

The translation (NRSV) does not contain verse 11 because most scholars think that persons in the early church added verse 11 ("For the Son of Man came to seek and save the lost.") after the time of Matthew.

The chapter first describes the setting of the sermon and the conversation leading to it. The annotated sermon follows.

The Setting of the Sermon
Since I teach in a theological seminary, most of my preaching takes place when I visit congregations on weekends. The sermon below was prepared for a weekend of preaching and teaching in a congregation in a county seat (population 5,000) in the midwest. The pastor and the body of spiritual leaders in the congregation, the elders, asked me to focus the weekend on what the church should do and be.

Because I was not familiar with the community, I talked with the planners about their situation, about why they sought such a weekend, and their hopes for it. I tried to be a long distance priestly listener.[1] About a year

259

before, a new pastor had come to the congregation. The new pastorate brought a period of renewal to the community. In the midst of the rebirth of spiritual energy, the pastor and the congregation's spiritual leaders in the congregation (the elders) asked me to focus on what the church should do and be. They wanted the fresh energy in the church to focus on the church's primary call. Although they did not use this language, they wanted the weekend to help the congregation remember the nature and purpose of the Christian community.

Although I thought that a series of doctrinal sermons would serve that occasion, the elders specifically requested expository sermons from the Second Testament. I turned to the Gospel of Matthew because it was the central gospel in the Revised Common Lectionary at that time, and I could presume that the congregation had some familiarity with it. Like the community in which I was invited to preach, the Matthean congregation is in a period of transition, though a more tense one. Matthew's church is working out its identity and its relationship to Judaism and the gentile world.

Preaching services were held Friday night, Saturday night, and Sunday morning. Bible study sessions took place Friday night (before the preaching service), as well as Saturday morning and early afternoon, and Sunday morning before worship. The meeting closed with the 10:45 a.m. Sunday service.

On Friday night, I preached on Matthew 5:14–16, "You are the light of the world." I talked with the community about the identity of the church (called by Jesus) and the vocation of the church (to be the light of the world). In the Matthean context, to be a light in the world means to witness to the manifestation of the rule of God through the life and ministry of Jesus, especially for the sake of Gentiles. The church is to model the reign of God in its own life and is to witness to God's rule in the larger setting. In the sermon below, I try to evoke the connection between this theme and searching for the lost by referring to this passage, "You are the light of the world."

According to the people with whom I talked prior to the event, most in the congregation were excited about the new prospects for the community, but some were a little anxious about the changes. The latter group had been quite happy with the congregation's former life. The prospects of change unsettled them. Although no one had left the congregation, the elders were concerned that a few of the members of the community might drift away. They specifically asked me to address that concern proactively. The sermon below is my attempt to do so on Saturday night.

On Sunday morning, I preached in conjunction with Matthew 28:16–20, the so-called great commission with its climactic affirmation, "I am with you always, to the end of the age." That sermon focused on the continuing presence of God as mediated through the risen Jesus in the community. In the Jewish tradition, God uses the phrase "I am with you," and similar expressions, to assure the community of the divine presence, leading, and trustworthiness. The passage assures the Christian community that through the living Christ we also experience God's presence, leading, and trustworthiness.

In the process of preparing the sermon, I discover that Matthew 18, the fourth major discourse of Jesus in Matthew, is something like a manual on how to live in Christian community with the purpose of modeling life in the reign of God.[2] Matthew 18:10–14 prescribes for the community to search for those who wander from it. God wants each person to enjoy the security of being a part of the divine flock. Just as God seeks us, so we are to seek one another.

While I study many words in their Matthean context and in their larger Jewish background, the notion of shepherd emerges as most important for this sermon. Jesus draws on the frequent use of shepherd in the First Testament to describe both God (the great shepherd) and leadership in the community (the leaders of the church are to be faithful shepherds).

This particular passage is appropriate to the gospel. It affirms God's love for each and all. It implies that God seeks justice for each and all in that God passionately desires for all members of the church to be in right relationship with God and with one another in Christian community. The passage is intelligible. We can grasp it clearly. It is consistent with other foundational Christian convictions. It is coherent with our worldview. The passage is also morally plausible. It calls for the moral treatment of all in its world. Therefore, I can adopt the interpretive relationship of running with the text with a minimum of explanation. My conversation with the pastor and leaders of the congregation leads me to think that the congregation will be favorably inclined toward the direction of the sermon, but have an inadequate understanding of it and may not know how to act in response.

With respect to the purpose of the sermon, I hope the message will interact with mind, heart, and will. I hope the sermon will provide the congregation with some clear information about the passage, its function in Matthew, and its applicability to the congregation's current and future situation. I hope that the community will feel being found by God and will feel empowered to find others. If members should stray from the community during the time of renewal, I hope that the sermon will prompt some members to seek them.

By talking with the pastor and others, I discover that many in the congregation have a traditional understanding of the parable as an affirmation that God seeks us. The sermon will offer a hearing that is, initially, unfamiliar.

After I read the text in the service of worship, I include a brief teaching moment in which I offer some brief exegetical remarks about details in the text so that the congregation will have this information as background, and will not be distracted by worrying over these details in the sermon.

The references to the angels in verses 10 and 14 derive from a belief in Judaism in the ancient world that God has assigned an angel (similar to the guardian angels of popular, contemporary Christian piety) to watch over each human community. In my view, ancient people used the figures of the angels as a way of speaking about the experience of ongoing providence. Matthew uses the phrase "little ones" to refer to disciples of Jesus.

A question that always comes up when I lead Bible studies on this passage: Why does the shepherd walk away from the ninety-nine sheep and leave them in danger to seek the one lost sheep? The answer: In those days, shepherds had pens built in wilderness areas to keep sheep at night. The shepherd provides for the ninety-nine. A flock of one hundred sheep is a modest size. The shepherd counted them each evening. As Psalm 23 says, the shepherd led them to water and food, tended their cuts, protected them from enemies (thieves and animal predators). Shepherds recognized each sheep. The shepherd lived through difficult conditions (cold in winter, excessive water during the rainy season, heat in summer) in behalf of the sheep. Judaism often spoke of God as a shepherd, and of the leaders of the community as shepherds.

The reference to "will" in verse 14 echoes the similar use of the word in the Lord's Prayer (Matthew 6:10b). In the prayer, the will of God is already being done in heaven. Biblical scholars describe the petition in Matthew 6:10b as eschatological: It is a plea for God to bring the apocalyptic cataclysm that ends this age of world history and inaugurates the rule (NRSV: kingdom) of God, a rule that is fully operative in heaven. In heaven, every relationship in every way is as God intends. God desires the same for the church, the community of "little ones" on the earth. This parable is a part of Jesus' instructions to the community in Matthew 18 about what to do when relationships in the church do not reflect God's will. The sermon is structured according to the Puritan Plain Style.

The Sermon: "Becoming a Community of the Found"

Beginning

Can you imagine a high school English teacher? 5 feet, 3 inches tall. Gray hair pulled back in a bun. Flower print dress. Those plump black shoes that older women used to wear. Glasses sparkling in the light, she taps her lectern, and says, "When you read a story, you nearly always identify with one of the characters. You experience the story through that character." Many of us identify with the lost sheep in the parable that I read a moment ago.

A very small child gets separated from its family in a crowded mall. Only 2 ½ feet tall, the child can only see trousers, skirts, and knees. Wide eyes, tears, a whimper, sometimes too frightened to cry. Lost. (short pause) In the nursing home with its smells — cleaning fluid, stale cigarette smoke, body odors — a person is wheeled into the sun room, and sits, and stares. Lost. (short pause) Called into the boss's office at 3:00 p.m. "The organization is making a change. You need to have your desk emptied and your key returned by 5:00 o'clock." Lost. (short pause)

As noted just above, many in the congregation have a traditional understanding of the parable as a story about God seeking us. In order to help people feel at home in the sermon, I decide to begin with the traditional affirmation. Later, I invite them to listen to the story from another point of view. The traditional interpretation does not conflict with the one that

I offer, but I want the listeners to have a good opportunity to move from the familiar to the unfamiliar. These images are intended to help the community experience being lost. I return to them in the paragraph just below in the hope of helping the congregation feel found.

Statement of the Direction of the Sermon

At one time or another, almost all of us feel lost. Sometimes we even feel like we've lost God, or that we're lost from God. We may feel that way, but Jesus is clear: You can never get so lost that the great shepherd will not find you. Like the shepherd in the story, God is with you. What a feeling — to be found. A mother's voice comes through the crowd. A hand on the shoulder of that person in the wheelchair brings a stirring of something familiar, something human. The interviewer picks up the phone and says to the vice-president, "We've found the person we need."

But what happens when we identify with someone else in the parable? The members of Matthew's church? Now, Matthew's church does not appear directly in the parable, but Matthew tells the story for them. But…why do they need to hear this story? After all, they are in the church. They are found. The answer to that question is intriguing, and it speaks directly to you and me. Consequently, I want us to explore this story as if we are members of the church of Matthew's day.

I hope that this statement will help the community shift from the traditional hearing of the story to the possibility of a fresh perspective. I do not, however, reveal the fullness of the point of view that is developed in the sermon.

Exposition of the Biblical Text

Many people in the days of Jesus believed that history is divided into two ages: old and new. The old world is corrupted by sin, and marked by alienation, pain, injustice. Nature is not even the way God intends. That is why weeds grow in your strawberry patch. God will replace the old world with a new one in which all things are the way God wants them to be. Joy in place of pain. Justice and peace in every relationship and situation. Nature a constant support.

Jesus manifests the rule of God.[3] "Here is my servant," God says. God's spirit fills Jesus to "proclaim justice to the Gentiles."[4] The miracles demonstrate God's rule. You might think of a miracle as a mini-instance of the rule of God. Jesus eats with outcasts and sinners, welcoming them into God's company. Jesus teaches how to respond to the divine rule through parables and other sayings. God's reign is "like yeast that a woman took and mixed…."[5]

Jesus calls the disciples and the church to witness to God's rule. "You are the light of the world."[6] The Christian community anticipates the new world. But, the church continues to live in the midst of the old. We go back and forth between the two.

As noted above, this sermon is the second in a series of three on a week-end of preaching and teaching. The material in the preceding three para-graphs is a reprise of themes from the sermon on the previous evening on Matthew 5:14, "You are the light of the world." I hope that its use here ties the sermons together and provides orientation for persons who are present at the present service, but were not in worship last night.

Matthew 18 is a manual on church life. This chapter gives instruction on how we can demonstrate the rule of God in our relationships with one an-other, especially when old world behaviors push aside the new.

"Become humble like this child."[7]

"If another member of the church sins against you, go and point out the fault...."[8]

Forgive one another seventy-seven times.[9]

When it comes to the parable of the lost sheep, Matthew says, in essence, "If a member of the church wanders away and gets lost, go after that person in the same way that the shepherd searches for the lost sheep. And when the lost sheep comes back, crank up the CD-player, break out the chips, light the candles, hang the streamers, buy some ice, and have a party."

Why would Matthew tell such a story? Evidently Christians saw some of their sisters and brothers drifting away from the community and were not doing anything about it. We do not have details as to who was drifting away or why. Maybe they gave up believing that God's rule would ever be com-plete. After all, they'd been waiting a long time. Maybe they were Christian Jews who found unbearable the tension between the church and the syna-gogue. Maybe they found it too difficult to be peacemakers, to turn the other cheek, to go the second mile. Maybe they were afraid to take up their crosses. Whatever the case, some drifted away while the rest of the congregation stood at the windows and watched, but didn't do anything about it.

But Jesus says, "No, No, No. The old world writes off people. But that's not the way it is in the rule of God. Seek them. Go to them. Do everything you can to help them. Go to them, like the shepherd who searched the mountain height. And if seeking them means forgiving something they have done to you, or asking forgiveness for something you have done to them, then do it."

We see the shepherd in the arid wilderness, searching. And we remem-ber. "The Lord is my shepherd."[10]   "God...will keep Israel as a shepherd keeps" the flock.[11] "I myself will seek them out," God says, " ...from all the places they have been scattered"[12] What does God call the leaders of Israel? Shepherds. And what does God want? True shepherds, who do in our every-day worlds what God does in the whole world.[13]

In Jesus Christ, God found you. Now, God calls you to go to those who have been found, but are in danger of being lost a second time.

I hope that the exposition clarifies the Matthean understanding of the text. I try to provide basic information plainly and directly. I hope that the congregation will hear these comments in light of the exegetical background that I discussed in the teaching moment at the time I read the Bible passage.

Application

I can understand some of the members of the church writing off people who drift away. A kid on a church league baseball team misses a couple of practices. Must not be interested. Coach doesn't call to tell her the day and time of the next practice.

The evangelism team is canvassing the town. They come to a street on which the front yards are small. The grass is worn through. The paint is peeling around the window frames. They see an old car sitting on concrete blocks. Somebody says, "Nobody from the neighborhood ever comes to our church." And so they go to the next street.

On Sunday afternoon, the elders take the Lord's supper to people in the hospital. At the patient information desk, the hospital has a file of the religious affiliations of the patients. The elders look in that file and find Sue's name.

"Sue. Who's that?"

"Haven't seen her in years. She was in a board meeting one time. Got in a big argument. Thought she was right. Stomped out. Hasn't been inside our building for years. We don't need to bother with her." We don't need to bother.

> *Because the exposition is (I hope) clear and uncomplicated, I can apply its point directly to the situation of the community. The application begins by helping the congregation imagine concrete situations in which we are tempted to write off people. I try to keep the application close to the everyday experience of the community.*

Jesus asks us questions. How can you forget a kid just because she missed a couple of practices? How can you pass by on the other side just because you see a car sitting on cement blocks? How can ignore a person lying in a hospital? You can't make them come to practice, or get them into a pew, or force the loaf and cup into their mouths. But you can let them know God loves them. The church wants them. You care. (major pause)

A funny thing happens to me when I write off someone. (pause) I discover that I go astray. I discover that I am lost. (major pause)

> *The point that we are lost when we write off others is a major idea in this part of the sermon. I try to emphasize it by setting it off with pauses.*

One July our family drove from Indianapolis to Oregon. A Subaru station wagon: two adults, four children, then ages six, three and two children in diapers. On a hot afternoon we stopped at Bear Lake, a little jewel in the corner of the Utah desert. Beautiful. We all got out of the car, took off our shoes, and waded into the cool water. Ah.

We got into the car and drove about 150 miles. One of the children asked for a Lifesaver, so Linda (my spouse) reached for her purse to get one.

Fumble. "My purse."

"What?"

"My purse…is gone." Her purse, containing our traveler's checks, our cash, our major credit card, and the detailed information about our trip. Had we left it at one of the innumerable roadside stops that you make when traveling with small children? (You wonder whether they have any bladders at all). Or did someone steal it while we were in the water at Bear Lake?

Neither Linda nor I said it at the time, but we both wondered who was to blame. Had she left it behind? Or was I responsible because I had not locked the car?

We stopped at a gas station to make the appropriate phone calls and started west again, keeping our eyes along the road for nuts and berries that we might eat. It is surprising how much hotter the sun was than before we lost the purse. The diapers that we had to change seemed to be the size of beach towels.

Linda was driving when the youngest child, then about four months old, began to cry. First whimpering, then little cries that got bigger and bigger until they hit storm-siren sound. I reached around to his child restraining seat and started to pull him out of his seat, "You little turkey, Thanksgiving is coming early for you this year." His little foot got caught in the mass of webbing that keeps the children in those seats. I gave him a jerk kin to a football player making a tackle at full speed.

Linda jammed on the brakes, pulled the car over to the desert shoulder, pulled him to her, and walked down the side of the road, away from me.

We had a AAA map, but we were lost.

After a long, silent trip, we reached a motel and called the person who was house-sitting for us in Indianapolis. "Oh, by the way," our housesitter said, "A police officer named Rindlesbaker in a town called Passenger, Wyoming called. He said something about having your purse."

In only the time it takes to breathe, the sun became cooler. The children became candidates for scholarships. And the diapers smelled sweet as cologne.

You know what? (pause)

That purse was found before we even knew it was lost. (pause)

And so am I. And so are you. (pause)

Through this long story, I hope the community will feel the movement from being lost to being found. I hope the experience of that movement will empower them to want to take the risk of seeking persons who wander from the community.

Ending

We are a community of the found. We are also a community of persons who seek those who are in danger of drifting away. It can be hard to go to them, especially when they've done something to you. Or when you've done something to them. You may not know what to say. You may not know what to do. Sometimes you need help from your pastor. But Jesus is clear. If we are found, then we are to search for those who are lost.

You do not go alone. "Where two or three are gathered in my name, I am there among them."[14] "I am with you always, to the end of the age." The one who found you goes with you. Who knows? In seeking someone else, you may find a part of yourself that is lost with them.

> *I hope that this ending encourages a reflective consciousness in which community members consider relationships in danger of being lost. It acknowledges the difficulties that attend seeking lost sheep, but reminds the community that the living presence of the risen Jesus is always with them as a source of strength. This sermon is followed the next morning by a sermon on Matthew 28:16–20, emphasizing Jesus' promise, "I am with you always, to the end of the age." I also hope that this ending helps the congregation anticipate the next sermon.*

CHAPTER SEVENTEEN

An Expository-Inductive Sermon
Mary Donovan Turner
Carl Patton Associate Professor of Preaching
Pacific School of Religion, Berkeley, California, U.S.A.

This chapter offers an expository-inductive sermon (see pages 99–113, 160–162). The text is Matthew 28:16–20:

> (16) Now the eleven disciples went to Galilee, to the mountain to which Jesus had directed them. (17) When they saw him, they worshiped him; but some doubted. (18) And Jesus came and said to them, "All authority in heaven and on earth has been given to me. (19) Go therefore and make disciples of all nations, baptizing them in the name of the Father and of the Son and of the Holy Spirit, (20) and teaching them to obey everything that I have commanded you. And remember, I am with you always, to the end of the age."

Background on the Conversation Leading to the Sermon
The Community. This sermon on Matthew 28:16–20 was first preached at a large, regional gathering of laity and clergy. While this denomination was not my own, it was similar to mine in theology and its spoken stances on social and political issues. As is usually the case, I would know but a very few of the several hundred gathered for the statewide meeting. I was in conversation only with those who had issued the invitation for me to come and with those who were planning worship. All others would, in some sense, be strangers. I could imagine that they represented a somewhat diverse group of churches steeped in different theological schools. I knew that regionally they were experiencing a change in leadership and that this event would be a time of naming and remembering recent and not-so-recent turmoil in their collective life. At the same time, it would mark a turn toward a new future. Because of my ongoing conversation with the wider church I knew of the struggles

and challenges these communities faced in being viable in this rapidly changing world.

With this information and being assigned the general theme of discipleship, I prepared to preach three times over a period of two days. This was the second of the three sermons. I chose the last verses from Matthew's Gospel and not the lectionary text for the week. I chose them because they looked back on the journey Jesus had made with the twelve. The verses also anticipated and propelled the disciples out into the future with the message that had been taught and lived out before them. I knew that for many hearing this sermon, the words of Matthew 28 would be familiar and comfortable. They would be able to recite the words with me, Bibles closed. For others, the commission could be embraced only partially because they would view it as a mandate to see other religious traditions as inferior.

Some in the community might have general notions of how these last verses differ from the endings of the other synoptics, and while many would know a conflated story of Jesus and his disciples, few would be aware of the particularities and peculiarities of the New Testament's first Gospel and its conclusion.

The Naive Reading. With this particular community in mind, I sat down and read and then spoke aloud the last five verses of Matthew. I knew that I must first read out of my own life experience and for the particular community I was addressing. My first recorded thoughts focused on several observations. First, the storyteller reminds us that there are now only eleven disciples; Judas is no longer with them (verse 16). This reminder alone brings rushing to the reader the emotions so intimately tied to the story of the last days in the life of Jesus and the betrayal by one of the twelve. We realize that even at the story's conclusion there is no perfect portrait painted of the twelve; the refusal to idealize them is, in some sense, our own good news. Even these first disciples gathered by Jesus were a curious mixture of indecision and fierce loyalty. This ambiguous portrait is confirmed by the response Jesus receives on the mountaintop in Galilee. Some worshiped, some doubted. I wondered what that meant — did the disciples doubt that it was Jesus with them?

I also wondered about the mountain in Galilee. Why would the gospel writer choose to have Jesus meet the disciples there? Had something of significance happened there before? I would need to do a search on the words "mountain" and "Galilee" to determine if these were, as I suspected, important places of revelation as the story had been told. What does it mean that "authority" had been given to Jesus (v. 18), all authority in heaven and on earth? What does it mean to go to "all nations" (v. 19)? Who are the "nations?"

I found myself intrigued by what has come to be known as the Great Commission (v. 20). It seemed to me that, in a succinct way., these final words of Jesus to the disciples encapsulated the entire gospel. The disciples are called to "make disciples." The gospel has in many ways been a story of the "making of disciples," and having watched Jesus with the twelve, we know that this is no easy task. Jesus is not talking about coercing or tricking people into quick conversion or cheap confession of faith. The "making of the disciples" in the Gospel of Matthew is a painstaking process of challenge and hope carried out by Jesus with patience and radical forbearance. It has to do with relationship.

The story about Jesus in Matthew's Gospel is, more than in other Gospels, a story about his teaching. Five major blocks of teaching material are woven into the narrative fabric of the text (see chapters 5–7, 10, 13, 18, 24–25). The disciples are being commissioned to do what Jesus has already done; they are to teach.

Jesus must know something about fear. He so easily recognizes it in the people around him. Often, as with the women who had witnessed the empty tomb, he acknowledges and, at the same time, tries to quell the fear that would keep them from living out the task that has been set before them. "Do not be afraid," he says to the women leaving the empty tomb, "go and tell my brothers to go to Galilee; there they will see me" (28:10). And then, following the commissioning of the disciples there is again the promise of presence (28:20). Here are the eleven, painfully aware of the ways they had abandoned and disappointed Jesus in the last days of his life, being commissioned to go out to all nations. The fragile, fleeing disciples are given so great a task. It is at the same time humorous and not. Regardless, the Jesus who they knew to be crucified was living and would be with them until, the gospel writer tells us, the end of the age.

So, what now did I see, hear, taste, touch, feel, and believe when I read this text? I saw disciples with furrowed brows who knew not whether Jesus had called them to the mountaintop to reprimand or forgive them. They are a mixture of fear and doubt, of wonder. Perhaps they were wondering how Jesus could have left them, wondering how he could now be alive, and perhaps grateful to see him once again. The words of Jesus sound strange to my ears. They are formal words, filled with imperatives, not what one would expect when friends are reunited after great trauma and tragedy. The disciples are silent, and we are left to wonder at their response. It is wondering about their own response that leads us to question our own.

There is little movement in this text. Jesus comes to the disciples after they have seen him, worshiped and doubted. The meaning is ambiguous, but perhaps the movement indicates not only a physical but also an emotional "coming together" of the twelve on the mountain. The fallible and frail disciples who have not been able to follow until the end are now given a global mission whose foundation is Jesus' cosmic authority.

I am captured by this portrait of the eleven; at the same time my attention is drawn elsewhere. I am plagued by a seemingly unrelated question that I cannot ignore. Who is missing? As Jesus stands with the eleven on sacred ground at this holy place of revelation – who is missing? It occurs to me that the women are missing. The twelve disciples have betrayed, denied, fallen asleep while Jesus wrestles with his fate, and finally they fled. But the women have stayed with him. These are women from Galilee, so why aren't they with

Jesus on the mountain? Mary Magdalene, Mary the mother of James and Joseph, and the mother of the sons of Zebedee were at the cross. The Marys went to the empty tomb. But in the last verses, they are not present. The mountaintop, I began to think, is barren.

For centuries, this text has inspired many a missionary movement around the globe. Armed with the command to baptize and teach, well-meaning missionaries have gone into cultures dissimilar to their own to convert the heathen. But I began to suspect as I read and reread these last five verses, that coming as they did at the end of a story detailing the complex and trying relationship between Jesus and the twelve, they did more than dictate the future relationships between disciples and the world. These last five verses told us something very important about the relationship between Jesus and the disciples. Much more. Since there is no mention in this text of Jesus' ascension I can assume that, for Matthew, there is something here of greater importance. Since the gospel ends in commission instead, I wonder what this means? The story doesn't end with a doxology, or a prayer, or a question, but with a commission, a task, a call, a challenge. This must have something to do with future, promise, commitment, community.

The Historical Context. Matthew was written by an anonymous author from and to an unspecified community. Perhaps it was written in Antioch, it is thought, in the closing decades of the first century. No theory can ever be completely validated. But about the community to which the author writes we know this: The community is trying to discern and delicately balance the importance of standing in and embracing tradition on the one hand and adapting to an ever changing and diverse world on the other. Written a half century after the crucifixion, the church faced important questions related to synagogue, church, and mission. In our text, Matthew 28:16–20, some of these themes culminate in a charge directed not just to one but to "all nations," Jew and Gentile alike. The call for baptism replaces the command for circumcision. The community is called to obey the commandments of Jesus and not the Mosaic law. The struggle between embracing the old and forging ahead toward the new took on different dimensions in the first century. It takes on different dimensions for the people I would be addressing. I was aware that they knew about the struggle between the old and the new, tradition and innovation. Church communities understand transition and resistance to it. Church communities of the twentieth century understand uncharted waters.

A Wider Conversation. Preaching need not be a solitary activity! Often my thoughts about particular texts are enriched by conversations with colleagues and students at Pacific School of Religion. Because they come from places international in scope and because life experiences are so varied, their perspectives shake me loose from time-honored assumptions that come with being a European American, middle-class woman who lives in the United States, who has been a lifelong member of a church community, who has been blessed with opportunities for study and growth. These conversations expand my sometimes limited peripheral vision, my horizons. In this instance I was touched by a conversation with a Samoan student who held this text close to his heart. Without a missionary's zeal prompted and fed by the great commission he would not now be Christian. A colleague responded to the "call to obedience" at the commission's end. What is commanded, he said, is to love neighbor, to love enemy, to reach out to those in distress. The command to obey he saw as the great equalizer, the call for justice. An historian reminded me of the horrors in the American West when the Christian community displaced and culturally replaced the rich and meaningful Native American ways of life with foreign and often unsatisfying ways. This was often done in the name of the Great Commission.

One professor remembered seeing a painting of this text in Jakarta, Indonesia. The disciples were seated on the ground and the Christ figure was hovering just above the ground addressing them with outstretched arms. All the figures were Asian. I was reminded that like an artist with canvas or photographer with camera, we see the biblical text from our own angle of vision. Other interpretations challenge our own conventions and assumptions, enrich our understandings. When reading the call to go to "all nations" this same person remembered tear-filled worship experiences where great masses of people were singing "O Come All Ye Faithful" in their native languages. It was for him a glorious reminder that the gospel belongs to no solitary individual, no single community, no lone nation, but to all of them. Different cultures live out and display the Christian message in varied ways that create a panorama of color and beauty, a symphony of sound, a rich mosaic. And doesn't this call to go out into the world, a friend said to me, signal that we can do more? That we can do more than we ever dreamed possible to bring about the realm of God that already *is*, but is also *not yet*? We are challenged by this text to work for transformation.

I can only imagine that if my conversations had taken me off the seminary campus and into the streets of Berkeley, responses to this text would be even more varied and revealing. This is the time in the reflective process for gathering, enriching, expanding, questioning, and imagining.

These and other images surfaced as I meditated daily on this text employing time honored spiritual practices. Using a practice developed by Martin Luther, for instance, I asked myself what word of instruction there was in this text for me. Did this text call me to thanksgiving? to confession? Was there anything that made me feel afraid? It was contemplating these questions morning after morning that brought me to a profound realization of the gratitude I feel for my own calling. It was also this practice that made me aware of the manifold ways I do not fulfill it. I realized, in spite of the way I live out my vocation, God keeps calling. We are chosen...again.

This personal reflection about my own ministry did not make its way directly and explicitly into the sermon text. But uncovering or recovering my feelings about call and my fulfillment (or lack of fulfillment) of it brought an energy and engagement that informed the sermon's embodiment. When I became convinced that the issue was not only relevant but also extremely important for my own understanding of self and of God, I could express through the sermon's delivery that passionate concern to the worshiping community.

The Literary Context. Matthew 28:16–20 is the last scene in the extended narrative gospel. They not only bring together a culmination of important narrative threads, but also give us important clues as to the purpose of the Gospel and how the preceding chapters are to be read. I find it useful, even mandatory, to read the entire Gospel in light of a single text. New images are raised, new narrative strands are discovered, new insights are gleaned from the once-again reading. In this instance, some of my initial questions of the text were answered. Yes, mountaintops are important to Matthew. Sermons are delivered there (5:l), Jesus prays there (l4:23), God speaks there (l7:1), people are fed there (15:29), and disciples are now commissioned there. And Galilee? This was where the saving light was made manifest, where the new light was to dawn (4:12–16). Perhaps for this reason Matthew as well as Mark are insistent that the post-resurrection experiences of Jesus take place here (unlike in the Luke-Acts narrative where the disciples remain in Jerusalem so that the spirit will come upon them and they will be filled with power). And, yes, we find that this Gospel is about the authority of Jesus (see 7:29, 9:6, 21:23–27). With this authority the disciples are lent a power, something stronger than their own, which will undergird their ministry and help them carry out the tasks to which they are called. To all nations? Yes, as a reader of the Gospel we witness a swelling momentum in the thought of the evangelist who portrays Jesus' mission first as one to the house of Israel (l0:6), but who, as the story closes, sends the disciples into the world, all of it. The baptismal formula – *in the name of the Father, Son, and Holy Spirit* – would take on additional importance, I decided, if this sermon was being written for Trinity Sunday, year A, its usual placement during the three-year lectionary cycle. The reading answered these questions but rendered other important information as well; new questions were forged and new insights born.

Scholars have found connecting strands between the end of Matthew's Gospel and its first two chapters. They note the emphases on presence, for instance, in l:23 and 28:20 as indications that the gospel writer intends for us to begin and end our reading of the story with the assurance that God has been, is, and will be with us. But it was the relationship between Matthew 4 and 28 that most intrigued me. In the former, the first four disciples are virtually unknown to us, but we are captivated by the relative ease with which they follow Jesus' command to drop their fishing nets by the side of the sea and follow. Immediately, Matthew tells us that they do. I am struck this time as I read at how willing they are to follow; they seem strong. But somehow also naive. They have no idea what is before them. And I wonder if Jesus knows how much time and energy and effort, how much perseverance it will take to "make" them into disciples. According to Matthew, making disciples takes a great deal of instruction. I am intrigued by the initial command to the disciples in chapter 4; it is to *come*. They are called to spend time with Jesus. In chapter 28 it is to *go*. The disciples, prepared by Jesus, are commissioned to teach.

As I read through the Gospel of Matthew, I watched for two narrative strands. First, the disciples as they live out the call they so immediately accepted. Do they follow? What kind of followers have they been? What happens between the initial calling and the last commissioning? And second, the women. Are they important to the story? How? Were they chosen? Where have they been? Where are they as the Gospel comes to a close?

Matthew directly and intentionally answers the first set of questions. The disciples follow, he tells us. They do not return to the seashore to resume their previous day to day existence. They follow until they, with Jesus, reach Jerusalem. Whatever is asked of them there is too great.

In response to my questions about women, I found a sensitivity and awareness of women from the beginning of the Gospel where, in his genealogy of Jesus, Matthew unexpectedly mentions five of them. By doing so, he forever secures their importance in the history of redemption. Throughout the narrative, women play a sometimes subtle, but nonetheless important role, as the ministry of Jesus unfolds. As the Gospel comes to closure, women take on a more privileged place as a woman anoints Jesus before his death (26:6–13). Women are there at the cross, looking on from a distance, and then as the first day of the week was dawning, they go to see the tomb. They are the first witnesses of resurrection. Their importance in the passion narrative is undeniable as their presence provides a marked contrast to that of the fallible disciples. Receiving a commission from the angel and then from Jesus who makes his first post-resurrection appearance to them, the women faithfully follow through on the task given to them. "Do not be afraid; go and tell my brothers to go to Galilee; there they will see me." Their faithful obedience and their fierce loyalty makes their absence on the mountain in Galilee a contradiction, maybe an irony or paradox. Why aren't they present when the final and consummate commission is spoken by Jesus? To embrace the commission but lament the women's absence on the mountaintop is to find the text only partially congruent with one's understanding of the gospel.

The Sermon: Purpose and Direction. In considering these two different but plausible interpretations, I became aware that two possible sermons were developing out of reading Matthew 28:16–20 in the context of the gospel. One focused on the unconditional love Jesus demonstrated for the disciples as he chose them **again.** This interpretation was certainly appropriate to the gospel as I understood it, was intelligible, and morally plausible. The other sermon had to do with justice. It focused on the absence of the women as the commission was made. This interpretation required that I take a different stance, one that was against the text which, in this respect, did not represent the all inclusive gospel as I had come to understand it. The juxtaposition of this text with other inclusive ones (even ones in Matthew) would provide the "disequilibrium" from which a thought provoking sermon could move to resolution.

I was aware that these were two very different sermons! While they both had to do with discipleship, a sermon on the unfailing love of Jesus toward the disciples would have as its function to inspire and encourage. It would invite listeners to "hear again" the voice of God calling them out for their own particular ministries, no matter what kind of followers they had previously been. It would be a sermon of grace, of forgiveness; it would impart a "second chance."

A sermon about the absence of women would challenge the last verses of Matthew and also the listeners to envision a mountaintop where all were present and felt called, embraced and sent out into the world. This would be a sermon about breaking boundaries, enlarging our vision, expanding our awareness about the "ins and outs" of our own communal living. One sermon could **not** effectively do both these things, and knowing that part of good preaching (and sometimes the hardest part) is letting go of a story, an illustration, even an interpretation or major theme for the sake of clear focus and function, I chose to follow the life of Peter and Andrew, James and John through the Gospel story. This, I felt, was in keeping with the context and needs of the community I was addressing. It was a community in need of healing, yet poised with new leadership toward the future. Thus, the focus statement for this sermon was the following: Despite the frailties and failures of his disciples, the resurrected Jesus chooses them again to go out into the world.

The Sermon Form. The purpose of the sermon is to allow the community to feel and experience what I had come to understand as the radical and grace-filled invitation to the disciples to continue being disciples, I knew that listeners would need also to experience the travels of the twelve as they first so obediently began to follow in the footsteps of Jesus. I also knew that they would need to experience the steps of the disciples as they became more deliberate, more cautious. They would need to know that as the last scenes in the crucifixion drama unfolded, the disciples had disappeared. They had chosen to no longer be a part of the story. How then would the news that Jesus was calling them back feel to them? What would they be thinking? These are probably not joy filled disciples, but disciples riddled with guilt, misgivings, fear. I wanted to use an inductive form that would allow us to move toward the sermon's focus; only by following in the footsteps of the disciples could we understand the radical, grace-filled nature of their final commissioning.

I wanted to create anticipation for the sermon by juxtaposing the first call of the disciples and the last — they are different people by the story's end, not wholly faithful and not wholly committed, but different. I wanted to do that by talking about their fear which was so noticeably and surprisingly absent in chapter 4, but which overwhelms them as they travel through Matthew's narrative. This is not what we would expect from a Gospel story — this movement from certainty to doubt, from faithful following to flight.

I decided not to move back and forth between the contemporary world and that of the first century, but rather to live fully into the world of the disciples, using language that would help us see our own faithfulness and faithlessness mirrored in their own. I would not begin with the end of the Matthew's story, but I would take people there — slowly — just as the disciples arrived there after painstaking lessons and disappointments and failures. I would take the listeners on the same journey of discovery I had experienced as I read through the Gospel of Matthew.

The Sermon: "Chosen Again" [1]

It's like a video on fast forward — that part of Matthew 4 that recounts the calling of the first four disciples. With an unbounded energy, the story begins and goes full speed ahead. No pauses, no places where the reader can stop and ask her questions. We are off and running to hear what happens to this person named Jesus. In the first three short chapters he is born and grows to adulthood. He is baptized. He changes his residence, moves to Capernaum, and his ministry begins. He preaches, "Repent for the kingdom of God has come near." Matthew can't tell us the story fast enough.

In chapter 4 we find Jesus on the edge of the Sea of Galilee. Walking along, he passes two fishermen, Peter and Andrew, who are casting their nets into the sea. Jesus says, "Follow me." They do! Immediately, Matthew tells us. Immediately, they laid down their nets and they begin to follow Jesus who continues his walk along the seashore.

He finds two more brothers with their father sitting in the boat mending their nets, and says to them, "Follow me." They do. Immediately, Matthew tells us. Immediately, they laid down the nets and they began to follow this Jesus.

As a reader of this story I want to cry out. I want to say, "Stop! Wait! I have some questions that need to be answered! Why does this Jesus need these people to follow? And why has he chosen these? Why Peter and Andrew and James and John? Why take them away from their fishing nets? Why take them away from the work that has provided security and consistency in their lives day after day? Why do they have to leave their father who silently sits there and watches them go?"

Peter and Andrew and James and John, if I could line them up in front of me, I would ask them some questions, too. I would say, "Why did you go? Had you heard about the preaching of this man called Jesus or was there just something compelling in that voice? Did you have no hesitation, was there no caution in your step? Did you not want to say, 'Well, I'll go along for a day or two and see if this works.' Wasn't there a part of you that wanted to tuck that fishing net ever so safely under your arm just in case you might need it again someday?"

We want to know more, but the storyteller is eager to move us along. There is no time for detail. No time to tell us why Jesus called these. No time to tell us why they decided to accept that incredible invitation. What is the urgency? We who love security and control and knowledge about the future, we would love to ask them more. We want to see their faces. Hear them speak. Listen to them tell us what they are thinking. What they are feeling. If I had them here right in front of me I would put my hands on their shoulders and lock my eyes squarely upon theirs, and I would ask them the one question that plagues my heart and my mind — "Weren't you afraid?"

The four disciples were quickly plunged into a world they had never known, one they could not possibly have imagined, as they dropped their nets by the seashore and began following that stranger from Galilee. They got in step behind him, walked behind Jesus as he went out through Galilee to preach and to teach and cure all diseases. They watched as the crowds began to gather around Jesus, people with every possible kind of illness — the demoniacs, the epileptics, and the paralytics, people with every kind of disease and pain. They all came and surrounded this Jesus who could heal them. The disciples must have wondered, "Does this Jesus…could this Jesus expect us to be healers, too?"

They sat with Jesus on the mountainside, and they heard those words that he spoke, words they often did not understand, words that didn't match the reality of life they had always known. "Love your enemy." "Turn the other cheek. Blessed are the meek. Blessed are the poor in spirit." They must have wondered, "Does this Jesus…could this Jesus expect us to understand what he is teaching us? And worse, does this Jesus…could this Jesus expect us to teach as he teaches?"

They must have been trembling as they watched Jesus reach out and touch that leper — "Does he…? Could he…?"

But they followed; they continued to follow. They followed Jesus to the seashore and into the boat that was riding those angry waves. They thought his life and theirs were hanging in the balance. And they followed him to the top of that mountain, where suddenly and mysteriously they heard the voice of God.

As we reach the end of the Gospel we continue to watch these disciples. We listen to them. We follow along with them, and finally our question is answered. Were those disciples afraid? You bet. They had found that to be a follower of this Jesus sometimes takes us to very frightening places. And as they turned that corner toward Jerusalem, their pace slowed. Those fishermen who had immediately dropped their nets by the side of the sea — we can see their pace slowly — slowly — slowly — become more cautious and more measured. Following this Jesus meant walking to the edge of life…staying with a friend while he walked to the edge of his life. And now Matthew tells us the disciples are following…but at a distance…

And then they flee.

They can follow no more. That fear. That fear was just too great.

Were they afraid that it would be too hard to watch their friend and companion Jesus walk toward that cross? Perhaps. Or, were they afraid that they weren't strong enough inside to face whatever life might bring them? Maybe. Or are we all, as Nelson Mandela suggests, not fearful that we are inadequate but fearful that we are really powerful beyond measure? Whatever it was, for our four disciples it was easier to run away. And they fled....

As readers of the story we think that perhaps for these disciples it is over. But, of course, it is not because this is the gospel. This is good news! This is the place where beginnings come out of endings and where strength comes out of weakness. And as the Gospel comes to a close, Jesus takes those disciples to the top of a mountain, and he speaks to them. He delivers the Great Commission. He takes those disciples, the very ones who had abandoned him, who had followed at a distance and then who had run away...he takes those disciples up to the top of the mountain, and he sends them out to teach and to baptize the world over. This is not just a commission! This is a moment of profound, radical, amazing grace for those who stumbled as they tried to follow in the footsteps of Jesus. Jesus takes those disciples, and he gathers them around himself on the top of the mountain. It is as if he says to them —

- "I know you were afraid to speak when a word needed to be spoken.
- I know that you left my side when I needed you most.
- I know you were afraid to reach out and welcome the stranger.
- I know that your knees were weak, your hearts beating with fear as you watched me travel toward that cross.
- I know.
- But now...I choose you...again.*"*

In Retrospect

It is not possible for the reader of this sermon (or the preacher) to know the full effect of its telling. I know only this: The sermon was met with silence, a lengthy one. I cannot know what each person heard or felt. I can only hope that in broad stroke the retelling of the story of the four disciples helped the community recognize the ways they had not been faithful followers. And I can only hope that in so doing they were somehow freed to embrace the call that is issued time and time again by a God who forever loves and is hopeful that we will work with God in creating a new world. That's what I heard anyway. The preacher was preaching to the preacher. She was chosen... again.

CHAPTER EIGHTEEN

A Topical-Deductive Sermon

René Rodgers Jensen

Co-Pastor, First Christian Church (Disciples of Christ)
Omaha, Nebraska, U.S.A.

This sermon is topical-deductive (see pages 113–117, 159–160). The topic in the sermon is an aspect of the doctrine of God: the relationship between God as transcendent and immanent. The movement is deductive.

The Setting of the Sermon

This sermon was preached at First Christian Church (Disciples of Christ), Omaha, Nebraska, in July 1997. It was part of a sermon series called "Meeting God Again for the First Time," a title borrowed from Marcus Borg.[1] The sermon series grew out of a discussion in an adult Sunday school class following the Heaven's Gate mass suicide. Heaven's Gate was a religious cult that sought to advance beyond this human realm. They looked for a new home in the heavens and believed that they would be given a sign when someone would come from beyond this world to take them to the higher world. Their religion was a blend of new age thought, eastern mysticism, and themes drawn from science fiction. Their leader believed that the Hale-Bopp comet would be followed by a craft to take them to the next level. In order to be ready for their trip, the members of the cult took their own lives in San Diego, California in the spring of 1997. Among the suicides was the daughter of a prominent Omaha family, so the senselessness of this tragedy hit home in a particularly vivid way.

As the class discussed Heaven's Gate and the peculiar theology behind their actions, it became increasingly clear that while people felt that the Heaven's Gate theology was wrong (clearly it had to be wrong to lead to such tragic consequences), the members of the Sunday school class, made up primarily of baby boomers, were unable to articulate exactly what was wrong with the cult's theology. Like most boomers, the class members value tolerance and openness to other ideas. Yet here was clearly a case where the "you do your thing and I'll do mine" credo of the sixties and seventies was inadequate.

Because the Christian Church (Disciples of Christ) is historically a non-creedal denomination, it is especially important for its members to be able to understand and articulate the foundational elements of the Christian faith. Members of this adult Sunday school class, most of whom had grown up in the church and were faithful attenders of both worship and Sunday school, were unable to speak with any assurance about the nature of God, the meaning of salvation, or what we mean when we say that Jesus is the Son of God. The summer sermon series was designed to review these basics of the Christian faith.

Questions and comments about Heaven's Gate came up in pastoral calling, in meetings at the church, and in casual contacts with members and friends. These comments revealed that many people had perspectives that were similar to those of the class that had sparked me to begin thinking toward this series, and this sermon in particular.

I decided to take a topical approach in this sermon because I wanted to speak, in a basic way, about an aspect of the doctrine of God (God as ever immanent and transcendent) that helps interpret the situation at Heaven's Gate, and that helps interpret many other questions concerning what we are to do from the standpoint of what we most deeply believe. This doctrine grows from biblical perspectives, of course, but it reaches further than the sweep of any single text. In the sermon, I review several key passages from the Bible. They are the fountainhead of an even deeper, broader theological current that can help us out with questions about God's presence and purposes.

I review with the congregation some popular notions of God that derive from Greek philosophy, but that have made their way, unhelpfully, into popular Christian thought. I compare and contrast these notions with the heart of Christian teaching.

In the latter phases of the sermon, I try to help the congregation consider ways in which our beliefs about God — especially God's constant presence — have very practical outcomes. On the negative side, we do not have to resort to attitudes and behaviors like those at Heaven's Gate. On the positive side, we have the assurance that God is always with us. I close with an image that is intended to help the congregation feel God's presence.

The approach is deductive. In the beginning of the sermon, I identify the issue with which the sermon is concerned: how we understand God. I state clearly my perception that certain popular notions of God are unsatisfactory. I indicate that I will review the unsatisfactory character of these notions, and that I will offer a better one. The sermon then develops along those lines.

Clark Williamson, one of my theology professors in seminary, said over and over again, "Ideas have consequences." One of the goals of this sermon, and the whole sermon series, was to help people realize that what we think shapes how we act.

The Sermon: "God: The Beyond in Our Midst"

My husband Rick and I were watching "Politically Incorrect" late one night, and comedian George Carlin was on. I don't remember the subject they were discussing, but somehow religion came up. George Carlin went off on a real tirade about God. "God is a grumpy old man who lives up in heaven, he watches every move you make so that when you make a mistake he can send you to hell. He causes war and disease and lets little children die. And, oh yeah — he loves you." Yikes! What a portrait of God!

This opening illustration is intended to help ease the congregation into the sermon. It is also designed to help listeners realize that the popular media offers a variety of images for God. Similar images are also found in popular Christian piety. We need to be able to recognize and evaluate these images and to realize when they may be painting a picture of God that is false to Christian understandings of God.

It reminded me of one of my theology professors in seminary, Norman Pittenger, who told us about once having a discussion about God with a friend who was an atheist. Frustrated at his friend's absolute insistence that there was no God, Pittenger finally asked the man to describe this God he didn't believe in. The man's portrait of God was not unlike George Carlin's: God is angry, judgmental, unforgiving, up there, out there, and indifferent to human pain and suffering. Pittenger listened carefully to the atheist's description of God, and then said, "Well, I don't believe in that God either."

Since then I have used Pittenger's question, "Tell me about this God you don't believe in?" with people who are questioning God's existence, and I have almost always found that the God they do not believe in is a God that I could not worship, either. A God who is far away, who either causes human suffering, or is indifferent to it. A God who is uninvolved in the world and unmoved by its plight.

I want to talk with you this morning about where this notion of God came from and about some of its negative effects. And I want to hold out a very different image of God, an image of God that is drawn from the Bible, and that gives us encouragement and positive guidance for life.

This notion of God has its roots not in the Bible, but in Greek philosophy. The Greek philosopher Aristotle talked of God as "the Unmoved Mover." This notion of God, which played a role in Christian theology for centuries, suggests that God created the world, like a great clock maker, who sets the gears in motion, then stands back and lets the creation tick away on its own. God creates or moves the world, but is not moved by it, not touched by it, not affected by it. Thus the picture of God as the Unmoved Mover.

This very Greek notion of God has deeply influenced centuries of Christian theology. The problem is, it is not a biblical description of God. The early church, as it expanded into the Roman Empire, which was dominated by Greek philosophy and ways of thinking, was influenced by Greek philosophers like Aristotle. Early Christian theologians adopted some of these Greek notions about the nature of God, and the God they painted was a God who was far away, unmoved by the human condition. Some theologians speak of God as "wholly other" in such a way as to suggest that God is completely divorced from the world.

> *In this very brief history of an aspect of Christian thought, I am trying to help the congregation name an attitude about God that is widespread among church members. I also try to help the community understand that our theology has a history, that it didn't just spring up from anywhere, and that understanding of the development of that theology helps us to critically appropriate the theology. As I suggest in the upcoming paragraphs, I hope the congregation will agree with me that early perspectives are more faithful and more helpful for today's believers.*

The problem is, this is not a biblical notion of God. Yes, the Bible does speak of God as transcendent, as the Creator who can call worlds into being with just a word, as great and mighty, so glorious that even to see him is to die. But the Bible also speaks of God as immanent (i-m-m-a-n-e-n-t), which means God is among us. The word "immanent" comes from the Latin root which means to dwell within. We get our word "mansion" from the same Latin root. God who is immanent dwells among us. The Gospel of John speaks of immanence when it says, "The Word became flesh and lived among us." (John 1:14). Similarly, in the 21st chapter of Revelation, another John says, "Behold, the dwelling of God is with men and women." According to that passage, God dwells with us. We are God's people. God wipes away every tear from our eyes. (Revelation 21:3–4).

Remember that one of the names for Jesus is "Immanuel," which means "God with us." The prophet Isaiah, speaking to the Israelites in exile in Babylon and sure that God had abandoned them forever, relays God's message of comfort and hope, "For I am the LORD your God, the Holy One of Israel, your Savior.…Do not fear, for I am with you" (Isaiah 43:3, 5).

The scriptures abound with stories of God's intimate involvement in the world. The apostle Paul visited Athens on one of his missionary journeys. Strolling around the city, everywhere he found idols dedicated to different gods. He even found one idol inscribed, "To an unknown god." When Paul preached to the Athenians, he told them that this unknown god is the God that he wanted them to know. This is the God who made the whole world and everything in it, but this God did not live in shrines. This God dwells in us and we dwell in God. This God "is not far from each one of us," Paul said, "for in [God] we live and move and have our being" (Acts 17:22–28).

Indeed, even God's name suggests that God is always with us. In Exodus 3, God calls Moses to lead the children of Israel out of bondage in Egypt. Moses asks God, "What is your name?" (Exodus 3:13–22). The Hebrew phrase that is God's response is very difficult to translate, but is usually rendered "I AM WHO I AM." But Martin Buber, one of the best-known Jewish religious scholars of this century, contends that the Hebrew verb in this phrase means the one "who will be there." God's name, then, should be translated, "I will be present as I will be present." God's name suggests that God is "present in every now, and in every here."[2]

I begin this discussion of scriptural backgrounds by acknowledging a thematic similarity between the Bible's pictures of God and the earlier image of God as the Unmoved Mover: God is the transcendent creator, who is always more than we imagine. However, I also quickly draw upon several significant, representative biblical texts to contrast their pictures of God as always with us, always involved in the world, with the earlier image of God as Unmoved Mover who is unaffected by the world and uninvolved in it. While the perspective that I advocate is biblical, it is not controlled by any single biblical text.

This motif does not mean that God is not still transcendent. God is both transcendent and immanent. God is more than everything (and thus transcendent) and yet everything is in God (hence God is immanent). God is right here, but God is also more than "right here."

It is important to keep both the transcendent and immanent in balance as we talk about God. If we talk about God as only immanent, then we fall into sloppy, soppy New Age kinds of theology, in which God is reduced to a kind of power or force or source of energy that suffuses all things, like "the Force" in the *Star Wars* movies. But if we speak of God as only transcendent, then God becomes an absent, indifferent, and uncaring Being. And in terms of having a personal relationship with God, there is little difference between an absent God, and no God at all. God is both transcendent and immanent. God is, in Dietrich Bonhoeffer's lovely phrase, "the beyond in our midst."[3]

Sometimes our religious language falls into the trap of making it seem as if God were only transcendent. For example, we begin our worship service each week with an invocation, which is traditionally understood as invoking or inviting God's presence for the worship service. But that's really kind of odd, don't you think? As if we had to remind God to show up for church! Of course, we don't. What we should properly invoke is our heightened awareness of God's presence. I fall into this mistaken way of speaking about God myself from time to time. I am most conscious of it when I pray with someone in the hospital and sometimes ask God to "be with" the person as they are in the hospital. But God is already there with them, feeling their pain, sharing their suffering. What I should be praying for is that the person who is sick will become more fully aware of God's unfailing presence.

I use these examples to illustrate ways in which we use language imprecisely. I hope that the congregation will move from these examples to reflect on all our language for God. Because our language plays a key role in shaping how we perceive God and how we act in relationship to God and one another, I hope that the community will want to use language that bespeaks God's constant presence and faithfulness.

In fact, it is precisely because of God's unfailing presence that we sometimes fail to be aware of God. We are like the fish swimming in the ocean. Often, we are no more aware of the God in whom we live and move and have our being, than the fish is aware of the ocean. Yet, God is always with us. Our challenge is to open ourselves up to a fresh, new, heightened awareness of that unfailing presence.

The irony is that sometimes people believe that they have to go hunting for God, as if God were someplace else, distant and hidden from us. Susan Strom, the Omaha woman who was among the suicides in the Heaven's Gate cult, once told a friend, "I'm out chasing God." Even her death was a desperate attempt to find God, to go to God. What a tragedy that she didn't understand that God has already come to us. We don't have to chase God. God chases us. God constantly seeks us out. In "The Hound of Heaven," poet Francis Thompson writes of how he tried to elude God, but God always found him.

> I fled Him, down the nights and down the days;
> I fled Him, down the arches of the years;
> I fled Him, down the labyrinthine ways
> Of my own mind; and in the midst of tears...
> Shade of His hand, outstretched caressingly,
> "Ah, fondest, blindest, weakest,
> I am He Whom thou seekest."[4]

I use this excerpt from the poem partly because it communicates a motif that is needed at this point in the sermon. I also use it because the poem is somewhat familiar in the congregation. I hope that people in the community will transfer their familiarity and security with the poem to the notion that is developing in the sermon. I hope they will recognize the direction of the sermon is not altogether new, but is a focusing of ideas that are already in their well.

The word became flesh and dwelt among us. God so loved the world, that God came to the world in the form of Jesus Christ to share our humanity and manifest God's presence and purposes. We don't have to go out chasing God as Susan Strom did. Sometimes all we have to do is just stand still long enough to let God find us.

Another poet, Robert Browning, in a burst of good feeling about the world, once wrote,

> The lark's on the wing;
> The snail's on the thorn:
> God's in His heaven —
> All's right with the world![5]

God has given us with this beautiful world. But our sense of the "rightness" of the world comes not only in knowing that God is in God's heaven. God is never just up there, out there, somewhere else. God is also in the midst of the muck, and dirt, and pain, and general messiness of our world.

The most painful and difficult time in my life was when my sister, then eight months pregnant, and her two children were killed in a car accident. I want to let you know one way that I experienced God's presence in the midst of that terrible and difficult time. The accident occurred during my last semester in seminary. Before we left Indianapolis, where we were living at the time, to fly to Texas to be with my family, I called a seminary friend to tell him what had happened, knowing that he would let my other friends know. When we got to my parents' house, there was a bouquet of flowers from my seminary friends waiting for me. To this day I do not know how they got those flowers to my mother's house. They didn't know my parents' names. They certainly didn't know their address. I'm not even sure they knew the name of my hometown. But like a message of hope and comfort and love, the flowers were waiting. Attached to them was a card that said, "We love you and we are with you. And so is God." I slipped that card into my pocket and carried it with me constantly during the next difficult days. Whenever I felt overwhelmed by grief and pain and loss, I would slip my hand into my pocket and touch that card, and know that I was not alone.

None of us ever are.

I chose to use this closing story after considerable thought and struggle. It is always difficult to know how self-revelatory to be in a sermon, particularly when talking about a deeply personal grief. However, in a sermon that dealt with as seemingly an abstract concept as the nature of God, it seemed important to bring it home in a very personal way: This is how I experience God's presence. Otherwise the sermon becomes mere intellectual speculation. This story is an example of an "evidential experience" (page 59).

CHAPTER NINETEEN

A Topical-Inductive Sermon

Reginald C. Holmes

Senior Pastor
New Covenant Christian Church (Disciples of Christ)
Denver, Colorado, U.S.A.

This sermon is topical (pages 113–117). It deals with the issue of injustice that results from racism. It is inductive in movement (pages 160–162).

Background on the Conversation Leading to the Sermon

The sermon was developed for the New Covenant Christian Church (Disciples of Christ) in Denver, Colorado. The sermon is one of a series designed to help the congregation interpret the sequence of events set in motion by the trial of four European American police officers for excessive use of force when they pulled over Los Angeles' African American motorist Rodney King. A videotape recording, repeatedly broadcast on national television, showed that the officers forced King on the ground and struck him repeatedly with clubs. The trial was held before a jury made up of ten European Americans, one Hispanic American, and one Asian American in a largely European American suburb, Simi Valley. The jury declared the officers "Not guilty," immediately prompting dismay in the African American community, and among many European Americans. Shortly after the verdict, an uprising took place in urban Los Angeles to protest the verdict and its larger racist symbolism. The protest resulted in face-to-face confrontations among people of different races and ethnicities, violence, and considerable destruction of property. In a memorable news conference, King thrust aside his prepared remarks, looked straight into the camera, and with depth and passion asked, "Can't we all just get along?"

In other sermons in the series, I tried to help the congregation name and process its feelings, thoughts, and behaviors in the wake of the verdict and the uprising. This sermon, which came toward the end of the series, is designed to address particular dynamics within the congregation.

286

New Covenant Christian Church (then known as Park Hill Christian Church) is predominantly African American. I am forty years old. About 40 percent of the congregation is made up of persons who are age forty and older. About 60 percent of the congregation is composed of persons who are younger than forty. These age-related statistics are important for reading the sermon because I take account of differences in the ways different generations experience and respond to injustice that results from racism. Through priestly listening, I discovered that many younger members of the congregation (and some older ones) were so pessimistic about improving race relations in the United States that they were reluctant to struggle against it. Some members were essentially saying, "What's the use?" This sermon is intended, in large degree, to encourage them.

I chose a topical approach because the issue of injustice manifest through racism spreads a wider net than is encompassed in any one biblical text. As noted in the sermon below, racism based on skin pigmentation is a relatively recent human phenomenon. People in the world of the Bible, and well into the 1600s, did not denigrate one another on the basis of color. While the Bible deals with slavery, the Bible does not explicitly deal with the contemporary phenomenon of racism and its injustices. Contemporary theologians posit a host of ways of understanding racism theologically, e.g., as sin, as idolatry, as a demon, as a principality, as a perversion, as a strategy for self-service and self-protection, as a systemic force. I recognize value in all of these approaches, but seek a wider theological basis for helping the community interpret its situation. In addition to the Bible and Christian history, I draw on my denomination's contemporary study of racism.

Through priestly listening I also discovered that many in the community have an idea of justice that is less than the notion of justice that is central to the Bible and to Christian tradition. As the title implies, the sermon attempts to help the congregation enlarge its sense of vision to understand justice from God's perspective.

I hoped that the sermon would become a part of the congregation's ongoing conversation about how to respond to racism and its injustices. I intended to reinforce older members of the community in their long, and sometimes wearying, struggle for a just world. I particularly hoped to encourage younger members of the congregation to want to join, or continue the struggle. At the least, I hope that younger members would not become cynical. The sermon attempts to be very realistic: naming painful aspects of injustice that many people in the congregation experience on a daily basis, but recalling important passages, themes, and images from the Bible and Christian history and theology that point toward reasons for hope. I am quite honest in acknowledging that progress takes place in fits and starts, and will last into the foreseeable future.

I organize the message inductively as a way of helping the congregation move past initial resistance to the possibility of investing their time and energy in efforts toward a more just community. I did not begin the sermon with a direct challenge to continue or join the struggle for justice. Instead, I begin by recollecting how that struggle has gone in our own lifetimes. The older members of the congregation will, likely, identify with these scenarios. I hope that both older and younger members identify with manifestations of injustice that the preacher describes in the middle of the sermon. In particular, many members know persons who suffer discrimination from the police and courts as described in the middle of the sermon. By the last third of the sermon, I hope that all in the congregation have found a place in the conversation, and are receptive to the suggestion to continue or join the witness toward a just community. For purposes of publication, some of the examples in the sermon are updated.

I mention Emmitt Til and Medger Evers — workers in the civil rights movement in the late 1950s and 1960s, both of whom were killed as a result of their work. Toward the end of the sermon, I refer to National City Christian Church, Washington, D.C. This congregation is well-known in the Christian Church (Disciples of Christ). The sermon also refers to the office of Regional Minister in this denomination. A Regional Minister is a middle judicatory minister, a counterpart of the executive presbyter or Bishop.

The Sermon: "God's Version of Justice for All"

Most of us who are above forty years of age grew up very patriotic. We were moved when we heard the national anthem. To be honest, I am still moved when it is played. Those of us who can remember the days of all-black schools can recall the daily, almost ritualistic, recital of the Pledge of Allegiance to the flag. Even when prayers were not offered, we would always stand, put our hands over our hearts, and pledge what many of us believed to be sacred words. Even while enduring the injustice of "Jim Crow" and the segregationist policies of the south and the north, we continued to pledge our allegiance. Through the murders of Emmitt Til and Medger Evers, we pledged allegiance to the flag. In spite of the conspiratorial charges surrounding the assassinations of Martin Luther King, Jr., and Malcolm X, we pledged ourselves to the flag and all that it was supposed to represent. Though painful to admit now, many of us believed that the words we recited actually included us. "One nation, under God, with liberty and justice for all."

The sermon begins by recalling practices and attitudes with which many in the congregation — especially older members — can identify.

In the midst of all that has taken place in race relations in this country in the last thirty years, I am forced to stop and reflect on whether or not this national proclamation is true. In the United States, we think of justice in connection with the way people are treated. In a just world, people should be treated fairly. The playing field should be level. People should get a square deal. They can get what they deserve. At the very least, as Rodney King says, we ought to be able to get along.

Yet, for many years, it has been self-evident to my generation, and the generations before me, and the generations after me, that while all people may be created equal, they are not treated equally in this country. My generation and the generations before me have been willing to struggle because we think that things can get better. But now we have a generation of African American children and young people on the verge of slipping into cynicism.

We all know the words. "America, America, God shed His grace on Thee, and crown thy good with brotherhood from sea to shining sea."[1] "My country 'tis of thee, sweet land of liberty of thee I sing...."[2] "One nation, under God, with liberty and justice for all." We know the words, but are they true for African Americans and other traditionally excluded racial and ethnic groups? Will the words be true for a generation that witnessed the beating of Rodney King, and the subsequent verdict that came forth from Simi Valley? To what degree are the words true for a generation of African Americans, and other racial and ethnic groups, who are witnessing the virtual abolishment of affirmative action? A question that many African Americans, Hispanics, Asian Americans, Native Americans, and others want answered is: What is justice? And when will it come about? And how?

> *The preacher helps clarify the topic being discussed in the sermon, but does not give away the direction or the conclusion. The preacher introduces a notion of justice that is popular, but inadequate. Later, the preacher will help the congregation consider an enlarged concept of justice drawn from the Bible and the wider Christian tradition.*

Many of you grew up, like I did, singing and proclaiming these patriotic words with great belief that they applied to us. We know now that these pledges were not interpreted to include the issues of black people. The United States is still, largely, a society that is white and black, white and other races and ethnicities that have been pushed to the margins. Historically, we all know what this means. It means that black folk deal, and are dealt with, from a position of weakness rather than a position of strength. I like the way a task force in our denomination recently put it: "Racism is prejudice plus power."[3] We live in a society in which prejudice toward African American people is coupled with the power to work against us.

It hasn't always been this way. How did this second class situation come about? Many scientists believe that the continent of Africa is the birthplace of the human race. Some of the oldest signs of human life are found there. Africa had large, prosperous, and progressive civilizations centuries with arts and learning and science while Europeans were still living in huts. Many of our ancestors were kings and queens. In the world of the Bible, the dark-skinned peoples of Africa and the lighter-skinned peoples who dwelled around the Mediterranean Sea lived alongside one another in respect and co-operation. The Bible mentions people of color and honors them. Moses' wife was a Cushite, a black woman. The Queen of Sheba was, likely, African. The prophets looked forward to the day when Ethiopians and Hebrews would stand alongside one another in God's presence. Simon, who carried Jesus' cross, was from Cyrene, modern-day Libya. Africa. Africa played an important part in the early church. The Coptic Church is one of the oldest continuing Christian bodies. Augustine, one of the church's most influential thinkers, was an African. In that ancient world, people did not separate themselves on the basis of color.

In fact, the modern notion of race did not appear until the seventeenth century. Linnaeus, the famous European who created the system of classification of plants and animals, was the first to classify human beings according to skin color. This notion of race developed at the same time that farming and industry in Europe and in North and South America needed inexpensive labor. The notion of race came about so that one group of human beings could enslave another for the sake of cheap labor. The darker races, they said, were inferior. White Christian ministers North America even interpreted the Bible to justify the superiority of light-skinned human beings over darker skinned ones. That's when they interpreted the curse of Ham to be skin color. Today, we know that text gives no indication — zero — that the curse of Ham was dark skin. But that only goes to show how powerful self-interest can warp Christian reading of the Bible. In the United States, these ministers and Christians did not hear a contradiction between the words, "Slaves, be submissive to your masters," and the words, "all people are created equal…entitled to life, liberty, and the pursuit of happiness." These ministers did not notice a contradiction between "Slaves, be submissive to your masters," and these words, "the truth will make you free."

The middle passage. Being sold like cattle on the slave block. Husbands separated from wives. Children torn from their mothers. Bought and sold like cotton. Long days under the hot sun. Long nights in cold cabins. The lash. After the Civil War, sharecropping. Jim Crow. Separate but equal. Oh, I know there have been some bright moments. Montgomery. "I have a dream." But some people in our culture want to peddle backwards. Affirmative Action is under attack. In California, state universities are no longer required to honor quotas for African American students, and so next fall those universities will have the smallest number of African Americans in their entering classes for many years.

> *In the preceding paragraphs, the preacher sketches a minihistory of changes in attitudes toward color and race, especially as they relate to the practice of injustice against African Americans. This history helps the congregation develop a framework within which to think about racism. This minihistory has the effect of increasing the potential for hope in the congregation. Racism is not inherent in the human condition. It is a learned, interconnected system of attitudes and behaviors. It can, therefore, be unlearned. Change is possible. Efforts to participate in change are not pointless.*

One of the most glaring examples of the continuation of our need for struggle is the court system. Everyone here probably knows at least one person who has had to deal with the legal system. Historically, African Americans have never been treated justly by the legal system in this country. This fact becomes blatantly obvious when you look at the cases in which blacks are pitted directly against whites. It has made little difference as to who was plaintiff and who was defendant. In direct confrontation within the judicial system, blacks more often than not come out on the losing side. In eighty percent of those cases the verdict came out in favor of whites. Of course, many European Americans raise the question, "But what about O. J.?" But you and I know that O. J. was the exception. Rodney King is the rule.

In the same ABC poll from which I drew these statistics, 79 percent of African Americans believe that police deal differently with African Americans than they do with European Americans. In cities across the nation, black folk are constantly faced with the question: Is this truly a just land? If not, what will it take to make it just?

The prison system is full of young black males who have committed crimes that are similar in proportion to the crimes of their European American counterparts. But, for the same crime, a black receives a disproportionately longer jail sentence than a white. Black people, as a whole, make up a little more than 20 percent of the population in this country, but we make up 50 percent of the prison population. In cases of murder, black males are far more likely than white persons to receive a death sentence. Such statistics would lead both blacks and whites to believe that black folk are committing over 50 percent of the crimes in the United States. This is simply not the case. The sheer numbers of whites who are charged with felonies is twice that of blacks.

I speak as a pastor in the inner city. I witness first hand the way the police and the courts deal with African Americans and the way they deal with European Americans. Beyond the shadow of a doubt, it is different. I spend hours in courtrooms as advocate and witness. And I can tell you that there are differences in the ways many judges and lawyers treat African Americans. For the most part, I find the indignity that blacks are shown to be appalling and reprehensible. From what I have seen in some parts of our justice system, I conclude that some European Americans believe that blacks are only three-fifths human.

In the United States, we think of justice in connection with the way people are treated. In a just world, people are treated fairly. People should get a square deal. They should get what they deserve. At the very least, as Rodney King asks, "Why can't we all just get along?"

I wouldn't want to turn back the clock to 1953, or 1923, or 1862. We've got a long way to go to a world in which everyone is treated fairly. But as a Christian, as a student of the Bible, and as a pastor, I also know that justice is more than a matter of behavior. Justice is more than the way people are treated. Justice is more than a matter of just getting along.

The sermon now introduces the wider vision of justice that God intends for the world. The preacher draws on the Bible, on helps that interpret the

*Bible, and on Christian history and contemporary theology to help ar-
ticulate this perception clearly and persuasively.*

For so long, we have held out hope that if we could enact laws and create
policies that call for the equal treatment of whites, blacks, and all others in
this country, relationships would become what they should be. So, we
marched. We faced the firehoses, the billy clubs, and the dogs. We went to
jail. We lobbied. We pounded on the doors of the congress and the courts.
And in some ways, things are better. We have more rights than we had in
1953. But things are not the way they could be, are they? Now that all can
use the same toilet, are race relations in the United States the way they should
be? Now that we can all go to the same public schools, are race relations the
way they could be? Now that all have access to higher learning, does that
mean that race relations are they way they should be? Now that blacks and
whites are living side by side in many communities, does that mean that race
relations are the way they could be?

African Americans know all too well that the above mentioned examples
do not indicate the wellness of race relations in the United States. These items
are, so often, not much more than window dressing. We may be able to wash
our hands together, but are out hearts together? What measure of wellness is
integrated public schools, when increasing numbers of European Americans
send their children to private schools, and when some European Americans
who teach black children believe that black children are naturally inferior?
What advantage is it to young African Americans, and other racial/ethnic
groups to go to school with European Americans and receive the same education, and yet not be able to compete in the job market? We may live next door
to each other, but we are often far from being neighbors.

*The preceding paragraphs help the congregation realize the inadequacy
of the prevailing notion of justice.*

Here is where the Bible and Christian teaching help us. According to the
Bible and Christian tradition, justice is a community with the kinds of relationships that God wants. Justice includes getting along. It includes people being
treated fairly, playing on a level field, getting a square deal, and receiving
what they deserve. But it's even more. Justice is people living in the relationship with one another that God wants. These are relationships of love, building up each other, encouraging one another, working with one another out of
care and concern.

One Bible dictionary points out that justice in community is founded
upon God's justice for the world. God created the world to be a place in which
everything works together for the good of all.[4] The way God relates to the
world is the way we are supposed to relate to one another. And when we do,
then every relationship in the world will be just. God not only treats everybody fairly, God loves everybody, and wants everybody to love one another
and to have the best life possible. That's why the Bible is full of instructions

for the community to provide for the orphan, the widow, the poor, the stranger, the outcast.

According to the Gospels, Jesus reinforces this understanding of justice. To some people, according to Matthew, he says, "Woe to you.... For you tithe mint, dill, and cumin, and have neglected the weightier matters of the law: justice and mercy and faith. It is these you ought to have practiced without neglecting the others."[5]

When some in the community do not enjoy fullness of life, the community itself is diminished. Racism diminishes the whole community. It diminishes the lives of African American people. It also diminishes the lives of white people, many of whom live in fear of African Americans, Hispanics, Asians, Native Americans. The white suburbs get larger and more protective. Sometimes you have to drive through a locked gate to get into a housing area. People send their children to private schools. They put their children into private sports programs rather than have them on teams in the public schools. They don't drive through certain parts of town .These things eat up a lot of money that could go toward building up the community. They are driven by fear. Think of the positive ways that energy — emotions, time, commitment, finances — could be used if it could be transferred from fear into vision. African Americans and other racial and ethnic groups suffer the most. But the whole community is diminished by racism and injustice.

This just community, what Martin Luther King, Jr., called "the beloved community," seems a long way off. Why should we continue in the struggle? Why should we encourage our children to continue to struggle for it? It would be easy to slip into cynicism and despair.

We continue because the God who created this world continues to work to make it a more just place. God is faithful. God doesn't give up. I have to admit that I wish things were happening faster. I am impatient. But if I have learned one thing from the Bible and from our history, it is that God keeps at it, even when things don't look like it. As the old song says, "We've come this far by faith, leaning on the Lord.... [God's] never failed me yet. O, can't turn around."[6] Can't turn around!

As the preacher develops the main point of the sermon (encouraging the congregation to continue or to begin witnessing for a just world), the preacher draws on familiar symbols of hope in the community — the song cited just above, the scripture texts, images, and ideas below. The mention of these familiar motifs is intended to evoke deep resonance in the congregation. They are empowered as they associate previous experiences of empowerment with the preacher's implicit call to action.

Many in my generation thought that our society would become progressively more just. We know now that isn't true. We gain some, and we lose some.

The children of Israel were enslaved in Egypt for 400 years before liberation. I can imagine they had a lot of hot days and cold nights. But they were freed. Jesus was crucified on a hard, splintered cross on a lonely hill outside Jerusalem. They laid in him a tomb, stone dead. But God raised him to life. Many of our ancestors were stolen from the land, stolen from their families, locked in the hold of ships without food or water, sold, starved, whipped, and lynched. But here we are in God's house, in the faith that what God has started, God will finish.

Of this I am convinced: We work with God we when we continue to struggle. The struggle needs to take place in every area of life. We need to talk to the people we see one-to-one on our streets and in our stores. We need to visit the schools and confront teachers and principals and students. We need to write letters to the editor, get on talk shows, lobby legislators, and march. When someone is about to be executed, we need to protest.

Of this, I am also convinced: If we give up, we give God less to work with. We bring defeat on ourselves. We leave the rest of the community to rot from the inside out. If we fail to struggle, we give the forces of injustice that much more room to pervert the world. The hard fact, as one of my teachers used to say, is that if we don't stand up for justice, no one else is going to stand up for us.[7] Oh, there will be some Hispanics, Asian Americans, Native Americans, and even some European Americans who will stand with us. But we've got to keep moving. It's like another one of my teachers, a European American said in class one time, "If you [African Americans] don't keep the heat on us, we [European Americans] will soon forget. Given the pressures of contemporary life and the many claims on our time, attention, and energy, even the best intentioned of us lose sight of our priorities. We need reminders. And sometimes we need big and forceful reminders."

Discouraging? Yes. Hopeless? No. Once in a while we see signs that are hopeful. Just last summer, our denomination instituted a "process of discernment" to help us discern the spiritual forces at work in racism. We are seeking to discern what racism is, how it operates in our church and world, and what God empowers us to do about it. For fifty years, our denomination has been passing resolutions condemning racism and calling for a just church and world, but this is the first time we are putting in motion a process to help every member, every congregation, and every agency to name, confront, and deal with its racism. We don't know what will result from this process, but at least it gives us a chance to deal openly with injustice in the church.

> *The sermon now offers three examples (one above, and two following) of events that are happening in the church that the preacher interprets as "signs" that the struggle is bearing positive fruit. The implicit message is that our witnesses for a just world can have practical effect. The preacher acknowledges that some impulses toward justice continue to be frustrated by calling attention to the nonelection of an African American as Regional Minister of Georgia. There is reason to take action in hope, but not all action will immediately bear the desired fruit.*

National City Christian Church, in Washington, D.C., has recently called Alvin O. Jackson as their pastor. Reverend Jackson had been pastor of the largest African American congregation in our denomination. National City is predominately European American. Pastor Jackson hopes that National City can become a prototype of the just church, the church in which all peoples and relationships support one another as God intends. Thirty years ago, twenty years ago, even ten years ago, this development would have been unthinkable in our church.

As I said a few minutes ago, we lose some and we gain some. A nominating committee nominated an African American to be Regional Minister in Georgia. But the board turned him down. Most observers believe that racism was the reason he was not confirmed by the Regional Board. A few months later, an African American was nominated and elected as Regional Minister for the state of Washington and the surrounding area. We take a step backward here and a step forward there. If we keep struggling, we keep the water fresh. We keep alive the possibility for refreshment, cleansing, change. If we stop, the water becomes stagnant and loses its capacity for freshness.

Justice is not a choice you make. You do not choose to give it to some of your citizens and withhold it from others. Justice is not an option Christians can choose. Justice is required of all of us. We are not required merely to talk it, but we are called to do it. Justice must be for all people, regardless of race, color, or creed.

Christians believe that justice is fundamental to the Hebrew tradition. The life and teaching of Jesus compel us to do justice. The cross and the resurrection compel us to love one another and to be gracious to all whom God loves. God's love is for the whole world and not a select few. God is not the God of some, but of all. God will bring justice for all. God gives us the opportunity to do our part.

I began this sermon by referring to the Pledge of Allegiance to the flag. I still pledge allegiance. But now I pledge allegiance to God's vision of a just world. And I pledge to continue the struggle. How about you?

Endnotes

INTRODUCTION

[1]Charles L. Rice, *Interpretation and Imagination: The Preacher and Contemporary Literature*, Preacher's Paperback Library (Philadelphia: Fortress Press, 1970).

[2]For this way of formulating the gospel, see Clark M. Williamson and Ronald J. Allen, *A Credible and Timely Word: Process Theology and Preaching* (St. Louis: Chalice Press, 1991), 71–90; idem., *The Teaching Minister* (Louisville: Westminster/John Knox Press, 1991), 75–82; and especially Clark M. Williamson, *A Guest in the House of Israel: Post-Holocaust Theology and the Church* (Louisville: Westminster/John Knox Press, 1993), 18–16, 22–23.

[3]I take this suggestion from David Buttrick, *Homiletic: Moves and Structures* (Philadelphia: Fortress Press), xi.

CHAPTER 1: ANXIETIES OF BEGINNING PREACHERS

[1]Barbara Shires Blaisdell in Ronald J. Allen, Barbara Shires Blaisdell, and Scott Black Johnston, *Theology for Preaching: Authority, Truth, and the Knowledge of God in a Postmodern Ethos* (Nashville: Abingdon Press, 1997), 79.

[2]Hans Van Der Geest, *Presence in the Pulpit*, trans. by Douglas W. Stott (Atlanta: John Knox Press, 1981), 40–50.

CHAPTER 2: WHY PREACHING IS IMPORTANT

[1]Clark M. Williamson, *A Guest in the House of Israel* (Louisville: Westminster/John Knox Press, 1993), 248.

[2]See further Clark M. Williamson and Ronald J. Allen, *The Vital Church: Teaching, Worship, Community, Service* (St. Louis: Chalice Press, 1998).

[3]Barbara Brown Taylor, *The Preaching Life* (Boston: Cowley Publications, 1993).

[4]The phrase is from Craig Dykstra, "Reconceiving Practice," in *Shifting Boundaries: Contextual Approaches to the Structure of Theological Education*, ed. by Barbara G. Wheeler and Edward Farley (Louisville: Westminster/John Knox Press, 1991), 35. This enhanced sense of practice is fueled by Alisdair MacIntyre, *After Virtue*. 2nd ed. (Notre Dame, Indiana: University of Notre Dame Press, 1984), 187.

[5]*Practicing Our Faith: A Way of Life for a Searching People*, ed. by Dorothy C. Bass (San Francisco: Jossey-Bass Publishers, 1997).

[6]Dykstra, "Reconceiving Practice," 47.

[7]Craig Dykstra and Dorothy C. Bass, "Times of Yearning, Practices of Faith," in *Practicing Our Faith*, 5. Authors' emphasis.

[8]*Growing in the Life of Christian Faith* (Louisville: Presbyterian Church [USA], 1989), 27–28. Dykstra is not named as the author of this book in this work, but is acknowledged as such in *Practicing Our Faith*, 205.

[9]Dykstra and Bass, 9. My emphasis.

[10]Dykstra, "Reconceiving Practice," 54–55.

[11]John Calvin, *Institutes of the Christian Religion*, ed. by John T. McNeill, trans. by Ford Lewis Battles (Philadelphia: Westminster Press,1950), 4.1.5, vol. 2, 1017.

[12]J.L. Austin, *How To Do Things with Words*, ed. by J. O. Urmson (New York: Oxford University Press, 1965).

[13]Alfred North Whitehead, *Modes of Thought* (New York: Capricorn Books, 1938), 45.

[14]Hans Van Der Geest, *Presence in the Pulpit: The Impact of Personality in Preaching*, trans. by Douglas W. Stott (Atlanta: John Knox Press, 1981), 113–114.

[15]*Revolutionary Theology in the Making: Barth-Thurneysen Correspondence 1914–1925*, ed. by James D. Smart (Richmond: John Knox Press, 1964), 45, though Barth laments the difficulty of seeing connections between the worlds of the Bible and the newspaper.

[16]Bonita L. Benda, *The Silence is Broken: Preaching on Social Justice Issues* (Th.D. Diss., Iliff School of Theology, 1983).

[17]Frederick Buechner, *The Alphabet of Grace* (New York: Seabury Press, 1970), 43–44.

CHAPTER 3: THE CHURCH AS A CONTEXT FOR PREACHING

[1]Craig Dykstra, "Reconceiving Practice," in *Shifting Boundaries: Contextual Approaches to the Structure of Theological Education* (Louisville: Westminster/John Knox Press, 1991), 49–50.

[2]Mary Catherine Hilkert, *Naming Grace* (New York: Continuum, 1997), 44–57.

[3]Those who need immediate start-up knowledge about preaching in their tradition can make good beginnings in *Concise Encyclopedia of Preaching*, ed. by William H. Willimon and Richard Lischer (Louisville: Westminster John Knox Press, 1995).

[4]Robert Waznack, "Homily," in *The New Dictionary of Sacramental Worship*, ed. by Peter E. Fink, S. J. (Collegeville: Liturgical Press, 1990), 552–558.

[5]John Wesley, *John Wesley's Works*, ed. by Albert C. Outler (Nashville: Abingdon Press, 1984), vol. 1, 104.

[6]For fuller discussion, see Clark M. Williamson and Ronald J. Allen, *Adventures of the Spirit: A Guide to Worship from the Perspective of Process Theology* (Lanham, Maryland: University Press of America, 1997).

[7]Craig Dykstra and Dorothy Bass, "Times of Yearning, Practices of Faith," in *Practicing Our Faith: A Way of Life for a Searching People* (San Francisco: Jossey-Bass Publishers, 1997), 9.

[8]St. Augustine, *Tractates on the Gospel of John 55–111*, trans. by John W. Rettig. The Fathers of the Church: A New Translation (Washington, D.C.: The Catholic University of America Press, 1994), vol. 90, 80.3, 117.

[9]Charles L. Rice, *The Embodied Word: Preaching as Art and Liturgy* (Minneapolis: Fortress Press, 1991), 62.

[10]Leander Keck, *The Bible in the Pulpit* (Nashville: Abingdon Press, 1978), 61, 64.

[11]For representative works, see Allison Stokes and David Roozen, "The Unfolding Story of Congregational Studies," in *Carriers of Faith: Lessons from Congregational Studies*, ed. by Carl S. Dudley, Jackson W. Carroll, and James Wind (Louisville: Westminster/John Knox Press, 1991), 183–192.

[12]Leonora Tubbs Tisdale, *Preaching as Local Theology and Folk Art,* Fortress Resources for Preaching (Minneapolis: Fortress Press, 1997), 64–77.

[13]A highly structured approach to listening to the congregational stories and conducting interviews is found in Jackson W. Carroll, Carl S. Dudley, and William McKinney, *Handbook for Congregational Studies* (Nashville: Abingdon Press, 1986), 24–25.

[14]Mary Field Belenky, Blythe McVicker Clinchy, Nancy Rule Goldberger, Jill Mattuck Tarule, *Women's Ways of Knowing: The Development of Self, Voice, and Mind* (New York: Basic Books, 1986). See Tubbs Tisdale, *Preaching as Local Theology and Folk Art*, 133–143.

[15]James W. Fowler, *Stages of Faith* (San Francisco: Harper and Row Publishers, 1981).

[16]The generational designations are drawn from William Strauss and Neil Howe, *Generations: The History of America's Future from 1584 to 2069* (New York: William Morrow, 1991). The chart is adapted from Ronald J. Allen, *Preaching for Growth* (St. Louis: CBP Press, 1988), 52; idem., "The Social Function of Language in Preaching," in *Preaching as a Social Act: Theology and Practice*, ed. by Arthur Van Seters (Nashville: Abingdon Press, 1988), 183.

CHAPTER 4: THE LARGER WORLD AS A CONTEXT FOR PREACHING

[1]A fuller discussion of these phenomena can be found in Ronald J. Allen, Barbara Shires Blaisdell, and Scott Black Johnston, *Theology for Preaching: Authority, Truth and Knowledge of God in a Postmodern Ethos* (Nashville: Abingdon Press, 1997).

[2]This typology is drawn from Walter Ong, *The Presence of the Word* (New Haven: Yale University Press, 1967).

[3]Tex Sample, *Ministry in an Oral Culture: Living with Will Rogers, Uncle Remus, and Minnie Pearl* (Louisville: Westminster John Knox Press, 1994).

[4]Edward Farley, *Ecclesial Reflection* (Philadelphia: Fortress Press, 1982), 165–170.

[5]Charles W. Allen, "Contemporary Theology" (unpublished paper).

[6]Clark M. Williamson, "Confusions in Disciples Thought and Practice: Theology in the Life of the Church," *Discipliana* 55 (1995): 5.

[7]Bernard E. Meland, *Fallible Forms and Symbols: Discourses of Method in a Theology of Culture* (Philadelphia: Fortress Press, 1976), 54.

[8]Neil Postman, *Amusing Ourselves to Death: Public Discourse in the Age of Show Business* (New York: Penguin Books, 1985), 16.

[9]Lyle Schaller, "How Long is the Sermon?" *The Parish Paper* 1/11 (1994): 1–2.

[10]Philip Wheelwright, *The Burning Fountain: A Study in the Language of Symbolism* (Bloomington, Indiana: Indiana University Press, 1954), 25–29, 55–59.

[11]Wade Clark Roof and William McKinney, *American Mainline Religion* (New Brunswick, New Jersey: Rutgers University Press, 1987), 22, 171–172.

[12]Marsha Clark Witten, *All is Forgiven: The Secular Message of American Protestantism* (Princeton: Princeton University Press, 1993), 53.

[13]Clark M. Williamson and Ronald J. Allen, *The Teaching Minister* (Louisville: Westminster/John Knox Press, 1991), 17.

[14]D. Newell Williams, "Future Prospects of the Christian Church (Disciples of Christ)," in *A Case Study of Mainstream Protestantism: The Disciples' Relation to American Culture, 1880–1989*, ed. by D. Newell Williams (St. Louis: Chalice Press; and Grand Rapids: Eerdmans, 1991), 563–570.

CHAPTER 5: THE LIFE OF THE PREACHER AS A CONTEXT FOR PREACHING

[1]Bernard Meland, *Fallible Forms and Symbols: Discourses of Method in a Theology of Culture* (Philadelphia: Fortress Press, 1976), 76.

[2]Alfred North Whitehead, *Process and Reality.* corr. ed., ed. David R. Griffin and Donald W. Sherburne (New York: The Free Press, 1979), 15.

[3]Mary Catherine Hilkert, *Naming Grace: Preaching and the Sacramental Imagination* (New York: Continuum, 1997), 52.

[4]Ibid., 53.

[5]Hans Van Der Geest, *Presence in the Pulpit: The Impact of Personality in Preaching*, trans. Douglas W. Stott (Atlanta: John Knox Press, 1981), 117–121.

[6]Joseph Sittler, "The View from Mt. Nebo," in *The Care of the Earth and Other University Sermons* (Philadelphia: Fortress Press, 1964), 75–88.

CHAPTER 6: PREACHING AS THEOLOGICAL INTERPRETATION THROUGH CONVERSATION

[1]Justo and Catherine Gonzalez, *The Liberating Pulpit* (Nashville: Abingdon Press, 1994), 47.

[2]For nuances in the contemporary preaching community's growing understanding of preaching as conversation, see Ronald J. Allen, *The Teaching Minister* (Louisville: Westminster/John Knox Press, 1991), 94–96; John S. McClure, *The Four Codes of Preaching: Rhetorical Strategies* (Philadelphia: Fortress Press, 1991), 68–71; William E. Dorman and Ronald J. Allen, "Preaching as Hospitality," *Quarterly Review*14/3 (1994): 295–310; John S. McClure, *The Round-Table Pulpit: Where Leadership and Preaching Meet* (Nashville: Abingdon Press, 1995); Lucy Atkinson Rose, "Conversational Preaching," *Journal for Preachers* 14/1 (1995): 26–30; John S. McClure, "Conversation and Proclamation: Several Resources and Issues," *Homiletic* 22/1 (1997): 1–13; Ronald J. Allen, "Why Preach from Passages in the Bible?" in *Preaching as a Theological Task: World, Gospel, Scripture*, ed. by Thomas G. Long and Edward Farley (Louisville: Westminster John Knox Press, 1996), 180–182; Lucy Lind Hogan, "*Homiletos*: The Never Ending Conversation," *Homiletic* 21/2 (1996): 1–10; Lucy Atkinson Rose, *Sharing the Word: Preaching in the Roundtable Church* (Louisville: Westminster John Knox Press, 1997); Clark M. Williamson and Ronald J. Allen, *Adventures of the Spirit: A Guide to Worship from the Perspective of Process Theology* (Lanham, Maryland: University Press of America, 1997), 113–158; Eugene L. Lowry, *The Sermon: Dancing on the Edge of Mystery* (Nashville: Abingdon Press, 1997), 26–28. I am particularly indebted to the work of John S. McClure. For an example of a sermon that is generated by means of conversation between the preacher and members of the congregation, see John McClure's message in *Patterns for Preaching: A Sermon Sampler*, ed. Ronald J. Allen (St. Louis: Chalice Press, 1998).

[3]Reuel Howe, *Partners in Preaching* (New York: Seabury Press, 1967), 47.

[4]Ibid., 53.

[5]Hans-Georg Gadamer, *Truth and Method*, trans. by Garrett Barden and John Cumming (New York: Crossroad, 1982), 330.

[6]Ibid., 347.

[7]Ibid.

[8]David Tracy, *Plurality and Ambiguity: Hermeneutics, Religion and Hope* (San Francisco: Harper and Row, 1987), 18.

[9]Ibid., 19.

[10]Clark M. Williamson, *A Guest in the House of Israel: Post-Holocaust Church Theology* (Louisville: Westminster/John Knox Press, 1993), 13.

[11]McClure, *Roundtable Pulpit*, 70.

[12]Tracy, *Plurality and Ambiguity*, 22–23.

[13]Scott Black Johnston in Ronald J. Allen, Barbara Shires Blaisdell, and Scott Black Johnston, *Theology for Preaching: Authority, Truth, and Knowledge of God in a Postmodern Ethos* (Nashville: Abingdon Press, 1997), 104.

[14]Walter Brueggemann, *Cadences of Home: Preaching Among Exiles* (Louisville: Westminster John Knox Press, 1997), 79.

[15] For an example of a sermon that takes a revisionary approach, see Marjorie Suchocki's message in *Patterns of Preaching: A Sermon Sampler*, ed. by Ronald J. Allen (St. Louis: Chalice Press, 1998).

[16]In this discussion, I am indebted to Susan Ackerman, "Isaiah," in *The Women's Bible Commentary*, ed. by Carol A. Newsom and Sharon H. Ringe (Louisville: Westminster/John Knox Press, 1992), 165–168.

[17]Ibid., 168.

[18] For an example of a sermon that takes a postliberal approach, see Serene Jones' sermon in *Patterns of Preaching*.

[19] Stanley Hauerwas and William Willimon, *Resident Aliens* (Nashville: Abingdon Press, 1989), 24.

[20] For elegant statements of this approach, see Charles L. Campbell, *Preaching Jesus: New Directions for Homiletics in Hans Frei's Postliberal Theology* (Grand Rapids: Eerdmans, 1997), and Scott Black Johnston's contributions to Ronald J. Allen, Scott Black Johnston, and Barbara Shires Blaisdell, *Theology for Preaching*.

[21] For an example of a sermon that takes an approach based on liberation theology, see the message by Carolyn Ann Knight in *Patterns of Preaching*.

[22]For an example of a sermon from an evangelical perspective, see the message by Bryan Chapell in *Patterns of Preaching*.

CHAPTER 7: THEOLOGICAL CRITERIA AND INTERPRETATIVE RELATIONSHIPS IN THE PREACHING CONVERSATION

[1]For the derivation of these criteria, see the sources in the Introduction, note 2.

[2]Clark M. Williamson, "Preaching the Gospel: Some Theological Reflections," *Encounter* 49 (1988): 191–192.

[3]Ibid., 194.

[4]Ibid.

[5]Clark M. Williamson and Ronald J. Allen, in the *Teaching Minister* (Louisville: Westminster/John Knox Press, 1991), 78.

[6]This approach is developed further in Ronald J. Allen, Barbara Shires Blaisdell, and Scott Black Johnston, *Theology for Preaching: Authority, Truth and Knowledge of God in a Postmodern Ethos* (Nashville: Abingdon Press, 1997), 62–69.

[7]Williamson, "Preaching the Easter Faith," 199.

[8]Clark M. Williamson and Ronald J. Allen, *Interpreting Difficult Texts: Anti-Judaism and Christian Preaching* (London: SCM Press; and Philadelphia: Trinity Press International, 1989), 2.

[9]Eugene Lowry, *Living with the Lectionary: Preaching Through the Revised Common Lectionary* (Nashville: Abingdon Press, 1992), 18–19.

CHAPTER 8: STARTING POINTS FOR SERMON PREPARATION

[1]James A. Sanders, *Canon and Community: A Guide to Canonical Criticism*. Guides to Biblical Scholarship (Philadelphia: Fortress Press, 1984), 21–45.

[2]Karl Barth, *Church Dogmatics*, trans. by G.T. Thomson (Edinburgh: T & T Clark, 1936), vol. I/1, 51–110. Note esp. 91.

[3]Chapter 16 contains an example of a sermon in the Puritan Plain Style. Thomas G. Long offers an example of a Puritan Plain Sermon and Fred B. Craddock models a sermon that exemplifies preaching verse by verse in *Patterns of Preaching: A Sermon Sampler*, ed. by Ronald J. Allen (St. Louis: Chalice Press, 1998).

[4]For a case study of a sermon in which the form of the text shapes the form of the sermon, see Alyce McKenzie's contribution to *Patterns of Preaching: A Sermon Sampler*.

[5]For the full table of readings, see Consultation on Common Texts, *The Revised Common Lectionary* (Nashville: Abingdon Press, 1992).

[6]James A. Sanders, "Canon and Calendar: An Alternative Lectionary Proposal," in *Social Themes of the Christian Year*, ed. by Dieter A. Hessel (Philadelphia: Geneva Press, 1983), 257–263.

[7]Eugene L. Lowry, *Living With the Lectionary: Preaching Through the Revised Common Lectionary* (Nashville: Abingdon Press, 1992), 39–43, 57–63

[8]Ibid., 25–26.

[9]Diane Turner-Sharazz develops a sermon on a biblical theme in *Patterns of Preaching: A Sermon Sampler*.

[10]Edward Farley, "Preaching the Bible and Preaching the Gospel," *Theology Today* 51 (1994): 90–103.

[11]Thomas G. Long, *The Witness of Preaching* (Louisville: Westminster/John Knox Press, 1989), 63.

[12]William B. McClain shows how a preacher can effectively coordinate the gospel with such an occasion (homecoming) in *Patterns of Preaching: A Sermon Sampler*.

[13]For further examples of topical approaches, see sermons from the following preachers in *Patterns for Preaching:* Thomas H. Troeger, Barbara Shires Blaisdell, Kathy Black, R. Scott Colglazier, Ronald J. Allen.

[14]For another example of a doctrinal sermon, see Barbara Shires Blaisdell's message on repentance in *Patterns of Preaching: A Sermon Sampler.* William B. McClain's sermon in the same volume draws on the doctrine of the communion of saints in a teaching context.

[15]Sally Brown illustrates preaching on a Christian practice with her sermon on music and worship in *Patterns of Preaching: A Sermon Sampler.*

[16]David G. Buttrick, *Homiletic: Moves and Structures* (Philadelphia: Fortress Press, 1987), 420–424.

[17]Kathleen Black models preaching on a personal situation in her sermon in *Patterns of Preaching: A Sermon Sampler.*

[18]Nora Tubbs Tisdale demonstrates preaching on a social issue in *Patterns of Preaching: A Sermon Sampler.*

CHAPTER 9: DEVELOPING THE DIRECTION OF THE SERMON

[1]Paul Scott Wilson, *The Practice of Preaching* (Nashville: Abingdon Press, 1995), 127.

[2]See especially Thomas E. Boomershine, *Story Journey: An Invitation to the Gospel as Storytelling* (Nashville: Abingdon Press, 1988); and the resources in Chapter 13, note 4.

[3]I am grateful to Jon L. Berquist for several insightful comments on this passage.

[4]The discipline of form criticism also uses the term "form" to designate distinct types of material found in the Bible in a way that is similar to literary and rhetorical criticism. Examples of typical forms are miracle story, parable, controversy story, legend. However, the form critics are more interested in the history of these forms prior to their inclusion in the Bible than are the literary and rhetorical critics. The form critics tried to identify the setting in life that gave rise to particular pieces of material. Literary and rhetorical criticism focus not on the history of the text, but on the text as it is before us. Further, form criticism, whose heyday belonged in a prior generation, concentrated on the interpretation of individual passages, and did not focus extensively on the place of the individual passages in whole books of the Bible.

[5]See *Word Biblical Commentary*, ed. by David A. Hubbard and Glenn W. Barker (Dallas: Word Books, 1982–), 53 volumes.

[6]Martin Luther, "Galatians 1519," in *Luther's Works: Lectures on Galatians 1535, Chapters 5–6, and Lectures on Galatians 1519, Chapters 1–6.* ed. by Jaroslav Pelikan, associate editor Walter A. Hansen (St. Louis: Concordia, 1964), vol. 27, 220.

[7]Martin Luther, "Galatians–1535," in *Luther's Works: Lectures on Galatians 1535, Chapters 1–4,* ed. by Jaroslav Pelikan, associate editor Walter A. Hansen (St. Louis: Concordia., 1963), vol. 26, 404.

[8]Walter Brueggemann, "Pain Turned to Newness," in Charles L. Campbell, *Preaching Jesus Christ: New Directions in Homiletics in Hans Frei's Postliberal Theology* (Grand Rapids: Eerdmans, 1997), 259–264.

[9]Joanna Dewey, "The Gospel of Mark," in *Searching the Scriptures: A Feminist Commentary*, ed. by Elisabeth Schüssler Fiorenza (New York: Crossroad, 1994), vol. 2, 482.

[10]Sandra M. Schneiders, "Does the Bible Have a Postmodern Message?" in *Postmodern Theology*, ed. Frederic B. Burnham (San Francisco: Harper and Row Publishers, 1989), 64.

[11]I first heard the phrase "vested interests" in connection with the interpretation of the Bible in a lecture in Lincoln, Nebraska, by Walter Brueggemann about 1980.

[12]Pablo Jimenez cites an incident in Puerto Rico that illustrates how vested interests can operate in a particular situation in *Patterns of Preaching: A Sermon Sampler*, ed. by Ronald J. Allen (St. Louis: Chalice Press, 1998).

[13]Paul Ricoeur, *The Symbolism of Evil*, trans. by Emerson Buchanan (Boston: Beacon Press, 1957), 25–46.

[14]Rudolf Otto, *The Idea of the Holy*, trans. by J. Harvey (London: Oxford University Press, 1950), 122–123, passim. For a fuller account of the experience of uncleanness, see Mary Douglas, *Purity and Danger: An Analysis of the Concepts of Pollution and Taboo* (New York: Praeger Publishers, 1966)

[15]Bruce J. Malina and Richard L. Rohrbaugh, *Social-Science Commentary on the Synoptic Gospels* (Minneapolis: Fortress Press, 1992), 210.

[16]Ibid., 223.

[17]Kenneth T. Lawrence, Joann Cather Weaver, Roger Wedell, *Imagining the Word: An Arts and Lectionary Resource* (Cleveland: United Church Press, 1994), vol. 1; Susan A. Blain, Sharon Iverson Gouwens, Catherine O'Callghan, Grant Spradling, *Imagining the Word: An Arts and Lectionary Resource* (Cleveland: United Church Press, 1995, 1996), vols. 2 and 3.

[18]Diane Apostolos–Cappadona, *Encyclopedia of Women in Religious Art* (New York: Continuum, 1996), 391.

[19]Barbara Chaapel, "The Lesson and the Arts," *Lectionary Homiletics* 2/7 (1991): 37–38.

[20]Thomas H. Troeger and Carol Doran, "The Scantest Touch of Grace Can Heal," *New Hymns for the Lectionary: To Glorify the Master's Name* (New York: Oxford University Press, 1986), 24. Troeger wrote the text; Doran the tune.

[21]Brian Wren, "Woman in the Night," in *Chalice Hymnal* (St. Louis: Chalice Press, 1995), 188.

[22]For illustrations of how experience can make its way directly and indirectly into the sermon, see Chapters 5 and 12.

[23]Several of the sermons in *Patterns of Preaching: A Sermon Sampler* exemplify ways in which the sermon and the Christian year mutually relate, e.g., the sermons by Paul Scott Wilson, Barbara Shires Blaisdell, Sally Brown, and Serene Jones.

[24]Wilson, *Practice of Preaching*, 150–151.

[25]Eugene L. Lowry, *How to Preach a Parable: Designs for Narrative Sermons*, Abingdon Preacher's Library (Nashville: Abingdon Press, 1989), 35.

[26]Ibid., 37.

[27]Ibid., 32–37, passim.

SECTION FIVE: PUTTING THE SERMON TOGETHER

[1]Kenneth I. Pargament and Donald V. DeRosa, "What Was That Sermon About? Predicting Memory for Religious Messages from Cognitive Psychology Theory," *Journal for the Scientific Study of Religion* 24 (1985): 190.

CHAPTER 10: ENGAGING THE CONGREGATION IN THE SERMON

[1]Susanne K. Langer, *Philosophical Sketches* (Baltimore: Johns Hopkins University Press, 1962), 89.

[2]Idem., *Problems in Art* (New York: Charles Scribner's Sons, 1957), 15.

[3]For steps 22 and 24–26, see further Thomas G. Long, *The Witness of Preaching* (Louisville: Westminster/John Knox Press, 1989), 106–111.

[4]Fred B. Craddock compares inductive preaching to taking a journey in his landmark book *As One Without Authority*, 3d ed. (Nashville: Abingdon Press, 1979), 57–58.

[5]David Buttrick, *Homiletic: Moves and Structures* (Philadelphia: Fortress Press, 1987), 285–303.

[6]Henriette Anne Klauser, *Writing on Both Sides of the Brain: Breakthrough Technique for People Who Write* (San Francisco: Perennial Library, 1986).

[7]Fred B. Craddock, "Praying Through Clenched Teeth," in *The Twentieth Century Pulpit*, ed. by James W. Cox (Nashville: Abingdon Press, 1981), 48.

[8]Ibid., 49.

[9]Barbara Brown Taylor, *The Preaching Life* (Boston: Cowley, 1993), 121.

[10]Rita Nakashima Brock, "The Courage to Choose/The Commitment to be Chosen," in *And Blessed is She: Sermons by Women*, ed. by David Albert Farmer and Edwina Hunter (San Francisco: Harper and Row, 1990), 109.

[11]Emphasis in the original, by I. Carter Heyward, "The Enigmatic God," in *Spinning a Sacred Yarn* (New York: Pilgrim Press, 1982), 107.

[12]Gardner Taylor, *How Shall They Preach?* (Elgin, Ill.: Progressive Baptist Publishing House, 1977), 141–142.

[13]Cited in Harry Emerson Fosdick, *For the Living of These Days* (New York: Harper and Row, 1956), 92.

[14]Charles R. Blaisdell, "The View from the Streets," in *Preaching Through the Apocalypse*, ed. by Cornish R. Rogers and Joseph R. Jeter, Jr. (St. Louis: Chalice Press, 1992), 48–49.

[15]William D. Watley, *Sermons on Special Days: Preaching Through the Year in the Black Church* (Valley Forge: Judson Press, 1987), 109–110.

[16]Ibid., 110.

[17]Fred B. Craddock, Sermon on Romans 9:1–15, in a collection of audiotapes, *Sermons Preached at the Altar* (JBC Cassette Service).

[18]Brown Taylor, *Preaching Life*, 174.

CHAPTER 11: A SMORGASBORD OF PATTERNS OF MOVEMENT FOR THE SERMON

[1]See Horton Davies, *The Worship of the American Puritans, 1629–1730* (New York: Peter Lang, 1990), 77–114.

[2]For another example of a sermon in this style, see the homily by Thomas G. Long in *Patterns of Preaching: A Sermon Sampler*, ed. by Ronald J. Allen (St. Louis: Chalice Press, 1998).

[3]For an example of a sermon that is structured by the quadrilateral, see my sermon in *Patterns of Preaching: A Sermon Sampler.*

[4]On the quadrilateral as a theological source, see Albert C. Outler, "The Wesleyan Quadrilateral—in John Wesley," *Wesleyan Theological Journal* 20 (1985): 7–18.

[5]In Wesleyan circles, experience is often discussed with specific reference to experience as illumined by the Holy Spirit as a source for the knowledge of God. Wesleyan writers sometimes speak specifically of religious experience as a part of the quadrilateral. Since God is omnipresent, I think more broadly of general experience as a theological source. Religious experience is included, for it is a part of human experience.

[6]For a sample sermon whose heart is verse-by-verse exposition, see Fred Craddock's message in *Patterns of Preaching: A Sermon Sampler.* For a fuller discussion of this approach see Gilbert L. Bartholomew and Ronald J. Allen, *Preaching Verse by Verse* (Louisville: Westminster John Knox Press, forthcoming).

[7]For a sermon that, essentially, gives a line-by-line exposition of a poem, see Thomas Troeger's sermon that centers on a poem by George Herbert in *Patterns of Preaching: A Sermon Sampler.*

[8]The classic work on inductive movement in preaching is Craddock, *As One Without Authority,* esp.51–76.

[9]L. Susan Bond provides a model of a simple inductive sermon in *Patterns of Preaching: A Sermon Sampler.*

[10]For guiding perspectives, see Thomas G. Long, *Preaching and the Literary Forms of the Bible* (Philadelphia: Fortress Press, 1988); Sidney Greidanus, *The Modern Preacher and the Ancient Text: Interpreting and Preaching Biblical Literature* (Grand Rapids: Eerdmans, 1988); *Preaching Biblically,* ed. by Don M. Wardlaw (Philadelphia: Westminster Press, 1983); cf. Ronald J. Allen, *Contemporary Biblical Interpretation for Preaching* (Valley Forge: Judson Press, 1984), 49–59.

[11]For a sermon in this genre, see the homily by Alyce McKenzie in *Patterns of Preaching: A Sermon Sampler.*

[12]Paul Scott Wilson, *The Four Pages of the Sermon* (Nashville: Abingdon Press, forthcoming).

[13]We can see a sermon in this format from Paul Scott Wilson in *Patterns of Preaching: A Sermon Sampler.*

[14]Buttrick, *Homiletic,* 276–77, 296–97.

[15]A clear example of Buttrick's approach can be seen in his sermon in *Patterns of Preaching: A Sermon Sampler.*

[16]Buttrick, *Homiletic,* 285–303.

[17]Ibid., 23–82.

[18]Ibid., 358.

[19]Henry H. Mitchell, *Black Preaching: The Recovery of a Powerful Art* (Nashville: Abingdon Press, 1990), 116–122.

[20]Three sermons in *Patterns of Preaching: A Sermon Sampler* particularly manifest this quality: those by Henry Mitchell, Frank Thomas, and Ella Pearson Mitchell.

[21]Mitchell, *Black Preaching,* 117.

[22]See Henry H. Mitchell, *Celebration and Experience in Preaching* (Nashville: Abingdon Press, 1990).

[23]Ella Pearson Mitchell takes this approach in her sermon in *Patterns of Preaching: A Sermon Sampler.*

[24]Martha Simmons preaches a group study in her sermon in *Patterns of Preaching: A Sermon Sampler.*

[25]Eugene L. Lowry, *The Homiletical Plot: The Sermon as Narrative Art Form* (Atlanta: John Knox Press, 1980).

[26]Lowry proffers such a sermon in *Patterns of Preaching: A Sermon Sampler.*

[27]Thomas H. Troeger, *Imagining a Sermon,* Abingdon Preacher's Library (Nashville: Abingdon Press, 1990), esp. 44–52. Barbara Lundblad develops a sermon as movement of images in *Patterns of Preaching: A Sermon Sampler.*

[28]Craddock, *As One Without Authority,* 57.

[29]Ibid., 57–58.

[30]Paul Ricoeur, "Biblical Hermeneutics," *Semeia* 4 (1975): 67. I am inspired in this direction by Ted Peters, "Hermeneutics and Homiletics," *Dialog* 21 (1982): 121–129. Cf. Ronald J. Allen, *The Teaching Sermon* (Nashville: Abingdon Press, 1995), 116–125.

[31]Pablo Jiménez develops a sermon in this pattern in *Patterns of Preaching: A Sermon Sampler.*

[32]Allen, *Teaching Sermon,* 109–116.

[33]Joseph R. Jeter, Jr., has a sermon in a jigsaw pattern in *Patterns of Preaching: A Sermon Sampler.*

[34]For a case study of a sermon developed in this fashion, see Jana Childers' contribution to *Patterns of Preaching: A Sermon Sampler.*

[35]Delwin Brown, "Struggle till Daybreak: On the Nature of Authority in Theology," *Journal of Religion* 65 (1985): 27, my emphasis.

[36]Eugene L. Lowry, *How to Preach a Parable: Designs for Narrative Sermons.* Abingdon Preacher's Library (Nashville: Abingdon Press, 1989), 37.

[37]Sermons in *Patterns of Preaching: A Sermon Sampler* exhibits this quality. Ella Pearson Mitchell develops a sermon that tells the story of a biblical character.

[38]Roger N. Carstensen spun this story into a twenty-minute sermon at a week of preaching at First Christian Church (Disciples of Christ), Fort Collins, Colorado, in 1979.

[39]R. Scott Colglazier develops a sermon in points in *Patterns of Preaching: A Sermon Sampler.*

[40]Wilson, *Practice of Preaching,* 207.

[41]James Harris, *Preaching Liberation.* Fortress Resources for Preaching (Minneapolis: Fortress Press, 1995). Harris models this approach in his sermon in *Patterns of Preaching: A Sermon Sampler.*

[42]Frank Thomas, *They Like to Never Quit Praisin' God: The Role of Celebration in Preaching* (Cleveland: Pilgrim Press, 1997). For a sermon utilizing this approach, see Thomas' contribution to *Patterns of Preaching: A Sermon Sampler.*

[43]Ronald J. Allen, *Preaching the Topical Sermon* (Louisville: Westminster/John Knox Press, 1992), 81–84.

[44]Ibid., 90–92.

[45]H. Grady Davis, *Design for Preaching* (Philadelphia: Muhlenberg Press, 1958), 154–157. Davis presents five organic forms: a subject discussed, a thesis supported, a message illumined, a question propounded, a story told.

[46]Allen, *The Teaching Sermon,* 103–109. Readers of Socrates' dialogues often chuckle at the simplicity or self-service of Socrates' questions. Despite such qualities, many people still use Socrates as an example of a question-asking, dialogical teacher.

[47]Craddock, *As One Without Authority,* 124–25, 146; cf. Allen, *Teaching Sermon,* 96–103.

[48]W. E. Sangster, *The Craft of Sermon Construction* (Philadelphia: Westminster Press, 1951), 87–92. Sangster offers a wide array of the classification of sermons according to subject matter (biblical interpretation, devotional, doctrinal, philosophical and apologetic, social, evangelistic), structural type (exposition, argument, faceting, categorizing, analogy), and psychological method (authoritative, persuasive, cooperative, subversive).

[49]Charles L. Rice, *Interpretation and Imagination: The Preacher and Contemporary Literature* (Philadelphia: Fortress Press, 1970), 58. Rice helps preachers relate sensitively to stories in various media in his *The Embodied Word: Preaching as Art and Liturgy.* Fortress Resources for Preaching (Minneapolis: Fortress Press, 1991), esp. 93–114. For a sermon that shows the integration of preaching and the arts, see Rice's message in *Patterns for Preaching: A Sermon Sampler.*

[50]Lowry, *How to Preach a Parable,* 43–170.

[51]Long, *Witness of Preaching,* 126–130.

[52]Ibid., 129

CHAPTER 12: STORIES, IMAGES, AND EXPERIENCE IN PREACHING

[1]Edmund A. Steimle, Morris J. Niedenthal, and Charles L. Rice, *Preaching the Story* (Philadelphia: Fortress Press, 1980). These authors contend not that the sermon should be a single narrative, but that the various parts of a sermon work together in much the same way that the parts of story work together.

[2]W.B. Gallie, "The Historical Understanding," *History and Theory* 3 (1963–64): 150–151.

[3]Stephen Crites, "The Narrative Quality of Experience," *Journal of the American Academy of Religion* 39 (1971): 297.

[4]Ibid., 304.

[5]Ibid., 307.

[6]Thomas G. Long, *The Witness of Preaching* (Louisville: Westminster/John Knox Press, 1989), 161–177.

[7]Author's translation.

[8]Lucy Atkinson Rose, *Songs in the Night: A Witness to God's Love in Life and in Death,* comp. and ed. by Ben Lacy Rose (Columbia, GA.: CTS Press, 1998).

[9]I cite this story from memory from an audiotape of a sermon by Craddock that I can no longer locate.

[10]Fred B. Craddock, *Storytelling Workshop* (notes from audio recording).

[11]Fred B. Craddock, *Preaching* (Nashville: Abingdon Press, 1985), 204.

[12]I owe this observation to John S. McClure, "The Narrative Function of Preaching," *Liturgy* 8/2 (1989): 48–51. McClure draws on John Dominic Crossan, *The Dark Interval: Towards a Theology of Story* (Niles, Ill.: Argus Communications, 1975), 59. McClure insightfully uses these categories for the larger task of speaking about the purposes of particular sermons.

[13]John S. McClure, "The Other Side of Sermon Illustration," *Journal for Preachers* 12/2 (1989): 2–4.

[14]Ibid., 3.

[15]Fred B. Craddock, "Amazing Grace," *Thesis Theological Cassettes* 7/5 (1976).

[16]Susanne K. Langer, *Feeling and Form: A Theory of Art Developed from Philosophy in a New Key* (New York: Charles Scribner's Sons, 1953), 212.

[17]Ibid., 292.

[18]Charles L. Rice, *Interpretation and Imagination: the Preacher and Contemporary Literature.* Preacher's Paperback Library (Philadelphia: Fortress Press, 1970), 86.

[19]Craddock, *Storytelling Workshop.*

[20]Kenneth Burke, *A Rhetoric of Motives* (Berkeley: University of California Press, 1969), 55–56.

[21]David G. Buttrick, *Homiletic: Moves and Structures* (Philadelphia: Fortress Press, 1987), 139–140.

[22]Ibid., 138–139.

[23]Ibid.

[24]Ibid., 137–138.

[25]The office of the Network of Biblical Storytellers is at 1810 Harvard Boulevard, Dayton, OH 45406.

[26]For fuller discussion, see Richard L. Thulin, *The "I" of the Sermon,* Fortress Resources for Preaching (Minneapolis: Fortress Press, 1989).

[27]Buttrick, 141–143.

[28]Personal conversation.

[29]Wilson, *Practice of Preaching*, 272.

[30]Craddock, *Storytelling Workshop.*

[31]Ibid.

[32]Ibid.

CHAPTER 13: EMBODYING THE SERMON

[1]*Learning Preaching: Understanding and Participating in the Process*, ed. by Don M. Wardlaw (Lincoln, Ill.: Lincoln Christian College and Seminary Press for The Academy of Homiletics, 1989), 158.

[2]Richard F. Ward, *Speaking From the Heart: Preaching with Passion.* Abingdon Preacher's Library (Nashville: Abingdon Press, 1992), 77.

[3]*Learning Preaching*, 160.

[4]Among the most helpful books in this arena: Ward, *Speaking from the Heart*; Charles F. Bartow, *The Preaching Moment: A Guide to Sermon Delivery* (Dubuque, Iowa.: Kendall/Hunt Publishing Co., 1995); idem., *Effective Speech Communication in Leading Worship* (Nashville: Abingdon Press, 1988); idem., *God's Human Speech: A Practical Theology of Proclamation* (Grand Rapids: Eerdmans, 1997); G. Robert Jacks, *Getting the Word Across: Speech Communication for Pastors and Lay Leaders* (Grand Rapids: Eerdmans,1995).

[5] This quote is attributed to Arthur Schnabel on the weekly worship bulletin of Augusta Christian Church (Disciples of Christ), Indianapolis, Indiana, U.S.A.

[6]John S. McClure, *Sermon Sequencing: A Workbook to Increase Your Homiletical Options* (Louisville: The Bookstore at Louisville Presbyterian Theological Seminary, no date), 59.

[7]For a detailed development of this approach, see Pamela Moeller, *A Kinesthetic Homiletic* (Minneapolis: Fortress Press, 1993).

CHAPTER 14: LEARNING FROM THE CONGREGATION, COLLEAGUES, AND CONTINUING EDUCATION

[1]On ministry as theologically reflective, see the overview and bibliography in David Polk, "Practical Theology," *A New Handbook of Christian Theology*, ed. by Donald W. Musser and Joseph L. Price (Nashville: Abingdon Press, 1992), 375–377.

[2]The process that John S. McClure proposes for feedforward preparation can be adapted to feedback groups. See his *The Roundtable Pulpit: Where Leadership and Preaching Meet* (Nashville: Abingdon Press, 1995).

CHAPTER 15: MISCELLANIA

[1]For similar models for formatting a sermon manuscript see the sermons in *Patterns of Preaching: A Sermon Sampler*, ed. by Ronald J. Allen (St. Louis: Chalice Press, 1998).

[2]Charles L. Rice, *Interpretation and Imagination: The Preacher and Contemporary Literature*, Preacher's Paperback Library (Philadelphia: Fortress Press, 1970), 139–40.

[3]Lyle Schaller, "How Long is the Sermon?" *The Parish Paper*1/11 (1994): 1–2.

[4]Charles Rice, *The Embodied Word: Preaching as Art and Liturgy.* Fortress Resources for Preaching (Minneapolis: Fortress Press, 1991), 117. Cf. idem., *Interpretation and Imagination*, 103–106.

[5]On the funeral and the wedding, see Paul Scott Wilson, *The Practice of Preaching* (Nashville: Abingdon Press, 1995), 285–289.

[6]For an illustration of preaching at a funeral, see Mary Alice Mulligan's sermon in *Patterns of Preaching: A Sermon Sampler.*

[7]Lisa Leber provides a sermon for a wedding in *Patterns of Preaching: A Sermon Sampler.*

[8]See further Ronald J. Allen, "The One-Shot Preaching Assignment," *Preaching* 7/2 (1991): 41–46.

CHAPTER 16: AN EXPOSITORY-DEDUCTIVE SERMON

[1]For the approach I took to long distance priestly listening, see Chapter 15, note 5.

[2]For my fuller perspective on this story see my comments on "The Lost Sheep" in *The Storyteller's Companion to the Bible: The Parables*, vol. 11 (Nashville: Abingdon Press, forthcoming).

[3]E.g., Matthew 4:17.

[4]Matthew 12:18.

[5]Matthew 13:33.

[6]Matthew 5:14.

[7]Matthew 18:4.

[8]Matthew 18:15.

[9]Matthew 18:22.

[10]Psalm 23:1.

[11]Jeremiah 31:10.

[12]Ezekiel 34:11–12.

[13]E.g. Numbers 27:16–17, Psalm 78:70–72; Ecclesiastes 12:11; Jeremiah 10:21; 22:22; 23:1–4; 25:34–38; Ezekiel, 34:1–10; 37:22; Zechariah 10:3; 11:4–17; 13:7.

[14]Matthew 18:20.

CHAPTER 17: AN EXPOSITORY-INDUCTIVE SERMON

[1]This sermon first appeared in *Pulpit Digest* 78/4 (1997): 41–44. It appears here by permission.

CHAPTER 18: A TOPICAL-DEDUCTIVE SERMON

[1]Marcus J. Borg, *The God We Never Knew: Beyond Dogmatic Religion to a More Authentic Contemporary Faith* (San Francisco: HarperSanFrancisco, 1997), 1.

[2]Martin Buber, *Moses* (Oxford: East and West Library, 1946), 53.

[3]Dietrich Bonhoeffer, *Letters and Papers from Prison.* Enlarged Edition, ed. by Eberhard Bethge (New York: Macmillan, 1972), 282, cited in Borg, *The God We Never Knew*, 32.

[4]Francis Thompson, "The Hound of Heaven," *The Works of Francis Thompson* (New York: Charles Scribner's Sons, 1913), vol. 1, 107.

[5]Robert Browning, "Pippa Passes," *The Reader's Browning: Selected Poems* (New York: Selected Book Company, 1934), 17.

CHAPTER 19: A TOPICAL-INDUCTIVE SERMON

[1]Katherine Lee Bates, "O Beautiful for Spacious Skies," in *The Chalice Hymnal* (St. Louis: Chalice Press, 1995), 720.

[2]Samuel Francis Smith, "My Country, 'Tis of Thee," in *The Chalice Hymnal* (St. Louis: Chalice Press, 1995), 721.

[3]Steering Committee for the Process of Discernment on Racism, *Business Docket and Program: General Assembly, Christian Church (Disciples of Christ), July 25–29, 1997*, 93.

[4]Temba L. J. Mafico, "Justice," *The Anchor Bible Dictionary*, ed. by David Noel Freedman et. al. (New York: Doubleday, 1992), vol. 3, 1128.

[5]Matthew 23:23–24.

[6]Albert A. Goodson, "We've Come This Far by Faith," in *The Chalice Hymnal* (St. Louis: Chalice Press, 1995), 533.

[7]The preacher is referring to Rufus Burrow, Jr., Professor of Church and Society, Christian Theological Seminary, Indianapolis, Indiana, U.S.A.